'One of the best books recently published in Au

Judith Brett, *Overland*

'*Struggletown* is marvellous. Tragedy and farce, comedy and drama, pride and shame, they are all to be found in Janet McCalman's wonderfully vivid and compelling account of everyday life and politics in the inner Melbourne working-class suburb of Richmond.'

John Knott, *Labour History*

'McCalman's history of 20th century Richmond is first class. She has effectively blended "oral" with conventional history to produce a unique account of Richmond from 1900.'

The Age

'The sort of book that gives flesh to the bones of history. McCalman uses the most rewarding source of all—people.'

Newcastle Herald

'There can be little doubt that *Struggletown* was and remains one of the most significant interventions in how Australian historians imagine writing about place, class, gender, politics and the tenor of ordinary lives. *Struggletown* was concrete and humane at a time when other people writing about working people didn't seem to have met many. In part because of the richness of its oral histories, it encouraged us to approach the people of the past on their own terms. It told us the benefit of listening. It was warm, brilliantly written, aimed at a public beyond the academy, and determined to do justice to its subject and its subjects.'

Mark Peel

'Seamus O'Hanlon was a young student working in the Richmond Hill Cellars when the book was released. He recalls the immense popular reception amongst locals, who felt pride that their Richmond was worthy of a book and given a new dignity and interest through its gaze. Ultimately this is arguably the most important legacy of an historical work based upon oral history interviews; that the people who are the living historical source material for the book agree with the way they are presented. And just possibly the eulogy to resilience, empathy and respect that is *Struggletown* gave one historian, and the community she wrote about, the opportunity to be re-imagined as something greater than they hitherto conceived.'

Carla Pascoe-Leahy

'Both informative and entertaining. The author's insight into the broad spectrum of this working-class community's battle to survive is a monument to professional research.'

Ballarat Courier

'Explores the impact of history on private experience by following a generation born under the lingering blight of the 1890s depression. They see two world wars, the even greater economic disasters of the 1930s, the post-war boom, and ... the first wave of non-British immigration.'

New Zealand Star

STRUGGLE TOWN

Private and Public Life in Richmond 1900–1965

JANET McCALMAN

MELBOURNE UNIVERSITY PRESS

For my parents

MELBOURNE UNIVERSITY PRESS
An imprint of Melbourne University Publishing Limited
Level 1, 715 Swanston Street, Carlton, Victoria 3053, Australia
mup-contact@unimelb.edu.au
www.mup.com.au

First published by Melbourne University Publishing 1984
First paperback edition 1985
Penguin edition 1988
Reprinted 1994
Published by Hyland House Publishing 1998
This edition published 2021

Cover design by Philip Campbell Design
Cover photo: *Richmond. Children's playground*, circa 1935. F. Oswald Barnett Collection, State Library Victoria.
Back cover photo: *Three children with dolls*, circa 1935. F. Oswald Barnett Collection, State Library Victoria.

Typesetting by Solo Typesetting, South Australia
Printed in Australia by McPherson's Printing Group

NATIONAL LIBRARY OF AUSTRALIA
A catalogue record for this book is available from the National Library of Australia

9780522877182 (paperback)
9780522877199 (ebook)

By the same author

Journeyings: The biography of a Middle Class Generation 1920-1990 (1993)

Sex and Suffering: Women's Health and a Women's Hospital (1995)

What Happens Next? Reconstructing Australia After Covid-19, co-edited with Emma Dawson (2020)

Awards

Struggletown

1984 Shortlisted for Age Book of the Year

1985 Ernest Scott Prize, University of Melbourne, for best book in Australasian History

1985 Victorian Premier's Award for Australian Studies

1985 Fellowship of Australian Writers' Local History Award

1992 The Max Crawford Medal, the Australian Academy of the Humanities

Journeyings

1993 *Age* Non-fiction Book of the Year

1994 Shortlisted for South Australian Premier's Award

1994 Shortlisted for Victorian Premier's Award for Australian Studies

Sex and Suffering

1999 Victorian Community and Local History Award, best publication category winner

1999 Winner NSW Premier's History Awards in Community and Regional History

1999 Shortlisted for *Age* Non-fiction Book of the Year

Journalism

1997 Shortlisted for Editorial and Opinion category, Walkley Awards for Journalism

1999 Media Award from the College of Educational Administration (Vic) for outstanding contribution to public discourse on education

Contents

1927–1939

1939–1955

1956–1965

Preface

It is almost forty years since *Struggletown* was first published, and in that time the Richmond it depicted has all but disappeared. Most of the people who spoke in the book have passed away, with their places taken by a new, sophisticated middle and upper class. Richmond has become very expensive, and the old Struggletowners, if they could see the suburb now, would not believe their eyes.

Those I interviewed whose lives had always been a struggle declared that they had never been so well off since they went on the Age Pension. In old age the worst was behind them: one had made sure she bought her first home in a street with trees and would lie in bed at night counting her household taps after a lifetime of having only one cold tap in the back yard. Her friend had repaired the hole in the hall floorboards that her son's university friends blithely hurdled. That her son had gone to university was a miracle, made possible by post-war state investment in education; her education had been snatched through secret reading in bed by candlelight.

By the early 1980s, Richmond was a world of widows, their men having died young after a lifetime of hard work, and for some, hard living. The newer families were mostly migrants from southern Europe, with another population beginning to arrive from South East Asia. Richmond hosted two population waves: original inhabitants moving to better housing and prospects in the suburbs, as they had been doing since the late 1940s; and Anglo-Celtic middle-class professionals, 'trendies', moving in to renovate. It was a profound class switch.

Richmond has always been a political place and has returned Labor members of parliament for the last 120 years, with the exception of the Anti-Communist Labor Party (DLP) win in 1955. Politicians' backgrounds changed from Anglo-Celtic to Greek then Vietnamese, and the trendies fell in with the cause of Labor, often reforming local branches. But since 2002, with the emergence of the Greens Party, drawing votes in equal measure from the Liberal Party and Labor, Richmond developed a new, more subtle class divide. These are the politics of gentrification, so that while modern Richmond may now appear homogeneously affluent, renovated and smart, the underlying problems of class, poverty and exclusion have not gone away: rather they are now focused on residents in public housing and on the lost souls of the streets.

Struggletown is a book about class: a topic most Australians avoid. The old Richmondites had no illusions, however, that class was powerful in their Australia from 1900 to 1980. Only the middle class contends that Australia is a classless society and nothing like the United Kingdom. For the born poor, their life experience is of being blocked and casually disdained. Poor people are still accused of being leaners not lifters, or of refusing to 'have a go' so they can earn a 'fair go', and if they live in public housing, they're accused of having nasty habits. The Struggletowners always told a different story. They remembered lives of punishing labour, of shame and despair and tears when they could not find work, of bullying from bosses, of dangerous work conditions that saw limbs smashed and heads scalped, of fear when illness or disability struck, of panic when a purse was lost in the street, and of the long, long days, weeks, months and years of the Great Depression. They remembered too that many could not cope and drank too much, and gambled too often, and lost their rag, and bashed their families, and stole things and got into trouble. Surviving poverty requires a daily self-discipline that the better-off could not imagine.

Struggletown was rescued by World War II. Suddenly people were needed in the factories as well as the forces. With full-time work and overtime, workers were able to save for the first time in their lives. Some were trained in trades, many learnt new skills. Others found new self-confidence in the armed forces and war industry. And when the war was over, post-war reconstruction ensured that the jobs continued, that government money could be invested in housing and schools and that the post-war babies need not end up like their parents. This was the big break in the cycle of Australian poverty, as industry expanded and government instrumentalities grew their permanent workforces with unionised workers protected by awards and the law. For the first time in Australian history, unskilled men and women had secure jobs with paid holidays and sick pay and eventually, superannuation.

The biggest change in post-war Richmond, aside from gentrification, has been the investment by the state in housing. People who are poor—because they lost their jobs at a bad time, fell ill, went bankrupt, had a nervous breakdown or a personal tragedy, whose families were toxic, and who either never had, or lost the personal capital to fund their own home—have the right to shelter provided by society. It is not ideal that apart from the more recent in-fill housing, most of it is acutely visible in tower blocks of apartments and a ready source of continuing stigma.

Within these tower blocks people form the same strong bonds they once formed in the streets of old Richmond, but as before, their peace can be disrupted by the unsupported mentally ill, the substance addicts and the petty criminals. This was always a part of Richmond life, and if it provided salacious pleasure to outsiders, it was always a strain to live next door to alcoholics and to hear women and children being abused. Neighbours then and now hate the screams and curses that penetrate dividing walls, and the desperate, wild youth with light fingers. The difference today is that society knows better how to support people with problems, although it still refuses to provide enough.

One brave reform and a local flashpoint has been the medically supervised injecting room operating out of the North Richmond Community Health service. Lives are being saved and the streets are being cleaned up, but while a privileged, noisy minority wants the clinic moved to someone else's patch, others, including families from the adjoining primary school, have been strongly supportive. These are the class tensions of the twenty-first century in the inner city.

This new edition of *Struggletown* belongs to the age of COVID-19—an historical disruption that, combined with the climate emergency and rampant global inequality, threatens to inflict a depression deeper and longer than that described in this history of working-class generation. Please let us not return to the Struggletown of the 1930s.

Preface to New Edition

In the fourteen years since Struggletown was first published, its subject looks very different. Richmond has become one of Melbourne's most desirable addresses for the sophisticated and cashed-up. The decaying factories have been remade as warehouse apartments; luxury dealerships have replaced the used-car yards; Bridge Road has become a mecca for the fashion-buyer and the latte drinker. In Swan Street, Dimmey's survives, but all around it premises cater for a different customer. The northern boundary is another world again, where Victoria Street has become a 'little Vietnam', alive seven days a week with Asian foods, goods, furniture and people.

In the streets everywhere the Victorian and Edwardian houses have been restored and renovated, often now for the second or third time. A 'period home' in 'original condition' is hard to find. New townhouses, some displaying the most avant-garde architecture in Melbourne, squeeze into tight spaces in narrow streets. Even the silos that tower over the Yarra have been converted into apartments. Many of the great factories—the Rosella, Bryant & Mays, the Pelaco, the Skipping Girl—have been transformed into apartments and up-market offices, with their icons reframed as 'industrial chic'. The Vickers Ruwolt site on the river bank is becoming a new town of luxury living.

The government high rise flats are still there, but the low-rise housing estates have been rebuilt or remodelled to look smarter and friendlier. Old Richmondites can be found in the housing estates, but many more residents are new to this country, overwhelmingly from South East Asia. And already these newest New Australians have made their mark not just in commerce and the professions, but also in all areas of community life including politics.

The politics look very different. Richmond lost its local council in the Kennett government's reforms of Victorian local government, and is now represented in the more-corporate style City of Yarra, along with its neighbours Collingwood and Fitzroy. Even the football team faced extinction until a public appeal restored its financial position.

Richmond is still a special place however; its residents still love it despite the choking traffic and impossible parking. The shopping streets now buzz; it is alive at night in a way it has not been since before World War I when pubs and shops stayed open late. Its football fans have not lost their Tiger roar when the boys are at their best. Its heart is still Labor, even if election nights are drowned in Chardonnay rather than beer. And not a few of those drinking Chardonnay are the grandchildren of Struggletowners who 'made good' after the war out in the suburbs, and who now can afford to move back.

It is very tempting to revise a text that was written when times were different and one's understanding was different also, but I have decided not to do so. The text must stand as one of the 1980s looking back. A new edition would require a whole new section on Australia since the 1960s and that would not fit the book's original structure and purpose. Similarly I have come to regret that I did not include more of nineteenth century Richmond in the story, but that also is for another time.

I have just one matter of interpretation that I believe should be revised. Australian attitudes towards racism and xenophobia have changed in the last fourteen years. We are now in the midst of an unparalleled national conversation about multiculturalism, assimilation, racism, and the need for reconciliation. I have come to realise that I was too quick to condemn Old Australia for its hostility to New Australians, especially in our Struggletowns. It is very easy to spot evidence of prejudice; less easy to appreciate the countless acts of kindness, the jokes over the factory work bench, the helping out with neighbours—all the moments of human contact and warmth that built Australia's real multiculturalism and which began where New Australians first encountered Old Australians. Those moments are rarely laid down in the historical record, yet they happened far more often than did the intolerances reported in the press. Multiculturalism did not begin in expresso bars and middle-class restaurants; it began in workplaces, hospitals, schools, in road works, on building sites—in all the places where people had to work together and make a life together. Of course there were nasty remarks, blows, hurts on both sides; but there was also friendship, jokes, teasing and when times were tough, mutual support. It has been an immense achievement.

Therefore a mixed-ethnic and mixed-class community like Richmond is a peaceful place. There is still crime because there is still unemployment, frustration and greed. But there is also still community and belonging. And I remain grateful for all that Struggletown has taught me about my own country and about life.

Preface

The history of the Australian working class before World War II cannot be separated from the history of its local communities. A communal history can tease out the social intimacies that were once the hallmark of the working class; a study that ignores the daily connections between public and private life tells only half the story. This book is an attempt to construct a social history of twentieth century working-class life by means of a group biography of a generation and its community. Readers seeking a comprehensive account of the Melbourne suburb of Richmond may be disappointed, as may those expecting an orthodox labour history. Certainly many Melbourne people, especially after the publicity recently given to corruption in the Richmond City Council, will find the particulars of Richmond intriguing, but it is hoped that others will detect resonances with Balmain or Leichhardt, Spring Hill or West End, Port Adelaide or Woodville, Fremantle or Battery Point, Maitland or Wonthaggi.

There is a further dimension to the study of public and private life. One of the salient facts about the twentieth century is that it has seen even the most isolated people drawn into national and global events. No longer is it possible for people to remain unaware of national upheavals as it was for many of the common people during the English Civil War and the French Revolution. The two world wars and the Great Depression afflicted the entire nation and this book endeavours to explore the relationship between public events and private experience. To do this I decided to impose upon the story the chronology of a human lifespan, to take a generation of people born in a specific place and to see how they fared as they lived through the two wars, the Depression and the post-war economic boom.

It is hoped that the lives of individuals and their home town can illumine in a fresh way the history of the Australian working class since Federation.

To explore private experience it has been necessary to use oral evidence in addition to the customary literary sources. There is nothing new or revolutionary about oral history; historians have always used it when it was available and helpful. And like all forms of evidence it has vices as well as virtues, some of which are discussed in Chapter 6. None the less, for a labour historian trained in nineteenth century British history, this venture out of the printed record of working-class struggle into the oral remembrances of daily struggle has been a sobering lesson in how little politics matter to most people. It is also chastening to write about people who are alive and able to read the interpretations placed upon their testimony. It is not as easy to pass judgment upon the living as upon the dead and in producing a book such as this, the historian is taking an enormous liberty with the privacy and dignity of the informants. Consequently a number of safeguards have been taken. Rather than barge in as a total stranger armed with a tape recorder and a battery of compulsory and intimate questions, I decided to allow the informants to tell as much or as little of their life story as they wished. People vary greatly in what they are comfortable about revealing to the outside world, so the interview had to remain in their control. Sometimes they requested that testimony not be divulged or they expressed opinions that, while honestly held, they would be reluctant to have broadcast. Sometimes, too, they revealed themselves to be foolish and such instances have been incorporated into general comments to lessen their subsequent embarrassment.

A further advantage of allowing the informant to control the shape and depth of the interview was that some quickly revealed themselves to be gifted observers of their life and times. These old people were born into a rich oral culture: some are compulsive talkers; others are vivid raconteurs to whom the printed version cannot do justice. Women seem to find it easier to talk about themselves than do men, but the men and women who stood out are all distinguished by their capacity to remain in touch with their emotions and to generalize about experience. Some are sensitive observers of others and reticent about themselves; some are valuable for their ingenuousness. If I were to deny the differing quality of the informants by being scrupulously fair about the extent to which each is quoted, it would deprive the outstanding informants of the opportunity to make their special contribution to the book.

Finally, there is the problem of veracity. Memory is notoriously unreliable, but the combining of oral testimony and printed records can assist us to verify most matters of substance. In fact, much of the oral evidence amounted to emotion recollected in tranquillity, a rich source for the way people cope with life experiences. A small number of white lies have been detected; probably there are more. Some readers who have lived through the same times will contend that this is not 'how it was' for them, but these must stand as legitimate differences of opinion. For legal reasons no hearsay evidence about the activities of the Richmond Council, the Australian Labor Party and the Democratic Labor Party has been used. This book must stick to the public record, even if what is now established as part of the public record is but the tip of the iceberg. The postscript summarizes the findings of Mr Alastair Nicholson Q.C. from the *Board of Inquiry Relating to Certain Matters within the City of Richmond* (Melbourne, Government Printer, 1982) which examined certain allegations about the Richmond Council which have been in circulation since 1961.

All the informants, apart from those who have held public office, have been given pseudonyms (in italics), as have people mentioned by them in circumstances that might occasion embarrassment or constitute slander. The pseudonyms have been selected to match the character and ethnic origin of their real names and some married women have been given a pseudonymous maiden name to identify their sibling relationship to other people in the book. The reference to each interview is cited only once in the notes and all subsequent appearances in the text, except where stated otherwise, relate to that initial reference.

There are many people to thank. My greatest debt is to the informants themselves. First among them is Angus Wishart, founder and secretary of the City of Richmond and Burnley Historical Society from 1972 to 1983. Angus introduced me to many of the informants, and with his wife Elma, never ceased to offer advice, support and hospitality. I also thank: James Beament, Harold Blundy, Tom Bradley, Jim Cairns, the late Irene Chalk, the late Gus Coloretti, Mary Cranston, Gertie Daly, Ron and Linda Edwards, Rene and Alf Elliott, Grant Forsyth, Mavis Giles, Ray Grace, Jean and Eric Green, Muriel Harris, Thelma Hoffert, Sophus and May Jones, the late P. J. Kennelly, Laurie L'Estrange, J. A. (Jimmy) Loughnan, the late Samuel Loy, Emma McIntyre, George Newman, Robert Parker, Margaret Perry, Lil and Alma Pincott, Thelma Roddy, Charles Roseby, Kevin Rush, Doreen Shaw, Frances Shaw, Marshall Slattery, Vi and the late Henry Tevendale, H. C. (Ossie) Timewell, Len and Hilda Topp, Isabella Wilson and the late George Winter.

I also wish to thank friends and fellow historians who had a part in the completion of this project: Stella Barber, Dr Ian Britain, Geoff Browne, Stephen Henderson, Wendy Lowenstein, Mike Salzberg, Paul de Serville and Eric Timewell. I am grateful to Professor Graeme Davison and Dr F. B. Smith for reading and commenting upon the manuscript in its final stages, as did Dr John Powles, Angus Wishart, Arthur Lonnquist and Laurie and Hélène McCalman. Molly Rimmer typed a long manuscript beautifully and patiently. My thanks are due to Hyland House for permission to quote (on pp. 163-4) from *Weevils in the Flour* by Wendy Lowenstein; and to Dr Serge Liberman for permission to quote (on p. 287) from *On Firmer Shores*. I also wish to thank the La Trobe Library, the Carringbush Library, the Town Clerk and Rate Collector of the Richmond City Council, the University of Melbourne Archives and the library and Features Department of the Herald and Weekly Times.

This book was written with the assistance of a grant from the Literary and Historical Committee of Victoria's 150th Anniversary Celebrations, and published with the assistance of the Victorian Ministry for the Arts.

My final debt is to my husband, Al Knight, whose wisdom as a book-man and deep understanding of working-class life inform this book throughout. If I have 'got it wrong' after all this, it is nobody's fault but my own.

1900–1914

1

Birthplace

The Place

When I was a kid we used to go to parties in the suburbs.
—Where do you come from?
—Richmond.
And the next thing you'd be dropped like an oily rag.[1]

In 1905 E. C. Buley described the journey by train to the city of Melbourne of a squatter politician in town for parliament. As the train passed through the suburbs it took him on a tour of the class structure of the metropolis:

> Next to his own suburb is one of detached villas, each with its own garden; then comes a region of wooden cottages, all neat and comfortable; and finally, stucco terraces, rather dingy and crowded, and many of them with cards in the window proclaiming that 'board and residence' may be obtained within. Suddenly a corner is turned and the city area is reached.[2]

That dingy and crowded place was Richmond.

Three decades later, in the midst of the Great Depression, a schoolboy, who would become a politician of a different hue from the squatter, was introduced to his future constituents by a similar bird's-eye view from the train. James Ford Cairns was never to forget the desolation he witnessed on those first forays into *Struggletown*:

> I went to Northcote High School, travelling by train from Princes Bridge to Merri through West Richmond, North Richmond, Collingwood and Victoria Park. It was a world that looked somewhat threatening, somewhat foreign, and after a while I decided to get off the train and walk round for an

> hour. One of the things I remembered was the Reserve behind the Richmond Town Hall. Whenever I went there there were always several hundred men hanging about on the Reserve. They'd sometimes play football if anyone ever had a football; they had little stalls where they used to sell kinds of meat pies for a penny; they had something—I'd never heard the word before—a gymkhana, and even then I became aware that there'd be someone who'd either pinch the proceeds or something like that would happen. And almost every street had dozens of 'to let' notices sticking out on a pole or a stick so that you could see it from the footpath.
> And around the Vine Hotel on the corner of Bridge Road and Church Street, there were always a hundred or so men standing outside with half-a-dozen in the bar—picking up the smell of it.[3]

Most Melbourne train travellers remained content with their bird's-eye knowledge of Richmond. By the 1950s it presented an aerial aspect of a town of corrugated iron: roofs were patchworks of rusting oddments kept down by bricks, bits of grey timber, jerry cans and car tyres; corrugated iron also replaced the fences that had been torn down for firewood in the Depression. Invidious comparisons with the spacious, ordered and sanitary family life in the garden suburbs were irresistible. And the aura of working-class dirt was made almost tangible as the outsider was assaulted by Richmond's industrial stenches. Eastern suburban commuters hit what seemed like a wall of lime and tannery foulness at the Burnley station; the north wind served up to the plutocracy of South Yarra and Toorak across the river an olefactory cocktail of tomato sauce and burning malt; and on hot days the bourgeoisie of Hawthorn savoured the tanneries and the smouldering contents of the Horticultural Gardens' tip.[4]

The rise of motor transport was to force a closer acquaintance with Richmond which had the misfortune to contain four major arterial roads as well as generating its own industrial and commuter traffic. While daytime economic life revealed an innocuous if decrepit community, night brought menace and alienation. In 1954, when a Hawthorn woman was fined £5 for failing to stop after an accident, she tendered as her defence:

> My only thought was to get home safely. I was very frightened as there had been so many bandits in the Richmond district, and being shortly after the hold-up in Hawthorn Glen, without reasoning about it, I just kept on going, wanting to get out of Richmond where the bandits seem to live.[5]

Yet when outsiders did manage to penetrate class lines and meet the bandits of Richmond, they were in for a surprise. Dr Jim Cairns's second encounter with Richmond came with his sudden election for the federal seat of Yarra in 1955:

> They were better off than I expected them to be. There was less alienation amongst them than amongst the people with whom I'd lived in the country.

> They talked to one another more. They knew much more about one another. There was a lot of gossip, of course, but what they didn't have in money and material things they had in personal relations.

That was Richmond's magic. Poverty and prejudice welded its people into a richly human community. Yet they remained haunted by their image in the outside world as it inspected their back yards from the train and peered nervously down their side streets. A resident despaired in 1916:

> The aspect presented to the train traveller between Richmond and South Yarra is one of most unsightly backyards, and the mental impression of this city conveyed is that it is a slum neighbourhood excelled in unsightliness by nothing else between here and Sydney. Where it is not slum it is advertising hoardings, and the odours are certainly not those of Araby the blest.[6]

This resident's plea for reform would be typical of the protests made by fellow citizens throughout the twentieth century: the pain of class stigma was as deep as the nastiness of slum life. They knew they did not deserve to be dropped like an oily rag.

Like all Melbourne's first suburbs, Richmond's social fate was determined by its topography, yet it commenced life as a settled white community with considerable advantages. The municipality, which includes the small suburb of Burnley, lies about four kilometres south-east of the Melbourne G.P.O. Its northern and western boundaries are the arterial roads of Victoria Street and Hoddle Street; its southern and eastern borders are formed by the romantic meanderings of the Yarra. At the suburb's heart rises a handsome hill with commanding views of the Yarra valley and of the distant Dandenongs. But the hill occupies only a small area of the city and the land falls away sharply to the south and the west and flattens to the north and the east to form an unremarkable plateau. Richmond's first settlers were the pioneering gentry like the Hentys and the Dockers who were attracted by the hill's fine views and natural drainage. By 1851 this select society was served by Richmond's first Anglican church, St Stephen's. Towards the river the lush but flood-prone river flats invited grazing, and still on the high land in South Ward stands a small community of wide-verandahed colonial homesteads and some fine bluestone town houses which once overlooked a picturesque river valley. But that large expanse of flat and water-logged ground, enriched by the domestic filth from the élite on the hill, nipped in the bud Richmond's career as a preserve of the gentry. By the 1860s small local industries had begun: bootmaking, furniture making, an organ builder, a maizina plant, a brewery and, significantly, a wool-washing plant and a tannery. The wide river flat proved irresistible to noxious trades seeking both a river frontage and a captive pool of labour living on their doorstep, who were too fearful to complain about pollution. Richmond's fate as a working-class suburb was sealed.

None the less, Richmond's palmy days were not yet over. The 1880s boom saw prosperous local merchants and manufacturers erect vulgar mansions and elegant spacious terraces on the hill. Religion too had its most prestigious premises on its commanding heights, but St Stephen's was now dwarfed by a more representative denomination ministered to by the Jesuits from their Gothic bluestone St Ignatius', consecrated in 1870. Designed by William Wardell, the architect of St Patrick's Cathedral, it is unquestionably Richmond's finest public building and arguably the most splendid parish church in Melbourne. Richmond's other pocket of gentility was in Burnley Street where Nellie Melba's father, David Mitchell, was joined by small businessmen, professional men and office workers in taking advantage of what was left of the river scenery. But the major development in the boom years was in workers' dwellings which spread all over the municipality. Developers and building societies erected terraces and free-standing workers' homes throughout the suburb. It was common practice also for a building tradesman to erect a pair of houses in his free time, live in one and sell the other. In some of the first settled areas existing early colonial dwellings and hovels were demolished and the sites redeveloped. A few of this first generation of workers' homes can still be found in the low-lying part of West Ward and in Centre Ward, distinguished by their low ceilings, high-pitched roofs and absence of passages. Many of these pioneers' cottages had to go to accommodate the new surveying of the street plans; some which survived the boom were secreted away down back lanes and behind new houses which conformed with the infant building regulations. Richmond as it stands today was a creation of the late Victorian boom and its true origins are now only occasionally visible.

By 1900 Richmond was a fully-fledged suburban community of 37 824 inhabitants. It had had local government since 1855 and had been a city since 1882. It was exceptionally well served by public transport in cable trams along its arterial roads and in two railway lines with five stations within the municipal boundaries. Such public transport enhanced Richmond's industrial role and extended the suburb's life as a major shopping area long after the decline of its affluent population. Swan Street and Bridge Road had both classy and cheap department stores that drew shoppers from all over Melbourne. Two essential amenities of modern life were also coming to Richmond in the early Edwardian years: sewerage was replacing the foul open drains and the Richmond City Council embarked on the still continuing saga of surfacing roads. Swan Street, the most prestigious shopping street, was first with a skin of wood blocks completed in January 1901 at a cost of £5000. Municipal inefficiency and neglect of road maintenance and street cleaning were to be the bane of residents and business people for decades to come. In 1902 210 streets needed name plates, and with poor lighting, finding the way home after dark was an art.

£25 would have paid for 210 new name plates and repaired the existing ones but the Council pleaded poverty, deferred the matter to the 1903 estimates and spent £250 on renovating the Town Hall instead.[7]

On paper, however, Richmond looked like a prosperous and well-served community. In 1900 it boasted twenty private schools (only three of them Roman Catholic) and five state schools, a United Friendly Societies' free dispensary, two free libraries (although the lending branch had 3000 volumes compared to Prahran's 11000), an array of friendly societies and lodges, sporting clubs, social clubs and even exclusive dancing assemblies, debating clubs, and a multitude, of church organizations. There were municipal heated swimming baths which also provided a bathroom service and the city's business was conducted from a fine Italianate brick town hall. Vaudeville companies played in local halls and everywhere there were dances. A lively and comprehensive local press that would endure almost without a break for the next sixty-five years informed and bonded the community. A pony racecourse owned and operated by John Wren was eager for punters' cash as were the legions of illegal Starting Price (S.P.) bookmakers. And for those who needed solace, no fewer than sixty-five pubs offered hospitality.[8]

Environmentally, too, Richmond was unusually advantaged as a working-class suburb. On its south-west boundary lay Yarra Park, in 1900 a planted park containing the Richmond Cricket Club and the Scotch College grounds and the Friendly Societies' oval. Local dairymen grazed their cows and draught horses on the lush river flats and Richmond children chased rabbits in its unkempt corners. Upstream past the tanneries lay Survey Park, 153 acres of natural bush, an exquisite refuge from urban dirt, noise and ugliness. It gave access to delightful swimming spots and picnic retreats and the Twickenham ferry linked Burnley with Toorak on the opposite bank. By the 1920s the Survey Park contained twenty cricket pitches, all packed with players every weekend. Next door was the Burnley Horticultural Society's Gardens of thirty-six acres. Established in 1863, it was one of Melbourne's oldest institutions. Finally, towards Yarraberg, there remained some of the Chinese market gardens which served Melbourne and its inner suburbs with fresh vegetables. Within Richmond the City Reserve behind the Town Hall was a scruffy apology for a park but the Barkly Gardens in South Richmond, developed from a filled-in quarry, attracted crowds of two thousand on Sundays to listen to band recitals in its rotunda.[9]

But in the streets where the people of Richmond conducted their lives, the quality of life was far from advantaged. On the hill gentility was in retreat. The 1890s depression had driven many of the better-off into more salubrious suburbs east and south-east. The mercantile élite, with some eccentric exceptions, was being replaced by a professional élite, of doctors, lawyers and dentists who practised in Richmond and identified with it.

Many of the grand houses had become seedy boarding houses. And while the housing stock built in the 1880s boom was still in good condition, pockets of acute poverty and vile slums could be found all over the municipality. As the economy recovered in the Edwardian years, the residential character of Richmond would come under attack from expanding industry. Burnley and East and South Richmond would suffer most but in 1900 South Richmond already evidenced the urban decay that would blight the entire community by the end of the 1930s.

On the flat, South Ward, still flooded after heavy rains in the Yarra's catchment area, housed the very poor. The unmade streets, many the narrowest in Richmond, were alleys of dust, chaff and dried horse manure in the summer and foul mud in winter. By the Church Street bridge lay Richmond's worst rookery, 'Irish Town', where respectable Protestants feared to enter lest they be showered with 'Irish confetti' of half-bricks. The natural drainage down the hill conferred on South Richmond so much putrid surface water that people dammed it in their back yards to keep ducks. The rabbitos and fishos cleaned their wares in the streets and threw the remains into the gutters for the cats and dogs. When 'Richmond Resident' walked along Cubitt Street on 24 February 1916 he found it 'full of horse manure, waste papers, empty tins) rabbit entrails, dead cats and such-like flotsam and jetsam, whilst the channels contained a quantity of malodorous slush'. And if the outside world was offended by the smells of Richmond, its torments were nothing compared with those of its hapless inhabitants. While South Richmond endured the tanneries, the boiling down works, the cork factory and the tip, in 1904 the residents of Abinger and Lyndhurst Streets on the hill were driven from their homes by the stench of the effluvia of a nearby jam factory.[10] As 'Richmond Resident' walked the streets of Richmond on that February day in 1916 he recalled the poet's words:

> I counted four and twenty stinks
> All well defined and various stenches.[11]

This then was *Struggletown*.

The People

The 1901 Census counted 37 824 people in Richmond—18 074 males and 19 970 females—housed in 7908 dwellings. By 1966 Richmond would have only 33 020 inhabitants but they would be better housed in 9616 dwellings.[12]

Already by 1901 Richmond was a stoutly white Australian community. Not one Aborigine lived within its boundaries after only half a century of white invasion, yet 70 per cent of Richmond's inhabitants were born in

Victoria and a further 6 per cent in other parts of Australia. In its middle-class neighbour, Hawthorn, both these proportions were slightly lower. In Richmond 11 per cent were born in England, 3 per cent in Scotland and 5 per cent in Ireland; Hawthorn's British-born were 13, 3 and 4 per cent respectively. Richmond had 233 Germans, 32 French, 56 Scandinavians, 67 Americans, 57 Italians and 63 Chinese: the non-British ethnic mix would have changed significantly by 1966. In sex ratios Richmond was decidedly more masculine than was Hawthorn with its live-in servants and high proportion of unmarried gentlewomen. Males exceeded females in Richmond in the economically active years between thirty-five and forty-five, but their lower life expectancy led to an excess of females over the age of forty-five. Richmond also had more children: 33 per cent of its population was under fifteen compared to 30 per cent in Hawthorn. Religion, however, was a keener measure of the demography of social class. While 40 per cent in Hawthorn and 39 per cent in Richmond described themselves as Church of England, Roman Catholics comprised 26 per cent of Richmond's population and but 14 per cent of Hawthorn's. Hawthorn was 15 per cent Presbyterian and 11 per cent Methodist; Richmond's Presbyterians and Methodists both comprised 11 per cent. Hawthorn had twice as many Baptists and Congregationalists as Richmond, but Richmond exceeded Hawthorn slightly in members of the Church of Christ and the Salvation Army. But above all it was population density that measured class differences and the side of a square accommodating a hundred people was 573 feet in Richmond and 1059 feet in Hawthorn.[13]

Richmond in 1900 was still largely a community unto itself. Not only did most residents earn their living in their home suburb but many worked for employers who also hailed from Richmond. Nineteenth century Richmond was not unusual as an industrial suburb in having a resident and visible ruling class that dominated commercial and professional life, governed the community through the Richmond Council and exerted social leadership through the churches and local organizations. At the turn of the century the élite was in political decline as the infant Labor Party began to challenge its hold on the Council, and by 1914 it would be routed, but its social significance for the poor of Richmond was far from over.

The significance of the Richmond élite had as much to do with communal mythology as it did with the actual exercise of economic and political power. The presence of an élite added spice to class relations. Working-class Richmond people remained fascinated by success in fellow Richmondites, relishing their disgraces, deploring their pretensions, revering their triumphs over poverty and insignificance. Many have a repertoire of such success stories and these fortunates succeed, in folk memory at least, far beyond the average and become 'top men', 'top surgeons', 'top accountants'. Ordinary people could derive deep comfort and gentility by association from the presence of the 'silk department' on the hill: perhaps being born in Richmond did not mean being socially doomed. Hence it is not uncommon for people who have left Richmond to retain fantasies of it as 'a rather elegant lovely place'. 'There were lovely mansions—some beautiful homes', one woman recalls, who left after a frightful life as a young mother during the Depression.[14]

Burnley, too, has spawned a legion of fantasists who recall its pleasant but undistinguished streets and putrid atmosphere as the 'Toorak of Richmond'. This desperation for significance also took an inverted form in the curious pride that even the respectable take in 'Squizzy' Taylor, the 1920s gangster. Nearly everyone has their Squizzy story, no matter how remote the connection: 'I can remember the night that Squizzy's fruit shop in Bridge Road was blown up: I went out to the front gate of our house in Coppin Street and I heard this big bang'.[15] Squizzy and his kind provided free entertainment for poor people, but also he was a Richmond boy who became famous, as though even notoriety was better than obscurity.

Of Richmond's legendary élite, few of the oldest families remained by 1900. Some who stayed were probably too old to move like the Saunders of malt fame who lived in 'Ernestine' in the Vaucluse hidden behind St Ignatius', one of the most beautiful and private residential closes in all Melbourne. Mrs Henty-Wilson clung on in Waltham Street as the last remnant of the gentry of St Stephen's. When she died in 1921 she left an estate of £2895 realty and £15 850 personalty. One of Richmond's most famous self-made men was Herbert King, the undertaker. He had come to Richmond in the early 1880s and when he died at his residence. 'Kingsley', in Lennox Street in 1913 he left a massive £15 659 realty and £5235 personalty. He was a businessman to the end, for although an Anglican, he left generous bequests to his colleagues at St Ignatius', St Stephen's and the Presbyterian church. Small business could be lucrative and the canny invested their profits in property, as did Charles Jago, a butcher and mayor of Richmond in 1893–94 and 1901–2. He moved to rural Springvale and died in 1914 leaving real estate including the Rising Sun Hotel and other Burnley properties worth £18 546 and a personalty of £9180. A fellow councillor, Edwin Crawcour (mayor in 1903–4), grew up on the Victorian goldfields and came to Richmond where he opened a pawnshop. His name can be found on many title deeds of small Richmond houses as the mortgagee. He died in 1923, described as a 'financier' of Mathoura Road, Toorak, leaving £28 684 personalty and £5302 realty. A lively and provocative public figure, he had made his mark as the master of the Duke of Richmond Lodge, president of the Jewish Mutual Aid Society and a life governor of the Melbourne, Alfred and Women's hospitals. His co-religionist on the Richmond Council in the early Edwardian years, Moses Alexander, was the patriarch of one of Richmond's most loyal wealthy families. At the circumcision of his nephew Benjamin Alfred in 1902, the Loyal Toast was proposed with a proud acknowledgement of the adherence to the Throne and the Empire of His Majesty's Jewish subjects and of the many honours possessed by Jews throughout the Imperial Dominions. Baby Ben would grow up to found the family's menswear store and preside over Richmond, beloved for his kindness and generosity.[16]

In Burnley Street, the towering figure was David Mitchell of the ominous sounding 'Doonside' and the toughness he passed on to Melba made him the very stuff of legend. *Bill O'Reilly* recalled one:

> And Davey Mitchell was a fine big man . . . everybody liked him . . .
> He lived in one of them two-storey houses too. His brother John used to tipple a bit and this particular day he'd had a little too much. Davey came home and said:
> —You've had a bit too much John.
> —No I haven't Davey.
> —John, what is 'enough'?
> —What you got Davey.
> —No, said Davey.—'Enough' is what I've got and just a wee bit more.
> And that was a millionaire's definition of enough.[17]

Yet when David Mitchell died in 1916 the Richmond Council did not like him enough to attend his funeral and the *Richmond Guardian* reminded posterity of his loathing of 'the monarchy of unionism' and of his haste to bring in scabs when his cement workers went on strike. Revering the self-made man, Mitchell encouraged his apprentices to get on and one, Clements Langford, established one of the biggest construction firms in Melbourne. A leading layman at St Stephen's and a member of the Synod, Langford capped his career as a master builder in 1928 when, despite advancing age, he climbed and fixed the lightning conductor to the first completed spire of St Paul's Cathedral. Two years later he died, leaving realty of £55 305 and personalty of £126 327.[18]

A modest business that flowered into a vast family dynasty was McConchie's timber yard. Mr and Mrs David McConchie arrived from Scotland in 1871, bringing with them the first charter for the foundation of the Independent Order of Good Templars. Sixty-five years later, in 1936, 172 of their 220 direct living descendants signed the register of the South Richmond Methodist Church in a family reunion. The family even fielded their own cricket team in local competition.[19] But the presence of such an affluent and dominant family in a working-class church created inevitable tensions. *Florence Smith* remembers with mortification:

> The McConchies liked to feel well dressed and so it caused quite a bit of jealousy in the congregation—'Mrs So 'n so's got a new hat'. My sister was a great one for dressing up and she'd go down to Dimmey's: 'Oh I like that hat', and the lady that served her had been there many years, knew her and

> would say: 'Oh that suits you—that really looks smart'. 'Yes, I'll take that—on appro. That'll be all right won't it?' So she'd take her hat, get a new dress and go all dressed up to church and on Monday morning be back to Dimmey's with the hat: 'So sorry, my husband didn't like it on me at all'.
> I was so ashamed to think that my sister would do a thing like that—just to outsmart the McConchies.[20]

A means of gaining wealth not open to such Protestants was hotel-keeping. A significant number of Richmond publicans made a lot of money and launched their children firmly into the middle class. In 1903 Mr and Mrs William Malone sold up and returned to Ireland to see their relatives and from there established their son in Edinburgh to further his medical studies. Georgina O'Meara, the daughter of the 'esteemed' publican of the Railway Hotel in Swan Street, matriculated at sixteen, completed her music studies two years later and by 1910 at the age of twenty-six was a star in the Nellie Stewart Company.[21]

The enduring strength of the Richmond élite, however, was in the professional men and the senior public servants who identified with Richmond and resisted the temptations to seek a better address. Of course some local professional men did eventually prefer to live elsewhere as did the L'Estrange family, one of Richmond's pioneers, yet they too remained close to Richmond's community life and politics. It was significant that Catholics slightly predominated in Richmond's professional élite, for the sectarian bigotry that divided Australian society made acceptance of Catholics by their Protestant peers difficult. If successful Catholics stayed in Richmond, however, they could enjoy a secure and respected role as the social leaders of their community. Poor parishioners enjoyed the rivalry between the better-off at St Ignatius': 'Oh she was a picture of herself', recalls *Lilian Campbell of* one dentist's wife. 'She used to come up to church with the great hats and the feathers and the Lord knows what—God!'[22] Yet, this social leadership could have unfortunate consequences: when a Richmond solicitor was caught misusing his trust fund, fellow parishioners all over Richmond lost their money. Patients remained loyal to professional men who were incompetent, senile or even alcoholic. One dentist spun out a simple filling for months—doing a little bit and 'letting it wait'.[23] There was money to be made by practising in Richmond, however: a Dr Boyd, formerly of Erin Street, left £82799 to his wife in 1936.[24] As elsewhere, there were a few doctors who took advantage of being in a poor suburb and provided services to prostitutes for venereal disease and illegal abortions. Some doctors took liberties of rudeness and roughness with working-class patients that would have alienated middle-class people, but most were kind, attached to their patients, and angry about the slums and poverty that harboured fatal infectious disease. As the best educated people, other than clergy, whom the poor had anything to do with, they were deeply respected and provided inspiration and encouragement for bright students hoping for scholarships and betterment. Growing up in a lower-middle-class family on the hill, Dr *Brendan Ryan* was inculcated with 'a great deal of respect for education and the educated man in public life; that in fact was a horizontal cleavage line in society as far as the family was concerned, in many ways more important than money or possessions'.[25] None the less the Edwardian élite knew their place and expected the lower classes to know theirs. *John Brown*, who worked as a leather dresser at the old Richmond firm of Kennon's for fifty years, recalls his early days:

> They had this idea that they had to lower themselves to speak to the workers—you'd see them in the street and they'd just pass you by. As the years went on they were more friendly to you and after the First World War things began to change . . .[26]

Bridging the gap between the élite and the vast working-class majority was an uneasy class of low-paid white-collar workers, self-employed tradesmen and small shopkeepers. They were sprinkled throughout the suburb, sometimes staying only briefly in a poor street—on their way up to better things or on their way down because of illness, unemployment or alcoholism.[27] *Hamish Roberts* remembers a bunch of double-fronted weatherboard houses being built in Twickenham Crescent just before World War I: 'Very few people had telephones then but these people did and we thought they must have been very rich . . . however, they were still working people, one was an engine driver'.[28] It did not take much to set yourself a bit above the common standard and those who wished to, took advantage of every possible means of social distinction. *Dot* and *Edna Wilson*'s father was a plasterer who through shrewd investment and hard work established a prosperous building firm and in 1921 moved his family to middle-class Malvern. As members of a rising family in Burnley the girls were acutely aware of their superiority to the poor children at Burnley school who were often dirty and had no handkerchief: 'You hated to be near them at school'.[29] When the *Murphy* brothers' business at the Richmond abattoirs flourished, the three families bought new large houses. *Emma* and *Alice*'s parents bought a house in Barkly Avenue with a built-in wooden copper: 'It had a pipe going through into the bath so you could fill it direct from the copper and didn't have to use a bucket—we always thought it was such a luxury'. Their mother was now able to employ a neighbour who was 'married and struggling' to help with the washing, although the purpose was more to help a friend rather than lighten her own domestic duties.[30] *Kevin Maloney*, as the son of a successful Swan Street bespoke tailor, remembers 'the weekly banking ritual' as one vital display of social distinction between the white- and blue-collar worlds. Working-class people never possessed a cheque account and paid all bills in cash; those who did have a cheque account wore it as a badge of gentility: 'You looked on them as people of means; they may not have had a penny in the bank but they had a cheque account'.[31] In 1910 the residents of Manton Street, Burnley, 'regarded as one of the select streets of the district', protested that a proposed Salvation Army barracks in their street would reduce the value of their property and afflict them with band noise and the comings and goings of the good people of the Army. Their protests were in vain and those barracks are in use still.[32] Yet the genteel were not so removed in moral life and ambitions from the working class for, class distinctions aside, the great and most significant divide in Richmond life was between the respectable and the rough. And if we are to understand the mental landscape of the people of Richmond in the twentieth century we must explore the values and ideals that shaped the Australian working class.

The ideal of respectability was amongst the most important cultural baggage brought to Australia by immigrants hoping for dignity and prosperity in a new land. The impact of the ideals of respectability on the behaviour of all classes had been one of the most significant social transformations that came in the wake of the industrial revolution. Respectability prescribed disciplines in behaviour which could alter the conception of the self. In demanding cleanliness, sobriety, extramarital chastity, thrift, time-consciousness, self-reliance, manly independence and self-responsibility, it promoted an ego that was self-regulating, responsible and mature. The respectable workman might still drink and gamble, but now he did so to a budget. Even more, the respectable workman might seem to have accepted the values of his masters, but he might also be now better equipped to think for himself. If, on the one hand, respectability encapsulated moral qualities which were needed by the new industrial state, on the other respectability offered the poor but honest some sort of psychological defence against the humiliations of insignificance and the frustrations of helplessness. Respectability taught self-discipline, but self-discipline did not necessarily imply social and political deference.[33]

In the workplace, industrialization needed a workforce that was sober, punctual, obedient and capable of observing set routines and safety regulations. Gone were the days of artisan independence, of drinking on the job, of taking 'Saint Mondays' for the weekend hangover. Many nineteenth century working people found new disciplines and habits forced upon them and the falling consumption of alcohol is one of the few statistical indices we have of these changes in behaviour. However, many working-class people took readily to respectability and were keen to partake of its psychological benefits as well as of its economic advantages. Those above the economic margin of respectability, who chose to follow its other moral prescriptions, found a path to self-respecting, manly independence—the emotional status of being fully adult. John Vincent has identified manliness and independence as the great moral idea of

Gladstonian Liberalism; and when nineteenth century British people called someone 'respectable' they really meant that he or she was fully human or civilized. However, in a Britain where the social classes were becoming ever more exclusive in the face of economic and social change, undertaking what Kitson Clark has called 'the consolidation of caste', the respectable working man, poor but honest, clean and sober, found himself still relegated to the political and cultural margins of received public life. Society still refused to acknowledge his true worth as a human being.[34] An American, Henry Tuckley, lamented of England in 1893:

> In this contest for the maintenance of social dignity, the working man was nowhere, and had no chance of getting anywhere. To be sure he is a man for all that; but it can hardly be compatible with a sense of manly independence to be made to see and feel all the time that his lines are cast among people who hold him to be their natural servant, and whose invariable attitude towards him—excepting when they want a favour at his hands—is that of undisguised contempt.[35]

Hence working-class respectables who found no solace in religion, politics, trade unionism, Secularism or domestic retreat, evidenced their frustration by having the highest suicide rate of all the classes, and by emigrating in droves.[36]

Respectable English—and Scots and Irish—came to Australia in the hope not only of fortune, but also of social dignity. Few found fortune and most discovered the greater democracy of manners to be but a superficial gloss on a social and economic structure just as limiting as in the old country. The average respectable working-class immigrant found himself still relatively poor and powerless, and the struggle to maintain social and economic respectability continued as before. And in the competition for work, especially in times of depression, working-class people were forced to fight for their respectability at the expense of their less fortunate fellows.

Keeping respectable meant that people lived with a perpetual sense of threat—not just from their employers and social betters, but also from their inferiors, the dirty, drunken, casual poor. 'There but for the grace of the Victorian Railways go I.' Or as many said to themselves: 'Thank God my parents were English and Chapel or Scots and Kirk and not Irish and Catholic'. Sectarianism and racism towards the Irish were to prove added complications in the character and political consequences of working-class respectability as it was practised in Australia. In England the Irish were often regarded as a race problem rather than feared as a social and political threat: their Popery was but a symptom of their congenital moral degeneracy. [37] In Australia the larger Catholic presence was a different matter. Here bigoted Protestants had to concede that the Irish Catholic population encompassed the same range of capacities and aspirations as did other ethnic groups and was growing in confidence. Certainly Catholics were over-represented in the working class and their anti-social behaviour was more often brought to the attention of the police: 46 per cent of those arrested for drunkenness in Victoria in 1901 were Catholics, whereas only 31 per cent were Church of England.[38] In Richmond the Catholic community was small and cohesive enough to isolate as a conspiratorial minority and big enough to be feared by poor Protestants struggling to maintain respectability and fearing Irish contamination. Hence some poor Protestants sought to use sectarianism as a social divider and thereby as a stepping stone to respectability.

Within the Catholic community, however, there were many respectable people who felt doubly discriminated against both as working class and Catholic and who deeply resented the racist image of the drunken and 'Dirty Irish' (a phrase one of my informants still uses to describe relatives by a mixed marriage). Dr *Brendan Ryan* is still 'irritated at every stage Irishman being a boozer (even Dave Allen)' and recalls the civilized and careful enjoyment of alcohol practised in his and many Catholic families. Respectable Catholics, therefore, were fighting battles on two fronts: first, against Protestants who discriminated against them because of their religion and, second, against the unrespectables in their own religious community who sullied the collective reputation of their church and ethnic origins. These tensions over class and respectability, between Protestant and Catholic and between Catholic and Catholic, were to bedevil Richmond politics for the next sixty years and would play a major role in the 1955 split in the Labor Party.

Yet when we step outside the arena of public conflict into the private world of Richmond people, we find sectarianism much softened. Many people did not take the sectarian conflict seriously—or as seriously as their politicians and church leaders said they should. Many in fact saw it as an evil, even if they still hoped their children would not contract a mixed marriage. The pervasive social tensions of the working-class private world were over respectability and survival—the integrity of the personality and the family, the good regard of the neighbourhood and employers. People who learnt about respectability as Edwardian children now rarely use the word 'respectable'. Twentieth century parlance has changed and these people tend to use 'respectable' as an ironic description of the pretentious middle class. However, when pressed, they certainly know the difference between respectable and rough in working-class life. The law courts continued to use evidence of 'respectable character' as a justification for leniency well into the 1940s, but twentieth century working-class Australians prefer to speak of 'nice people' and 'good families' and 'no-hopers' and 'bad eggs'. Therefore, when we look into the private world of Edwardian Richmond as these old people now remember it, the issues and obsessions are the social legacy of the nineteenth century, described in the language of a later age.[39]

Bill O'Reilly was one of eleven children, he never wore shoes and rarely ate meat, yet the *O'Reillys* considered themselves respectable and relatively fortunate because their father was a permanent labourer on the railways: 'Everybody thought that Government jobs, especially the Railways, was a good job because it was wet or dry and you got paid'. Families like the *O'Reillys* saw themselves as superior to the unrespectable casual poor, such as those who worked at the Rosella jam and sauce factory when the tomatoes and the fruit came in, *Isabel Williams*, as a devout Protestant, life-long Liberal voter, and by her own admission, an unworldly spinster, once had to take work at the Rosella:

> Some of these women, including my friend Ollie, were pretty hard cases and they'd tell these little dirty yarns, but they never told a yarn in front of me. Strangely enough they used to say to me: 'You put all your peels in the kerosene tin while we tell a yarn'. My young brother used to say: 'Low class people work at the Rosella'—I'd never have that. A friend said to me: 'Fancy you going to work at the Rosella—a different class of people to the way you were brought up'. But I never had a word said out of place by the men or anyone.[40]

This stigma upon casual workers was based upon hard practical facts. An irregular income strained and disturbed family life. The casual poor were constantly on the move, searching for work, doing midnight flits because of rent arrears and debts. In Mary Street, a mixed street of double- and single-fronted houses with some real hovels, the population was divided between those who stayed for years (not only as owner occupiers but also as respectable tenants), and a population that was entirely unsettled. In 1901 35 out of 111 occupied households changed occupants at least once, in 1902 59 out of 107 and in 1903 39 out of 104. Moreover these changes were mostly occurring in the same houses where it seems landlords were more lax about the character of their tenants.[41] Consequently children were often changing school and mothers had to start afresh to establish credit at the corner store and build a community network that was the working-class family's greatest support in times of illness, stress and unemployment. The casual poor lived from week to week, the worst off from day to day. There was no point in planning for the future and the whole rhythm of family life was utterly different from that of a breadwinner in good health on regular wages. As a Victorian Board of Inquiry into unemployment warned in 1900:

> Irregularity of employment has a demoralizing effect upon the worker exposed to it. The existence of a listless, helpless and idle class on the fringe of the unemployed population is largely due to this cause. Men, otherwise industrious, deteriorate physically and morally when exposed to long and frequent periods of compulsory inactivity.[42]

When a family on irregular wages had a good week it was only human that they blew some of their cash at the pub or with the S.P. bookie. Yet it was often the drink and gambling that trapped a family in the casual economy, and much casual work, in particular fellmongering and day labouring, attracted alcoholics. There were, of course, gradations of respectability and roughness and not a few families straddled the dividing line with a respectable woman married, usually unhappily, to a rough man. At work and at the pub respectable men often associated with the rough, loyal to relatives and childhood friends who had fallen victim to hard times. People moved between the two social worlds: elevated by good luck and regular work into respectability, reduced by unemployment, illness and stress into the ranks of the casual poor. At the bottom, dissoluteness and defeat were manifest in dirt, and domestic filth and body odour were for all the immediate daily hallmarks of the rough. The ultra-respectable, however, had little sympathy for the dirty, the unchaste and the drunken—these were self-disciplines that cost nothing. And the respectable widow who battled to keep her children clean and decent despite the direst poverty could find herself the most esteemed member of the street community.

Jean Fowler's father worked in the bush in a sawmill and his large and near-destitute family only saw him once a fortnight when he brought back to Richmond

> about 35 shillings for the fortnight and a couple of bottles of wine. And that would be all we'd see of him. Off he'd go—it didn't worry him. It was my mother who had all the trouble. Of course I've been all around Richmond—White Street, Green Street, Durham Street, Somerset Street, Edinburgh Street, even Swan Street on top of a butcher's. My mother would have to shift because they never had the money to pay the rent.

Jean grew up on the margin of respectability; only her mother's will and self-discipline kept the family clean, fed and clothed somehow. But there was little time left for affection and fun: 'too many kids for any of that sort of business'. At St Ignatius' School *Jean* was treated as one of the reprehensibles because her mother could not pay even the minimum fee of sixpence a week, but one of her most vivid memories there was to encounter a shattering social incongruity:

> These people on the hill who lived in Charles Street and Elm Grove—I can remember one girl from there [at school]. I never even had a book—I didn't have the money to get a book and the nuns would say read from the girl next door'. I remember trying to read and [this girl] put her arm out [so I couldn't see]. And she was just walking in lice and they were on the desk and I'm back like this. Because my mother, she was marvellous—we'd get home of a night and she'd comb and comb our hair and put kerosene on it.

> She was very clean like that. But this girl's just sitting there and they're falling off her—I wouldn't go near her again. *She was meant to be clean—they had money.* I don't know what her mother was doing.[43]

Jean's friend, *Muriel Thompson*, recalls how as mothers during the 1930s and 1940s the two of them banded together to fight off the demoralization of life in the worst pockets of South Richmond:

> There's a little gang of us that sort of keep together. *Jean*'s kids and my kids went to school here, and we'd go down to the beach, right down the end of the tram. And you'd keep together and lead a clean life. We never sat round pubs like some of them—but a lot of our cobbers did. At Christmas time we went around the pubs from the church singing carols. 'You frightened to go into the pubs Mrs *Thom*?' I said, 'No, my husband used to go in them, but I never went with him'. Perhaps if we had gone in with our old man we might have been a bit better.[44]

The minority—and it was a minority—who did take to drink, compulsive gambling, crime and prostitution, were a constant reminder to the respectable of the dangers of letting go. Below those capable of work in 1900 there was a small but very visible army of vagrants, alcoholics, opiate addicts and the mentally and physically incapacitated. In winter, as unemployment rose, so also did convictions for vagrancy, and the law took a dim view of wilful destitution. In 1903 the Richmond magistrate, Mr Keogh, asked a certain Louis Tammie how he lived: 'I starves', replied Tammie who was promptly sentenced to 12 months hard labour. And Thomas Biggs who had been transported to Van Diemen's Land, was also sentenced to 12 months for vagrancy, three months short of his hundredth birthday.[45]

Destitute children, orphaned or abandoned, wandered the streets, begging and stealing. In 1903 John Hunter, a 'wee lad', was charged with being a neglected child. Constable Strahan told the Richmond Court:

> The mother of the boy had died six months ago. She was a woman of ill-repute and the putative father refused to have anything to do with the boy. The lad had been in charge of in turn two persons, but they had each got sick of him and turned him out. Latterly he had been wandering about the streets, subsisting on what he could beg and pick up and sleeping out under verandahs.[46]

The previous year Alice Jenkinson was charged with being a neglected child. The court was told that 'her father was dead and she had not seen her mother for eight years, during which time she had worked for her living. Lately she had become very deaf and was unable to find a situation. She had been wandering about and the police took up the case for her own protection'. Alice agreed to go to the Convent of the Good Shepherd.[47]

Many near-destitute and alcoholic families did have homes of a sort—often hovels tucked away down lanes or behind newer dwellings. They may have been one household in a respectable street, vivid warnings of the dangers of relaxing self-discipline and control. Drink and dirt usually went together. As *Ruby Kane* recalls: 'You'd always find where the drink was—the house was neglected'.[48] *Lilian Campbell* remembers one:

> There was one on the corner of Abinger Street and Lyndhurst Street—we used to call it Cockroach Terrace—houses with fences right on the street. The one on the corner—she was a drinker. She became pregnant and my brother came home to Mum and said 'Oh Mum you should see Mrs "So and so"—she's out like that with beer'.

The tragedy of the alcoholic wife was even more appalling than that of a boozing husband, for a mother with good mental health and physical resilience could do much to protect her children from the ravages of a drunken father. The children of a sober father, left at home with an alcoholic or disturbed mother, fared far worse. Of course, as it is still the case today, it was common for both man and wife to have alcohol problems. None the less, respectable people often did extend friendship and support to the innocent victims of a disturbed family, but seeing the depths that people collapsed into left many children with a horror of drink for life. *Lilian Campbell* was the daughter of a labour aristocrat—her father earned £10 a week as a felt hatter in the 1920s—yet *Lilian* still made friends with the traumatized child of an alcoholic family:

> In Palmer Street there was a little lane that went right through to Murphy Street and there was one house in that little lane, the *Trevelyans*'. And *Dollie Trevelyan*—her mother was a drunkard and *Dollie* had no control over her bladder. She wet, wet, wet all the time and it used to run down her legs. It was a dreadful smell, I went to their house one day and the only furniture, or bed was a heap of straw in a corner—that's where *Dollie* slept. Nothing else in the room. There was only a kitchen table and a couple of chairs in the house full stop. And Mrs *Trevelyan*—she was neglected. She'd have her dress undone and I remember one day seeing her bust and I thought 'Isn't she rude'—but the poor thing was drunk half the time.

Moreover it was much more difficult for working-class people than for the better-off to hide moral disgrace and disturbed behaviour from their neighbours. Most people turned a deaf ear to everyday family noise and to sounds of intimate relations that came through party walls or flimsy weatherboards, but fighting and bashings were harder to ignore. *Friedrich Smith* still wonders at the double standards over family violence:

> It was quite common for men to bash up their wives and the strange thing was, if you were to kick a dog another man would kick you. But if you were

> having an argument with your wife, nobody would interfere. During the First World War, one Friday night I was down in Swan Street and there was a fight going on outside a hotel at the corner of Docker Street. And this fellow was cleaning up his wife and another fellow who knew the family went to her assistance (he was in military uniform) and she turned round and belted him for belting up her husband. This was the way it was—you couldn't understand why.[49]

Many respectables could never comprehend the perverse loyalty of those victims of wife-bashing who refused not only to seek police protection but even to admit to friends and neighbours what was going on. One wife-basher who did end up in court was Walter Crowley, who in 1912 was convicted of assaulting his wife, Lena, and threatening her with an axe. Neighbours in Gwynne Street told police that there was trouble in the house every night of the week: '*The crying of the children was continuous and sometimes it could be heard hundreds of yards away*', they said. Crowley got off with a suspended sentence, the magistrate admitting that if he did go to prison, 'his wife and children would suffer and if fined, the wife and children would really pay the penalty'. Three years later Crowley was finally sent to prison for three months, after Constable Strahan, hearing the noise from the street, entered the house to find Crowley with his hands round his wife's neck, banging her head on the floor and threatening to kill her.[50]

Such hideous public displays underwrote working-class respectability, especially the bitterness of wives and daughters who *believed* their menfolk drank to excess, even if their excesses were only occasional. Of course, living on an inadequate income—and all working-class incomes were inadequate—there was never really enough money to spend on alcohol and cigarettes. Nearly every elderly working-class person today *believes* that they had a relative who drank to excess and the visible tragedy of alcohol abuse explains the high incidence of teetotalism in this generation of Richmond people, especially among women, both Catholic and Protestant. The enormous decline in alcohol consumption up till the 1940s in this country is all the more remarkable, in that for much of that time alcohol and opiates were the only chemical relief readily available for chronic pain and depression and anxiety.[51]

Poverty and frustration also laid people open to the temptations of crime. The known criminal families appalled the respectable, even though they found a certain morbid entertainment in their exploits and behaviour. *Florence Smith*'s Methodist family were terrified of the *Briggs Mob* in their street:

> A big family of cousins, aunties and uncles and that. They were drunkards really. Saturday night mostly they'd have a party and get drunk and it would end in an all-in brawl. One night in particular, we watched from across the

> road—we didn't dare cross over to that side—and one of the *Briggs* brought his woman out by the hair of her head. He was dragging her along the footpath.

But if Richmond's small criminal community provided colour and excitement they were a problem for the people they lived among. Parents dreaded adolescent sons and daughters being drawn into anti-social behaviour; neighbours feared the violence; the respectable winced for the damage they did to Richmond's collective reputation. Mostly the respectable could do little about it but there was no doubt of the social tensions generated by the conflict between the respectable and the rough. In 1909 a middle-aged man, Richard Wynne, was fined £5 for using obscene language while he lay in his own bed in his own house because he could be heard fifty yards away. And in 1912 the now 'ultra-respectable' residents of Little Smith Street pleaded for its name to be changed, first because of the bad name it had earned in wilder days and second because they objected to the necessity 'to parade the limits of their narrow thoroughfare by publishing the prefix "little" throughout the whole course of their correspondence'. Honour was restored with a change to 'Flevill Street'.[52]

As for the larrikin pushes, even respectable women remain rather indulgent towards them, emphasizing that they never harmed girls and that women were always safe on the streets. Respectable men, however, are far less forgiving, for many were themselves victims of push violence. *Hamish Roberts* has no illusions:

> The pushes were groups of larrikins who had just left school and started work. They invariably used to get together on street corners and their language would be vile. They had nothing to do on Sunday evening so they would get on a street corner and look for trouble. They used to get opposite the church in Burnley and wait for all the girls to come out of church. Of course we'd be the target for them, looking for a fight.
> This applied all round Richmond. One of the pushes even had their own football team—they used to call themselves 'the Coppins' because they all came from around Coppin Street. They played football against us and chased us home with bike chains afterwards. They were opposite to the churchgoers—there was a definite division between those who went to church and those who didn't. A lot of the unrespectable—the larrikins—were against the government and the law. And in a lot of cases they were drunkards. They liked to break up things and were jealous of people who got on.

Hamish Roberts is a man who did get on, but who also has remained a good Labor man.

All this was the background to the obsessions that pervade respectable working-class life, especially in women: cleanliness, sobriety, no 'language', premarital chastity, the hatred of debt, the desperate importance of good character. Women often assumed the role of moral guardians, sometimes regarding grown men—their own husbands—as self-indulgent children who always wanted to go out to play—at the pub. This often led to resentment in men who worked long hours in tiring, boring jobs only to come home to a nagging, sexually frightened wife. In some, respectability degenerated into neurosis. *Jean Fowler* confesses: 'If ever I go into Coles and I pick anything up, I always drop it because I'm frightened. I'd die if ever I was accused of thieving or anything'. *Isabel Williams* says her 'blood runs cold' when she hears the 'bad language kids use today in the street'. But one of the saddest pathologies of respectability was the house-cleaning obsession—the fanatics who scrubbed and scrubbed: 'They didn't last long', *Ruby Kane* remembers; 'they went mad'. For some like George Montgomery who threw himself into the Yarra from the Anderson Street bridge on a Tuesday in December 1902, life itself was not as important as respectability. His suicide note read: 'I cannot . . . [sic] this life any longer and go to seek the unknown. This is the result of trying unsuccessfully to live and keep honest and upright'.[53]

Ultimately the pressure to remain respectable was both spiritual and material. In such a close-knit community the known character of a man affected his chances of work, especially of permanent jobs. The very fortunate, usually tradesmen, did possess the 'Open Sesame' of written references but most had to rely on verbal recommendations and *Kevin Maloney* maintains that any man known as a 'bit of a player' was adjudged unreliable. This, he emphasizes, is why people tried to hide personal problems, even though the neighbours had their suspicions, for skeletons in a working-class cupboard had an economic dimension.

But above all it is *Muriel Thompson*, who has battled through the acutest poverty, who sums up the greatest value respectability held for survival: 'I found out there was a lot of love in Richmond. There was a horror of—you know—but if you were a nice person, you had plenty of love around you'. And it was this love that made life bearable and ensured you both emotional and material support in bad times, for the respectable trusted each other and shared food and money, knowing it would one day always come back.

The story of this Richmond generation's lives is shot through with the themes of the struggle to keep their self-respect, no matter what tragedies or deprivations faced them: It was a battle for the integrity of the personality, the moral achievements one did not need wealth to buy. And for most Richmond people these needs and conflicts were to be more important in daily life than politics or religion, even if political and religious leaders played on these ideals and debased them into prejudices. But above all respectability gave some inner relief against the stigma of being working class, of coming from where the bandits lived and from being dropped like an oily rag.

The Economy

The surest path to respectability lay in the gaining of a regular job but for many Richmond people economic respectability remained elusive and precarious. Even in times of economic prosperity most outdoor work, especially labouring, was casual and therefore below the margin of respectability. Even though Richmond was a stiff walk from the port of Melbourne, many Richmond men sought work on the wharves and not a few still worked in the bush, leaving their wives and children to fend for themselves in the city. But the Edwardian years culminating in World War I saw Richmond and its fellow industrial suburbs in a state of economic transition from an essentially pre-industrial manufacturing structure reliant on sweating and small units to a modern factory-based industrial system. And while this would do much to reduce the sweating evil, it would also mount an effective attack on skill and artisan independence. It would create more regular jobs for women, juveniles and some men, but it would do so at the expense of skill.

The devastating 1890s depression fostered a new Factories and Shops Act in 1896 which, through the establishment of Wages Boards, succeeded in abolishing much of the sweating in the clothing and footwear trades that were the backbone of Richmond and neighbouring Collingwood. As prosperity returned, manufacturers had to accommodate the new Act and reorganize their enterprises. By the time the Wages Boards were investigated and reviewed by the Royal Commission of 1902–3, production was increasingly being transferred from outworkers' homes to regulated workplaces and for those who continued to work at home the Wages Board rates gave them a living wage for an eight-hour day.

Not that sweaters had given up easily. One dogged survivor was Charles Edward Robinson, a heavy boot manufacturer in Richmond, who employed about twenty men. Evasive and pleading ignorance of such essentials as the wholesale and retail prices of his boots and the output of every worker, he claimed that his employees were not on piecework and that they received £2 2s a week. Yes, his father had been prosecuted several times under the Act so that two years ago the business was registered under his name; and, although confident that his workmen were in 'comfortable circumstances', yes, it was true that the factory opened only on Tuesday, Wednesdays and sometimes Thursdays; and no, he did not know what the men did during the balance of the week.[54]

Bigger fish than Robinson were equally determined to oppose and circumvent the Wages Boards. John Bedggood, the founder of one of Richmond's biggest boot factories, started sending his samples to be copied by the lower paid workers of free-trade New South Wales: 'I am not going to break my heart bootmaking. I am as courageous as anyone in the city, but I am not going to keep a hospital for people'. But the new factories were no hospitals as employers retaliated by instituting the 'task system'. Workers were set a task to complete in the eight-hour day and the standard was based on the speeds of the fittest and fastest. Slow workers were sacked or kept on if they agreed to hand back to their employers a portion of their pay after the wages book had been entered up to the satisfaction of the factory inspectors. In the boot trade cases were reported of men taking home twenty-five to thirty shillings when the Wages Board rates were £2 14s and £2 15s. A youth was getting fivepence a pair of boots when the log was eightpence and one old man took home only ten shillings, a fifth of the wage entered in the employer's books. At the other extreme, highly skilled workers complained that the Wages Board had destroyed their advantage as the minimum award was also observed as the maximum, regardless of quality of workmanship. The task set workers was always too severe and they found themselves forced to work harder in the factories than ever before. One tailoress confessed: 'You are in continual dread that you are not making the money up'. The Commission concluded: 'The task system was really piecework at a lower rate than the log'.[55]

The nastiest reaction to the Wages Boards came from the tanning and fellmongering industries led by the great Richmond firms of Kennon's and J. Dale and Co. As soon as the Act came into force all the tanneries closed down and reopened only when the Act lapsed. J. Dale and Co., the largest establishment in the colony, declared it would have to fold once the forty-eight-hour week replaced the sixty-hour week, and the employers' representatives on the fellmongering Wages Board resigned and refused to co-operate. And while the captains of noxious industry played politics, men from all over Richmond were out of work. But the unions were determined to keep their Wages Boards, for these noxious trades were still largely casual, the pay absurdly low and the working conditions disgusting and unhealthy. Robert Hunter, an employee of Dale's and president of the Operative Fellmongers' Union, told the Commission of the pullers and the sweathouse men forced to work on decomposing skins. The foreman worked most of his sixty-hour week in the sweathouse delivering the pelts to the pullers for which Dale's paid him thirty-six shillings before the Act: 'The foreman is now in hospital'. The Commission remained unimpressed by the employers' fears of financial ruin and J. Dale and Co., despite the forty-eight-hour week, in fact had decades of prosperity ahead.[56]

The success of the Wages Boards was confirmed and their jurisdiction was to be extended to still unregulated industries like milk carters and dairy workers where hours were up to a hundred a week. In 1907 the Basic Wage was put into operation and the fundamental wage- and condition-fixing structures that controlled working-class economic life for the rest of the century were in place. But the real problem facing the working class was more than inadequate pay and poor conditions. The largest problem was the immaturity of the economy and the shortage of regular and suitable work for all those desiring it. Even in good years, unemployment stood at levels that would be quite unacceptable by the 1960s. An analysis of the 15000 unemployed in the winter of 1899 revealed the alarming fact that 52 per cent of them were artisans or skilled labour, 47 per cent were unskilled and 0.08 per cent white-collar workers: 20 per cent of these were assessed to be first-class workmen, 50 per cent as fair to medium workmen and 30 per cent as either too old, too weak or too lightly built for heavy work. The economic development of the next fourteen years would do little to provide work for many of these people. The new factory system had no place for slow workers and technological advance was to result in the de-skilling of processes, replacing skilled men and women with juveniles.[57]

Food processors and the clothing and footwear trades were leaders in the de-skilling of work. In jam factories girls under a male foreman even made jam tins; in clothing factories apprentices were prevented from learning to make a garment right through because fragmented specialization speeded production; in the boot trade Frank Anstey estimated that five people produced more boots in 1911 than did six in 1909. Union protests were usually in vain: only the pastrycooks had a victory when they forced the registration of Swallow and Ariell's employees under the Pastrycooks' Wages Board. Yet had the Wages Boards never existed, the modern factory system would still have proved irresistible to employers. William Sutherland's vinegar, pickle and cordial factory had planned its economies of scale and processes so cleverly that when the Wages Board came into operation their unskilled girls on nine and fourteen shillings a week were earning above the log. The brand new Rosella factory erected in 1905 followed Sutherland's example, and using seasonal female labour, impressed as 'probably the largest factory of its kind in the Commonwealth'. Between 1904 and 1910 the proportion of females in Victorian factories per hundred males rose from 50.90 to 54.09; the nearest figures were in New South Wales with 27.27 to 32.26. By 1913, with the highest number of women in factories in Australia, Victoria had the lowest average wage, and along with New South Wales, the fastest declining birth-rate. The strain of work on expectant mothers was blamed for a rise in prematurity and increased maternal and infant deaths and *Labor Call* saw only dangers of 'race deterioration' in the increasing participation of women in the new factory system. Women themselves far preferred the regulation and companionship of the factory to the tyrannies and isolation of domestic service. The factory girl valued her freedom out of working hours and domestic service increasingly became the refuge of the desperate or of single supporting mothers with young children.[58]

Much of the industry developed in this brief Edwardian period was to endure until the present day. In 1909 the magnificent Bryant & May's match factory was built by Clements Langford. Bryant & May's promised to abandon the use of white phosphorus (if other match factories followed suit) and reconstituted their chemical formula so that 'suicide by drinking match heads in solution is now impossible'. Up to four hundred workers enjoyed central heating and insulation against the summer sun, a two-storeyed recreation hall which included a games room, library and dining room, a 'top quality bowling club', tennis courts and a pleasant garden. Fun at work, it was hoped, would distract workers from the size of their pay packets. Marshall's Shoe factory and the Braeside Shirt factory (Pelaco) set new standards in mass production. At Braeside lavish Christmas parties, and a fortnight's (unpaid) leave each year were intended to reconcile the girls to their semi-skilled status and disguised piecework rates of pay.[59]

Fun and fellowship as an antidote to discontent was not an invention of the new factory system. Most large Richmond employers set great store by their Christmas excursions and parties and ruled their workforce with conscious paternalism. Richmond abounded in family firms like Bosisto's, the eucalyptus oil manufacturer, Kennon's and Dale's, Harding's Crumpets, Wertheim's piano factory and a score of others. Workers in small establishments tended to suffer the worst conditions and the highest incidence of accidents but their intimacy with their employers sometimes made industrial action impossible. Richmond's most prominent paternalist was G. H. Bennett, the cordial manufacturer and M.L.A. A former mayor as well as parliamentarian, Bennett's work picnics were lavish and ostentatious. In 1900 thirty gaily decorated wagons took the four hundred Picnickers to the Royal Agricultural Showgrounds. The Richmond City Brass Band headed the procession through Richmond's principal streets and at the Showground employees in jockeys' silks competed in handicap trotting races while their families amused themselves at the sideshows, merry-go-round, shooting gallery, or the fortune teller, and listened to the minstrels. Bennett's workers were so grateful for their 1904 picnic that one hundred assembled at his home. 'Stonehenge', on the hill and presented him with a 'handsome claret jug and silver salver inscribed'. During working hours, however, G. H. Bennett's drivers had less fun: in 1914 the firm was fined for working carters for more than sixty hours a week without a permit—one unfortunate had put in eighty-two hours in a week. *John Brown* remembers Squire Kennon taking the Wages Board through the tannery and lying through his teeth: 'this and this isn't very hard work'. Yet Kennon's were never so stingy with their parties: to mark their Diamond Jubilee in 1923 they spent £2000 on a day's picnic at Mentone, slaughtering two hundred turkeys for the feast.[60]

The other area of industry that began to develop in those years was engineering. Messrs Ruwolt moved from Wangaratta to Richmond to manufacture dredges for alluvial gold fields, and between 1908 and 1921 they built twenty-eight massive dredges, exporting many to Malaya. Jaques

Bros, after insolvency in the 1890s depression, recovered once the new gold discoveries called for complex mining equipment. The two world wars were to expand the metal industries dramatically, and with the growth of the automotive trade) engineering would provide the most secure employment for skilled men in Richmond in the twentieth century.[61]

But the Edwardian revival that did most for the tradesmen and labourers thrown into destitution by the land crash was in the building trades. Large firms like Clements Langford won contracts for new factories, theatres and office buildings: in 1915 Clements Langford were to complete the £40 000 'palatial' Hoyts theatre in Bourke Street, Melbourne, in a record twenty-four weeks. Jobs and the new Wages Boards were putting money into consumers' pockets and by 1910 the expanding retail trade had encouraged large stores in Richmond like Love and Lewis and Head's to rebuild and expand. The first Maples furniture store opened near Richmond people's doors and one of Richmond's best known landmarks, the gold ball on the dome of Dimelow and Gaylard's Model Store twinkled over Swan Street for the first time as the new Dimmey's rose from the ashes of the old. Today Dimmey's is the sole survivor of the great Edwardian department stores in Richmond. In July 1911 alone a new match factory was being built for E. L. Bell and Co. in Burnley, Marshall's Shoes were extending, as were a Tennyson Street confectioner, A. McNair's pottery works in Bendigo Street, Saunders' Malt Extract and a rubber works in Rooney Street. The increased demand for electric power now forced the Melbourne Electric Supply Co. to add new machinery to the Green Street power house.[62]

Workers began to return to Richmond and many on regular wages were able to leave the shared cottages and boarding houses they had fled to in the Depression. The demand for housing exploded. By 1912 the local labour market was reported by estate agents to be 'entirely absorbed'; rents rose 50 per cent in Richmond between 1907 and 1912 and speculators moved back into the provision of workers' homes. All over Melbourne the toothless gaps left in suburban streets by the Land Crash were being filled with Edwardian villas sprouting sensuous fretwork and extravagant chimney pots. In Mary Street (Centre Ward) thirty-three new houses were built between 1907 and 1913 to add to the existing 109 in 1904. In December 1911 one large firm commenced building a terrace of cottages in South Richmond with rents fixed at fourteen shillings a week. Within a few hours of posting the 'to let' notices, deposits had been paid on the whole row and the rents were raised a further shilling.[63] The 1912 valuation revealed the extent of Richmond's recovery:

	Net Valuation	*Population*
1880	£113 000	21 756
1890	£311 000	36 488
1899	£171 000	34 310
1912	£289 181	40 651[64]

But the flurry of building and the lines of sanitized factory girls in smart uniforms peeling peaches and chopping tomatoes could not hide the thousands still trapped into poverty by the seasonality of production and the immaturity of manufacturing industry. The 1911 Census still found 14 930 unemployed males in Victoria, the majority of them between the ages of fifteen and thirty. And while the better-off congratulated the State on its new prosperity and told the trade unions that there was no 'genuine unemployment' in Melbourne, the working class knew their lives to be as precarious as ever before. But the brief Edwardian boom established the industrial structure that would shape the economic destiny of the children born in Richmond in those years for the rest of their working lives. Not until World War II would working conditions and opportunities enter a period of equivalent change and development.[65]

The Politics

Politics were to be more important in Richmond during the twentieth century than in most Australian suburban communities, and the focus of that political energy overwhelmingly parochial rather than parliamentary and national. Not that Richmond's parliamentary representatives were of no great consequence in national affairs. On the contrary, of its four Federal members between 1901 and 1965 one was a Prime Minister, one later a deputy Prime Minister, one a leader of the Federal opposition, and one, had he not led the 1955 splitters into the Democratic Labor Party, was believed destined by A.L.P. power brokers for the prime ministership. The Federal electorate of Yarra was one of the safest Labor seats in the country until the 1955 Split when it was temporarily threatened by the D.L.P. Similarly the State seat of Richmond has been Labor since 1908 apart from being the sole D.L.P. seat between 1955 and 1958, and its State member between 1962 and 1977 was the leader of the State parliamentary Labor party for ten years. Until the Split Richmond's parliamentarians' contests were for pre-selection rather than for election and only the Split forced parliamentary candidates to work in the electorate to win support. Such a safe seat released parliamentarians for high political duties and local political life turned inwards to the complex world of Labor machinations and local government. Yet here too, once Labor gained control of the Richmond City Council in 1913, there remained little point in opposition from conservatives and independents. Local people with political ambitions saw no alternative to being 'Labor' and the Richmond Labor party embraced some improbable bed-fellows over the years. Personal power was the business of Richmond politics, power based on family feuds, faction fights and back-room deals. Loyalty was the highest virtue in Richmond life: 'being Labor' was like barracking for 'the Tigers', Richmond's Australian Rules Football Club—it was politics of the heart rather than of the intellect. And the issues that bonded and divided Richmond people were loyalty to family, to friends, to the party and to the church. By 1955 loyalty to the A.L.P. and the Catholic church were to become tragically incompatible, turning Richmond into one of the bitterest and most damaged battlegrounds of the whole disaster.

Within a decade of Labor winning control of local government, the Richmond City Council had acquired the evil reputation for corruption, electoral fraud, intimidation and criminal associations that has dogged it ever since. This was undoubtedly a calumny on many of the men and women who had held municipal office in Richmond but there were fires to produce some of the smoke that has captivated outside observers and mythologizers. Certainly the metropolitan press took delight in Labor's fall from grace in Richmond: nearly every press report chronicling the decline into mental illness and alcoholism of one of Richmond's most disputatious and colourful local politicians is headed: 'Ex-mayor on Assault Charge' or 'Ex-mayor in Court'. The Victorian A.L.P. found Richmond an embarrassment but chose only to intervene in its worst excesses. The late Pat Kennelly, when State Secretary of the A.L.P., decided that Richmond's 'rough stuff was not of great consequence:

> They all did it—put in a vote, drag in someone from another ward. You have to be used to it. They talk about selection ballots and how 'crook' they were in the old days, but if there were 5 per cent of the votes that were 'crook', that's the most there were . . . That's all. They joined the branches, they held their meetings and they sent in balance sheets that I didn't believe, but still, why wake the world?[66]

While the M.H.R. for Yarra, Jim Cairns, also decided to tolerate the Richmond machine, but his reasons were more those of an academic:

> The machine itself worked because of corruption, because of 'jobs'—not a bad sort of corruption I suppose—jobs on the Council and other things the Council could do. That sort of corruption is different. In other areas like Hawthorn, Camberwell and Kew councillors don't accept £10 or £50 like they do in Richmond, but they benefit from being on the Council through

> their business activities and thereby get far more money, many many times more money as a result. But they don't even see it to be corruption. However, people in Richmond were always aware that it was corruption and had a conscience about it and in some ways would not go as far, would stop short and would like to change. But no, they wouldn't like to change or stop short in Hawthorn. Having a neatly pressed suit—never blue like Jacky O'Connell used to wear—was evidence [in one councillor's case] that he wanted something better. Unfortunately the thing he wanted was to be middle-class, really bourgeois, but no one in Hawthorn wanted to be something better in the sense of being something different—they wanted more of it. But those people who were corrupted in Richmond were uncomfortable about getting more of it. They had never lost the instinctive feeling that that was wrong, and that applied to their physical violence too.

The story of Labor's blemished record in Richmond tells more of the special problems of working-class communities than it does of proletarian moral viciousness. Society tends to expect greater virtue in Labor politicians and remains blind to the pressures that afflict and tempt them. The poor need intelligent, fair and efficient administration more than the rich. In Edwardian Victoria local government bore responsibilities for social welfare, sanitation and drainage, food and drink adulteration, roads and quarries, town planning, building regulation and slum control, infant welfare and pasteurized milk, health and cultural enlightenment—a burden far in excess of its financial and human resources. The 1919 Spanish Flu epidemic and the Great Depression would force State and Federal governments to assume some of these duties, but this did not alter the fact that poor local government damaged the social well-being of the working class. Irrespective of the quality of local politicians, a city council like Richmond's was doomed to fail many of its constituents; consequently it is not surprising that local politics quickly came to fulfil other, less expensive but also less admirable needs. The poor have to exploit whatever resources that are at hand. Just as the poor in the West End of London regarded the rich not as their oppressors but as a fortunate resource to live off—like coal—so also has Labor-controlled municipal government in Australia often been regarded as a fortunate and legitimate source of jobs, political patronage and financial kickbacks. Such petty corruption was a natural extension of the sub-legal deals, lurks, favours and of the bounty that 'fell off the back of trucks' that thrived in the masculine pub culture of working-class communities. Poor people would insist that such lurks were essential to survival; equally, working-class councillors would assert that municipal office imposed financial burdens of entertainment, transport and the maintenance of a telephone in their homes that a working man's wage could not remotely pay for. Moreover, large-scale corruption cannot flourish when there is little money in the municipality. The few allegations of bribery that were investigated and proven before 1960 all concerned remarkably small amounts of money. That would change, however, in the 1960s.

But if the spoils of office were small beer, the psychological consolations were immense and even more corrupting. Politics offered excitement, achievement and prestige to working men trapped in menial occupations that could not fulfil their talents. For this Edwardian generation it was almost impossible to move out of the working class by intellectual attainment. The paths to upward social mobility were few: small business, self-employment for a tradesman, public service examinations, elementary school teaching, the church, sport and, of course, politics. The working class possessed a vast reservoir of frustrated intelligence and creativity and when such men and women achieved political or trade union office, they clung to it with a desperation not felt by their conservative colleagues who had legal practices and business directorships to return to. Vanity more than cupidity was to be the undoing of many of Richmond's champions of Labor.

The Edwardian period in Richmond witnessed the capture of political power by the working class. Of Richmond's two Victorian members of parliament in 1900 one was a benevolent capitalist, the other a working man turned class traitor. G. H. Bennett, the cordial manufacturer, did little for Richmond beyond the provision of extravagant public entertainments that simultaneously advertised his wares: seven thousand children attended his party to mark Queen Victoria's jubilee and each year he sponsored the St Ignatius' school picnic. Bennett inspired genuine affection amongst people still so deprived that philanthropic largess evoked gratitude rather than wariness and his funeral cortège in 1908 comprised nearly two hundred vehicles and extended one and a half miles on leaving St Ignatius'. Bennett's colleague in the two-member constituency of Richmond was an altogether more complex character. William Arthur Trenwith was born in Tasmania of a convict father and rose to prominence as a new type of aggressive trade union leader in the 1880s while secretary of the Operative Bootmakers' Union. Pugnacious but ambitious for gentility, his relations with his union members were always stormy. In 1889 he was elected to the Victorian Legislative Assembly as the first Labor man in the parliament. He assumed leadership of the growing Labor group, but devoted to the ideal of a 'Lib-Lab' alliance, he disdained the independent Labor party and on Federation entered the Senate under the wing of Alfred Deakin and went with the Fusionists to form the first united conservative opposition. He died in 1925, vilified by the Labor movement that had launched him into public life, but the material rewards of £4330 realty and £3345 personality must have been some consolation. Yet Trenwith did leave one legacy to his Labor successors that endured—protectionism. Richmond's politicians, culminating in Jim Cairns, continued as conspicuous champions of protectionism on behalf of an electorate whose footwear and textile trades had much to fear from cheap foreign imports. The protectionist legacy made sound political sense and defensible economic sense, but, tragically, it also served to legitimize the instinctive xenophobia of ordinary Australians.[67]

On Bennett's death in 1908 the Labor Party captured the State seat of Richmond with the election of E. J. Cotter, a cooper working in Sutherland's Vinegar factory. Ted Cotter held Richmond for thirty-seven kindly but undistinguished years: parliamentary conviviality rather than social ambition was to be his undoing. There are suspicions that he had connections in the 1930s with John Wren, but his early and best years in politics reveal him as no captive of the millionaire sportsman and his shady political machine. Something quenched the fire in Cotter's belly, however, and in the twilight of his career he did little other than inspire some of Richmond's dirtiest tricks as rivals conspired to defeat him for the preselection.

The new Labor politician to stamp himself effectively upon Edwardian Richmond was the M.H.R. for Yarra, Frank Tudor. Tudor was the archetypal respectable artisan radical. A lifelong teetotaller and the deacon of the Congregational Church, he had a moral breadth that embraced Home Rule for Ireland, to the horror of many Richmond Protestants. At the time of his election to parliament he was president of the Melbourne Trades Hall Council. His fellow parliamentarian, R. A. Crouch, assessed him as 'not a good or deep speaker, but a good friend and an indefatigable member for his constituents'. His house was always open and his unfailing kindness secured Yarra as a Labor stronghold. He never missed a local meeting or gathering and, like all wise Richmond politicians, involved himself in sport. In 1913 *Labor Call* was impressed by 'the strong odour of Labor sanctity' in the Richmond Football Club: 'at the last annual meeting Customs Minister Tudor was in the chair and moved the adoption of the balance sheet, Gordon Webber M.L.A. seconded it, while the mover of the adoption of the report was M.L.A. Cotter'. Tudor served in three Labor ministries as Minister for Customs but it was to be the Conscription crisis in World War I that would thrust greatness and the leadership of the Federal A.L.P. upon him.[68] With Richard Ignatius Loughnan, the founder of the Builders' Labourers Union, as his campaign secretary, Tudor quickly built up a solid Labor following in Richmond. *Ted Sullivan*, who was to spend many years as a Richmond councillor, remembers of Tudor:

> I cut my teeth hanging on to my father's hand listening to the man speak from the back of a wood carter's truck with a hurricane lamp, expounding the policies. And to get them there they used to borrow the auctioner's bell and go round the streets. And they'd come out in their hundreds—there were no pictures or TV in those days—the peasants liked to listen to their

> parliamentary representatives and they'd stay there until 10 or 11 at night. I think it was a better world then because people weren't blasé—they were genuinely interested in the Labor philosophy of life.[69]

Tudor's solicitousness and organization rewarded him with a steady growth in his majority until 1914 when he stood unopposed and still commanded a 72 per cent turnout. Some voters established proud local traditions like Miss Godwin of 'Yarra' in Coppin Street: the first woman to vote in Richmond after the enfranchisement of women, she saw to it that she was the first woman to vote in every subsequent election.[70]

As Tudor reaped the benefits of the creation of the Richmond Labor organization, so also did the working class use it to gradually capture the Richmond City Council. The Richmond branch of the Political Labor Council was formed in February 1901. Four unofficial Labor men were already on the Richmond Council: Councillors Sutch, Sheedy, Carter and P. J. O'Connor (who was to be the first 'Wren man' in the Victorian parliament). In July 1902, under the presidency of Phillip Halfpenny of the teetotal Richmond Workingmen's Club, the Richmond P.L.C. nominated its first official Labor candidates for the August Council elections. The commercial élite on Council became alarmed. Councillor Charles Jago, the butcher who hired brass bands to advertise his meat, deplored the greed of the Workingmen's Club in its appetite for power and the support offered by State and Federal parliamentarians.[71] Councillor Herbert King, the non-sectarian undertaker, found himself heckled by the radical, Dr W. D. Carnegie, during his election speech to the 'silk department' of West Ward:

> Dr Carnegie: Is the candidate in favour of children being sent to a school that has been reported by none other than the Council's Health Officer as being reeking with scarlatina?
>
> Cr King: Even though I am an undertaker, I would not favour such a thing. (laughter)[72]

King lost his seat; but not to a Labor man, as West Ward was considered too ambitious for the P.L.C. However, a burst of 'tremendous cheering' greeted the announcement of the result when R. H. Solly, President of the Trades Hall Council, won North Ward in an extraordinary election, and Robert Hunter thrashed the popular publican, George Male, 739 votes to 439 in South Ward. It would take eleven years for Labor to win control of the Richmond Council and elect the first Labor mayor.[73]

The élite was not slow to perceive the Labor threat and, ironically in view of subsequent history, the Labor men discovered some peculiarities in the Voters' Rolls: Frank Tudor had been 'accidentally' omitted and the dead were generously represented. In 1904 and 1908 Councillor Edwin Crawcour succeeded in banning *Tocsin* and the Sydney *Worker* from the two Richmond libraries: the people, he opined, 'wanted something to improve their minds and educate the rising generation, not vitiate them'.[74] Almost as a gesture of defiance, Crawcour threw two mayoral balls during his 1904–5 mayoralty. It did mean that his wife had to wear her dress twice but its proliferation of detail could stand a second viewing:

> . . . a handsome gown of black-spotted crystal chiffon over white glace silk worked with black Chantilly lace and chenille, the trained skirt draped round the foot with deep Chantilly lace, caught with sequin motifs and showing frills of white, edged with black ruching. The bodice was handsomely trimmed with lace and medallions of sequin with rope of black chenille, finished with jet drops.[75]

When Gordon Webber M.L.A. was elected as Richmond's first 'Labor mayor in 1913 he banned the mayoral ball and sent all the children of Richmond to the seaside instead. Thus began the annual Parents' and Citizens' children's picnic, one of Richmond's most delightful and enduring traditions. The Melbourne *Herald* seized on Webber's ban as an example of how Labor mayors would create disastrous financial losses. *Labor Call* estimated that the drapers of Richmond lost up to £4000: 'Gordon practically threw the money into the sea, when he sent all the Richmond school children to the seaside, to learn, amongst other things, mixed bathing'.[76]

Gordon Webber was one of the most talented Labor politicians to emerge from Richmond in the early years of the P.L.C. Elected to the Richmond Council in 1908 at the age of twenty-three, he had started in business as a perambulator maker, but by 1912 when he was elected M.L.A. for Abbotsford, he was secretary, of the Soap and Candle Workers' Union and one of the most popular leaders in the Victorian Labor movement. A teetotaller, a Unitarian, and to the private glee of the establishment, a republican, he belonged to a nineteenth century tradition of puritanical artisan radicalism that had but a short reign in Richmond Labor history. Deaf to the pragmatic pleas of Labor colleagues, Mayor Webber refused to make Loyal Toasts at functions. The outraged Richmond magistrates refused to sit on the Bench with him, questions were asked in Parliament and the conservative Melbourne daily paper, the *Argus*, had a field day. The Richmond Ladies' Benevolent Society, a repository of conservative virtue, clashed so violently with Webber and his Labor councillors over the allocation of their Council grant that the police were called to bring order to the Council Chamber. Only the outbreak of war would force Webber to recant and deprive the establishment of such an inflammatory political weapon.[77]

But for all the theatricality of Labor's rise to power in the Council, the real business of local government muddled along with little change. Ever worried about increasing rates, by 1912 the Council was in a dilemma.

Although Richmond's indebtedness was less than half that of Prahran or South Melbourne, councillors on both sides knew that Richmond had to improve its services and roads and that they had left the running until too late. The war hastened the use of motor transport and with sharply rising costs Richmond faced a financial catastrophe. By 1912 Richmond looked enviously at Prahran where Chapel Street had been wood-blocked for eighteen years, literally paving the way for the heavy investment in shopping and industry. Swan Street was sealed and a great success, but every winter Bridge Road was ankle deep in mud and the cost now of surfacing it was £13 000. That year Council hoped the problem would simply go away and decided to spend money on the enlarging of the Town Hall and the abattoirs and the acquiring of a refuse destructor and a tar distilling plant. Labor would be equally slow to react to Richmond's needs, and ideals often faltered in the face of financial stringency. The resources to better working-class life and work were so limited that Labor councillors were often faced with impossible choices and unsatisfying compromises. In January 1913, for instance, Webber and his Labor colleagues were embarrassed when the Minimum Allotment Anti-Slum Crusade congratulated the conservative Richmond councillors for refusing building permits for two houses on pocket-handkerchief allotments in Brougham Street. Webber defended his vote on the grounds that the housing need was so great and that the plans allowed for 300 square feet at the back of the houses, but the criticism still stung.[78]

One Labor innovation in 1913 was the commencement of public lectures on the City Reserve on Sunday afternoons. Dr David Rosenberg, Richmond's most loyal scholarship boy, was chairman of the P.L.C.'s lecture committee and organized talks from Dr W. S. F. Bottomley on National Health schemes. Professor Osborn on 'Food Facts and Fallacies', Mr Mullaney on 'Democratic Facts' and C. J. Bennett, President of the Trades Hall, on 'Drink, its Causes and Cure'. The tone was self-improving and intellectual and the attendances 'very sparse'. The lectures continued well into the war and became increasingly anti-conscriptionist; only Adela Pankhurst, speaking on 'War' in April 1914, attracted a good audience and on one Sunday in June 1914 Frank Anstey was to speak and altogether failed to appear. Artisan self-improvement had little appeal; in Richmond the acquisition of power was the thing. As to what Labor politicians would do with that power was not so clear. Renown more than reform preoccupied many Richmond politicians, an obsession born of class stigma. And that stigma was real: the *Richmond Guardian* said in 1915 of the late Councillor Jack Street, the first Labor councillor to die: 'He was only a workingman, but he was above temptation'.[79]

By the outbreak of war, the Richmond Labor movement had begun to assume the character and structure it was to maintain until the present day. The puritan artisan tradition inherited from England and Scotland was in retreat. In its place were rising the networks of families and factions like the Loughnans and the O'Connells. The first Geoff O'Connell entered Council in 1913; the talented Heagney family had its first politicians in office. The composition of the Richmond Labor movement was becoming more Catholic and some local politicians were finding patronage from John Wren. The push from the Catholic Federation had already exploded in the State Political Labor Council. The war would bring battles over hotel hours, State aid to Catholic schools, conscription and Irish nationalism, that would further strengthen the sectarian complications of Labor in Richmond and add fuel to the class hostilities cloaked under Protestant purity.

2

Childhood

The Family Home

The family homes of this Edwardian generation of children would be much the same as those in which they would commence their own child-bearing and would inhabit until old age. In their lifetime only the Victorian Housing Commission would provide a significant number of new habitations, and with the exception of those wards which have given way to industry, the housing stock in place by the outbreak of World War I is largely intact today. Comfort and convenience would improve but not until the 1950s and 1960s did incomes become sufficient to install hot water systems, gas stoves and fires, to add bathrooms and proper laundries and to buy washing machines and refrigerators. The earliest improvement, however, came with the reduction of family size, for the chic cottages coveted by the young sophisticates who have rediscovered Richmond were hardly adequate for the Victorian and Edwardian families for whom they were built.

In Edwardian Richmond 52 per cent of the houses had three or four rooms, another 22 per cent had five and a mere 1 per cent had one or two. The standard worker's home was a single- or double-fronted cottage, 54 per cent of the housing stock being wooden. Richmond, with its pockets of large houses, ran third behind Fitzroy and Collingwood in population density for the Melbourne metropolitan area: 37.14, 30.02 and 28.28 people per acre respectively. But these three were still far ahead of the next most densely populated suburbs of South Melbourne and Prahran with 19.99 and 19.55.[1]

Pressure within the home was somewhat relieved by a dramatic fall in the Edwardian birth-rate after the peak of the 1880s boom. In 1909 the

Richmond birth-rate was only 23.3 per thousand compared with 41.89 per thousand in 1889. By 1913 it began to rise again to hover around 30 per thousand, reflecting the Edwardian economic recovery.[2] Large families of five or more children were still common, however, even among Protestants, and old people now marvel at how they were all fitted in. *Hamish Roberts* was sixth in a family of seven boys and three girls, and when the family moved to the Burnley cottage their father was buying at 10s a week through the State Savings Bank, the girls had one bedroom, three boys the other, two were in a bungalow in the back yard and two had already married. The *Smiths* were even more cramped in their still smaller house in Francis Street. Five sons and a lodger slept in one bedroom, their parents and the youngest and only daughter slept in the other. By the age of seven *Phyllis* was too old to share her parents room, especially as her father drank in bed and had bouts of violence, so she slept on the front veranda behind a blind and with the window open in case she became frightened.[3]

Bathrooms were rare in Edwardian Richmond and most houses had no internal supply of water, only a tap in the back yard. Water pressure was appalling—it could take a quarter of an hour to fill a bucket in some areas. All water had to be heated either on the stove or in a wood-fired copper in the back yard. Most families bathed on bath night, usually a Saturday in preparation for Sunday school, a cleansing ritual of more than physical significance for some.[4] *Lilian Campbell* at thirteen and 'like a string bean', was still bathed by her mother in a galvanized tin bath in front of a roaring fire and rubbed down afterwards with camphorated oil 'Poor mum used to have to bring in the bath'. The *Smiths* had primitive washing facilities in the laundry:

> Lack of privacy was a problem to all and that was why you learned to live naturally. Take us—there were nine people living in a four-roomed house. The bathroom and washhouse was all in one and to get to the W.C. in the back yard you had to go through the kitchen and the washhouse. A curtain was put across and that was the only difference. Very often you'd be in the bath and mum or your sister would say 'I'm coming through', and they'd just mind their business as they went past. You took no notice of each other—you weren't exhibiting yourself but it gave you a feeling of comradeship.

Many families failed to take such lack of privacy so easily and some women remained afflicted with pathological sexual modesty for the rest of their lives.

The heart of the working-class home was the kitchen. Big families in small houses meant that front parlours were often sacrificed for bedrooms so the kitchen was the only communal room in the house. Most had one-fire stoves although gas stoves bought on hire-purchase were making an appearance. With a table, a sink or work-bench and perhaps an easy chair, a clothes horse and numerous pairs of long, restless male legs, it was a tight fit. *Lilian Campbell*'s family were better off in their double-fronted house in Stawell Street where their large block enabled them to run poultry and keep a pony and jinker. The family room was dominated by a big table and a black monster of a stove. The bath stood waiting in the corner, and crockery and food were kept in a pine chiffonier-type safe. *Lilian*'s fey Irish mother one day took a dislike to the pantry ' "That pantry's dark—knock it down", and I knocked it down and made the room bigger'. Next door was the Preservene Soap factory:

> I'd hop over the fence and throw all the barrel pieces back and Mum would light the fire with them. Well, if Mum set fire to our mantelpiece and the chimney once, I think she did it regularly every week. On would go the wax and wood and then BOOM!

Outside the back door was the ubiquitous Coolgardie safe for storing milk and meat, but at *Lilian*'s the back door had the added charm of being framed by chicken carcasses 'Mum was always pulling the chickens' necks, and hanging them up at the back door—"bleeding", she'd call it'.

Most working-class families were weekly tenants. In Mary Street the percentage of owner occupiers stayed around 35 per cent and Dingle and Merrett's study of the Collingwood ratebooks revealed a level of tenancy in 1911 in excess of 70 per cent, with the poorest ward reaching 82 per cent. Their findings suggest that the 1890s depression did not significantly raise the level of tenancy because many of the repossessions by banks and building societies were of landlords' holdings. Home ownership was not to rise until the early 1920s. Richmond's landlords fell into two broad categories: working-class people who built or bought one or two properties to provide an income in old age, and large-scale operators who did make a lot of money. Some big landlords were also employers who gained both income and industrial harmony from their investment. Daniel Barrett, a Mary Street landlord, owned twenty-one properties in Richmond when he died in 1921. They ranged from substantial brick terraces and a seven-roomed house with stables on the hill to tiny cottages in the meanest streets in South Richmond, and, with rents from thirty shillings for the hill house to £1 for the terraces and nine shillings for the worst cottage, he netted £18 0s 6d a week. Yet such handsome returns were no incentive for landlords to maintain their properties in good repair, for the rates were assessed on improved values.[5]

The Edwardian slum problem was different from the neglect and decay that pervaded the whole suburb by World War II. Much of the Edwardian housing stock was relatively new and still in good condition. The slums surveyed by Constable Koetsveld in 1914 for the Royal Commission on the Housing Conditions of the People were the remnants of early colonial Richmond left after the development of the 1880s. The worst slums he found were hidden down lanes or behind newer houses:

> Little Wellington Street Nos 35 and 37, three rooms each, rent 8s. each; three adults at No. 35, and two adults at No. 37; no bath copper or troughs; land 30 feet by 51 feet for the two of them. Dove Street: This is another very bad place you go into a right-of-way leading off into another right-of-way. No. 26, four rooms, rent 10s.; parents and seven children. No. 28, four rooms, rent 10s.; parents and three children. No. 30, four rooms, rent 10s.; parents and six children . . . These three places are on land 33 feet by 66 feet.[6]

Few of these residential lanes and their cottages remain today, but one rare survival is Theresa Street off Mary Street, a terrace of four three-roomed cottages built in 1916 by a local furniture retailer, Patrick Macauley, after an earlier terrace was condemned. The access lane and right-of-way are still unmade.

The slums were the refuge of the incapacitated, the alcoholic, the senile and the plain dirty. And as many of the Edwardian slums were the remnants of the early colony, so too were many of the eccentrics who lived in spectacular dirt, relics of a ruder world. Ann Kelly, 'with a rope around her belly', who lived in a hut in Utopia Lane near Burnley school, provided endless pleasure to taunting children. She scandalized the modern by squatting in the open to urinate, and once when bricks were thrown at her and she was spat upon, she found herself before Richmond Court for using 'insulting words'. The Court was indulgent after Mr G. F. A. Jones reminded the Bench that 'She lives in Utopia, but her life there has not been nearly as happy as we might expect'; and Ma Kelly invoked her associations with the gentry in a last clutch at dignity: 'I have served some of the best families in the State, including the a'Becketts'. In 1908 the Health Inspector, using a ladder, climbed over the barbed-wire-encrusted fence of Mary Hoare, an old woman of 67 Charles Street, and found twenty-one goats, two dogs and forty fowls in her average-sized back yard. Inside the house he found that the goats' bedroom was the front parlour and that her feathered companions were equally at home in the kitchen where there 'was a puddle frequented by ducks and fowls'. The court found Mary Hoare less endearing than Ann Kelly and fined her £5.[7]

The dirty and unrespectable were far more of a trial for the people who had to live near them. Dirty households harboured vermin and respectable families waged constant war against lice, bed bugs and rats that were not of their making. And they were forced to live under a moral stigma that was equally not of their making. Constable Koetsveld spoke as a Richmond man more than as a policeman when he pressed the Royal Commission to understand that most of the inhabitants of the slums he had surveyed were respectable people driven there by the shortage of cheap healthy accommodation. When asked outright whether there were slums in Richmond, he replied defensively: 'Of course it just depends what you call slums; we have no brothels—not one—we have no prostitutes; the last brothel was broken up three years ago in Richmond'.[8] Working-class sensitivity to the stigma of 'the slums' was to bedevil the housing debate until after World War II. Too many middle-class social critics saw slum life as synonymous with vice, and while they did much to bring about housing reform, they did so at the expense of the self-respect of the poor. The Reverend Charles Neville, superintendent of the Presbyterian Mission in Fitzroy, told the Royal Commission in 1914:

> Our experience is that moral apathy and religious indifference go hand in hand with poverty and bad housing conditions. We find there is no inducement in such surroundings given to the people to overcome temptation, but the tendency is to make them liable to yield to drink, gambling and licentiousness. Intemperance is as much an effect as a cause of bad and over-crowded houses. With better homes people become more alive and responsive to agencies of all kinds that offer service.[9]

Nowhere in his evidence to the Royal Commission did he cite low income as the root of the evil, for there was a fundamental conflict between what social reformers and poor saw as the solution to the slum problem. The poor wanted sufficient income to negotiate their own lives; the reformers wanted to change the environment so that good plumbing could bring the poor within the pale of civilized society. Consequently, the working class and their political representatives were ambivalent about the anti-slum campaigners. In 1936 the Communist, Dr G. P. O'Day, in a deputation to the Minister for Transport, spoke of the dangers to health in Melbourne's inner suburbs: 'One of the first things which he learnt about infectious diseases in Melbourne was that infantile paralysis etc., always formed in Richmond'. The Labor Richmond Council was outraged: 'Councillor Huckerby, as a man who had lived in Richmond and brought up four children there, considered the statements as scandalous. Councillor Fitzgerald said that the houses in Richmond would compare with those in any other suburb'; and Councillor O'Connell spoke from the heart: 'I come from a little village called Yarraberg and it would compare favourably with other suburbs'. But perhaps not a little guilt prompted these protestations for until the formation of the Victorian Housing Commission, local government with its responsibilities for community health and services was the sole political authority which could mitigate some of the miseries and dangers of slum life. Undermanned and legally underpowered, they faced great difficulties. Above all, they knew that there was simply not enough low-rental accommodation available to the very poor; and if they were tardy, as they often were, to condemn houses as unfit for human habitation, it was not entirely due to timidity or laziness. On the eve of the outbreak of war in 1914 the shortage of housing had reached such a stage that the now Labor Richmond Council decreed it legal for householders to erect tents in their back yards to accommodate members of their family.[10]

The Edwardian Baby

The babies born in Richmond between 1900 and 1914 were the most biologically fortunate generation so far. The first twenty-five years of the twentieth century saw a halving of the Australian infant mortality rate in a period, according to Professor Douglas Gordon, that 'witnessed the greatest explosion of health ever experienced by mankind'. That is not to say that the Edwardian baby was not exposed to hazards to life and limb that are much reduced today. Diphtheria, scarlet fever, whooping cough, typhoid, tuberculosis, measles, as well as the two great killers of young babies—infections of the gastro-intestinal tract and of the upper respiratory system—still visited working-class communities on a disproportionate scale. Working-class babies were—and are—more liable to congenital defect, prematurity, low birth weight and perinatal death; their mothers are more likely to be young, single or married in haste or at risk after four or more pregnancies. But the working-class baby's real problems began in the home.[11]

The infant death-rate from what were called 'non-preventable causes' like congenital defect and prematurity, remained unchanged; it was the fall in deaths after the first week of life from infant 'diarrhoeal and wasting diseases' and from respiratory diseases like pneumonia, bronchitis and whooping cough that brought the total mortality rate down. These were the diseases of environment and maternal competence. Working-class babies lived in over-crowded homes, damp and dark, where respiratory disease flourished and they were more likely to have consumptive mothers. But the gravest dangers came when breast-feeding failed. Wet-nursing by relatives and neighbours still occurred in working-class communities: *Friedrich Smith*'s mother wet-nursed a neighbour's baby after her own died, and 'she said it was the hardest thing she ever did in her life'. Most had to rely on cow's milk, however, and safe cow's milk was scarce in poor communities. Above all, the working-class mother faced immense practical difficulties in keeping milk fresh and feeding bottles and tubes sterile. This Richmond generation still see a baby's first summer as the most dangerous period of a child's life: 'If you can get him through the summer without dysentery he'll be right'.[12]

In 1901 there were 107 dairies and milk stores in Richmond alone and the Council officers waged a constant war against contaminated and watered-down milk. The best dairies kept a special healthy cow known to be free of tuberculosis for milk for babies and sick children; the worst were a nightmare. *Alice* and *Emma Murphy* used to be sent down to Paddy Maloney's dairy every Sunday after Sunday school to collect the milk. He would milk the cow direct into their billy, his hands black with grime between the fingers. In 1908 the Lady Talbot Institute began supplying safe but unpasteurized milk with an ice-chest to families with a doctor's recommendation. Then in 1911 the Richmond Council decided to withdraw its support from the Institute and to contract the Willsmere Milk Company to provide pasteurized milk. Habits died hard, however, and in the first six months only nineteen parents availed themselves of 1945 pints of the Council's milk while the Lady Talbot Institute continued without subsidy to supply 13 607 pints to Richmond families. The State government, in conjunction with the Institute, then introduced its own pure milk scheme which required that the municipalities pay two-fifths of the cost of the milk and provide trained nurses. The demand for milk in Richmond was in excess of all other suburbs and the Council baulked and renewed its contract with Willsmere. In March 1913 the Lady Talbot Institute withdrew its services from Richmond altogether, leaving the Council with the sole responsibility for the provision of safe milk. When the Richmond municipal health officer produced his health report for 1914 the Richmond infant death-rate had risen slightly, and non-significantly, from 71.8 per thousand to 83.5. Opponents of the Council blamed the milk row, the M.O.H. produced a special report, and the controversy alerted some Richmond mothers to the dangers of unpasteurized milk. In 1915 the use of the Council's milk more than quadrupled and the infant death-rate fell back to around 65 per thousand, where it remained for the next few years.[13]

But the reasons for the fall in infant deaths were more complex than pure milk. There certainly seems to have been an improvement in domestic hygiene. This generation of Edwardian mothers was the first to come under the compulsion of the 1872 Education Act. Bearing in mind that many working-class children benefited little from school and that the Census did not test functional literacy, none the less the 1901 Census found that 9.23 per cent of women over forty in Richmond were illiterate or able to read only, but in the age-groups fifteen to forty only 1.92 per cent were in this category. (In Hawthorn, even with its large number of servants and quarry workers' families, female illiteracy over forty stood at only 4.4 per cent.) Possibly more important was the bubonic plague scare of 1900. In London cholera was regarded as 'the best of all sanitary reformers'; in Australia the bubonic plague scare hastened good hygiene all over the country. In Richmond special house-to-house inspections were conducted by the Council and a general clean-up occurred throughout the municipality. A bounty of twopence a head for dead rats was offered by the Council, inaugurating one of the great pocket-money lurks for Richmond children who quickly became expert rat-catchers. The M.O.H., Dr Bransom, declared the plague scare a 'blessing in disguise', and 1900 saw the best health report in the city's history. By 1903 Dr Bransom was confident that most people boiled all milk and water. In 1909 the infant death-rate was the lowest ever recorded in Richmond to that date: 77.58 per thousand compared to 90.0 for the whole metropolitan area. The installation of sewerage also helped and, although reticulated sewerage is no guarantee that people will observe better hygiene and many do manage open pans with safety, it did help reduce fly-borne disease. House flies were bad beyond belief: *Hamish Roberts* can remember his father carving Sunday roasts black with flies (fly-wire screens did not appear in most homes until the 1930s). But most important of all was the decline in family size: the fewer the women to have five or more pregnancies, the fewer the birth complications and the fewer the babies at risk from tired wombs.[14]

The ruling élite, led by a clutch of prominent medical spokesmen, saw only danger in a declining birth-rate, however. Infant mortality was deemed not so much a private tragedy as a national calamity. Australia must populate, and populate with vigorous exemplars of the white race, clean and healthy in body and mind. The nation had a duty to protect the newborn from the incompetence and negligence of bad mothers; and bad mothers, they believed, abounded in the working class. Working-class mothers were suspected of drunkenness and dirtiness, of dosing fretful babies with opiates and alcohol, of feeding them dangerous and wrongly mixed foods. Calls were frequent for the legal prohibition of the lower-class habit of keeping young babies in the marital bed where they could be 'over lain' and suffocated. (Although murder by drunken parents and death from dehydration of neglected babies cannot be ruled out, most such deaths were from what is now known as Sudden Infant Death Syndrome.) 'Good' working-class mothers, on the other hand, were suspected of being over-indulgent and too generous with the breast, failing to inculcate regular habits and orderly behaviour as a preparation for efficient adult life. The campaign for maternal education, however well-intended, was authoritarian in effect and denigrating in implication. Yet by the time the Infant Welfare movement became established throughout urban Australia, the most dramatic fall in infant mortality had already taken place.[15]

Richmond mothers were in fact the first in Melbourne to be offered maternal education. In 1910 the Richmond Council, in conjunction with the Australian Health Society, organized a series of public lectures commencing with the value of breast-feeding and the necessity for pure milk. The Richmond Creche and Free Kindergarten (now the Dame Nellie Melba Kindergarten) inaugurated infant care and cooking classes in 1912. The year before, however, the Women's Christian Temperance Union had started a School for Mothers in Richmond with lectures from a disinguished group of women doctors, Dr Mary De Garis, Dr Lucy Kilvington and Dr Isabel Younger (Ross). By 1917 Dr Younger and Mrs Hemphill of the W.C.T.U. had started a new school for Mothers in St Matthias' schoolroom in Church Street and in early 1918 succeeded in persuading the Richmond Council to subsidize the Victorian Baby Health Centre Association, bringing about the first Baby Health Centre in Victoria. By July the Centre had moved to Cremorne Street in South Richmond and a new one opened at the Town Hall. In its first year the Richmond Centre cared for five hundred new babies, nearly half the babies born in the suburb that year. By 1920, with new branches in East Richmond and in Burnley, it was an institution, and baby care so important that a weekly column catered for the modern mother in the *Richmond Guardian*. But for all the undoubted good gained from the Infant Welfare movement, it did signify a direct invasion of the integrity of the family. It marked the beginning of the intervention of middle-class experts in working-class family life, an intervention that would later expand with the social workers, social planners and bureaucrats of the welfare state.[16]

The fact that infant mortality fell so significantly before the Health Centre began its work testifies also to the growth of economic respectability and its domestic advantages in working-class life. Poverty rather than maternal ignorance remained the gravest danger to the newborn, and if Edwardian working-class babies were doing better than previous generations, they still faced a worse biological future than did their better-off cousins. In all forms of illness and accident this working-class generation would succumb more often and earlier in life. And by the age of fourteen their disadvantage could be seen by the naked eye: in 1907 the average working-class lad could be up to three inches shorter and a stone lighter than his upper-class compatriot.[17]

Mothers and Fathers

If the Edwardian working-class baby possessed a better biological future than ever before, so too was his subsequent childhood likely to be more loving and secure than that of his forebears. The growth of respectability in the Australian and British working classes had profoundly improved the quality of family life, an advance still measurable in the comparison of the rough with the respectable majority. *Isabel Williams* grew up in a South Richmond boarding house run by her aunt and, as a respectable family, they viewed with horror and compassion the misery of the alcoholic and disturbed families all around them:

> Women hid things in those days from you. You could have women who didn't drink at all and their husbands would knock them about. And you would hear they were being belted up—we heard it in our let rooms—but if

> you said anything they would always stick up for the husband and they'd be knocked about hellishly.

Isabel's neighbour often talked of her childhood with an alcoholic father—of the midnight flits and the waiting on Saturday nights to see how much of his wages paid that day remained after the pub:

> And when he came home mother used to lock some of the kids in the toilet because he'd want to bash us up too. Mother was a good singer and she'd sing him to sleep, but many a night at seven or eight years we'd walk the streets of Richmond, just to get away till the morning and he'd be sober again.

Fear was part of childhood, as was shame. *Jean Fowler*:

> I remember down here in Durham Street I never had a pair of shoes to go to school in, so they got me these high boots with buttons all down the side and you had to do them up with a button hook. I got them half cut off so they wouldn't look so bad. I walked all the way up the back lanes—I knew I had to go to school but I used to cry every morning because I had these damn shoes on. It was shocking. I never had anything.

Even more pitiable was the plight of the respectable widow or deserted wife. Work compatible with motherhood was scarce. Office and factory cleaning in the small hours of the morning helped some; others turned to domestic service, where they could bring their babies, or to washing and sewing. There were no widows' pension or deserted wives' allowances until the institution of the Commonwealth Widow's Pension in 1942. All a destitute mother could do was to have her children declared 'neglected' by the courts and either taken into custody by the Department of Neglected Children or boarded out to her. By 1936 Victorian Child Welfare payments to 'neglected children' boarded out on the State were the lowest in Australia. Contemporary medical evidence estimated that the average cost for a normal diet for a child of twelve to fourteen should be 8s 9d, or with the meat ration halved, around 7s 8d. The average Child Welfare payment in 1936 was 7s 1d, yet this comprised the entire income for many fatherless families.[18]

The presence of a male breadwinner with a regular wage and a strong commitment to his family made a vast difference to the quality of family life. But it was the management of daily expenditure that determined the family's fate for, even for skilled workers, the margin for error or accident was small indeed. If a housewife lost her purse with the week's housekeeping or the husband lost his pay packet it could spell disaster. *Mary Davis* remembers:

> Once my sister had to go to the grocer's and she had a pound and was fooling round with a boy and she lost it. And was there blue murder. Of course we reckoned it was the boy who pinched it out of her pocket.

> But that was really upsetting to lose a whole pound. Nobody had it to lend to you—you just had to go without to make it up.[19]

According to her husband *Doug*, in later years if a man lost his wages, his workmates would whip round to help him out. Even worse was when a father went on a binge in a time of stress. Some children developed a horror of strikes because of the sudden loss of income and security. *Monica Rinoldi* adored her magnetic and devoted Swiss father but she came to hate his politics:

> Why I dislike strikes today is that the Gas Company then always seemed to be on strike and my father was a very good unionist. He was rather one-eyed like that and stubborn. He'd go away to a meeting and come home in a real bad temper and we'd all have to toe the line and his meal would have to be there. I think a certain bitterness came to us children in that—he'd be out all day at a meeting, bad temper, and yet although there was no money coming into the house and my mother would be up till 12 o'clock sewing, he would still have his hot meal waiting there for him and then he'd just take himself off to bed.[20]

Monica has never voted Labor in her life.

In the eyes of their dependants—wives and children—'good fathers' were those who turned all their wage packet over to their wives and 'bad fathers' kept some or most for their own pleasures. Today it is still a point of pride in some working-class women that they get the pay packet unopened. The whole question of respectability and the management of household expenditure was intertwined with people's perception of sexual roles and money easily became a battleground for marital resentments. For the respectable Edwardian working class and for many of their children for the rest of their lives it was the man's role to provide and the woman's role to spend, but most women perceived, often bitterly, that it was a man's world. *Lilian Campbell* observed that in her youth:

> Women were just there to bear children, be in bed when the man wanted her to be in bed, have the dinner on the table when he came home from work, and boil up the copper and do the washing as best she could. And if the prop broke and the washing came down in the mud—bad luck—get another prop and prop it up as best you could. No, things were not easy—my poor mother was a slave.

Yet *Lilian*'s family were relatively well off. For *Jean Fowler*, from a family in real poverty because of a weak father, the irrationality and injustice of sexual roles was even more incomprehensible:

> It was always a man's world. 'You go and ask your father—he'll tell you whether you can go out or not.' It was always 'ask your father'. And the boys wouldn't raise their hand to do a thing in the house—the women had to do

> the lot. The boys would just sit around and play cards or go down the street or something, come home—'what's for dinner'—always. I taught my sons to wash up and do things here—they'd get me a cup of tea in bed if I was sick. Yet my mother thought there was nothing like the boys—she said she'd rather have boys any day, and yet the whole three of them just bludged on her while the girls did everything for her.

It is not uncommon for women of that generation to have early developed a 'set against men' which has blighted their own marriages and family life. But this 'man's world' was essentially the outside world. As *Lilian* quips: 'The men had up-the-pub of a Saturday afternoon; the woman's place was in the home, full stop'. Even the most devoted fathers felt emasculated by having to change a nappy, for if woman's place was in the home it was also where woman ruled. The working-class family was most commonly a matriarchy where women bore the major responsibility for the expenditure of the family income, the care of the children, the quality of family life. Women sometimes regarded their husbands as one of the children except that they slunk out to play at the pub or with the S.P. bookie. Battling against poverty bred often formidable middle-aged women who towered over their feckless and immature husbands. The vast majority of men regarded it as a matter of pride that their wives did not have to go to work, and their wives agreed with them: a working wife signalled masculine failure. None the less, men could resent their role as compliant and barely tolerated providers. *Kevin Maloney* is a perceptive observer of the Richmond he knew as a child:

> You can understand that a hotel is like a club—if they felt that they were not wanted at home, they'd wander down to the pub and that starts a lot of unhappiness. But you've got to be understanding of why people do fail—there's something missing or they're driven to it. Of course, on the other hand, you could have a nagging woman that would drive a man up the wall—'where've you been?' and all that type of thing. And they'd have to bring the pay packet home unopened.

This strict division of sexual roles tended to elevate the moral status of women at the expense of men. *Kevin* expounds the ideals of Christian motherhood in his youth:

> A woman was regarded with respect. She was the wife, she was the mother and she was the manager of the household. The man went to work and brought in the money; the mother would maintain the house. The woman would be on a pedestal. Generally she would be happy to be in charge of the house and a lot of these women were wonderful managers because they had to make do with a mere pittance at times. I can recall a case where the husband was a bit of a no-hoper and the woman had a large family, but she would go out to work as a charlady and that was how she made some money

> for the kids. And they grew up wonderfully because of their love for their mother and they would never do anything to hurt her.

The struggle to feed, clothe and nurture a family on a grossly inadequate income imposed a burden of relentless effort that seems almost unendurable today. Being working-class meant (and still does) having to do an enormous amount of heavy exhausting work, most of it tedious and repetitive. The good working-class mum had to cook on a wood-fired stove that had to be lit every morning before even having a reviving cup of tea. All water had to be heated on the stove or in the copper in the back yard. Most houses lacked even a cold tap inside. Meal preparation was slow and washing up with cheap soap seemed interminable. Phyllis *Smith*, as the only girl, had to help her mother and did resent it 'a little bit':

> I didn't think it was right that the men sat and talked and played cards of a night while us two women would gather all the dishes and wash them up. We'd already had the pleasure of cooking all the meal. My father was very fussy. If he went out and found dishes that weren't washed thoroughly, he'd wash it again before he'd use it. Everything had to be spotless and shining.

When *Phyllis*'s mother got a gas stove, it 'was a miracle'. The Monday wash meant a draining day of lifting, stirring, mangling and carrying sodden sheets, towels and clothes. Many women had the added burden of washing work clothes impregnated with cement, plaster, mud or oil. Then there was the battle to dry it all in Melbourne's unreliable weather in tiny back yards—and as *Lilian* says, 'if the prop broke and the washing came down in the mud—bad luck'. Few kitchens had the room to dry a whole wash on a clothes horse in front of the stove and the wash had to be completed quickly because the poor often had only two changes of clothes. *Jean Fowler* remembers having only two sets of clothes and as soon as she returned from school she would have to change into 'any old thing you could find to go out and play'. She took pity on one girl at St Ignatius' School in the early 1920s who turned up in a bag dress 'made into a skirt and top. I don't know how she wore it because it would stick into you—a rough bag. It had a fringe—it looked nice but the poor girl had to go in that—I couldn't have borne it'. In *Muriel Thompson*'s family, clothes were put in the oven to dry and 'first up, best dressed' was not a joke in her family; it was to be the same for her own children in their turn in the 1930s. In between cooking, washing and cleaning, women sewed, mended, made rugs—every household item that could be home-made usually was. And all this labour was performed by women frequently pregnant, overweight, tottering on swollen ulcerated legs with varicose veins, wincing with bad backs, stricken with arthritis and often poor-sighted. Their daughters, themselves accustomed to hard work, are now overwhelmed by the burdens so patiently borne by such working-class women. *Phyllis Smith*:

> My mother used to get up at the crack of dawn and by the time she got the supper over, it would be almost dawn before she got to bed again. But my mother [despite a serious heart condition] never had a breakdown. She had nine pregnancies—a child every two years including a breech birth and three deaths.

As we shall see later, one price paid was their daughters' schooling.

The intense effort needed to feed and clothe a working-class family tended to force people to measure the quality of parenting, especially of mothering, in material rather than in emotional terms. For *Alice Murphy* the 'good mother' always had food ready: 'that's what we always used to say—no matter whenever you went to my mother's, like mothers of those times, there was always plenty to eat'. Even young children sensed the closeness of destitution and of not having enough to eat. In large families there was rarely enough for second helpings and every meal represented a triumph of one more day against poverty and insecurity. The cheapest and most sensuously satisfying way to fill tummies was with refined carbohydrate stodge. Sweet food often came to fulfil emotional rather than physiological needs, especially in families that did not drink—sugar was the curse of the non-drinking classes. An ample table of puddings, pies and cakes, especially at the high tea that followed the Sunday roast, was a deeply satisfying celebration of another week survived. Sunday was also the day for family visiting. *Hamish Roberts*:

> In those days the families were close together; the relatives visited. We had a team of people coming to our place on Sunday afternoon and they'd all stay to tea. They'd all crowd into the dining room and we'd be pushed out into the kitchen. We'd be sitting at the kitchen table and one of my brothers would say, 'we're going steerage tonight', and we'd just get the left-overs. All the others would be having what we considered to be a big banquet. My parents' brothers and sisters all came—there was no entertainment—it was just all talk, talk, talk, about family and relatives. That sort of thing doesn't apply today.

Food and conversation were fatally linked. With both men and women working long hours, meals were the most important times for family talk. As with alcoholics for whom all social interaction becomes intertwined with drink, so did food for many become associated with the expression of relationships. The quality of family talk was often high, especially in political households like the *Ryans'* where the Irish Question was as much a passion as sport. Social and educational inequality trapped many fine intellects in menial occupations and their children not infrequently received a better education over the kitchen table than they did at school. At the *Ryans'*, a lower middle-class family:

> The whole family sat down in a civilized manner so that the children were taught how to hold their knife and fork. The food was ample. Specially do I remember roasts and Irish stew and rabbits—they were a shilling a pair. Also hash made from cold lamb and plenty of onions. At meal times I was very much the child—seen and not heard—but not infrequently I was allowed to remain up, on the rug in front of the fire, and listened to the conversation of the elders.

In the *O'Reilly* home, one of the respectable poor, the talk was much the same as at the *Ryans'*, but the food was very different:

> In those days we didn't get any fancy foods to eat. They talk about calories in these days and it makes you laugh because we ate what was put in front of us, and sometimes it would be only stewed vegetables because vegetables were cheap. A two-pound tin of jam was only fourpence. We ate a lot of bread—no butter, it was too dear at a shilling a pound—and potatoes. We didn't get much milk—milk was kept for the younger ones. We never had much meat. even on Sundays, only cheap cuts. We used to buy a lot of mutton flaps and boil them, take the bones out and press them—they were only about a shilling a pound then. That was nice—we'd enjoy that. I don't remember eggs, and as for fresh fruit—only what we could pinch.

In *Jean Fowler's* family their only treat was a sixpenn'orth of stale cakes bought from a shop near Lennox Street as it closed on Saturday mid-day.

The quality of working-class nutrition is difficult to assess as we have no reliable figures on family diets. Yet even amongst small families on a skilled man's wage, there were likely to be some vitamin deficiencies through over-cooking vegetables. The vast majority of families managed to fill children's tummies somehow, although many school children had little or no lunch. It was not uncommon for men and working adolescent sons to be given the lion's share of meat and egg protein, while mothers and daughters had to fill up on stodge; and, in an age when pregnant women believed they had to eat for two, obesity was common. Only the heavy physical work performed by both men and women reduced the threat to health of a diet too high in refined carbohydrate and fat. But food meant success, happiness, reassurance and solace and as the working-class standard of living began to rise in the 1940s these rituals, once based on life-sustaining needs, degenerated into self-indulgence. The size of the meals and afternoon teas consumed by this generation today can be truly astonishing, and the fact that the memories of childhood food are often the most vivid of all testifies to the emotional importance of food to the poor.

The demands of working-class motherhood seems to have drained some women of all affective emotion. There were women, however conscientious, who performed like domestic robots. *Thelma* and *Irene Clark*'s mother had had the responsibility of rearing her blind brother and younger sister. She never went to work and married at fifteen. She then had a large family, but in three stages so she did not finish her childbearing until late middle age. With little education and bad eyes she never read and never wished to leave the house. She even refused to go to the theatre with her husband. Her daughters blamed her early life:

> She never had any life. When she was going out with Dad Grandma would deliberately keep the meal late and she'd have to rush out and not do the dishes. And when she came home the dishes would all be waiting for her still—she often told us about that. Things were hard and she'd live on bread and dripping and if there was any butter in the place her eldest brother used to put it up in a high cupboard so Mum couldn't get it.

She performed the tasks of motherhood punctiliously:

> She used to take my sister and me to school over at Burnley and we always got a ha'penny to spend and we'd go off to the lolly shop. If it was raining there'd always be a pair of dry socks in her pocket. And at the end-of-the year prize-giving she was always there. Every day she used to bring our lunch over and sit and have lunch with us (she wasn't the only mother to come). Then she'd be back again at four o'clock to pick us up—she was frightened of us crossing Swan Street in those days—of course it's three times as bad now.

But she couldn't show love. *Thelma* felt it acutely: 'I don't think Mum could open up—there was a shell there—she couldn't let herself go'. *Thelma*'s husband similarly had lacked love as a child and they were to give each other in marriage the warmth they had been denied as children. Mrs *Clark*'s remoteness similarly cut her off from the street community and when in old age the help and support of neighbours could have made her life easier, she had no friends. Her only contribution to the street community had been in the grim role as a layer-out of the dead. She had one pleasure—gambling: 'Mum loved horse racing—she used to study them; even when she was confined to the house she liked a little bet—no one knew of course—those were the days of the S.P. bookie up the lane'. Mrs *Clark* was a superb cook, but she never tried to pass on her skill to her daughters. Perhaps she was unwilling to make her daughters work as she had to do, but perhaps, too, she feared losing her monopoly of the one great thing she could do for her family.[21]

Monica Rinoldi's mother similarly could not show love; but in her case she had 'married beneath her station' when she ran away with the vital and charming *Jack Rinoldi*, foreign, working-class and Catholic:

> My mother was cold. She was brought up, what you might say, a lady. She went to a private school and they had a cook and a maid and my mother didn't have to do anything. In those days, in her father's eyes, she had married out of her station, not only out of her religion and he was very hard on them for years. She had a pretty hard life then.

It was *Monica*'s father who gave the children real love and care: 'If we ever had a pain or were sick during the night, it was never my mother who would come and give us a dose of medicine or console us, it was my father; I don't know if she was rather shy, but she would run away from sickness'. Certainly her life was grim: 'My mother's pleasures were non-existent, I'd say; she did have her own friends especially when the kids had grown up; she'd go to the football and the pictures and to church but nothing else'. It was no until adulthood that *Monica* appreciated her mother's qualities and problems:

> My mother always seemed to be rather dowdy whereas my father was very smart and elegant. But when she got older and was left alone I used to look at her and think, 'Your're beautiful, you know'; but that didn't occur to us when we were young. I think she was overshadowed—she could have been rather disappointed in life.

For all the feckless, selfish or lazy fathers, there were many who were attentive and passionately committed to their families. It was not unknown for men to contribute to the housework and cooking in recognition of their wives' burdens. *Phyllis Smith*'s father was a good father and a bad husband, finally deserted by his wife once *Phyllis*, the youngest, was married. Born into a rich German family, he had run away to sea and by the time he settled and married in Australia, he spoke seven languages. He worked on the waterfront until World War I when his British naturalization could not save him from being persecuted as an enemy alien. The whole family suffered; but the father, highly intelligent and cultured, also brooded over the loss of his first daughter who had died in his arms from diphtheria:

> I loved my father you know. He was a fine good-looking man and being the only girl I suppose he spoilt me a bit. But everything I learned to love in the way of ballet or music he taught me. Although he had that drinking problem, he never lost his job because he'd never drink on the job. But he'd leave Richmond Station and go in and buy a bottle of wine and when he went to bed at night he'd drink that bottle and it'd be gone in the morning. But he'd be sober and do his job the next day. And he'd never drink when he took me out. Mother would dress me up in the best clothes and he'd take me out—we saw all the musical comedies and the ballets. Once he took me to the Bijou Theatre and Stiffy and Mo were on and I got marched out. He called me 'Biddy' because he put me in a sweep when I was born. He took me to violet farms and I'd gather violets, and up round Warrandyte when all the

> wattles were out, so I did learn my love of beautiful things from my father. But I was more afraid of my father than my mother. My father never hit me in his life, but he'd a great big belt that he'd wear and he'd sit at the head of the table to carve and I'd be sitting next to him and he'd say, 'Right lass, what have you been doing today?' and I'd say I'd done so and so at school and he'd then say, 'Right, I don't want to hear any more from you, we're going to talk adult talk'. But I loved him and I was fascinated by him, but I didn't dare give him any cheek.

Phyllis's father was a traditional European paterfamilias yet even he on Sundays, his only full free day, would prepare a lavish cooked breakfast as a treat to the family. In the *Clark* household, despite the mother's assiduous housekeeping, the father washed and ironed his own work clothes; and after Sunday tea 'no one could move until he came in with the carpet sweeper to pick up the crumbs—Dad was a fuddy duddy'. Men often took over domestic chores when their wives were incapacitated. *Doug Davis*'s mother was asthmatic and unable to climb the stairs, so the sons looked after their own rooms and their father 'used to hop in with the cooking—make cakes and little pies'. *Muriel Thompson*'s parents had the exceptional problem that her mother had been blinded by measles at the age of three. She was just out of Blind School when she met her husband, 'a great big tall English gentleman' twenty years older then herself, who ran tea rooms in Lonsdale Street. They reared three daughters in great hardship as the father was forced on to the pension while the girls were still at school. With the little capital he had he bought three tiny cottages in South Richmond which were to be roofs over the family's heads for the next two generations. *Muriel*'s mother could read Braille and just see light; but there was little she could do for a young family. Their father, being a cook, took over all the domestic responsibilities easily. They were poor but very happy:

> He was like a father to her. He used to feed her with a spoon. He was an absolutely marvellous man. He never drank or smoked or sweared. She was a bit of a demon—imagining things and that—you do when you're afflicted in some way—but he was beautiful. I used to say he was an angel—I've never met many, but he was one because he was so kind to my mother.

For many of the very poor, however, a lack of family affection was one of the many prices of poverty: 'I think they had too many in the family to be bothered with that kind of business', as *Jean Fowler* says of her parents.

Emotional security came more easily with financial security. Will *Parker* grew up in a respectable Methodist family. His father was 'afraid of nothing and nobody in the physical and moral sense'; his mother he idolized:

> She was a lady. I still think the world of my mother. She was a wonderful person. In contrast to Dad who was up in fireworks in five minutes and as

> quick as lightning in doing anything he did, she was more placid and peaceful.

They taught their children to be practical Christians, considerate of the needs of others in this world and certain of their path towards the next: 'It didn't seem an unsettled or uncertain life or world to me. Never in my life have I felt insecure—that's funny isn't it'. That inner calm and self-confidence would enable *Will Parker* to take risks in business that made him one of the few Richmond men of his generation to make a fortune. And he remained a Christian gentleman to the end.[22] When the *Murphys*' family butchering business began to flourish, the children found themselves indulged: 'We were never deprived of anything—if we were sick we had bride dolls brought to us and our father once went to Sydney and brought us back a watch each—at ten and twelve years'. Even the very poor tried to give their children some treats—*Muriel Thompson* wonders how her blind mother ever managed the little birthday parties she threw for them: 'Hundreds and thousands on bread in the front room'.

As for *Lilian Campbell*, she could do no wrong:

> The local fisho, Mr Scott, used to cut the fish heads off and flick them into the gutter for the cats. And I picked up a fish head and it was huge like a football and I threw it at Elsie Munro, hit her on the side of the head and nearly flattened her. They complained to Mum and nothing was said; nothing was done. Another time I threw a rock at Ossie Sharples and it meant my Mum and Dad taking him to the Children's Hospital in the jinker to have his head stitched. And nothing was said to me—I remember hiding round the corner and watching them set off. I didn't want to hurt—it was just that I was a good shot. I was a tomboy—they used to call me Tom.

And when *Lilian* turned on the taps at Mrs Reid's dairy, 'and all the milk ran down Type Street', Mrs Reid's complaints fell on deaf ears: 'I can see Mum and Dad now with their elbows on the picket fence bored to tears hearing about me'.

As happened with *Lilian* and *Phyllis Smith*, the youngest child sometimes became spoilt after the death of an older sibling. Even though infant mortality fell so dramatically in the Edwardian period, babies still died at twice the rate non-Aboriginal babies do in Australia today. Older children were still whisked away by diphtheria, typhoid, pneumonia, peritonitis and tuberculosis. Death through accident, especially among boys, was also frequent. Children were increasingly being hit by motor vehicles, but drowning in the Yarra or in swimming holes in abandoned quarries was more common. Death was still a companion to young life and part of most families' experience. The suddenness of serious illness in young children was made even more fearful by the difficulties of seeking medical help. In 1911 there were only two slot telephones in South Richmond and they were closed to the public after 8 p.m. The only other phones were in pubs which most women disliked entering.[23] Household accidents were common, especially when water had to be heated on stoves and in coppers. *Phyllis Smith*, valiantly trying to help her mother, went to pour boiling water from a large pot of mussels into the gully trap. It was too heavy for a little girl and it scalded her legs. For three months she missed school, the only treatment being Carron oil on the burns: 'I can remember the agony—no tablets—no wonder we're tough people'. A neighbour left a baby's bath of boiling water on the ground for washing. Her two-year-old daughter crawled into it and *Phyllis* cannot forget the agonized screams: 'the baby was bandaged from head to foot but later died'. Fatal diseases like diphtheria were still such a threat that they entered children's folklore. One song, set to the tune of a World War I camp song, celebrated the Fairfield Infectious Diseases Hospital:

> Do you want to live in Fairfield
> For a week or two
> They give you porridge or stew
> And they stick needles into you.

When *Phyllis* was diagnosed as having diphtheria her mother fainted—they had already lost a daughter through it. Children who survived acquired heroic status:

> Violet McLoughlin—her mother had separated from her father so she had grandmothers and aunts and mother living with her. But her father sent her beautiful working models of stations and all sorts of things so Violet was the one who had several prams and dolls which we kiddies used to borrow to play mothers. She was the lucky girl of the street—fair and blonde and fragile. She nearly died of diphtheria, too, and had her throat cut.

The prolonged convalescence from serious illness deprived children of much schooling. *Monica Rinoldi* was stricken with typhoid just before her family moved to Richmond from the bush. She lost all her hair and still suffers from the after-effects on her bowel. *Isabel Williams* contracted diphtheria at five, not long after she came to live with her aunt in Richmond. The lodge doctor expected her to die quickly and advised her aunt not to bother to send her to the Fairfield Hospital. Her aunt put her on a couch in her own bedroom and kept a fire going night and day to assist her breathing. She was bed-ridden for three months and later had to be wheeled round in a pram. She started school nearly two years late and her aunt's devotion obliterated her relationship with her mother: 'After that I thought I could never leave my aunt because I couldn't remember my mother at all'.

Isabel had the not uncommon experience in the working class of being brought up by relatives, of being unofficially fostered. This was the fate of many illegitimate children or of families where one or both of the parents had died or deserted. In the early Edwardian years there appears to have even been some baby farming: in 1904 a young Richmond woman, Mrs Elfrida Gibbs, was fined £5 under the Infant Life Protection Act over the death of Henry Barr whom she had 'adopted' for the fee of £3. When the baby was handed over to her, however she paid only thirty shillings. She was not a registered nurse, and she wanted a baby as she had none of her own; yet this was her second conviction for a similar offence.[24] In *Isabel*'s case, her father was struggling as a selector and severe drought had placed the family in peril. Her aunt offered to take her to ease their burden. When she arrived at her aunt's boarding house in Dover Street, South Richmond, she had never seen a mirror and kept chattering at the other five-year-old girl through the glass. Her parents were relieved that she became so attached to her aunt, 'and it wasn't till I was leaving school that they showed any interest in me at all and asked me to come home because I was old enough to work'. She refused; and nursed her aunt and uncle through old age, returning the love they had so freely given her.

The callousness of *Isabel*'s parents exemplifies an important difference between Edwardian working-class family life and the present. The Edwardian working-class family was in a state of transition from an older, harsher world where children were seen as workers in the family economic unit rather than as cherished dependants for whom the parents worked. This is not to deny that most of these Edwardian children were not enjoyed and treasured by their parents, but many parents still expected to retain control over their children's time and activities which the State through the education system now compulsorily claimed.

The striking difference between the Edwardian family and today is in discipline. The elderly always tend to deplore the unruliness of the young, but there was a toughness in the average family that would now be unusual. Probably more than any other class in society, the respectable working class needed immense self-discipline to endure the uncertainties and trials that inevitably befell them. Very few of these Edwardian children grew up to find adult work that they enjoyed. To raise their own families they had to be able to tolerate a relentless routine and sustain a lifetime of moral effort. Escapism and self-indulgence could bring disaster. Hence most parents consciously or unconsciously knew that their children needed to be toughened to survive the future, and many children respected this rationale behind their parents' insistence on doing their duty to family life and needs. Girls were expected to start young in their share of domestic duties even if it meant truanting from school. Boys were expected to earn money—selling papers, running messages, caring for animals, doing odd jobs. Even spoilt children like *Phyllis Smith* and *Lilian Campbell* worked hard as very young children. *Lilian*'s joyful and free childhood never detracted from her capacity for self-discipline in maturity;

quite the reverse, for her enhanced self-confidence enabled her to fight and succeed where others were easily intimidated. But harsh discipline, even in humane respectable families, could misfire. *Mary Davis*'s father was 'very strict and stern and you never had any confidence'; and in retrospect she blames this for her poor performance at school. *Brendan Ryan*'s family believed that children should never be heard; and at school too 'personal expression was not encouraged'. Even after he had completed his medical studies he found self-assertion difficult, his psychological growth having been so stunted by his parents: 'I don't think every boy got quite as crushed down as I was'.

Of course, as always, children were pathologically abused and the more a family was under economic stress the greater the danger. *Jean Fowler* is bitter still towards her father who, 'like a lot of men, was terribly selfish and cruel'. She remembers once coming home from school late at a quarter to five after watching her older brothers fishing in the Yarra: 'My youngest brother was kicked up the stairs—it wasn't because it hurt him, it was because he was the man of the house; and he went for me and I just went out the other way'. Such violence was in part still accepted by society, for community standards had little respect for the rights of children. In 1901 Mary Scudmore was charged with beating her consumptive niece, Adelaide Place, who had been in her care after her mother's death. Adelaide had subsequently died—allegedly from the consumption, not the beating. Mary Scudmore pleaded guilty and the judge mitigated her penalty with an explanation of her behaviour that horrifies today:

> It is well known that persons suffering from consumption were most refractory and at times threw themselves about and behaved in a manner that persons in good health would not do. Very likely this child had herself caused the bruises on her. There was nothing to show that the defendant had done anything more than a parent would to a disobedient child.[25]

Mary Scudmore was fined forty shillings. The common themes running through the cases of wife and child abuse before the Richmond Court were of broken marriages, unemployment, drink, mental illness, illegitimacy, shot-gun marriage—the alienated residuum of society. For the majority of Richmond children their family life was loving if rigorous, ruled by mothers and fathers passionately devoted to the survival of their family and to the integrity of the clan, as *Hamish Roberts* remembers of his mother:

> In those days people kept in close contact and my mother knew everyone—she knew all their birth-dates—nephews, nieces. She was delighted to have them all—it was her whole life, especially after her husband died. And as each one married and had children, they'd come too—her whole life was centred round those children.

Play

The Edwardian working-class child grew up in a lively street community that the motor car has since destroyed. Mothers felt secure in the knowledge that the community kept a watchful eye for accidents, unexpected dangers and vicious fights. Elderly women now marvel at the safety of the streets from sexual predators; only *Phyllis Smith* remembers one man who exposed himself in the lane until a crowd of neighbours chased him away. Critics might deplore the incontestable dirtiness of Richmond's streets but the children did not care.[26] Their suburb was a giant playground, rich in excitement, adventure, spectacle and delight, and they felt doubly fortunate in having the river and its still beautiful bushy surrounds and parks on their doorstep.

The public play of children was governed none the less by gradations of status and respectability. Most respectable families insisted that their children be off the streets and in bed by 9 o'clock; the over-burdened and the unrespectable were more lax. *Jean Fowler* and her eight brothers and sisters 'used to chase around the street under the street light until 11 o'clock at night; we used to have a marvellous time and we never used to think of men chasing us or anything like that'. At the other end of the social scale, it was a mark of gentility to forbid children to play in the street. *Brendan Ryan*, growing up on busy Church Street in a lower middle-class family, had a different world of play from the poor. His was a domestic world, bounded at first by his parents' garden and later by the home of his best friend in Elm Grove. He retains a keen memory of the details of the garden—the texture and aroma of trees and plants, of tiles and the picket fence—the fruits of a solitary child's explorations of a limited environment. His later passion for football was satisfied at school.

Loneliness was rare for most Richmond children, however. In the streets they played the timeless games and recited the lore of the street children all over the industrialized world. Toys were few and basic—a doll, a top, a diabolo, a hoop, balls and home-made bats, carts, skipping ropes. They were great collectors—cigarette cards, marbles, cherry stones for cherry bobs. They learnt how to bargain and trade with their treasures and they learnt how to gamble with cherry bobs so that many later S.P. bookies ran their first Melbourne Cup books at school. But their most important toys were their imaginations and their physical environment and they early learnt to exploit them both creatively and very mischievously. *Albert Perkins* and his friends played games with the tram cables: 'we used to get the handle of a kerosene tin, make it into an S hook and try to catch the cable, then we'd tie a jam tin then a kerosene tin and away they'd go up the road.[27] Older boys made 'gee whiz' or billy carts, and the more genteel residents of Richmond Terrace and Lennox Street complained regularly at 'yelling youths' rolling 'recklessly at a mad pace' down their hills.

In 1916 Councillor Barcelo moved to ban billy carts from Elm Grove and the other hilly showpieces of Richmond, and the *Richmond Guardian* declared:

> One phase of small boy brutality, according to council by-law, is over, but it is terrible to reflect that the energy of these monsters will find some new outlet. Outside our offices in Lennox Street there are ten-year-old tyrants who have learned to whistle with two fingers in their mouths, and the noises are terrifying to young and old. Whistling should be prohibited. Others of these two-legged tyrants are able to catherine-wheel on their hands and feet, and a boy making his way along the path by this method of locomotion is apt to kick somebody's brains out. The Council should make catherine-wheeling a criminal offence. Then there are those young urchins who yell, making women faint and horses bolt; the boys who chase one another and who run full-tilt into innocent pedestrians—ought they not to be shot on sight?[28]

Boys were generally more adventurous than girls, free to roam and explore, to swim in the river or in the quarry. *Hamish Roberts* had a typical Burnley boyhood:

> At Burnley we had a place called 'the Sandy', just on the turn by Twickenham Crescent. It was a lovely sandy spot. We used to swim there and none of us had togs on. It would usually be on a Sunday and as soon as we saw a boat coming up from Princes Bridge with all the respectable people going to Hawthorn Tea Gardens [now Leonda], we used to get into the water and swim round the boat. There was another spot at the end of Burnley Street where there was a ferry going over to Williams Road. On the other side there was Glover's orchard and if you were good enough to swim across the Yarra, you were able to help yourself to his pears and apples. But finally he got a saltpetre gun and he'd fire at us and sometimes you'd get it on the bare bottom. When you think of it we were game because it wasn't unusual to come across something tied up in a bag—dead animals, a bag half unsewn with something smelly in it. Further round in Richmond people were up in arms at the big group of boys who'd swim there and there was some larrikinism—swimming with no togs on—and they'd be caught and fined.

The South Eastern Freeway obliterated all these haunts. *Emma* and *Alice Murphy* also have an abiding love of the river as a result of growing up in Burnley; for even if girls, out of modesty, could not join in the swimming, the river supplied adventure and relief from the searing heat of high summer, as *Emma* remembers:

> In the days of our schooldays—my word, the river was fascinating. And on a hot day at lunchtime there were no end of young boys drowned. We have gone down there and seen the boats with the police and the grappling irons.

> We've seen them pull them out in the nude. And strangely enough three of them were mates of our brothers.

The great floods were the greatest fun of all: 'We've seen pianos, everything under the sun, go down that river; one time there was a poor horse and its foal on the island down there and they had to row a boat to it'. But the sisters did more than watch the life of the river:

> Every time I think of it now I could be ill—we used to hire a boat from down there—2 shillings an hour for us kids. We used to row up the river—we even took our little brothers with us and I couldn't swim properly. We used to go up there where there used to be buffalo grass—beautiful on a hot day—cool—and pull in and get out.

The river had its more sedate attractions. A band played on the bank on Sundays and those who could afford it walked or took a boat to the Hawthorn Tea Gardens where the children could be diverted by the monkeys and the exotic birds. The Burnley Horticultural Gardens remained a great favourite. The Survey Park was increasingly being used for organized sport, but many Burnley children simply spent all their school holidays in it. At the western boundary of the municipality the cows and work horses grazed on the river flats, to the delight of the children; and over the river the Royal Botanic Gardens were already among the best of their kind in the world. *George Little* remembers being chased off the cricket pitches in the cow paddock by the police, because children-were forbidden to play there on Saturdays: 'Everyone jumped into the railway yards then went off to the Botanical Gardens and made a nuisance of themselves to the girls'.[29]

Richmond itself abounded in sights and scenes ripe for exploitation by inventive children. These children grew up watching a great deal of adult work, observing it with a pleasure that was sometimes quite sensuous: the horses being shod, the dairies with their gleaming basins of curdling milk, Mr Hosking fashioning billiard cues in his shed in Hosking's Paddock, the stone knappers breaking the great bluestones for road-making. Best of all for *Lilian Campbell* was the slaughterhouse at the Richmond abattoirs:

> The *Murphys* were our neighbours and on Friday Mrs *Murphy* would put Mr *Murphy*'s dinner between two plates tied up with a big handkerchief, and we'd harness Nancy up to the buggy and down we'd tear along Burnley Street to the slaughterhouse with Mr *Murphy*'s lunch and collect his wages because Mrs *Murphy* would want it for Friday shopping.
>
> Whilst we were down there we'd watch Mr Wren. He'd be spearing the cattle, then he'd hit the pigs on the snout and kill them. Then we'd go and watch the slaughtermen cut the sheeps' throats. And get a baby lamb that had just been dropped—bring that home. Then it would bleat all night and Mum lost a boarder over a lamb bleating all night, but Mum wouldn't care. And

> then we'd get a bladder and fill that up with water, and bring home some black puddings, tripe and sweetbreads, lambs fry.
>
> The slaughterhouse was a great place for playing—it had atmosphere!

Children derived enormous pleasure from tormenting adults—knocking on front doors and running away, tying string to knockers, setting booby traps of cans of water that descended on the unwitting heads of adult passers-by. *Friedrich Smith* put a lot of thought into his pranks. With some mates he built a cannon with some water pipe and a spring and mounted it on a truck. Guy Fawkes night provided the setting:

> In those days a threepenny bung bung was about six inches long and $1^1/_2$ inches thick and it had a hell of an explosion. We got some money, got one and went down to the Royal Hotel. We held open the bat-wing doors, put the bung bung in the cannon and just as it was about to go off, we let it fly right into the bar. There was a hell of an explosion and we ran like hell because we spotted our father at the bar and he came home hot and mad because he'd dropped his bloody pot of beer.

With the Richmond Council's twopenny bounty for dead rats, children became expert rat-catchers. But rats had other uses. Walking home from school one lunchtime *Lilian* caught sight of a neighbour's exquisitely polished passageway: 'You could see your face in it, and 1 had picked up a rat in my travels and I threw it. It slid down that passage and it went right from the front door to the back. I ran for my life'. Children teased and ridiculed the senile, the insane and the eccentric. *Bill O'Reilly* and his friends delighted in reminding old Mrs Pannell from the fruit shop of her husband's sad demise. She would raise her skirts to wipe away her tears and reveal an old colonial absence of underwear.

The great sport of Richmond children was theft; Australia could have been dubbed a nation of shoplifters. *Kevin Maloney*'s favourite target was Connell's Grocery on the corner of Swan and Church Streets because he could do a running dash through its two entrances and grab a handful of biscuits. That is until they got wise to him and doctored the biscuits with cayenne pepper and he fled home: 'Oh Mum—burning, burning'. When *Friedrich Smith* played truant from school he had to forgo lunch; but lightning raids on pubs for cheese and biscuits helped. *Lilian* was always enthusiastic about buying kerosene for her mother because Mrs Kennedy had to go to the back of the shop, giving *Lilian* 'open season on the counter'. Pinching fruit from Mr Bailey's cart she got down to a fine art, making forays from her hide in the arum lilies while he delivered his orders. *Lilian* also acquired an early distaste for wine:

> Ernie Boland (he was to become a mayor of Richmond) and I used to go down to Fatty Schmidt's to clean her windows. This day she had a big bowl of tomato and onion soaking in vinegar and she had a doctor visiting; she

> was sick. Old Dr *Irvine*, he was an alcoholic but we didn't know—we thought he was feeling the cold always in his overcoat—and there was wine for him. Well, I took a slice of onion and a slice of tomato and I got thirsty so I took a swig of wine out of the wine bottle. Then more cleaning of windows and sweeping the yard, more onion and tomato, more vinegar, more wine—my God I was sick and I haven't looked at red wine since.

Lilian was, of course, a tomboy who liked adventure, but many girls and boys played together, especially at night when under the street light the older children told ghost stories which sent the tiresome younger ones fleeing to bed and safety. Children were immensely inventive in their stories (skills now destroyed by television) and it always seemed to *Doug Davis* that his mother called him in for bed just as the story reached the best part. *Phyllis Smith* first met her future husband when they were five and six respectively. At first she found him 'a horrible little monster', and their romance commenced with a fight in the gutter. *Emma* and *Alice Murphy* knew all the boys and grew up to go out with them: 'They were never rude to us or said anything that we had to tell our mother about'. They felt under no special restrictions except that they were required to do many more household chores:

> I can't remember the boys having to do much. And we laugh remembering how we'd be playing with the boys and Mum would come to the gate and sing out, 'Come on you two, what about the dishes', and we'd sing back, 'the kettle's not boiling'. 'You don't have to have the kettle boiling'. We had to do our chores.

Such parental demands on girls must have played a part in adult patterns of psychologically strong-mothers and feckless fathers that are so common among the underprivileged. Many girls were more protected, and were restrained from joining the boys in river and quarry adventures.

Most children had to work for their pocket-money, running messages, fetching jugs of beer from the pub, doing odd jobs. In a portent of things to come, *Lilian* earned two shillings a week from the *Murphys* next door for sweeping the yard, buying the groceries and collecting Mr *Murphy*'s wages each Friday from the abattoirs: 'fifteen pounds they trusted me with—I was in the big time'. Other children had to work to help the family. *Arthur Coombes* shouldered big responsibilities for a small boy:

> They used to put shell-grit down for paths in those days and the shell-grit used to come from Portarlington. My grandfather used to scoop it off the beaches and send it up by boat. I used to deliver loads of shell-grit—I was only ten or twelve at the time—and I'd drive the horse-drawn lorry. It was a big thing then for a boy to be able to drive a lorry into town. And I used to hawk down in Yarraberg as a boy with a sixpenny basket. And when they'd open the door, 'Oh I don't want nothing today', and I'd jam me foot in the

> door and say, 'You haven't looked at what I've got to sell—a cabbage, a cauliflower, a bunch of carrots and a bunch of parsnips—sixpence the lot'. 'I'll buy your cabbage. How much?' 'Threepence.' 'Oh dear, I'll give you tuppence for it.'[30]

The *Coombes* family had a thriving business and it was more a matter of principle than necessity that *Arthur* worked as a child. Other children were thrown into the workforce when they lost their fathers or even both parents. *Harold Stephenson*'s father was killed at Gallipoli; and he started selling papers very young until, at the age of eleven, he obtained a special dispensation from the Education Department to leave school and work full-time. The paper selling was to remain a good standby, especially during the Depression, but it was not easy. The selling spots in the city were controlled by criminals like Squizzy Taylor in perhaps one of the earliest examples of business franchising in Melbourne.[31] Another means of survival for orphaned boys was as live-in dairy hands. For as little as 5s a week and their keep boys as young as ten rose before dawn to bring in the cows, milk them and then, with a special dispensation to leave school early, they took the cows back for the night. The 1902 Royal Commission into the Factories Act found dairy hands to be one of the worst abuses of child labour still in existence. In 1913 Sydney Adams, 'an anaemic-looking youth of seventeen', was convicted of imposition at the Richmond Court. Both his parents had died four years before and, to support his younger brother and two little sisters, he had posed as a deaf mute, carrying a letter purported to be from his widowed mother as he plied a trade as a hawker of postcards and race cards. After character witnesses had appeared for his defence, he was let off with a bond in view of the initiative he had displayed.[32] But the most common child workers were in family businesses—shops and dairies. *Isabel Williams* started her day at 5 a.m. and would have twenty lunches cut for her aunt's boarders before serving breakfast. That all done, she went off to school.

As working-class children had to assume adult responsibilities early, so too did some witness scenes unfit for their years. Obviously the children of disturbed families had appalling experiences; but a child like *Isabel*, growing up in a boarding house, saw 'a lot of life' too early:

> We had at least three married couples in the boarding house who were very well brought up people and yet, as soon as pension day came, they'd be getting their drop of wine. One man we had—Mr Donnelly—was a great reciter—all Shakespeare. You had it all for three days and you hardly ever slept. But you didn't tell him to get out because when he was sober he was so nice and educated. It never mattered what you said to him—he never got wild. He'd be reciting all *Hamlet* and so on. And his wife was a trained sister from St Vincent's and she was just as bad. She got to the stage where she had no modesty and would go without her bloomers. And Mr Curtis told me

> that when he was driving the dust cart he met her down Stephenson Street and she'd collapsed in the street—she'd got very thin because they weren't eating, just drinking—and he lifted her up into the dray and she had no pants on and was trying to pull her dress down. And he felt humiliated. In the end Mr Donnelly took a heart attack going up our stairs and fell down dead in the passage. I went to my friend Ollie to help me and we were trying to get him up—I was about sixteen then and didn't know he was dead. Then the police came down to the hotel opposite because it was six o'clock and I had to ask Constable Lowe would he come in and see Mr Donnelly because he'd collapsed. *You couldn't get an ambulance to come in those days unless you had a bed for them in hospital and they just wouldn't take you if you were old.* Anyway the policeman came and he got the ambulance quick and lively and when the ambulance man came he said, 'You want an undertaker'.

Isabel had to attend the morgue to identify the corpse but she was used to that, because years before she had had to identify the charred remains of a boarder who set alight to himself in bed.

Children were not only workers; they were also serious consumers. 'When you were a child all you thought about was a penny', *Mary Davis* remembers. When the moving pictures came to Richmond in 1912 a whole new dimension was added to life for both young and old.[33] On Saturday afternoons the fortunate got threepence for the pictures and a penny to spend, and if you caught a rat that was another twopence or 'if you found a lemonade bottle that was a penny and big news'. Saturday afternoon was the highlight of *Mary*'s week:

> You stood there an hour before the pictures opened—you never missed out—that was really 'it'. And did you spend that penny! You never spent a penny straight out—that was real extravagant. You'd stand there an hour and get a ha'p'orth of this and a ha'p'orth of that; six-a-penny lollies, silver sticks and silver sammies and bull's-eyes and you sucked them all day so you really got your penny's worth.

Phyllis Smith lovingly recalls 'The Hoadley's chocolates, big and luscious—the sweets are not the same now, they're tizzie; and the cake shop next door—for a penny you got beautiful big lamingtons, great big cream cakes and jam scones—really I thought I lived in a child's paradise'.

Where there was a little money to spare on entertainment, many parents made great efforts to take their children to the pictures, vaudeville and the city theatres. Many managed somehow to give birthday parties. At *Phyllis*'s 'everybody packed in, small house—it didn't matter—you'd have fifty children and my father was always very charming and would help turning skipping ropes or something—no drink that day, he'd be well and truly healthy'. But in *Mary Davis*'s family only adults celebrated birthdays and it was not until adolescence that she began to participate in family entertainments around the piano and the gramophone.

Finally, however, the abiding passion of Richmond people of all ages was sport, above all football. It would sustain many throughout their lives; for those who left Richmond and 'made good' it was one part of their hearts that would remain forever 'Richmond'. Children sneaked into matches without paying amidst the legs of sympathetic adults. Every open space had footballs soaring overhead every day of the week; but sport in childhood had its greatest significance in the schools, where for many it represented the sole path to achievement and the only thing that made school bearable.

School

However strong the traditional influences of family and, community may have been on the children of Richmond, the Edwardian working-class family was also truly modern in that it relinquished much of the intellectual, moral and physical training of its children to social institutions and professionals. The introduction of compulsory education had enabled the State and organized religion to invade the privacy and integrity of the family. The school was the social agency for the imposition of middle-class culture on the working class; it policed the shaping of future citizens. Of course, working-class radicals both here and in Britain throughout the nineteenth century had argued that free compulsory education was as important as the right to vote in the emancipation of the common people. Yet, when the 1870s brought national systems of education, some radicals perceived with dismay that the government schools were means of social engineering rather than beacons of enlightenment.[34]

In Australia the role of the churches in education complicated the matter. While the Protestant private schools educated the affluent and the powerful, the Catholic system catered for more than a quarter of the working class. Sectarian bigotry deluded some radicals that 'free, compulsory and secular' was achievement enough; and, while deploring the religious indoctrination of the Catholic schools, they remained blind to the social indoctrination of the State schools. Church and State were united in the endeavour of impressing obedience rather than independence on the poor. The role of the school was not to open up a new and fresh future for Australia which tapped the talents of all its citizens; education was to replicate the present, to ensure that working-class children grew up to be working-class adults. And if State school children weekly pledged themselves to 'honour the flag and cheerfully obey parents, teachers AND the law', whereas Catholic children were exhorted to obey the Pope and honour Ireland, they were equally expected to grow into complaisant fodder for the factory and the battlefield.

Without wishing to do violence to the complexities of the history of education in Victoria or to be unmindful of the dedication and imaginativeness of many administrators and teachers, the bare facts do speak for themselves. It was not until fifty-four years after the inception of 'free, compulsory and secular' education that Richmond boys had their own junior technical school so that they could become skilled tradesmen; two years later the girls were similarly endowed, albeit in temporary accommodation for twenty-eight years that was filthy, decrepit and eventually unsafe. But this was nothing to the ninety-five years it took for Richmond children to have their own high school which could open the door for them into the middle class. Successive Victorian governments voted with their feet on working-class education—it simply was of no importance and it was not until the 1960s that the electorate demanded strong educational policies of governments.[35]

When this Edwardian generation commenced school the State schools were barely forty years old; yet they were grossly overcrowded, unsanitary and already falling to pieces. Burnley school was doomed from the beginning; because the government architect had failed to evaluate the subsoil, and the three-storey brick structure was erected on subsiding ground. By the time *Hamish Roberts* started school there in 1909, cracks had appeared in the walls and it was declared unsafe; it was not closed and demolished until 1980. Instead of being the first buildings in Richmond to be sewered, the schools were among the last. Burnley crammed over eight hundred students into a building fit for half that number; at Yarra Park over eleven hundred children squeezed into the pocket-handkerchief playground that still exists today on the corner of Punt and Bridge Roads. In 1910 the *Richmond Guardian* was outraged that 'costly and handsome' new schools had been erected in Canterbury, Surrey Hills, Camberwell and Hawthorn and that 'the old-fashioned prison-like structures' in Fitzroy and Brunswick had been 'remodelled to bring them up to modern ideas'; yet 'not a single school in Richmond has participated in any of the grants'. At North Richmond, however, where an overflow of two hundred children had to be taught in an adjacent hall, a grant was made the following year: 'A wooden shanty of a lavatory has been erected which is a disgrace to the Department', while the only exit for children upstairs remained the three-foot-eight-inch stairway—a death-trap in a fire. A new infants' school was erected at Central State School in 1915; yet by only 1943, when the school shared accommodation with the Richmond Girls' Secondary School, all the buildings were declared unsafe, the worst being a building only ten years old where cracks were 'inches wide' and the walls and roof were 'moving daily'. By 1948 the falls of plaster were to be so dangerous that the principal would be forced to send the girls home.[36]

And inside these packed and decaying classrooms the children of Richmond were prepared for working-class life. They were given levels of literacy and numeracy fit only for the factory; they were instructed in hygiene to preserve the public health; girls acquired the domestic arts so that they could feed and clothe a family on an inadequate income; boys were trained in wood- and metal-work to get their hand and eye in early; they played team sports to build character and sinew and to relieve frustration; their art classes sought only to train them in accurate copying; their history rarely aspired beyond dates and propaganda about social classes and events that had nothing to do with common people like themselves; their geography was of climes and cities they would never see unless transported to far-flung battle lines; their nature study thrilled to the germination of a wheat seed on wet cotton wool and to the life cycle of the Emperor Moth but never hinted at more complex modes of reproduction; above all, they were taught to learn by memory and belief and not by question and investigation.

In his evidence before the Fink Royal Commission on Technical Education of 1900, the principal of Yarra Park school, Frederick Hayden, painted a portrait of an Edwardian Richmond school. He described a teaching staff crushed by the futility of its task and demoralized by an irrelevant syllabus and the iniquities of Payment by Results. He pleaded for more teachers—a ratio of one teacher and one assistant per one hundred pupils being essential for effective teaching. The curriculum must be reformed: working-class children should not be required to follow the formal syllabus of English grammar, geographical facts, and historical dates: they needed manual training. He thought that

> generally wood-work would develop a special aptitude (he displayed work done by one of his pupils, Lewis Evans) that showed that there must be some latent talent and genius that only required developing. There would be a great demand in factories and places of business for lads who had completed a course of manual training. There should be no attempt to teach a trade, only dexterity of the hand and an acquaintance with the use of tools. [Furthermore] a great many boys who now play truant would go to school if they had the chance to attend a manual training centre.

Yet perhaps the lack of technical education was not the only reason for the scandalous rates of truancy in the Edwardian schools. Hayden was a progressive but his description of Yarra Park's reformed drawing classes eloquently testifies to the oppression of the spirit in the schools for the working class:

> The present standard of drawing seemed fair enough to the average classes, but it might be improved by not having the younger children in second and third classes confined so much to the drawing of lines and curves. They ought to be, as soon as possible, taught to draw something from nature, if it were only a leaf or some object in the room, or sticks placed in different positions. There was too much of the mechanical idea of giving out books to

> a large class, and flat copies to draw from and the children did not take much interest in this class of work.[37]

Compulsory education signified a massive intervention by the educated and the affluent in the private lives of the poor, and it is clear that many working-class families initially resisted. In 1882 Yarra Park had 1742 children on its rolls and an average attendance of a mere 872. And while truancy rates fell over the next thirty years, many Edwardian children were spectacular truants, often aided and abetted by parents who resented the schools that sought to deprive them of their children's labour and company.[38] *Lilian Campbell*:

> I very seldom went to school. I was the youngest and my brother had died which rocked Mum. And she'd say, 'Oh, we'll go to the cemetery today', which was a day's outing because we'd take the tram to Pentridge and walk the rest of the way to Fawkner—take a thermos of cocoa and a few sandwiches. Then the next day Mum would be upset and she'd say, 'Oh, we'll go to the Market today', and that would be another trip up to the Victoria Market. Wednesday: 'Oh, we'd better clean up today', and we'd get stuck into the housework. Thursday: 'Well, you'd better put up an appearance today because Mother Augustine or Mother Claudia will see your sisters up at Sodality and might enquire where you've been all week.' Which I would do and trot up to Vaucluse—'Morning Mother—Morning Mother'—and let them see me. Friday: I'd say, 'Mum there's a test on today—I don't know anything'. 'Oh well, stop home today'. But if I managed to put in three days running at school I could catch up with my spelling, my dictation and my arithmetic. Mentally not much good, but I could catch up. One day I turned up for school with my bag on my back and they were packing up for the Christmas holidays and I knew nothing about it. Mr Meikle on his bicycle was always chasing Mum up—that was the Truant Officer—and I always had to go up to Mr Meikle with a note that I suffered from dysentery. If it was true that I suffered from all the dysentery that Mum attributed to me, there'd be nothing left of me. Oh, I knew Mr Meikle—I was an artist at dodging him on his bicycle.

Bill O'Reilly was a more typical male truant. Repelled by a brutal teacher at St Ignatius', Mr Macoby—dubbed 'Smackaboy' by the children—he went in the front gate each morning and straight out the back one, to pass the day watching men on the wharves or lying on the grass in the Fitzroy Gardens. Girls were kept at home to help their mothers with new babies or with family illness. Many parents saw little value in education that, in their view, wasted time on subjects and skills that were not relevant to paid work. The very poor needed their children in the workforce as early as possible.

But as compulsory attendance became a fact of life, acceptance of the authority of the school grew, because working-class parents came to realize that their children's best hope of escape from poverty lay in education. None the less, some of the Victorian and Edwardian parents who resisted the school's appropriation of their children's time dimly perceived, perhaps, that it was an attack on the autonomy of the family. For all the benefits of the increasing role of the Welfare State and the explosion of the helping professions, there have been some losses among the multitude of gains. Poverty and helplessness have not been abolished, only mitigated. People and families in need have lost some of their autonomy and dignity as politicians, bureaucrats and professionals diagnose and decide for them without asking what they would like. Successful protest through the ballot box only replaces these decision makers with another team who are still politicians, bureaucrats and professionals. And it has been the people of the working class who are least equipped to defend themselves against the modern policing of the family. Their poverty prevents them from making private arrangements to service their needs; their lack of confidence inhibits them from battling the indifference of politicians and bureaucrats; their ignorance intimidates them in the face of doctors, social workers and, of course, teachers.

The only immediate counter to this loss of parental authority was in collective action with other parents on school committees. The parents' support was vital to the morale of the teaching staff and where a strong tradition of parent involvement existed, such as at Brighton Street State School, the schools were able to offset central administrative neglect. Brighton Street held Christmas concerts, dances and juvenile balls and in 1905 was able to start a library. Endowed with generous grounds, the school was transformed by its magnificent garden—all the children's own work. In 1903 the *Richmond Guardian* noted with pride: 'very appropriately the cantata to be rendered by the children of the school at their concert on 13th November is connected with flowers, being entitled "The Flowers of the Forest"'. But strong parents' committees and 'Old Boy' associations did not emerge in all Richmond's Schools until the 1920s, by which time compulsory education had touched the lives of three working-class generations. At Burnley the parents campaigned, with some success, for new playgrounds and better road safety; at Central the Old Boys' Association donated prizes; at Cremorne Street funds were raised for scholars. By now all the schools held juvenile balls and fund-raising concerts in the Town Hall and had Miss Rose Allen, the dancing teacher, scurrying from school to school to prepare the performers. More than two hundred competitors starred at Burnley's Juvenile Fancy Dress Ball in 1926 where 'liberal prizes were offered for the best character sketches, fancy dress, original and comic representations including posters advertising various brands of manufactures'. When Mr S. E. Simpson, the determined headmaster of Brighton Street, retired in 1927 he could boast that 'the school garden is now the beauty spot of Brighton Street. It was a tip when he took over'. And during his headmastership he had placed Brighton Street among the best of Richmond's schools in scholarship and sport: 'many of the pupils have gained scholarships in the business colleges and some are now occupying good positions'.[39] *Muriel Thompson* was one Edwardian schoolgirl who was forced to leave at thirteen to Work in the Bryant & May match factory. In her turn as a parent, however, she was to make the Brighton Street Parents' Committee her life's work. It would begin when she enrolled her first daughter at the kindergarten and saw children there without shoes and pants. She ran house parties to raise money for shoes and 'one day I remember saying that there was hardly any shoes on my feet and I was buying shoes for the little people *because I didn't want them to be like me*'.

In a subtle way the school ethos attacked working-class life itself. In teaching middle-class drill, middle-class grammar, middle-class cleanliness and middle-class manners—'Sir' and 'Miss', 'girls before boys' and 'no swearing'—by implication it taught the poor shame. At the same time working-class children were blocked from entering the secondary schools that could enable them to escape proletarian life. Of course there were caring or eccentric teachers who, despite the vast classes, the fatigue, the low pay and the daily demoralization of school life, did manage to reach and inspire a lucky few. But even the best teachers could not hope to conquer the working-class child's most common barrier to effective learning—low self-esteem. Most working-class children were doomed to being processed, somewhat forlornly, through a system that did little for them. Many experienced only a vague yet bemused sense of failure; some spent their entire school lives in a state of war with authority; a few gifted and sensitive children, as we shall see later, were to perceive bitterly in later life that the only thing they learnt at school was that they were inferior.

The question of secondary schooling simply never arose for the vast majority of Edwardian working-class children. Richmond Boys' Technical School would not be opened until 1926 and the Girls' Secondary School until two years later. The new Continuation Schools charged fees, so the brilliant working-class child's only hope lay in a scholarship to the Continuation School or to a private school. In 1904 the Protestant private schools had savagely opposed the establishment of the State Continuation Schools: secondary education should remain in private hands because only the affluent had a right to it; the scholarship system was more than adequate to recruit the exceptional lower-class scholar. State secondary education for rich and poor alike was 'simply Socialism', opined the Reverend W. H. Fitchett, landboomer, champion of Empire and 'death in battle' and president of the Methodist Ladies' College.[40] Fortunately, we have a historian of the effectiveness of the scholarship system in recruiting working-class brains for higher studies. Dr David Rosenberg, the son of destitute

Russian Jews, had himself won a scholarship to Scotch College from Yarra Park State School. Keeping his own records, he reported in 1922: 'No school child has won a State School scholarship since Elsie Youll won one in 1901', and concluded: 'If that is not evidence of the decadence of the education of the Richmond school child, 1 would like to know of any better'.[41]

Low opinion of working-class intellectual potential was not confined to the personnel of private schools or to remnants of the high-Victorian intelligentsia. It would continue, and continue in high places that profoundly affected educational theory and practice. In 1931, before a Board of Inquiry into cutting Education Department expenditure because of the Depression, the anonymous headmaster of one of Melbourne's leading high schools declared that only one half of one per cent of the entire school population was intellectually fitted for higher professional work and another 3 to 5 per cent for lower professional work. Yet by 1931 the number of children receiving secondary education was between 10 and 15 per cent and the system was producing 'frustrated and disgruntled' men of culture who were 'socially objectionable and politically dangerous'. The headmaster supported his argument with the findings of the now infamous Professor Cyril Burt of the University of London. Burt was the leading educational psychologist in the British Empire, the author of the 'identical twins reared apart' studies and the father of intelligence testing and streaming in schools. We now know that Burt fabricated case studies, conducted in collaboration with fictitious female research assistants, in his desperation to prove scientifically that genetic inheritance is the sole determinant of intelligence and that the lower classes are congenitally inferior to the upper classes.[42]

If a working-class child had to be very bright it were best that he be male and a Roman Catholic. The financial plight of Richmond's Catholic schools exceeded that of the State schools. With an income of fees only, graduated according to parents' capacity to pay, the schools in working-class parishes faced appalling problems. The secular syllabus differed little from that of the State schools, with the exception of history, but religious instruction took up classroom time each day. The standards between primary school students in the State and Catholic systems probably were much the same, as both really attempted to teach far less than children under ideal learning conditions can achieve. Secondary schooling, however, saw many Catholic schools struggling to match the academic standards of the Continuation Schools and the Protestant private schools. *Brendan Ryan* went from St Ignatius' to Parade Christian Brothers' College where he learnt no Latin. At fourteen he transferred to the élite Jesuit college, Xavier, and found himself relegated to the lowest Latin class. Yet even at Xavier he did miserably in the Junior Government scholarship examination because his teacher had not read the syllabus correctly. But for all the deficiencies of the Catholic schools, the motivations of the Church hierarchy were a little different from those of the State. The Catholic church was anxious for its flock to elevate their position in society, and education offered a means of upward social mobility that would benefit the standing of the entire Catholic community. By 1900 the hierarchy was deeply worried that the proportion of children in the top three classes of the elementary schools never rose above 20 per cent and in the top class it was never higher than 2 per cent. One solution was to prepare Catholic children for public service examinations and coach them for government scholarships, and Archbishop Carr and his successor Dr Mannix directed the schools to seek out academic talent and coach it. It would be a long and painful process and not until the 1960s did the proportion of Catholics at university accurately represent their community: the poverty of the family proved to be an even greater waster of talent than was the poverty of the school. But scholarships could be found at a pinch for exceptional students and the religious life itself offered a way out for the brilliant and sensitive working-class child. (The number of ex-seminarians among academic historians who came from the urban or rural poor is still remarkable.) No Richmond State school could have boasted an equivalent array of the 'priests, doctors, lawyers, parliamentarians and high officials in the Public Service' who attended the inaugural meeting of the St Ignatius' Old Boys' Association in 1946, all of whom commenced their careers from humble beginnings in Richmond'.[43] Academic excellence was not the only reason for scholarships. One of Richmond's notable scholarship boys was its greatest Tiger, Jack Dyer, who was given a scholarship to De La Salle College to develop his football rather than his mind. (As his fellow football pundit, Lou Richards, claims: 'Poor Jack—he even failed plasticine'.) Secondary education for girls was to produce ladies, Christian mothers and nuns, but it was no less valued in Richmond. *Brendan Ryan*:

> The local convent, Vaucluse, was a Faithful Companions of Jesus establishment and it had boarders and day girls. All the people who could possibly go there went and they were very cheap. The boy of the family wouldn't go to the convent—he'd go into a trade or labouring, but the girl would. Now when they married in Richmond, my word they improved the social standard of behaviour in those families because the girl would have some idea of values.

The convent celebrated the feminine civilizing mission which drove an often unbridgeable gulf between the male and female spheres in both private and public life.

What did Richmond's schools do for—and to—this Edwardian generation? School broke up the democracy of the children's street community. It divided the affluent from the poor, Catholic from Protestant, even male from female: ideologies of class, religion and sex that would last a lifetime.

Richmond's tiny élite either commenced school at one of the big private schools outside Richmond or sought a more modest gentility in one of Richmond's three remaining academies. Clifton College was the only one to survive World War I and offered tennis and typing, elocution and music, and the clean air of the Hill where the college was 'healthily situated'. It too succumbed to hard times in 1928 and was little mourned.[44] *John Brown* knew a girl who went there: 'She really was a bit dull and she couldn't learn at the ordinary school—they took on a few like that; she used to skite about going there but it was only because she was difficult'. For the vast majority at 'the ordinary school', the academic quality of State and Catholic elementary education was much the same. Some people only remember school days that were oppressive and fruitless; others have fond, even joyful memories. Some of the bitterness towards Catholic schools really stems from a more general grievance against the Church that has been reinforced by adult experience. But in this admittedly small sample, those who are content with their schooling are more inclined to be politically conservative, either as Liberal or D.L.P. voters. It is possible that a full inquiry would reveal a significant role for working-class school experiences in the formation of adult attitudes towards authority, class and politics.

Those who praise their schooling are grateful for two things—the discipline and the practical utility of what they were taught. Perhaps they had low expectations of their own education but they do compare it favourably with what they see as the licence and vocational irrelevance of the schools today. The happiest memories are still of the fun and games in their own school days. Children who were good at sport were in their element. *Emma Murphy*:

> We loved school—the best days of our lives—we were in everything under the sun. We did Maypole; we were on the Melbourne Cricket Ground for the Prince of Wales coming here—beautiful displays. I was captain of the rounders team and I got a medal for the champion of Richmond in running—you wouldn't think it to look at me now.

Her sister *Alice*:

> I was captain of basketball and I got a gold medal at the Exhibition Buildings for the championship of basketball. And my brother *Vic* (later a famous Tiger) he was captain of the cricket and football teams and he represented the schoolboys in Sydney. And the other brother *Bill*—they were all in it. I loved school and—it really amazes me now to think of it—but we went through with all the same teachers and it was so different. Miss Beater—she was a wonderful person . . . Miss Brennan who had the 'little bubs' as she called it . . . There was Mr Skewes—they were fine men that went right through with each of our brothers.

For *Emma* and *Alice* school was secure and rewarding, as was their family. *Thomas Beauchamp is* grateful for sterner qualities. He now deplores the coddling of children with pocket calculators and visual aids. In his day

> . . . there were fifty in the class with the teacher out the front, no older than yourself, but she'd manage those fifty children. She was able to convey her message and we got the message all right because we learnt our tables and all that—sufficient to carry us through to the present day. Now they're reducing the ratio of pupils to teacher—they want 24:1—and she can't convey her message from what I hear—the children are over-ruling the teacher.[45]

Monica Rinoldi insists she had 'a marvellous education' at North Richmond State school. She was allowed to sit for her Merit Certificate (eighth grade) and she appreciates all the domestic science and sewing she did there: 'That was all in our State school education—it was very practical and very good'. *Dot* and *Edna Wilson* were in classes of sixty and seventy at Burnley, but 'they were very good—no noise; they were good teachers in those days—they taught every subject to their classes'. Children, who wished to please and knew how to, fared well.

In the Catholic schools—St Ignatius' and the little feeder schools of St Stanislaus' and St Louis'—respect for authority was intertwined with respect for the Church. For all the lay and religious teachers remembered with bitterness, there were religious, especially nuns, of genuine piety who made deep impressions on receptive children. Girls often admired the ladylike gentility of some nuns. *Ruby Kane* spent all her happy schooldays at St Ignatius':

> I was in the Maypole for the St Patrick's Day march and we won it two years running. It was lovely in those days. The nuns were not strict—they were firm. To my way of thinking they brought us up properly; they didn't let us be like a lot of animals which they are today—the nuns were lovely. I remember Mother Helena—she was a funny old dear. You weren't allowed to speak in the lines in those days—you had to walk along with great decorum. Of course I was a bit of a chatterbox and we'd talk and she'd say, '*Ruby*—what would your poor mother say if she could hear you talking. Pass on child, pass on'. We always say 'Remember Mother Helena'. I think she had the Irish in her.

Happy memories of school days abound in the minor triumphs of sport and maypole and spectacle. A sense of personal success was vital; but the means of success most open to working-class children were the accomplishments of eye and limb, not mind and spirit.

As Dr *Brendan Ryan* now sees it, he encountered at St Ignatius' Infants' School the 'first non-relative real influence in my life—an F.C.J. [Faithful Companions of Jesus] nun, Mother Josephine—a small, petite, angelic soul with infinite patience and high ideals'; but the curriculum left much to be desired:

> Teaching was by indoctrination. We learnt the ABC, the tables and the Catechism by this method and it had some credits as well as debits. Personal expression was not encouraged and neither was it at home and these were real debits.
>
> Periods of Nature Study at school were a welcome relief. I was able to experience the germination of a wheat seed and the emergence of a root radical from a bean. For a child that's interested, God it's an awesome thing, that. This gave me a feeling of awe, reverence and respect for living things that never left me—a never-ending source of pleasure. An illustration, of course, for me of the hand of God.

For *Lilian Campbell* the hand of God was found wanting at St Ignatius', however:

> There you were with the archangel—huge wings. It was Mass first Friday of the month and if you put a bite of food in your mouth after midnight you couldn't go to Communion. Sudden Death. I remember that I had to go to Communion and I'd eaten some green jelly after 12 o'clock and I thought this is where I'm going to be struck dead for sure. I went up the aisle to the altar rail, received communion, turned round to walk back to my seat—nothing happened. I sat in my seat—nothing happened. I was waiting for death. The Mass was over and I went out and my dad was waiting with the jinker and pony. I hopped up into the jinker. Now Dad's jinkers always went down at the back because the horse was too high in the front and when it lifted its tail and farted you'd get the full blast. Being tipped back in the jinker, I did feel sick and the horse was doing everything that comes naturally and I had to lean over the back of the jinker and bring up the green jelly. And I thought this is IT—DEATH FOR SURE. But I didn't die and I thought,
> 'Now . . . ???'

There were many working-class children who hated school and gained little from it. Children's performance at school was easily damaged by family problems, illness and emotional difficulties; and working-class children were—and still are—the most vulnerable to stress. The long recuperations after bouts of diphtheria, typhoid, scarlet fever and the other infectious diseases of childhood robbed children of months of schooling. *Phyllis Smith* saw little of school after the Spanish Flu in 1919, diphtheria, her scalding from boiling water and her mother's demands to help in the house. *Isabel Williams*'s terrible bout of diphtheria delayed her starting school until the age of seven. Then there were family problems. The death of a parent could so unsettle a child that learning was severely impaired, as happened to *John Brown* after his mother died and he was passed from relative to relative, changing schools each time. *Mary Davis* blames her father for a crippling lack of self-confidence: 'I had a very strict father and that's what I think kept me back. I never had a clue what the teacher was talking about; your parents never helped you with your school work—my father couldn't have anyway'. The school belonged to a world that, too often, both parent and child could not understand. Unbeknown to herself and to everyone else around her, *Isabel Williams* was a gifted child, but:

> I never had very much encouragement at school because I was never allowed to do homework. Auntie didn't believe in that—'You must learn while you're at school'. So if I had to do homework I had to get up very early and do it before I went to school [and before she cut the lunches for the boarders] or very late at night. There was no electric light—just lamps—it's a wonder my eyesight's still going.

The only help *Isabel* received was when her ailing aunt asked her to read the paper to her aloud, which expanded her vocabulary.

Above all, acute poverty itself could impair a child's ability to survive and succeed in the school system. *Jean Fowler* was another gifted child, but her alienation from the school and the Catholic Church began in the infants' class at St Joseph's, South Yarra, during one of her family's many moves:

> I went to school and I don't know what happened but I believe that I had a dirty neck. I wouldn't know—I was only a little thing in the first grade or babies. And I'll remember as long as I live—they took me in front of my brother up in the 5th or 6th grade and told a girl to come out and take me to the basin to wash my neck. And that was enough to turn anyone off the Church and my mother never let me go to school with a dirty neck again.

The nuns were hard on the very poor and the unrespectable. And they punished hard. *Jean* still smarts at the memory of canings on cold winter mornings: 'How they didn't break your hand I don't know; they were terribly cruel, the nuns, and I don't care a damn where you went, they were all the same'. There were no academic consolations for the humiliations of school life:

> We didn't learn much at St Ignatius' because as soon as we came in we had to say the Catechism. At some times of the year we had to say the Rosary before we went out and when we came in we had to say another lot. And we'd be kneeling on the forms—it was hell. I had no books and I couldn't read off anyone else's book—I was the dumbest thing on earth at school. I don't know how they ever put me up each year into the next class.
>
> I think I taught myself to read—I'm sure I didn't learn it at school because I had nothing to learn by. I loved reading and when I started school in Richmond we were living in Green Street and I'd read a book a night by the candle—from the little Swan Street library up here. And I'd say the words over and over again until I could spell them. I used to have a good

> memory—I'd know every flower—but since my heart attack I've had to wait for an hour for the name to come to me.

Jean Fowler's sons were both to prove gifted; she now attends the Uniting Church.

Religion could be a minefield for the children of mixed marriages. *Isabel Williams*'s father was a Protestant, her mother a Catholic. Initially her aunt sent her to Cremorne Street State School, but, according to *Isabel*, she was a 'sook' and was teased and bashed; so her aunt sent her to St Stanislaus', and into even more trouble:

> Sister Magdalene—she was so hard and made my life hell on earth. She'd have me in a corner and say, 'What are you going to be when you grow up?'
>
> 'A Protestant like my father.'
>
> 'You can't be, you've got to be Catholic like your mother—the only true faith.'
>
> And she'd keep me in playtime and lunchtime, but I had to buy the meat every day for the evening dinner, so if I was kept in and was late I got a hiding. But I couldn't dare tell aunt because she would have gone down and told them off and that would have been even more humiliating than being kept in the corner.

She was wrongfully accused of writing graffiti in the toilet because, as a Protestant, 'I was full of sin'. Then her Church of England Sunday School refused to give her a prize because she went to a Catholic school: 'I was heartbroken because it had lovely pictures in it'. Promoted to St Ignatius' school, the sequence of petty injustices continued. She developed a revulsion against kissing 'the cold marble feet of Christ in St Ignatius' Church'. Finally at eleven she fell ill, refused food and began sleep-walking. The Lodge doctor advised her aunt to send her back to the nearby State School so that she could walk home for a proper lunch. She needed special care, he said, because she would not live long. She survived, however, and at thirteen sat for her Merit Certificate:

> At the end of 8th grade we did our exams and then all the papers were taken over to Collingwood to be checked. We only had five girls and one boy in our grade and of course he gave this little Billy Nation extra tuition to what he gave the girls. When he came back after a week of correcting papers he said that the results were out and without any congratulations or 'I'm glad' or 'pleased' he said to me sitting in the front row (we were all spread out so we couldn't talk),[6] 'I'm surprised about you—you got the highest marks that went through the centre—176/180'. And this Billy Nation who they all thought would get very good marks—he didn't. Another girl got the next best.

> But you just took it as a matter of course and never thought about it and I promptly left school and stopped home.

The school was indifferent to working-class talent, especially female working-class talent: 'You never got very much credit for it from the teachers'. Not until she was in her fifties after she did exceptionally well in the Post Office examinations did *Isabel Williams* realize that she had a good brain:

> When you go all through your young life and then your adult life with no confidence—if you do get a little bit later it seems so unusual to have it. When I first went to the Post Office and they gave me this list to learn, I brought home this big list of the south-west country towns and realized that I had to learn it all off by heart, I cried. And I said to my young brother, 'I won't be able to do this', and he said, 'Of course you will'. Well I did, but I straight-away said to myself, 'I can't do it'. Some years later one of the girls I'd started with, Kate Murphy, said to me, 'I could kick you'. 'Why?' 'Because you've got ability but you've got no confidence in yourself.' Because when I was a kid, if anyone asked me if I could do anything, I'd say 'No'.

For *Isabel* the essence of 'working-class thinking' is having no self-confidence. Lack of self-confidence is the psychological mark of being working class, not class solidarity, not trade-union loyalty—just plain lack of self-confidence. And that for *Isabel* began at school, as it did for *Jean Fowler*:

> I remember at school, up at St Ignatius'—I don't care whether they know it or not—I was put in a room because I didn't have any money to pay them the sixpence a week for fees. I was on my own and put in a room to watch the other kids doing exercises. I was the only one they wouldn't let out for drill. I just sat in there by Mother Philomena and watched them. I did resent it. I said I'd rather send a dog up there than my kids—I sent them over here to Brighton Street.
>
> That's put me off them altogether—they did that to me and I'll never forget it. *It made you inferior. I think that's what was wrong with me all my life—until I got older and I got that mad that I didn't give a damn about anybody—I just went my own way.* And people said, 'You speak out', and I said, 'Well, I've been sat on all my life and why shouldn't I speak out now that I've woken up to myself'. I think this happened to me when I had my kiddies and I stood up for them. I was going to make sure they weren't sat on like I was—you know—pushed aside. When I was a kid, I had kids ask me to go back with them to this friend's place. And I was meant to be great friends with them, yet when I got there, they stayed inside and sniggered and went on—things like that. They were terribly hurtful kids and I thought I'll never stand that again.

When she grew up, *Jean* saw too many working-class people, through lack of confidence, resign themselves to poverty and helplessness:

They just sort of dropped their bundle and went along as they were. I've always wanted to get somewhere, do something. I can't sit back. My sister and I—we'd go to work and do housework, and pretty hard housework, round Camberwell. My sister just gave this up the other day—the doctor said she had to—she'd just turned seventy-six.

Isabel and *Jean* both bear scars. *Isabel* is a passionate Empire Loyalist: *Jean* has been angry and unforgiving all her life. And though they have both attained self-esteem in the twilight of their lives, the psychic damage inflicted by -poverty, church and school has exacted a fearful price in impaired health and inner anguish.

1914–1926

3

War and Peace I

Richmond Goes to War: 1914–1918

The declaration of war between Great Britain and Germany on 4 August 1914 marked the real end of the nineteenth century. The twentieth century has above all been the century of total wars and World War I was to drag an isolated human community like Richmond into a global theatre of shared suffering, dislocation and change. And the impact on a working-class community was necessarily different from that on the more affluent. Putting aside for a moment the private tragedies of lost lives and health, working-class people would have to do more than their fair share of the dirty work on the battlefield and in the factory: they lacked the cash to mitigate the inevitable hardships of war; working-class men were more likely to enlist because of unemployment; their death or incapacitation would inflict greater deprivation on their dependants. Even in those first months of heady patriotism, Richmond went to war with wariness and trepidation.[1]

The war was a mixed blessing for the Richmond economy. The knitting mills, textile and boot factories flourished under war contracts, the engineering firm of Ruwolt's began threatening the residential charm of Burnley Street. On the Hill arose the Pelaco shirt factory, a rude and ungainly blot on the Richmond skyline. As the Burnley Progress Association argued in the autumn of 1916, war industry was to be applauded as long as its factories did not appear the suburb's 'ideal residential areas'.[2] But a ratepayer from the Hill was to complain by 1918:

> Living in Rowena Parade, at the back of the Clifton Joseph's Cap Factory, our neighbours and myself can vouch for the nuisance it is. Our property, inside and out, is being spoiled with the black smoke and flakes from the

> narrow spout chimney . . . Sometimes we have to take the clothes off the line and rewash them.[3]

Yet despite the rush to enlist, the first months of the war saw an alarming rise in unemployment. War contracts took time to assign and implement. Export industries like the tanneries had to readjust quickly. Many small businesses, including home-building, that thrived on peace, floundered. And when the war contracts did come in, they favoured the skilled over the unskilled and often the female over the male. Only by the winter of 1916 did demands for relief on the Richmond Ladies' Benevolent Society fall significantly and the Town Hall have a mere eighteen men registered as unemployed. Yet by February 1917 *Labor Call* saw the problem as 'terrible in the extreme', as returned soldiers swelled the ranks of those seeking work. Even in prospering industries, young single men found themselves laid off by employers who hoped they would enlist.[4] The patriotic *Richmond Guardian*, which remained carefully neutral during the conscription crisis, paid this tribute to Richmond's first Victoria Cross winner, Private Thomas Cooke, a carpenter who left a widow and three children:

> He was an ambitious young man, and, though a skilled tradesman, who would have been welcomed into permanent employment in normal times, he believed that he would ultimately do better by launching out for himself. But the bursting of the war-cloud upset his plans. The building trade became slack. For any little contracts that were going there was keen competition. None of the big firms wanted men. They were putting off even their oldest hands. Private Cooke obtained temporary employment in the fitting up of transports, but it did not last. He put prices in for several advertised 'jobs', but without success. There was only one thing left. Private Cooke enlisted. That was in February 1915. The following day a letter was delivered at the Gardner Street house which offered him a contract, and which would have kept him going for at least six months. Private Cooke would have liked to stay near his wife and children. Private Cooke, our first Victoria Cross winner, was an industrial conscript.[5]

Civilians also had to cope with a burgeoning cost of living. Food prices rose by 40 per cent between 1913 and 1919, and footwear and clothing by at least as much. Wages rose, too, but the increases were not uniform and working-class incomes lagged well behind prices. War and drought had a devastating effect on meat prices and consumption: in 1913 137 783 sheep were slaughtered at the Richmond Abattoirs and in 1916 only 71 408. Pork consumption rose to plug the gap but by September 1915 a number of Richmond butchers had closed and the Richmond Council unsuccessfully petitioned the State Government to legislate powers for the importation of frozen meat from Queensland to be sold at a Council shop. The Council, however, did award employees a three-shilling bonus to offset the rise in food prices. War also brought taxation into working-class life. In

1915 the Government instituted the first federal income tax, an entertainment tax and a war-time profits tax.[6]

One Richmond business that did very well out of the war was the *Richmond Guardian* itself. Despite the loss of German and Swedish paper, it found enough to expand from a four-page local into a modern eight-page newspaper, replete with bold headlines, photographs and war news to rival the metropolitan dailies. But its greatest attraction lay in the letters home from Richmond boys at the front; and, in its eagerness to bring the war to Richmond, the paper ran foul of the War Precautions Act in early 1916. Censorship shielded civilians from many of the terrors of the war and Richmond read mostly of jaunty heroes: 'Happy Times In Trenches and Hospitals' headed the report of Christmas 1916. Inevitably, war-shocked survivors returned to a community which had little conception of what they had endured. Some old soldiers, like *Bill O'Reilly*, are still unable to talk about their war. And for some, only the wives who nursed them through the nightmares, understood the anger, the drinking and the violence that their children found unforgivable. Many returned servicemen were only to feel truly comfortable in the company of their fellows, a shared emotional isolation that fortified the Returned Servicemen's League for decades to come.[7]

The press did help break down some of the cultural isolation of the Australian working class. The war stimulated newspaper reading among people—especially women—who had not previously incorporated newspapers into daily life. By January 1915 the Richmond libraries reported a rush on their reading rooms as people scoured the press, especially the still uncensored American publications, for war news. Once the war became locked in stalemate, however, attendances returned to pre-war levels; but borrowing remained high, as people sought escape in books as well as in the new excitements of the cinema.[8] Above all, the soldiers' letters in papers like the *Guardian* were the first testimonies of working-class tourists. Only a handful of the Richmond élite had travelled abroad before the war and their travellers' tales had all the relevance of going to the moon. Now ordinary Richmond lads were seeing the world and their observations were absorbed into the national sense of identity. Private C. S. Penn remarked:

> If ever I was glad to have been a white man it was in Ceylon, when I saw the natives loading coal. They had to lift it up the ship's side, a bag at a time, and the wages are 1s. a day. Our wharf labourers do not know what work is.[9]

Private R. W. Young wrote from Mena of the fate that befell one Australian who lifted the veil of an Arab woman:

> He paid for it with his life. His throat was cut from ear to ear. The Arabs are handy with the knife, and some of our fellows will find it out to their sorrow if they don't watch out . . . [10]

Private Walter Hutchings, formerly a compositor on the *Richmond Guardian*, reported friendlier receptions after he was invalided from Gallipoli to England:

> The Australians seem to be looked up to here more than the English "Tommy". One only has to let visitors know he is an Australian and he has everything that is going and dozens of offers to call here with a car and show him around, treat him to tea, cigarettes, stamps, fun, etc. I have been offered money by several, but, of course, would not take it.[11]

The Anzacs' welcome was eventually to wear thin in England, but in these honeymoon days as colonial exotics they benefited from social intimacies the upper class could not risk with working-class British soldiers. But if the *Guardian* brought vignettes of foreign parts to Richmond, it also brought something of Richmond to the trenches. Corporal F. J. Maher wrote on behalf of ten 'Richmond lads' who were being sent the *Guardian* in Gallipoli: 'I can assure you it is real good to get your paper here, and although it is a month old when we get it, the news is quite fresh to us'.[12]

The *Richmond Guardian* certainly played its part along with the clergy, the schools and community leaders, in the 'manufacturing' of patriotism; but it reported as much as exhorted, and it now provides a valuable record of the impact of World War I on an Australian working-class community. And the story it reveals of Richmond at war is not one of unremitting patriotic enthusiasm, furious knitting bees, white feathers and Hun fever which was then split asunder by sectarian and class bitterness over conscription. Rather, it describes all these well-documented phenomena of the war operating over a mass of somewhat confused but decent people, in conflict between a simple sense of national duty and wariness as to what price they would really have to pay. And Richmond certainly did do its duty and paid an outrageous price in lives lost and maimed, a community sacrifice still visible on the Honour Boards of Richmond's schools. *Will Parker*, who served in France, saw something lost for ever:

> Oh, it was the pick of the country who went and all young men. And if you had false teeth you were no good; if you had glasses you were no good. It worried me to think that such fine and physically able and in character strong—so many to be killed, crippled, maimed.

At the beginning Richmond went to war with a vengeance. War was a godsend to community opportunists—politicians, charity workers, clergy, businessmen, teachers and the self-important. Within a fortnight of the declaration of war the Richmond Progress Association saw a chance of toppling Mayor Gordon Webber in the Council elections by impugning his loyalty. Webber trimmed his republican sails, began standing for the National Anthem and chaired a meeting of patriotic citizens to raise money for war victims. He was returned with a solid majority. The vicar of St Stephen's, the Reverend George Lamble, by early September was 'much impressed during the last few weeks by what he regards as signs of a growing seriousness in the life of the people'. Many Protestant clergy would be caught by their hopes that the war would inspire a religious revival and their efforts to justify the appalling losses in the name of God. Lamble himself did well out of the war, serving as an army captain-chaplain and busying himself on return with a soldiers' social club at Richmond House that later provided the nucleus for the R.S.L. in Richmond. The battle-hungry flocked to enlist and at Richmond's official farewell to its first 284 volunteers, a Boer War veteran, Corporal Gainge, promised that they would be 'proud of their soldier boys' for this was 'real war' whereas the Boer War 'was only bushranging'.[13] By late March 1915 nearly 1500 Richmond men had volunteered; yet, amidst all the enthusiasm before Gallipoli, a Red Cross function gave ominous warning of how working-class civilians really felt. The Ladies' Committee of the Richmond Red Cross was inspired to use George Coppin's former mansion, 'Pine Lodge', as the setting for a gala fête and, at night, a *palais de danse* reminiscent of the house's former glories. Respectful of Richmond's poverty, admission was set at sixpence, with threepence per dance and supper. Weeks of preparation and lavish publicity promised a splendid evening and hundreds of dancers were expected. They sold four tickets. Rather than see the food rot and the drinks go down the drain, they declared the dance free and only then did the crowds come. The *Richmond Guardian* was shattered:

> It was evidently sheer meanness and reluctance to part with a small coin. Trouble did not end there. Some unprincipled persons annexed four of the Oriental Lanterns that had been hired to illuminate the grounds, and on top of this some urchins forced their way in on Sunday and finished up all the unsold soft drinks and refreshments.[14]

Somehow £25 was raised for the Belgian Relief Fund.

Then came Gallipoli and the first Australian life lost was that of Captain J. P. Lalor, the 'frank faced son' of Richmond's Dr Peter Lalor and grandson of the hero of the Eureka Stockade. He died valiantly from shrapnel wounds and by his corpse lay six Turks shot to death and a seventh killed by the sword.[15] Five other Richmond men were on that first casualty list and the community armoured its innocence with defiance: the *Guardian* titled its first photograph of the landing as 'The Most Famous Feat of Arms in History'; later feats in France would bring only grief.[16]

Gallipoli invigorated the persecution of Germans in Richmond. Since the first days of the war the press and local patriots had taken it upon themselves to investigate the loyalties of prominent local Germans like Hugo Wertheim of Wetheim's piano factory. Like communities all around Australia, Richmond had early purged its street names of Hun associations but, with Gallipoli, Hun Fever really took off. In one sitting alone of the Richmond Court, two cases were cited as examples of inherent Hun brutality: one was a drunken Swede, and the other charges against two brothers, Edward and Albert Dennert, who had ordered a man out of a paddock behind their father's pub in Victoria Street. The *Guardian* headlined the Dennert case: 'The Huns at Home: Brutal attack on Peaceful Citizen' and the brothers were sentenced to three months gaol. A month later the Dennerts appealed and the Judge quashed their conviction, finding no evidence of undue violence in their actions. In May one Richmond girl preferred patriotism to respectability and was applauded for refusing to marry the German father of her baby.[17] German businesses were boycotted and German workers sacked, but for *Friedrich Smith* the consequence were lifelong:

> Being of German descent, I doubt if I did three years schooling of the eight I was supposed to do. The coming of the First World War changed everything as far as I was concerned and one thing I did learn was to defend myself. Even some of the teachers would come into the class and ask how your grandmother was in Germany—well we had no way of answering those sorts of questions. And kids would call you a 'dirty German' and one thing and another, and of course one would take a poke at you and another one would. So I carried the few books I'd need in those days and I had a wooden pencil case tied together with a long strap. Well if the kids got daring and there was more than I could handle, I'd swing the strap. And one kid, I cut his lip and knocked two teeth out. And his father came over to have a go at me but he didn't realize that my father was home and my father just picked him up over the front fence and said. 'If you come in here, you knock on the door like anybody else'.
>
> People who really knew us, they were damned sorry, but a lot of people were very bitter. My father had difficulty in getting local work. He used to go on the wharf, but being a naturalized subject, he couldn't continue working there, so he got a job in the Victorian Railways and he was working on the railway lines up round Bright and Rutherglen and he'd come home only occasionally.

There were to be some unexpected benefits from the war for working-class civilians. The medical rejection rate among Australian volunteers, and reports of the British Army where soldiers were unable to masticate coarse rations, alarmed the general public about the physical and dental health of the working class. Then in July 1915 the St Stephen's Harriers Club announced ashamedly: 'Quite a number of members have tried to enlist during the last few months, but in every case dental troubles have arisen'. A public meeting was convened at once and the Richmond Council made a deputation to the Minister for Education for funds to establish a dental clinic for Richmond State school pupils. The Minister was sympathetic but unable to help; the Council started its own fund but failed to raise enough for the clinic to open.[18]

Muscles fared better than teeth, however, especially female muscles. And the scene for the health and fitness campaign for the youth of Richmond was the municipal baths. (Not that these fresh-water baths were all that salubrious. In 1911 Annie Morcombe, aged thirteen, drowned in six feet of water, but the bathkeeper had to clear the 150 women and girls from the water, count them besides their bundles of clothes and then dive repeatedly before he could find her body.) The bathkeeper, Mr W. I. Bennett, had organized a life-saving club and in May 1916 photographs of the female members of the club appeared in the *Guardian* and the Melbourne *Herald*. The papers were besieged with letters from young men proposing rendezvous and marriage; and on meeting nights the 'girls gather round and the letters are read aloud'. The Richmond Council then launched what it claimed to be Australia's first Municipal Gymnasium to build a 'fit future Army for Australia' at the cost of only £1 per man. The gymnasium was for both sexes but the girls stole the limelight, and if the Army reaped little benefit from it, female emancipation did. Now respectable girls could publicly pursue and display physical excellence, an opportunity hitherto allowed only on the stage. Prudes, of course, wasted no time and Father Brennan banned a performance by the girls in St Ignatius' hall. Mr Bennett and his girls were undeterred and in January 1918 staged a swimming carnival at the baths to raise funds for a forthcoming Patriotic Carnival. A susceptible reporter from the *Guardian* was quite overcome by the vision of the 'new freedom' inspired by Annette Kellermann and Richmond's own Grace Buller, 'in the use and display of the female body'. Here were nice girls a chap could marry 'in skin-tight costumes which allowed a liberal display of leg, neck and arm, [who] looked the embodiment of physical perfection'. The 'new freedom' had still a long way to go, however. At the end of the carnival boys and girls jumped into the water together, and when Mr Bennett applied to the Council the following week for permission to run mixed bathing one day a week to promote attendances, the councillors unanimously refused. They had been disgusted by the way the carnival had 'degenerated' at the end, and feared for the moral welfare of the young people of Richmond.[19]

But the most significant effect of the war on Richmond was in the growing maturity of working-class politics. Gallipoli hastened the demise of unthinking jingoism. Now that war was real and awful, and the magnitude of the losses in the Dardanelles had weakened the Australian commitment to the Empire, serious appeals for volunteers had to be made for the first time; and in July 1915 the minimum height for recruits was lowered to five feet two inches.[20] In the first week in July, Prime Minister Billy Hughes addressed a recruitment meeting at the Richmond Town Hall.

The people 'crowded liked packed sardines around the passageways and the corridors'; Hughes was magnificent:

> No man need hesitate . . . They were in a life and death struggle. They had to kill or be killed. They had to crumple the despot that was now threatening to reduce all Europe to a shambles—a foe that put forces against civilization and Christianity . . . They lived here in Australia under a glorious charter of liberty and that had been won for them by the British race through years of perpetual struggle.[21]

The military mission for civilization and Christianity quite overwhelmed Richmond public life. The August Council elections passed almost unnoticed—'the war overshadows everything'.[22] Even John Wren was keen to do his bit and on 11 September the *Guardian* published a collage of photographs of 'Private Wren's First Day in Camp'—getting up, eating, digging and washing. Private Wren was also applying his singular talents to the Imperial cause: he was hon. sec. of the camp sports committee and was 'building an entertainment stadium' to keep the troops 'away from the lures of the city'.[23] On 21 July 1915 the working-class clubs in the Victorian Football League outvoted the middle-class clubs who wanted all football suspended for the duration of the war, but once the Grand Final was over, seven of Richmond's players, including the legendary 'Checker' Hughes, succumbed to the pressure to enlist. Most of the patriotic condemnation of spectator sport was aimed at working-class pleasures rather than cricket and racing, but in October 1915 the Richmond Methodists added their small voice and called for the cancellation of the Melbourne Cup.[24]

Yet, by the end of 1915, as the toll of dead, wounded and sick rose, evidence of war strain began to mount. Repatriated wounded and sick troops appeared in the streets and the public became alarmed by delinquency from soldiers on leave. Christmas saw a brutal riot erupt among four hundred people outside a hotel on the corner of Burnley Street and Bridge Road. Two men were given heavy sentences for bashing a soldier over the head with a bottle and a handkerchief full of broken glass. New Year brought news of the evacuation from Gallipoli and Richmond counted its cost: sixty-three dead, sixteen missing, two hundred and thirty-two wounded or ill.[25]

In January 1916 the country was in the thick of a recruitment drive for the new army of 50 000. Richmond was assessed to have 8000 men of military age and was set a quota of 428. By mid-January 4200 men had replied to the 8000 enlistment cards sent out. The *Guardian* published the results to date, hoping to shame shirkers into facing up to their duty. It was never to go into such detail again; for the responses only gave heart to the unwilling. Of the 1739 replies classified—113 were declared ready for immediate enlistment; 63 were prepared to enlist at a later date; 171

volunteered but were medically unfit; and 1168 refused outright; 708 of these were married and 459 single. The *Guardian* then cited some of the disgraceful replies of those who had refused:

> One man who has a wife and five children declared: 'Any man who is in such a position as me is always at war'. Several replies were received to the effect: 'I will enlist when all the Germans are discharged from Newport Workshops'. One man said: 'I refuse to leave my mother to the tender mercies of the Commonwealth' and others offered to go 'when all the Germans in Australia are interned'. Alleged conscientious objectors to the war are plentiful. The most concise, most original, and probably the most truthful reason given is expressed in one word only 'frightened'.[26]

In the midst of a heatwave in the last week of January, recruiting sergeants pounded Richmond's 'well scorched streets' only to find most men at work and many employers barring them from speaking to their workers. A massive rally at the Town Hall addressed by Senator Pearce yielded only twelve volunteers. When the new recruits marched through the streets a week later, only one hundred and twenty were to be counted. By March the final replies were in. Nearly eight hundred had not bothered to reply at all despite the severe penalties for not doing so. And Richmond had failed to fill its quota—defeated by lack of commitment to a middle-class war and by the poor standard of working-class health. The final statistics were never published and the campaign boded ill for the chances of raising the one hundred and sixty-six reinforcements needed from Richmond each month to keep the A.I.F. up to strength. Nationally the prospect of conscription loomed.[27]

In its last meeting for February, the Richmond Council reluctantly debated conscription. Councillor Strahan won over a majority vote for giving the voluntary system a fair trial: 'It is only a matter of wages', he argued. 'Pay the men £1 a day and you will soon get as many soldiers as you require.' Councillor Kemp, the Independent for prosperous West Ward, was shocked that pay was a 'disincentive . . . patriotism should be enough'. Six weeks later Councillors Strahan and Kemp were again at loggerheads over the war—this time in response to the Shire of Ripon's call for the banning of all sport for the duration of the war. And as debate over the war began to fall into class lines, the Army recruitment campaign descended to the plain macabre. Sergeant Pulford and his armless, eyeless 'sweetheart for life', Sergeant Ball V.C., began holding recruitment meetings in the streets of Richmond. Ball had won the V.C. at Gallipoli for bringing wounded mates in from the firing line and ended with seventy bullet wounds. With Pulford holding him up in the back of a lorry he made 'a pathetic appeal' while Pulford told 'the truth about Gallipoli': 'We didn't have to leave because we were beaten. We had to leave because we didn't have enough men to avenge the deaths of all of those brave comrades of ours who fell'. The ghastly pair did better than the politicians, though, and at their Victoria Street meeting won fourteen recruits.[28]

The gradual class polarization of the conscription debate was revealed by the struggles within the Australian Natives Association. In May the Richmond branch refused to endorse the A.N.A. Conference's policy on the grounds that the voluntary system had not yet proved a failure. A week later the branch president, R. H. Palling, addressed the Richmond Council. Councillor Burgess, as a member of the Home Defence Forces, demanded to know why Palling himself had not enlisted. Palling exploded:

> . . . as a married man, I do not as yet consider it my bounden duty to volunteer when thousands of parasites, more eligible than myself, with no intention of ever realizing their responsibilities, are loafing round Melbourne today. (Hear, hear) I am a conscriptionist. That system is the most equitable and democratic. By conscription I do not mean merely the conscribing of the manhood of this country, but also its wealth. I believe it is unfair to conscribe the eligible manhood of this country to fight, and to allow ineligibles, whether individual, firm or organization, to make exorbitant profits as a result of conditions arising from this war while others are giving life and limb for our country. Further, in my opinion, thousands of those who volunteered were conscripts in its worst and most deplorable form—men who were forced to enlist to provide the necessities of life for their dependants. They did not volunteer—they were conscripted.[29]

Community tension was rising. A curious case came before the Richmond Court in late July when three women alleged that a group of youths had insulted them outside the Richmond station the previous Sunday. The youths had teasingly called out 'Taylors' because the women were wearing the colours of the Taylors Jam factory football team. But the women were also wearing their husbands' battalion colours and when they accused the youths of disrespect to the colours and of shirking their duty, they were hooted and abused.[30]

In the first week in August the Richmond Council passed a resolution opposing conscription, but at the same time called a meeting in the Town Hall to mark the beginning of the third year of the war. The attendance was pitiful and [the] Mayor had to explain that Friday was a bad night for such a gathering: 'The women folk are all out shopping' he said, 'and most of the men have to stay at home to mind the house, if not the baby'. Then on 19 August the *Guardian* recorded 'Richmond's darkest hour'—the casualty lists from the slaughter at Pozières. In contrast to the 1915 municipal elections, voters all over Melbourne seemed galvanized into a new political awareness. Poll turnouts were astounding and in Richmond class lines hardened: in West Ward the Progressive Association's anti-Labor candidate and in South Ward Labor's Maurice Joyce both won with record majorities. And Palling entered the Richmond Council uncontested.[31]

A fortnight later Frank Tudor, the Minister for Customs, resigned from Cabinet and announced that he would campaign against conscription. Tudor had prevaricated for weeks, claiming he could not come out in the open until Cabinet had made up its mind. But his hand was finally forced by the Richmond branch of the P.L.C. who had committed themselves to the campaign and virtually presented their M.H.R. with an ultimatum. That weekend the news from France was even worse. The Richmond dead outnumbered the wounded; two brothers had been killed side by side; another two were missing.[32]

Tudor soon assumed the federal leadership of the Anti Conscription campaign. It helped that he was a teetotal Congregationalist, albeit one who had enraged militant Protestants in Richmond by supporting Irish Home Rule.[33] But he also presided over a P.L.C. that was fighting for its life. The Richmond P.L.C. came late to the conscription debate because it was preoccupied with defending the integrity of the party against assaults on two fronts-from the Catholic Federation and the Drink interest. Parallel with the evolution of war politics in Richmond ran a story of sectarian tensions within the Labor Party and of conflict over the role of the state in the regulation of morals. The result was a highly complex reaction to the war and conscription: the formation of a broad non-sectarian alliance against conscription and a split within the Catholic community over State Aid to church schools and the nature and role of the Labor Party. *Ted Sullivan*, whose family were in the thick of these battles within the P.L.C., sees the seeds of the 1955 Split as being sown during World War I. Alliances and prejudices were formed then, that in the family dynasties of Richmond Labor politics were passed from generation to generation—and still endure.

In 1914 the public leadership of the Richmond branch of the Catholic Federation had come from the èlite—men like Councillor G. R. Admans and Dr M. P. Macgillicuddy. Then, Ted Cotter, although a Catholic, refused to support State Aid in the 1914 State election and attracted enough Protestant votes to win by a record majority. The failure to win Catholic votes away from the Labor Party in the election persuaded the Catholic Federation that they should use Catholic Laborites to capture the party from within. In Richmond 'Jack' Brady, secretary of the Richmond Hibernians and a former secretary of the Richmond branch of the P.L.C., was promoted to leadership of the Federation branch. In November 1914 the Victorian Central Executive of the P.L.C. had proscribed members of the Catholic Federation, the Licensed Victuallers' Association, the Loyal Orange Lodge and the Women's Political Association as being within Rule 38 (g) which forbade membership of the P.L.C. The Catholic Federation and Dr Mannix campaigned furiously to have the ruling overturned at the 1915 State Conference, and in Richmond Brady threatened to stand as a Catholic candidate if 'Cohen and Co. do not mend their attitude'. But the

State President, Laurie Cohen, won a resounding victory at Conference and, the Federation was further thwarted by the resolution that any members of the party known to have worked or voted against endorsed candidates at the State election were to be expelled. The result was the founding of the Catholic Workers' Association, formed to educate the Labor movement from within in the merits of the Catholic cause. Hot on the heels of the Catholic Federation came the Liquor Lobby. In July and August 1916 the Richmond branches of the P.L.C. found themselves swamped with new members. George Vesper, secretary of the Richmond branch, was dismayed as over a hundred new members, 'nearly all of them employed at malt houses, breweries, bottle works and yards', were attending in force. A week later the conscription campaign began.[34]

Tudor spoke first to a record attendance at the P.L.C. branch meeting: the conscription campaign had fatally weakened the voluntary system, he told them, and 'as far as Richmond was concerned, it had given three thousand recruit—a record surpassed by no other city in Australia'. A committee was formed to collaborate with the Abbotsford and Collingwood branches to arrange meetings in Yarra. Prime Minister Hughes then called for the Mayor of Richmond to organize a pro-conscription meeting. Councillor Fear did not reply. In the next fortnight Richmond men attended in force for the Home Service call-up. Eventually 1503 were examined: 604 were declared fit; 329 were rejected; 510 were doubtful; 60 were found to be temporarily unfit. Exemptions were claimed by a further 885—mostly on grounds of being only sons, or of having to support parents or of working in war industry.[35]

On 11 July Tudor addressed a public meeting in the Town Hall. Even the *Richmond Guardian*, which Tudor accused of not reporting Anti meetings, could not ignore this one, for 'It was easily the biggest crowd that has ever gathered in or about the municipal building'. Mayor Fear led the procession of official Laborites. Tudor declared that being anti-compulsion was not being anti-war and spoke proudly of Richmond's contribution of volunteers. But also he told them that this was the most important meeting ever held in Richmond:

> The people were asked to decide a question that not only had an important bearing on their own history, but on the history of all nations. It was the first time in history that a question had been submitted to the people of a country as to whether they should adopt a system which until a very short time ago was absolutely unknown in any British country.[36]

The next evening T. Ryan, a South Australian Labor M.H.R., gave a pro-conscription address. He was abused and ridiculed with parodies of Salvation Army refrains until he was forced to flee under police escort out the back of the Town Hall through a 'howling mob of five hundred men'. When it came to the vote a fortnight later, 72.64 per cent of the civilian voters of Yarra said 'No' to conscription.[37]

The referendum over, the Richmond P.L.C. returned to its battle with the Liquor Lobby. The vote in State Parliament on six o'clock closing was imminent and the *Guardian* noted one of Richmond's political ironies:

> Richmond's parliamentary representatives are an enigma if not a conundrum. Tudor is a teetotaller who was present at the Liquor Trades' picnic. 'Gor Save' Webber now the M.L.A. for Abbotsford is also a teetotaller, but voted against six o'clock closing and Ted Cotter who will enjoy a drink with either a lord or a labourer voted for the Bill.

Cotter's opposition to the Liquor Lobby—intriguing in view of his alleged later attachment to John Wren—provoked a furious attempt to dump him as Richmond's M.L.A. The branch's new members, whose admission fees had been paid by their liquor trade employers, overturned all the rules of procedure, but Cotter managed to hang on. Snide suggestions that the Catholic Federation had collaborated with the Liquor Lobby to remove Cotter led to angry denials. The *Guardian* was unrepentant and alleged that the Federation and the Liquor Lobby shared a 'secret agent'—a certain Horatio Phelan. Phelan had come in 'as a silent worker in the last State elections', had subsequently associated himself closely with the Catholic Federation, and now reigned as a 'dictator' over the branch membership which had recently been 'so incontinently inflated'. The *Guardian* continued: 'In everyday life Mr Phelan is associated with the firm of bacon curers that have made such a feature of the shrewd and clever trade mark "Don't Argue". Mr Phelan does not act up to it at Labor League meetings'.[38] A fortnight later Phelan got himself made a delegate to Annual Conference and pledged himself—in order—to (1) seeing that Catholic schools got a fair deal for the payment of teachers (2) advocating the rights of the Liquor trade and (3) improving the Labor platform. The meeting exploded and the *Guardian* commented:

> What a mundane world it is, to be sure! Twelve months ago almost to a day, Messrs L. Kenny and McMahon were permitted to put the case for the Catholic Federation before the annual conference of the P.L.C. Mr Kenny stigmatized the delegates he was addressing as 'godless socialists'. The meeting fell upon him in indignation. Mr Kenny was proposed and accepted as one of the 'godless' at the last Richmond branch meeting of the P.L.C.[39]

The old guard of the Richmond P.L.C. took the only course open and walked out. George Vesper, Dr David Rosenberg and old Catholic Laborites like Richard Loughnan who refused to be drawn into sectarian politics set up a rival branch of the P.L.C., producing Richmond's first Labor split. The new branch became known as Vesper's League and it would take two years for the P.L.C. Central Executive's call for re-amalgamation to be heeded. (In February 1916 George Vesper had been appointed assistant rate collector for the Richmond Council amidst cries of 'jobs for the boys'. Then in early 1919 the rate collector, Mr C. R. Syle, was dismissed for alleged incompetence and for corruptly favouring certain ratepayers. Syle claimed that a vendetta had been conducted against him ever since he had successfully sued Gordon Webber for libel five years before. His protestations were ignored and Vesper became Richmond's rate collector, a position he held until his retirement in 1938. On retirement Vesper immediately stood for Council and died in office in 1943.)[40]

Simultaneously in these early months of 1917, the Left critique of the war was strengthening. Dr Mannix's deprecation of the conflict as an 'ordinary trade war' earned him the respect and gratitude of *Labor Call* and the Victorian Socialist Party, and the continuing resentment of loyalist Protestants. If Mannix's stand drove away as many Protestant votes against conscription as it won from Catholics, then certainly in Richmond Tudor's Protestantism seems to have fortified the non-Catholic Anti cause. And Tudor shared some of Mannix's doubts about the moral justification for the war. Certainly recruiting in Richmond was becoming ever more difficult. People still turned out for recruitment meetings—three thousand packed the Cinema Theatre in Richmond in early February when a young girl broke down after reciting 'Kitchener's Call'. Yet few replied to the invitations sent to every eligible man in the suburb and only an old man and a handful of boys offered themselves that night.[41] Recruitment meetings were by now no more than free theatre. A few days later Tudor spoke at a recruitment meeting at the Melbourne Town Hall. Of the war that two years before had been hailed as the means to a moral and religious regeneration of the nation, he now despaired.

> Today there was a bloodlust among the people. We saw red and thought red and were unable to reason as we did two and a half years ago. When we read of a number of enemies being 'wiped out' and sent to their Maker, we rejoiced. We did not think as we used to think.[42]

By April the country was in the thick of a Federal election campaign. Tudor was then leader of the fractured Federal Labor Party and at his first Richmond meeting on Sunday afternoon, 22 April, three thousand people crammed into Barrett's Cinema. But it was Adela Pankhurst, not Tudor, who captured the meeting:

> The landords of England believed in war, and were responsible for its declaration. They should see that the people at home belonging to those whom they were compelling to fight, did not starve . . . The war was being waged in the interests of the wealthy, and the poor would suffer for it for generation to come. Peace could never be obtained until the mass of the people in the belligerent nations desired it. For the sake of women, for the sake of international peace, the only people to govern the Commonwealth were those chosen by the Labor Party.[43]

The audience listened with rare attention and gave her 'prolonged applause'. News of the meeting inspired four thousand to attend the next one and when, the following week, the Director-General of Recruiting spoke in Richmond, he was howled down. Despite the national defeat for the Labor Party, Tudor's majority in Yarra was untarnished.[44]

Vesper's Labor League now formulated a radical position on the war and in June resolved that the Labor movement must safeguard and defend 'the industrial, civic and conscientious rights of the workers, which have been achieved through many years of toil and suffering, lest these be swept away by the rising torrent of conscription and capitalism which is gathering universal momentum'. Their fears were well founded in their own suburb alone. The following week a report on Richmond industry revealed an unprecedented high tide of prosperity'. Nearly all local manufacturers reported a higher turnover than before the war, even industries without war contracts were sharing in the boom. But the boom in capitalism was not being shared by labour. Adela Pankhurst spoke again to a full Town Hall in August on the deterioration of the working-class standard of living: since the outbreak of war wages had risen only 39$^{1}/_{2}$ per cent compared with the cost of living's 50 per cent. None the less, the recruitment campaign had dried up even the economic conscripts and by the end of July the *Guardian* was forced to admit that recruitment in Richmond was 'like flogging a dead horse'. The Victorian Socialist Party seized the chance to arouse public indignation at the unfair economic burden of the war. They engaged the Richmond Town Hall for a rally on 24 September and organized for a crowd to march from the Yarra bank to Richmond. Mrs Jenny Baines counselled the marchers before they set off: 'She did not tell them to break windows, but she advised them to do what they thought best. She said that if people wanted food they should go to the cool stores or to the bakers and the butchers and the other places and take it'. Under banners like 'Arrest the Profiteers' and 'Why starve when Mice and Rats grow Fat', they marched through Richmond. Curiously, the police were stationed on the wrong route and the demonstrators had free rein along Swan Street. Among the first plate-glass windows to go were those of William Angliss, the meat king. The furniture stores of Tye and Co. and Maples incurred £160 and £125 worth of damage and Dimmey's £55. Only three people were arrested and the four hundred marchers joined a mere two hundred in the crowning Town Hall meeting.[45]

Dr Mannix succeeded better at becoming the figurehead for the Anti cause. His Anti-Compulsory Service League welded Catholic conservatives and Laborites under a common banner and his extraordinary rally on the Richmond Racecourse propelled leading St Ignatius' laymen from the Catholic Federation into the campaign. The role of Irish patriotism is hard to determine. Dr *Brendan Ryan*'s family, within the privacy of the home, were still very Irish: 'Thomas Fitzgerald and Wolf Tone were household names; the romantic elixir of the brave was very much with us'; and the family remained unmoved by the general English patriotism of war-time Richmond. Yet when *Brendan* went to Xavier, even though the school's

Jesuits were an Irish province, he found that few boys shared his loyalties. The civilian Anti vote in Yarra in the second Conscription referendum reached 73.27 per cent and even if every single Richmond Catholic followed Dr Mannix's call, twice as many Richmond Protestants voted 'No' to conscription. For Richmond it was a class, not a sectarian, cause.[46]

1918 was to be a year of healing. With the conscription crisis over, public feeling returned to honouring and supporting the men at the front. Richmond's Patriotic Carnival raised £1605 for the blind soldiers in May.[47] Then in August a Civic Welcome was mounted for Richmond's returning soldiers, and a lone Richmond caterer, Mr J. Carmichael, prepared an extraordinary tribute to the working-class addiction to refined carbohydrates. While an Imperial Orchestra of thirty played all night in the Library Hall, Richmond's heroes faced:

Sandwiches

chicken and ham, egg and lettuce, ham, tongue, cress, roast beef, salmon, lettuce and ham, anchovy and sardine.

Chicken and oyster patties

Cakes

fruit meringues, amazons, spanish meringues, snow balls, Alexandrias, Othellos, Desdemonas, chocolate fingers, fan chousettes, Genoisse cakes, sponges, queens, halfmoons, Vienna pastry, assorted almond pastry, Pretoria shells, dice, macaroons, shortbread squares, French pastry ornamented in various shapes, pears and apples meringued, plain and fancy biscuits, assorted sponge fingers, plain seed and currant cake, ornamented French cakes—orange, nut, rose chocolate.

Desserts

golden jelly, champagne jelly, madeira jelly, Montpellier cream, charlotte russe, Italian cream, tutti-frutti, trifles en caramelle, fruit salads.

Ices

passion fruit, vanilla, strawberry,
Fresh fruits in season, dried fruits, nuts, confectionery.

Drinks

tea, coffee, aerated waters; Wine cups—claret, chablis, pineapple. (No intoxicating liquors were served, the claret cups and punch being the nearest suggestion to strong liquid refreshment.)[48]

As rumours of the impending Armistice spread, a last-minute rush of volunteers sought to save face. Then on the 11th of the 11th it was all over. Richmond's street celebrations were hosted by Mr Sid Gibb, 'well known in sporting circles' and dressed in a frock coat and silk hat. The crowd sang patriotic songs until up Church Street and into Swan Street came a tin band of 'Matchie girls' from Bryant & May, led by a bagpiper. And behind them, bashing away on normally scarce kerosene tins, came a gigantic tin band of all the children of South Richmond.49 In Burnley Rose Saddler, whose father worked hard to provide Burnley State School with an Honour Board of its war dead, was to remember that night as one of the biggest of her life:

> My brother came out from the city with the news and my father said, 'We'll ring the school bell', and of course people came out to see why it was ringing—it was about nine o'clock at night. So they marched around the streets and sang and got tins of boiled lollies and they scattered them round.
>
> The next morning my father got up and the school bell was rung again when we were to go to school, but he'd been round the shops and there was to be a picnic down at the Survey Park. We all went down there and our mothers were back getting lunch for us and Dad was at the school. And *Emma Murphy* said to me: 'I won a race that day and got two shillings', and I said: 'You're a pro now, *Emma*'.[50]

Richmond's first war was over.

Peace and Problems: 1919–1926

As with the Edwardian high noon before World War I, collective memory has endowed the Gay Twenties with an image of sparkling prosperity and emotional expansion that owes more to the contrast with the calamity that followed than it does to the intrinsic well-being of the period. The war, in fact, left a legacy of personal problems, social tensions and raised expectations; and life remained drab and difficult for the poor and the defenceless.

Obviously the immediate problems were of the returned servicemen themselves. Many were to carry physical and mental disabilities for the rest of their lives. Jobs were scarce and schemes for their rehabilitation often ill-planned and foolishly administered. *Will Parker* was one who was tempted to abandon Richmond for the independence of life as a soldier settler. Wisely, he first went bush and learnt something of farming. When he was offered a block he realized that it was too small and asked for two. He was refused and he joined his brothers in the family soft-drink business that eventually brought them real success. He had no illusions about returning to a land fit for heroes: 'It was only "say" to me. I expected I'd have a battle and that's what it's been'. After twelve months on his back in the Caulfield Repatriation Hospital, *Bill O'Reilly* was discharged as Totally and Permanently Incapacitated. A compulsive truant, he had little education to fall back upon, but he did have a flair for invention and good business sense. He now has no doubt that he would have done better in life had he not gone to the war; but he was saved by his marriage:

> Because my health wouldn't stand up to a full day's work I had to find the easiest way out and that was a business where the two of us could work. Shops, newsagents—we've been in everything. The only thing she wouldn't be in was a pub—I could have had two pubs but she said she wouldn't take children into a hotel to live and that was that. But she was a beautiful woman and a beautiful wife. I wasn't a scholar and she used to do all the clerical work—she was a pretty good scholar at school and that helped a lot. So between the two of us with my brain and her hard work, we jogged along from one business to another.

And there were subtler difficulties. Heroes they might be; but they did make some civilians uneasy. Some people were shocked, even repelled, by the maimed as they attempted to return to normal life. Even though his father had been killed at Gallipoli, *Harold Stephenson* was unable to envisage war until he saw its victims return: 'We never had TV to show pictures—if you got any news it was from the papers and then rumours'. The alcohol abuse and the horrific incidence of venereal disease in the forces stigmatized the entire A.I.F. in the eyes of some.[51] When *Monica Rinoldi*, as a vivacious sixteen-year-old, brought home her future husband, a twenty-five-year-old former Light Horse man, her parents were appalled. Not only was he a cradle-snatcher, but also a returned soldier; and returned men drank, carried 'soldiers' diseases' and had brought back a lot of English brides—'the English brides gave them a bad name'. *Monica* stuck to her Light Horse man and 'my husband was one of the cleanest and finest men you'd ever see 'in a lifetime'.

The servicemen themselves were changed men. Many had broadened their horizons, and acquired self-confidence and inner resilience. *Will Parker*, for one, returned from France more tolerant of religion and class:

> You didn't ask a fellow who was going out with you to mend the wires in the night what religion he was or where he come from. I don't care what a man's religion is. If he's a proper-sided fellow and he's sincere in what he believes and carries out what he professes, that's all. Going to war makes you more tolerant.

But it was not so for civilians like *Will*'s Methodist family; and the 1920s were to be disfigured by the social tensions over religion, class and personal liberty that had been exacerbated by the war.

The problems of the peace were not slow to manifest themselves. Hard on the heels of the Armistice came the Spanish Influenza pandemic. The first Richmond case was reported in late January 1919, and the community, warned by the overseas reports, responded quickly. Within a fortnight the Richmond Council had established a hospital in the Central State School and schools were to be closed for the next sixteen weeks and cinemas for the next five. And, as with the Bubonic Plague scare of 1900, the flu prompted a much needed clean-up of the community. After seven weeks the Richmond statistics stood at 1119 cases notified, 148 treated in hospital and twenty-six deaths. The revolting pneumonic symptoms and the justified fears of fatal infectious disease promoted panic and bizarre remedies. Urban working-class people were not to know that their crowded and dirty living conditions enhanced their immunity: healthy rural communities around the world were to succumb more drastically than were the urban poor. The press did not help by calling it 'The Black Death' and recollections of the Spanish Flu are redolent with medieval imagery.[52] Richmond Protestants were deeply impressed by the silent nuns from St Ignatius' who filed down the centre of Bridge Road each morning to nurse the stricken in the Central School hospital. *Friedrich Smith* recalls the terror of 'the Bubonic Plague' in an over-crowded Richmond cottage:

> A lot of people were really terrified. My brother and I were sharing a double bed. Harold next to me got it. My eldest brother got it. I nursed Harold at home; Jim went to the Exhibition Building emergency hospital. Willy, the second eldest brother, thought he had it and somebody told him that the best thing to keep it away was quinine so he bought a shilling's worth and took the lot. They took him to the Melbourne Hospital, then to the Exhibition hospital then back to the Melbourne—he didn't have flu—he had quinine poisoning.

Friedrich's wife *Florence* was thirteen at the time:

> I slept with my mother when she had the plague and she had pneumonia. And they go through a crisis, and this night she was singing the hymn 'In the sweet bye and bye' and I thought she was dying. When the doctor came the next morning she was all right, she'd gone through the crisis, but I thought she was going up to heaven.

By the end of March the flu had abated even though deaths were to occur into the winter. Richmond now faced the social and economic cost to the affected families and to local industry. The Council faced the cost of the entire emergency medical programme. Municipal authorities were still expected to carry the primary responsibility for health and social welfare and it would take the Great Depression to force State and Federal governments to relieve them of this impossible burden. The Richmond Council, scarcely able to carry out essential roadworks, by mid-August had a bill of over £3000 for medical staff, equipment, medicines, fumigation and inoculation. It called on the State government to pool the cost of all the municipalities and to contribute half. Instead, in November, the State government made a claim on the Council for £3663 9s. The councillors were 'staggered', but paid up.[53]

After the Spanish Flu came the national maritime strike. Richmond industry was hit hard: hundreds of workers were stood down; even the Jam Factory lost all its melon supplies for the season. By mid-July people were rushing to withdraw their savings and estate agents were implored not to evict tenants who had a good record of payment. Again the Council and local charities were expected to dispense relief, but by the end of July their resources were exhausted and the State government was forced to fund a relief depot at the Town Hall. The depot, in sixteen weeks, relieved 1115 cases, issuing 8962 orders for food and 384 orders for board and rent. Richmond business people donated £2460 and large quantities of meat and other perishables. None the less, the Richmond Council stood firmly behind the strikers. The Mayor, Councillor Barcelo, chaired the Victorian Socialist Party's meeting in the Town Hall when Tom Walsh expounded the seamen's cause and was arrested. The Council later refunded the V.S.P. for the hire of the hall.[54]

The 1919 maritime strike presaged the industrial unrest that punctuated the 1920s. The war had raised working-class expectations and political confidence but peace failed to bring a rise in working-class real wages. Working-class bitterness was vindicated by the Royal Commission into the Basic Wage when it reported in 1920 that a just basic wage, based on the Harvester Judgment's principles, should stand at £5 17s a week, whereas it was merely £4 2s. Ordinary Richmond people not only suffered from the paucity of their incomes, but also from the disruption to industry of the great strikes, especially the second coal and maritime strikes of early 1921, and of the gas workers. The gas strike of 1920 saw the Richmond Council quite unable to administer any local relief at all, and all cases were thrown on the mercies of the not so benevolent Ladies' Benevolent Society. (In 1921 the L.B.S. had a rule never to give more than six shillings a week because they were 'assisting not keeping applicants'; first applicants received only 2s 6d, and were then 'investigated by a member of the Society as to the level of their need and their moral character.[55]

The most socially alarming strike was the police strike of 1923. Young *Harold Stephenson* was selling *Heralds* in Swanston Street when the rioting started:

> Someone says, 'They're coming down here', and it was down near the Post Office, breaking windows and snatching coats and everything and a big crowd was welling up Bourke Street towards Swanston Street. A couple of other fellows selling papers said, 'We're getting out of this'. And they were punching each other and women putting on coats. Bang went the window of London Stores—then the Leviathan's. I run down the street to a cake shop, Lou Collins'—'They're coming down here'. People rushed out. Then I went down to the agent at Flinders Street Station and he says, 'I'm taking all the money and I'm going. Get out of town—this is serious'. We got out in time.

Richmond reported few 'outbreaks of vandalism and brutality' compared with some other suburbs; but a Richmond man was murdered outside Wirth's Circus on the Saturday night. The Richmond Council stood by the strikers and in February 1924 formally condemned their sacking from the Police Force. The community was well aware of the poor pay and conditions of the police and in 1922 the Council had estimated that Richmond needed at least five more policemen to ensure the safety of the suburb.[56]

Industrial militancy was but one manifestation of the uncertainty that afflicted the entire Australian economy during the 1920s. The Hughes government had recognized the need for tariff barriers to develop manufacturing industry and between 1921 and 1927 manufacturing employment rose by 24 per cent in Australia. Overseas firms that moved to Australia in those years included General Motors, Ford, Dunlop, Paton and Baldwin, Lysaght, I.C.I., Nestle, Cadbury, Kelloggs, Gilbeys and Philips and many Richmond people were to be either their direct employees or to work for their allied service industries. Yet tariffs and growth did not ensure security of employment. So much of Richmond industry had depended on war contracts that peace brought real hardship. By the winter of 1923, some of Richmond's boot factories were forced to be on half time. In the winter of 1919, the Richmond match factories had retrenched two hundred men and girls as their safety match market deserted them for Japanese matches. Yet, with protection in 1926, massive retrenchments again became necessary. After the distress of the unavoidable post-war slump of 1919 and 1920, the years 1922, 1923, 1925 and 1926 all recorded serious unemployment in Richmond. The Commonwealth Royal Commission into National Insurance in 1927 found this type of cyclical unemployment to be nation-wide between 1914 and 1925. The boom of the 1920s was an illusion. Professor Noel Butlin now sees overall economic growth in Australia as remarkably poor before the 1950s in comparison with the United States, in that each period of prosperity, including the 1920s, saw the economy only catching up to the levels of growth reached before the preceding slump.[57] Moreover, by the 1920s industry was short of skilled workers, a direct legacy of the political neglect of working-class education. In 1927 the Royal Commission into the causes of destitution found:

> An analysis of the particulars furnished by the various charitable organizations shows that 44 per cent of the applicants for relief were unemployed as the result of the shortage of work; 25 per cent were in distress as the result of sickness, accident, physical or mental defect and old age; 13 per cent were widows with young families; eight per cent were deserted wives and six per cent were in destitute circumstances arising from personal causes. The majority of the applicants are the dependants of unskilled labourers and reside in the industrial suburbs.[58]

For many working-class people the Great Depression was to be 'normal' only longer.

One industry that did boom in peace was building. Big money was being made in property development and home-building as new suburbs consumed market gardens and farm land to the south-east. Richmond people, who already owned property or who had saved, joined the move to McKinnon, Ormond and Glenhuntly. *Hamish Roberts* bought two blocks of land recently subdivided from market gardens in Moorabbin and Bentleigh and paid them off at five shillings a week out of his wages as a law clerk. This modest investment as a young unmarried man was to set him up for life and to secure his place in the middle class. But the property boom inflated rents as well as values; and the less fortunate struggled to find accommodation amidst an already grave housing shortage, further aggravated by the returned soldiers who were marrying and seeking a family home. By 1923 Richmond landlords were asking twenty-five shillings a week for houses that rented at fifteen shillings before the war. The Richmond Council campaigned against rent sharks by publicly exposing them: one they caught in 1922 had raised the rent of a house from 17s 6d to £1 10s in a mere six weeks. Inflated rents ate into already 'inadequate wages; over-crowding increased; dwellings physically deteriorated. Yet landlords used the shortage of accommodation and/or their alleged poverty the face of rising prices and inflated building costs as grounds for appeal against Council orders on condemned premises. The Richmond Valuer, George Vesper, was asked by the Royal Commission of 1920 into the Basic Wage whether Richmond was 'a reasonable residential suburb'. He had to answer 'no'; for most of it would have to be demolished and rebuilt to meet the Royal Commission's minimum standard. The passionate Dr David Rosenberg went further. He doubted whether six houses in the whole of South Richmond were fit for human habitation and alleged that in the worst part of North Richmond, one street—Mahony Street—was known as the 'valley of death' because diphtheria was close to being endemic there. The Richmond Council was far from grateful for this public condemnation of its community and even the M.O.H., Dr Haynes, protested that Dr Rosenberg had 'insulted the residents of Mahony Street'. Despite the apparent prosperity of the next six years, when the Central Executive of the Victorian branch of the A.L.P. made its own investigation into the housing conditions of Melbourne in 1926, it found no improvement at all in Richmond on the slums reported to the Royal Commission in 1914. They were not to know that the Great Depression and World War II would ensure that the housing stock of Richmond faced another thirty years of neglect.[59]

The 1920s also marked the beginning of the slow decay of Richmond as a human community. Along with similar industrial suburbs like Collingwood and Fitzroy, by 1927 the population was steadily falling.

Young Richmond couples hankered after 'pleasant, healthful homes in the outer suburbs where they find fresh associations and their children may grow up in helpful surroundings instead of being penned up in city dwellings'. Increasingly, those who stayed in Richmond did so because they had no choice. Industry accelerated its invasion of South Richmond and Burnley. Residential property was far cheaper than existing commercial sites and premises: in August 1920 a record price of £8500 an acre was paid for prime vacant industrial land in Swan Street; and the Rising Sun Hotel recorded a 145 per cent increase in sale price in less than three years by 1924. In April 1922 the Richmond Council was forced to adopt industrial zoning regulations to stem the erosion of the residential parts of North, South and East Wards. But the problem remained that a large number of inhabited houses were left in the factory zones and, apart from the pollution, noise and heavy traffic inflicted on the people, the fire risk was vastly increased.[60] *Muriel Thompson*:

> The Cherub shoe factory was next door to us—we had factories everywhere around us in this little street. The Cherub was burnt out—it was brick and we didn't get burnt that much. But we had canaries that were stiff in their cages. Then they threw all our stuff in the street—the piano was the first thing that went out. Then it must have been Christmas because somebody pinched our Christmas dinner that was in our safe.

After a long battle *Muriel* received a piffling compensation for smoke and water damage to her possessions, but during the spate of 'insurance fires' in the Depression, many found that they were ineligible for compensation from a factory fire next door if the damage was not directly caused by the flames but only by falling masonry. Tenants in the factory zones now found landlords refusing to carry out even the most basic and sanitary maintenance. The only joy for house-owners was that one day their cottage might be bought at factory prices for redevelopment. *Muriel Thompson* and her sisters had to wait more than thirty years for their homes to be coveted by their neighbouring Satanic Mills, but a least in old age *Muriel* has bought a cottage on the Hill, fulfilling her lifelong ambition to 'live in a street with trees'.

Another industry that boomed in peace was organized crime. In 1921 the *Richmond Guardian* blamed the war for teaching many men 'brutal licence' and fostering civilized humanity's 'primitive instincts', so that all over the world the social strains of war were now manifest in a wave of crime. In Melbourne the 'wowser' campaigns to abolish illegal totes and evening drinking had succeeded in providing deprived communities like Richmond with the lucrative industries of SP bookmaking, illicit gambling and sly grog that were to thrive until the late 1960s. As a poor suburb, Richmond had always had its share of petty crime and drink-related violence. Big money, however, could only be made in gambling.

By the 1920s John Wren had gone respectable and in his place appeared two talented professional criminals with strong Richmond connections—Henry Stokes and Leslie ('Squizzy') Taylor.

After a humble beginning as a horse-dealer and bookmaker living in Mary Street, Richmond, Henry Stokes turned himself into the 'Two-up King' of Melbourne. By 1919 he ran Melbourne's best two-up school in Goodwood Street, Richmond, with Taylor as a junior partner. In November 1919, while Stokes was interstate, the police raided the school and the fifty arrested gamblers were conveyed to the Richmond Police Station in a fleet of taxis only to find that a sympathetic crowd of three thousand had rapidly gathered to cheer them up. Another raid a few days later was nearly thwarted by angry locals milling around the fleet of cabs in Goodwood Street urging the arrested gamblers to escape.[61] However loyal his Richmond clientele, Stokes saw richer pickings to be had from the wealthy. *Norman Stevens*, as a man with form, a driving licence, a reputation as one of Melbourne's best street fighters and a good shot, worked for Stokes as his bodyguard:

> Stokes—he was an interesting character. He was well known for his ability for running a fair-dinkum two-up school. He set us the task one time of putting down a mat to play two-up on. And when we'd stretched it out (one thing interesting to note—Stokes would pay anything to a good tradesman) he'd say, 'I'm having blokes coming over from New Zealand', and we'd be pulling it up again and up again—it went on and on—to have a bit of bounce in it so the pennies would roll around and around on it—he was noted for that. And if you won—say you won a thousand quid—he'd mind it for you and you could come the next day and get it when you wanted to. He looked after his customers—oh God, why wouldn't he! Look at what he had—he had doctors and lawyers and Jack Doherty was a mate of his. They'd be finished at two in the morning and they'd ring up (fancy ringing a man up at two in the morning). He'd get out of bed and say, 'Well, how much will it be Jack? and he'd say, 'Three hundred'. 'Make it five.' You know—easy got—easy go. That was two-up. Now he went to gaol in Ballarat—a bank in Ballarat—he had a bit of trouble there and he hit the can. He got a good job out there—he was well looked after, he had contacts. When he got out of there, the baccarat was going and the two-up was going. He bought the Matears'—that's the fellow that's got 'The Australia' in Collins Street—he bought his house, lock stock and barrel—walk in walk out—in Queen's Road. All he had to do was the drinks—when you went in the door there was a sort of tray bar—and all he had to do to that place was to put a tenner's worth of gladiolus in the hall and get the tables built to play baccarat on. Well he got going. One day he said to me: '*Norm* will you go outside for me in Queen's Road—you know a bit about cars—just park them for me'. Anyhow—a top gambler come in, he was a Jewish fellow, a nice fellow, and

> he was noted on the racecourse for a long while—and he offered me two bob. Two bob—I saw the day when I'd eat it—-but it was an insult then.[62]

Notwithstanding *Norman*, Stokes was shot and thus ended the job of a lifetime.

But Richmond's own was Squizzy Taylor. Born in 1888, the second youngest child of a respectable coachbuilder, Taylor grew up in Richmond as an 1890s Depression urchin. At school he was said to be a timid, sly runt and his first easy money came as a 'crook' apprentice jockey in pony races. His first brush with the police was at the age of eleven and by the time he was twenty he had amassed a record of petty larceny and done time in a Salvation Army home. In January 1908 he was convicted of stealing ten shillings from the till of the still flourishing Cherry Tree Hotel in Balmain Street and was sent to gaol without option of a fine for giving cheek to the Bench.[63] Taylor, like Stokes, moved to bigger things, specializing in gambling, blackmail, intimidation and murder. Some believe that Taylor was really the front man for Stokes, the then 'Mr Big' of Melbourne. But his swagger and elegance and spectacular flair for evading the law captured the public imagination. He pressed dazzling bank notes into the hands of the down-and-out for petty favours: 'He was a criminal admittedly, but he had a very soft-hearted streak too', says the impeccably respectable *Ruby Kane* of this undoubted psychopath. Above all, he was a celebrity, and a celebrity from Richmond, who enabled the poor to enjoy a vicarious defiance of the rich and powerful who despised them. When Taylor was killed in a shoot-out with Snowy Cutmore in Carlton in 1927, the funeral cortège from his little house at 18 Darlington Parade on Richmond Hill was watched by a vast crowd that had collected since early in the morning. *Lilian Campbell* wouldn't have missed it for the world:

> The funeral was on a lovely Saturday morning and I had the two kids in the pram. His little widow was all draped in black with the widow's weeds and she had nice legs—that was the first thing I noticed as she came down the step.

Those lovely legs of Ida Pender were to bring her fame and respect as the wife and dancing partner of Mickey Powell.

Politically, the 1920s were afflicted by the class and sectarian tensions that had been aroused by the last years of the war. In Richmond class and sectarianism became fatally intermingled, an intermingling that damaged both sides of politics and in particular sullied the Protestant cause. But the 1920s also witnessed a decay of Labor integrity in Richmond that was to embarrass the Victorian A.L.P. for decades to come. At first the party in Richmond entered peace full of confidence and with a sharpened radicalism. In April 1919 Vesper's Labor League, soon to be restored as the only legitimate branch in Richmond, unanimously passed a resolution calling for the democratization of industry: i.e., the ownership and control of industry by the workers for the workers'. The party increased its majority in the next two Council elections, and Richmond conservatives realized that they stood no chance of recapturing the Council if they campaigned under their proper political colours. Their only hope lay in arranging themselves under the banner of Imperial loyalty and Protestant moral superiority. And the mounting confidence of Victorian Catholics under the leadership of Archbishop Mannix provided fruitful ground for bigotry and the manipulation of working-class Protestants.[64]

For the Federal election of 1919 the Protestant Federation placed hoardings around Richmond of 'Protestants—vote Protestant and Loyalty' until the Richmond Council voted to ban them as sectarian imputations on the loyalty of Catholics. But when the Irish-Ireland League requested permission to hold a meeting on the City Reserve the following year, the Council steered a middle course between the Irish patriotism of Councillor O'Connell and the Protestant loyalism of Councillor Davies and followed the lead of Councillor Barcelo who 'as an Australian of mixed ancestry, asked why the wrongs of Ireland should not be discussed as well as the wrongs of Servia or Belgium'. In 1920 Maurice Joyce, the Irish-born organizer of the Carters and Drivers' Union, was elected Mayor. Later a chairman of the Trades Hall Council, Joyce was and remained an ornament to the Catholic community and to the Labor movement. But Labor was recruiting to office in Richmond able politicians of all persuasions. In 1920 Gordon Webber retired from Council to concentrate on his parliamentary work and was replaced by Bruce Longfield, an accountant who had studied for the Methodist ministry. Longfield was to give long service to Labor on Council, but, significantly, was never elected Mayor. 1920 also brought Mrs Mary Rogers into the Labor team, the first woman elected to municipal office in Victoria, and at the conversazione held at the Trades Hall to celebrate this first for women and for Richmond, she called for an amendment to the Local Government Act to permit 'the municipalization of milk, fruit, vegetables and other commodities'. The next year Dr David Rosenberg was elected president of the Richmond branch and hopes were expressed that he would contest the next Legislative Council election. By early 1921 there were few grounds for accusing the Richmond Council and the Labor party of being a Socialist/Fenian conspiracy and when Councillor O'Connell called for the banning of three anti-Catholic novels by Lindsay Russell from the Richmond Library, his colleagues quietly dropped the matter into the too-hard basket.[65]

Four weeks later the Council made a fatal move. It granted permission to the Trades Hall Council and the Victorian Socialist Party to hold the May Day procession in Richmond after it had been banned by the Melbourne City Council. The Socialist Band headed two and half thousand marchers to the City Reserve where five thousand watched Maypole and Morris dancing. Within a fortnight 2800 signatures were collected and presented to the Council, protesting the holding of 'demonstrations that savour of disloyalty to the Crown'. The 'non-political and non-sectarian' R.S.L. informed the Council that 'over four thousand went to the war from Richmond; they were sent . . . [and] now the Richmond boys had come home to find the principle for which they fought outrageously attacked'. Councillor Robinson asked Mr T. Parkinson, the vice-president of the Richmond R.S.L., 'if it were not a fact that four thousand went from Richmond to fight for freedom in Australia and the rest of the world?' But Mr Parkinson 'was not prepared to admit that. The soldiers went to resist German servitude being imposed upon the British Empire'. The petition failed but, alerted to the conservative threat, Dr Rosenberg urged all lapsed party members to rejoin to help counter those who were organizing young men into the Australian Legion.[66]

With the R.S.L. licking its wounds, into the breach leapt the Richmond Council of Churches, bristling with new ammunition: to wit, the Richmond Council had desecrated the Sabbath by permitting the Royal Victorian Institute for the Blind to hold two charity picture shows. Every Protestant clergyman in Richmond pledged himself to denounce from the pulpit on 22 May the sins and iniquities of the Richmond City Council. On that fateful Sunday, many followed the example of the Reverend F. Delbridge of the South Richmond Methodist Church, who likened the imminent decline and fall of the Richmond Council to that of Ancient Rome. But the General of the Richmond Army of God was the Reverend Lamble of St Stephen's:

> I sincerely believe that for this city at least a Labor Council (that is a council which understands and appreciates and is in full sympathy with Labor's highest aspirations and ideals, Labor's need and possibilities) is what we need and the only one we want to have. But let them be men whom we can trust—God fearing, truthful men of integrity, able men—men whose mouths and whose language will be that of decency and dignity, not of oaths and blasphemy and filth; men whose minds are clear of covetous desire; men whose hands are clean from unworthy gain—whose eyes are clear to see the needs of all the men in this city; whose ears are clean, not clogged with party prejudice or noisy sectarian clamour; whose hearts are tender towards the great soul need of this undisciplined and untaught people whose ideals are high, whose principles are unselfish, whose purposes are strong, whose patience is great.

Protestant councillors were shattered. Councillor Bell declared he was ashamed to be an Anglican and withdrew his children from the church where their father's integrity was impugned.[67]

But Lamble's sermon was also a cunning political manifesto. He got himself interviewed by the *Herald* and announced that the Council of

Churches would contest the next Council elections. Their four 'true Labor' candidates included the patriarch of the South Richmond Methodist Church, Adam McConchie, the wealthy timber merchant. His solution to Richmond's slums was not reclamation but soap: 'The people should do their share towards keeping the houses clean'. When the elections finally came, all the Labor candidates won with only small dents in their majorities and Labor spokesmen entreated the Protestant leaders to join a united campaign to remedy Richmond's social ills. Dr Rosenberg even invited the Reverend Lamble to join the Labor party—he refused and two years later rose to higher things as a Canon of St Paul's Cathedral. The Protestant clergy had disgraced themselves and many ordinary Richmond people were appalled by their opportunism. Councillor O'Connell now succeeded in having anti-Catholic literature banned from the Richmond Library, fortified by Protestants who, dismayed by the spectre of Richmond sectarianism, had added their complaints. And at the same meeting the councillors decided, without a division, that the library should purchase the works of Karl Marx.[68]

One reason for this foolish foray into politics by the Protestant churches was that Frank Tudor was mortally ill and unable to exert his usual influence on the Congregational Church. He finally died just after New Year in 1922 and Billy Hughes as the Prime Minister was his chief pallbearer. Competition for pre-selection for the nation's safest Labor seat was intense. King O'Malley, E. J. Holloway and Alf Foster were joined by three locals, Councillors Joyce, O'Connell and Palling, but it was the earnest, self-improving and eloquent James Scullin that the party wanted securely in Canberra. Within five years he was deputy leader and, two years later, Prime Minister.[69]

Ironically, the Council of Churches had been premature in their attack on the integrity of the Richmond Council and the Labor Party. The next six years saw a dramatic decline in the character of local politics and the emergence of the dynastic machines. Two vast families now began to come to power. One was the Cremeans, upwardly socially mobile, ambitious and devoutly Catholic. They were related to the O'Connells by marriage; and H. M. Cremean, although eminently respectable, was close to John Wren. Only the 1955 split would conclude the family's distinguished career in the A.L.P. The other family were the Loughnans, equally ambitious and capable, but more independent of the Catholic Church. The patriarch, Richard Ignatius, was Squizzy Taylor's bondsman and local legend supplied Frank Hardy with the allegation that Loughnan was Taylor's co-driver in the Trades Hall murder of 1915. What *is* fact is that Loughnan was a character witness at the trial for the culprit, Richard Buckley, testifying that as organizer for the Builders' Labourers' Federation he had attempted to rehabilitate him. Richard Loughnan's son Cornelius Anthony (Con), was a drinking companion at the Vine Hotel of Taylor and a hairdresser and S.P. bookmaker, John Corry. Again Con Loughnan was never convicted of any offence with Taylor, but Corry was with both: of S.P. bookmaking with Taylor in 1925 and in August of the same year of acting as Loughnan's 'agent' in organizing boys from St Ignatius' School to distribute unauthorized election bills. A climate of suspicion hung around father and son that pained their respectable relatives and delighted their enemies.[70]

The first member of these two families to move into the Council was Con Loughnan. Endowed with a quick mind and a flair for words, he had entered a seminary and acquired a little higher education before losing his vocation. Chronically disputatious, impulsive and capable of sudden sadistic violence, he was clearly afflicted with a severe personality disorder that by middle age sank him into alcoholism. His crude voice belied his taste for stylish dress; in later life he would sport an elegant cane that concealed a rapier. In his final years of decline he was to be disfigured by a grotesque wen on his neck that completed the bizarre menace of his physiognomy.

Con Loughnan entered Council in a characteristically controversial way. In 1923, following the State Conference's policy on slum eradication, the Richmond Council passed a by-law limiting shop frontages to 16 feet and house frontages to 22 feet. Loughnan quickly saw that this would penalize home-owners whose houses were burnt down, preventing their being rebuilt. Nearly two-thirds of Richmond's houses were now in jeopardy and Loughnan stood against Councillor Kemp in West Ward in the 1923 election, warning of a Richmond scarred with vacant blocks that were useless except for commercial premises. He lost narrowly. Undeterred, he formed the Small Landholders' Defence League and deluged the press with anonymous letters exposing as class traitors the Labor councillors who supported the by-law:

> The day of reckoning is at hand. The Small Landholders' Defence League composed of Laborites and unionists only has been formed in every ward. The old pioneers of Labor are coming together, the old spirit of Labor is prevailing. 'David's' case will be brought before the workers, then goodbye to the spurious imitation of Labor, of whom one pioneer at our last meeting said: 'That we are entitled to deal with the crowd who vote against the branch who put them into office'.[71]

Ted Sullivan remembers the battle:

> They brought a by-law in here—rather stupidly—that any house that was less than 22 feet, if it was burnt down, couldn't be rebuilt. When the people of Richmond realized it, it led to a revolution. I was only a child at the time, but I went down with my father and I never seen a bigger pack of people outside the Town Hall. There were at least ten thousand people there.

> They were in the hall, they were up the stairs, they were in the Council Chamber. They were roaring, screaming and threatening. Anyway it was beaten.

In the 1924 Council elections Loughnan was elected unopposed for East Ward. Within a week he and O'Connell were a faction, the 'Young Turks', challenging the power of the old guard under the leadership of Councillor Bell and the pro-22 feet group led by Mary Rogers. The standard of Council debate plunged. At the meeting to elect the new Mayor, O'Connell first accused Bruce Longfield of joining the Labor Party to 'save his skin' against being conscripted and second, declared of Maurice Joyce: 'A few years ago Councillor Joyce was talking revolution on the Yarra Bank; now he was hobnobbing with the idle rich'. The ugly row permeated the Labor Party at all levels. The 1925 branch elections and Council pre-selection ballots abounded in smears, intimidation and accusations of branch stacking. The Loughnan/O'Connell Reform Party was using the Small Landholders' Defence League to build a machine and the factional fighting in the branches persisted years after the offending by-law was repealed. But Con Loughnan's erratic personality began to undermine his credibility as a champion of the people. For one thing he was known to carry a gun and obliged the police in May 1925 by firing four shots at a man suspected of breaking into a factory at 2 a.m.[72]

In March 1926 things suddenly went sour for him. First Councillor Dave Murphy publicly repudiated the Reform Party, 'because I refuse to be bluffed, bullied or bribed'. Within weeks Councillors Joyce, Rogers and Kennedy succeeded in having Loughnan 'severely censured' and suspended by the Victorian Central Executive of the A.L.P. for using defamatory leaflets in the 1925 pre-selection ballot in South Ward. The Richmond branch stood by him and Scullin delivered a eulogy at the next branch meeting. In March and April the *Richmond Guardian* published pages of prolix abusive letters from all sides of the internecine war. In August, after failing to obtain official permission from the Central Executive to hold a contested election for Mayor by all ratepayers, Geoff O'Connell was chosen by his colleagues as Mayor. By September 1926 the Labor Party in Richmond was in chaos: branch stacking was endemic and Con Loughnan was accused of working against the endorsed candidate for West Ward, H. M. Cremean. In October the Central Executive was forced to suspend all meetings of the Richmond branch until March 1927 so that new boundaries and rules of membership could be implemented. Even Geoff O'Connell, enjoying office with his sister Mrs Cremean as his Mayoress, turned on Loughnan and advised him to 'drop personalities': 'Cr Loughnan was a young man with a good future before him, but he was rowing a flat-bottomed boat without a rudder, and there was just a chance of him running ashore on no-man's land and becoming a Robinson

Crusoe'. After a furious battle, Con Loughnan lost the pre-selection for the East Ward in 1927 and Councillor Cremean had the satisfaction as returning officer of announcing the result.[73]

As Con Loughnan rose and fell, the family was quietly doing well. 1925 saw R. Loughnan appointed R.C.C. Inspector of Scaffolds and James Loughnan, 'one of the oldest and most respected inhabitants of Richmond', spending his declining years as Electoral Registrar for Richmond South and Richmond Central. On his death in 1928 Miss Gertrude Mary Loughnan succeeded him. In 1928 Con Loughnan himself reached the pinnacle of his trade union career when he was appointed General Secretary of the Hospital Employees' Association of Australia. (A month later he was convicted of illegally posting bills for an A.L.P. dance and fined £5 for perjury.) And in August his young brother Jimmy was welcomed as the Plasterers' Society delegate to the Trades Hall Council, where as the youngest delegate, he joined his father, one of the oldest.[74]

Meanwhile, back at the Town Hall, the Council applied some of its energies to local government. Many Richmond people were amused by the comic-opera of Labor politics; others became alarmed by the standard of financial management. In December 1927 an anonymous correspondent to the *Richmond Guardian* detailed the Council's steady decline into debt since 1924 and peculiar accounting procedures designed to disguise the mounting deficit. But the Council's gravest financial blunder was made in good faith. The Council, after inadequate research, decided to adopt an American system of concrete road-building. In the heat of all the grandstanding in 1926, the Council had not bothered to consult the City Engineer for technical advice and detailed estimates. In 1939 Jimmy Loughnan, by then himself a councillor announced that in the 1920s the concrete road system had cost the Richmond ratepayers £250 000, but it was also plain by then that the cost was only part of the disaster—the roads could not be repaired. Bitumen hot-mix temporarily plugged the widening cracks, ragged edges and ubiquitous pot-holes, but Richmond still is scarred by the incompetence of the Councils of the 1920s—it is renowned as having the worst roads in the whole metropolitan area. The City of Richmond was to enter the Great Depression with a disordered Labor Party tainted with petty corruption, and a monumental civic debt administered carelessly and impulsively.[75]

4

Youth

Work

> *We didn't have much chance when we were young because we were poor and as soon as you were fourteen you had to go to work. I used to wear stockings to go to work and then I'd go back to being a kid on Sunday and put socks on.*[1]

Adolescence represented something of a paradox for this Richmond generation. On the one hand, they were forced to accept adult responsibilities as workers very early; on the other, they were expected to remain at heart innocent children. *Bill O'Reilly* started work in the bottling department of the Shamrock Brewery at twelve years of age and brought home ten shillings for his first week's work:

> I remember my mother holding the half sovereign in her hand and she looked at me and said, 'My word, that's good money for you'. So you see I did do some good.

But he was only allowed to be half a man:

> I don't think we were allowed to grow up in those days—we were kept down, kept kids. A three-year-old would know as much as we would at fourteen. We didn't know anything about sex in those days—that was the last thing we thought of.

Yet once in the workforce these children had to negotiate a ruthless world that missed no opportunity to exploit their youth, timidity and inexperience. They were acutely vulnerable, above all because the working-class family needed income at almost any price, and for some the price paid compromised their safety, moral welfare and lifelong career prospects.

Not that the vast majority of working-class adolescents were unwilling to go to work. On the contrary, most were desperate to leave school as soon as possible. Some, however, were precipitated into the workforce by family tragedy. *Harold Stephenson* was granted an exemption certificate at the age of eleven so that he could help support his war-widowed mother and two younger brothers. But he was lucky. The Education Department required that he attend night school at a technical college where his flair for mathematics flourished with the more advanced teaching. He was to become a high-class boilermaker, concluding his career with casting sculpture. His other stroke of luck was more unusual. One day, he was cooeeing in the street with some mates when he was spotted by the choirmaster of St James' Old Cathedral. He was persuaded to audition and within a year was a soloist and receiving lessons in theory and practical music at the Conservatorium. Music became the abiding passion of his life until he became tragically afflicted by Boilermaker's ear—near-total industrial deafness. *Lilian Campbell*, predictably, had had enough of school:

> I left school at thirteen years eleven months. I said to Mum, 'I can't stick it out that extra month till I'm fourteen, can I leave?' She said 'of course', and I took myself up to Duncan's match factory in a lane just over Church Street. 8 a.m. to 6 p.m. with half an hour for lunch. Standing all day packing wax matches. I loved it. I was in the big time then, earning £1 a week.

Hamish Roberts was another who got a lucky break:

> I left school at fourteen—couldn't wait—I don't know why—to get to work. I remember seeing an ad in the paper, 'Wanted: an office boy in a solicitor's—ten shillings a week'. A lot applied—work wasn't very plentiful and they would gladly accept anything. I was luckily chosen—I think because the Scotch name appealed to the Scotch boss. He said it was because of my handwriting, but I can't believe that. My mother was looking forward to 7s 6d a week out of the ten shillings for board because it was needed at home. I remained there because I was lured on by the little rises each time—2s 6d here, 2s 6d there. Things were very cheap—you could get a three-course meal for 1s 6d, so your expenses weren't great and your railway fare was next to nothing.

So *Hamish* entered the white-collar class and manhood at one blow. He started in knickerbockers but soon graduated to long trousers: 'I thought everyone was looking at me—I had been so long in short trousers that I couldn't imagine myself as a grown man'. He was never to know unemployment and insecurity, but as a law clerk with a working-class education, he would eventually be grossly exploited as a solicitor on clerk's wages, performing all manner of work while the partners creamed off the professional fees.

The dilemma facing the working-class school-leavers and their families was whether to chase the quick money as unskilled labourers and factory juniors or whether to forgo a significant increase in the family income while they completed an apprenticeship. Most female apprentices in the clothing trades started on five shillings or 7s 6d a week—nothing like the pound *Lilian* got at the match factory. Boys started at about ten shillings a week as apprentices, but when *John Brown* started at Kennon's Tannery in 1906 his starting wage as a fifteen-year-old was five shillings. Families in dire need could hardly resist the lure of factory wages. *Muriel Thompson* left school at thirteen with an exemption certificate, 'to help my parents':

> I went to the match factory first. I was only a bit of a kid and he had me scrubbing floors and it nearly killed me. It was hard, all those wooden floors, but I had to get money somewhere—got about 12s 6d—and we had a navy blue uniform and a little cap.

The tragedy facing these juveniles 'in the big time' was that their value to the system lay only in their youth. *Muriel* found Bryant & May's clean and reasonably safe—'phossy jaw' had been eliminated but there were hazards if the phosphorus got on to the match boxes—however, 'I do know that when you turned twenty-one they'd hide you in the toilet or anywhere' when the factory inspectors and union organizers visited. *Mary Davis* is still bitter that she never learnt a trade; and when she entered the workforce in the early 1920s, the instability of the economy was forcing many factories to operate seasonally. The Cherub shoe factory operated only six months a year and 'then you'd have to fossick around for something else—the jobs didn't seem to last long in those days'. For the rest of her working life, even after marriage, 'you always had to put your age down'. One of the best jobs she ever had was in a knitting factory in seedy Moor Street, Fitzroy. There she earned £2 a week from which one shilling went in tax and £1 to her parents for board. Out of the remaining nineteen shillings she paid for her clothes, glory box and fares, so she would walk home to South Richmond each night to save the threepenny fare.

The large modern factories mollified their legions of semi-skilled and unskilled hands with good working conditions and plentiful organized recreation. They might hide their elderly juveniles in the lavatory, but they rarely stinted on fun; and the 1920s were great years for lavish work picnics and industrial competitive sport. The Bryant & May's Christmas party in 1918 was held in a vast marquee on the lawn and 'the tables looked very attractive with their decorations of yellow and black and vases of vari-coloured flowers'. In March 1923 the firm took 1100 match-workers and their friends on a boat excursion to Sorrento for the annual picnic; the Yarra Falls Spinning Mills a month before had hired an entire train to transport their workers to Frankston to run races and dance in the open air, and had scored a full page of photographs in the *Richmond Guardian* to record the event.[2] And on Richmond Hill the Pelaco shirt factory, that had prospered by diluting the shirt trade into mass-production piecework, even dared to bring fun right on to the factory floor when it permitted a thousand employees to have community singing in the lunch break to mark Music Week in 1922:

> Everything went with such a swing and everyone seemed to be enjoying themselves so much that the management hadn't the heart the ring the starting bell on time, and it was nearly half-an-hour before the manufacture of shirts and collars proceeded to the haunting lilt of 'Stumbling all around, stumbling all around'.

Pelaco happiness and prosperity came to a sudden end in 1928 when piecework was made illegal and the standing-down of workers because of slackness of trade was banned. The firm's industrial officer pleaded in vain that piecework meant higher wages (for the very fit few) and that in nineteen years not a minute had been lost in industrial disputes (not a minute had been lost for much else either, apart from Music Week). Now, faced with paying regular weekly wages, Pelaco retrenched nearly a quarter of its workforce in one blow.[3] Yet good public relations worked and *Muriel Thompson* was one of many young girls who saw advantages in factory life:

> They always had a union and they'd give you an overall and a hat and morning tea. And they did everything for you. I used to say about the factory: 'Well, we didn't know anything about office work and somebody's got to do the factory work'. [In the little sweat shops] they'd make them work all night, but we were right on the dot out there. If anyone did anything they'd go on strike there. Oh no—right on the dot and if you were a minute late they'd take off a quarter of an hour. In all I think they enjoyed themselves better than they do today.

The greatest danger to the unskilled was of being trapped in the seasonal economy. Unskilled men could only find security in a government or municipal job; those who failed were at the mercy of the building industry with its trade cycles, and of the waterfront. Female unskilled workers in Richmond had little option but the factory, and the food processors were almost entirely seasonal. The quick could earn high wages in the right season: *Jean Fowler* one year made £5 a week at piecework on the peaches: 'We thought we were made and my father used to be waiting for me to come home and give him some tobacco'. The food processors could always rely on the fear and desperation of their casual hands to maintain high production. *Isabel Williams* had stayed home to look after her ageing aunt and uncle; but once her uncle died and they lost his pension she had to find work at the Rosella factory. Her neighbour, Ollie, had experience on the fruit, and 'the Lord must have been looking after me' because she was taken on as Ollie's friend. The rate was 1s 6d per hundred tins of fruit filled:

> I got very adept at the work and we made more than anyone else and that was only a bit less than thirty shillings a week, but you thought that was marvellous. That was lovely because some of the others would make only five shillings a day. It was pathetic with some of them, poor things, and so they complained because we got too much and we had to go on the belt only half a day.

Before holidays, even Easter, everyone was given notice; but *Isabel* and Ollie were kept on for day work in the jam room: 'Oh, God must have been looking after us'. Their next promotion was on to the lemon butter: 'You had to be damned quick or you'd get your hands in the machine'. *Isabel* was kept on for four years: she was an exemplary worker—her health was precarious and each month she was afflicted with crippling menstrual cramps. But she never complained and never took time off; she even was too shy and afraid to ask the foreman for permission to go to the toilet. The foreman only knew of her afflictions when the combined smell of the cooked apricots and the solder for the tins caused her to faint.

They key to survival was self-confidence. *Isabel* knew that everyone's ambition at school was 'to get into the government', for even a labourer or a plate-layer on the railways was secure and was 'looked up to as being much above the ordinary person'. Yet even though she had been dux of the inner suburbs in the Merit examinations, *Isabel* and her young brothers, when they came down from the country, entertained no such aspirations: 'It was something that never entered our heads, *because our thinking as so basically working-class you never thought you had the ability to do those jobs*'. By contrast *Lilian Campbell*, who had seen so little of the schoolroom, found that her independence and sheer nerve equipped her magnificently to succeed in the factory system. After her flying start at the 'matchie', her mother decided that she needed a proper trade and sent her to the boot factory:

> I was quick to watch the others on the machines—I didn't want to sit trimming cottons all day—that was dull. So I watched a girl doing linings one day and I thought that's what I want to do—I want to get on a machine. So I watched her running the canvas round on to the fabric lining and I had a go at it and I thought, 'Oh, I can do this'. But the machine, being a power machine, was inclined to bolt and I had to learn to be very careful. And if it was a Singer I'd tell her I was used to a Jones and if it was a Jones I'd say I was used to a Singer because I didn't know how to thread up, but I soon learned. And then I learnt to do linings; then I watched them put on the toe caps and the back straps and I had eight jobs in twelve months and with every change of job I put my wages up 2s 6d. So my sisters, who'd served

> apprenticeships at the boot trade, were getting £2 6s 9d when they were in their twenties and here was I, sixteen and a half to seventeen, getting £2 17s 6d simply by promoting myself as a boot machinist. I wasn't very popular with my sisters but I was having a great time. Finally I was made a sample hand at Tascotts—Taylor and Scotts—in Collingwood so I must have been good at it.

Years later *Lilian*'s cheek was her undoing when she was sacked for cutting workmates' hair in factory time. Cheeky workers had to be careful. Apprentices were protected by their indentures, but once they were out of their time, the disrespectful and the lazy were the first to go. *Thelma Clark* was sacked for simply waving at some boys through the window.

Thelma may have been a little flirtatious; but, like most girls from respectable families, she entered factory life as a sexual innocent. Such innocents learnt the facts of life at work rather than at home and their ignorance and fear of dismissal made them vulnerable to sexual harassment. *Muriel Thompson* had to cope with the worldliness of the factory at only thirteen:

> Going right down I was really innocent because I'd never seen anything like that. But I must have had a lot of sense and I could follow it all and I used to say 'Grow up', whereas some people say, 'Oh yes', and you can grab them by the neck and drag them anywhere. That's the point. I'd never seen anything in my own home because my mum was innocent—she was blind. We had to learn in our own way.

The children of families just above desperate financial need had the best chance of being apprenticed to a trade or of entering a government office. Many Richmond boys entered local firms like Challingworth's iron works and remained there for the rest of their careers. Boys like *Thomas Beauchamp, Harold Stephenson* and *Doug Davis* who entered the metal trades were to be the most fortunate; for the metal-working industries were to expand enormously in their working lives. Even so, their early years were not easy. It was customary for apprentices to be sacked as soon as they completed their time, largely to avoid paying adult wages but also to force them to widen their knowledge. *Thomas Beauchamp* had the luck to be apprenticed to Anderson's, a firm with a large range of machinery, so that he came out of his time already widely experienced. None the less, he was determined to gain 'wider knowledge', and moved from firm to firm where other former Anderson's men were foremen and able to vouch for his training. He was to have a remarkable career in light engineering, early showing himself to be both an inventor and a natural foreman. For him, apprenticeship amounted to far more than learning a job: 'Our experience of learning trades taught us taking responsibility for our actions'. By the time he was thirty he had moved out of Richmond for ever and built a home in picturesque Balwyn. He remained in secure work throught the Depression and later rose into the ranks of management.

Harold Stephenson had a more typical experience, suffering periodic unemployment as he widened his knowledge, and did not really get on his feet until World War II. Ironically, apprentices to trades were more likely to suffer bad and dangerous working conditions than were the unskilled in the large modern factories. Small firms were notorious for having old and dangerous machinery, appalling toilet facilities and scant protection against the heat and the cold. *Doug Davis* remembers cooking soup in a kerosene tin over an open fire in the yard to give the workers some comfort in winter. Dirt floors were still common, even at the K.M. factory in *Harold Stephenson*'s time there. One day he had been using an electric drill all day when

> around twenty to five one of the chaps says, 'Can I have the electric drill?'—a younger chap from Footscray—and I handed it to him and he got electrocuted. They used to hose down the ground to keep the dust down for the next day. I had heavy working boots—no safety boots were supplied in those days—but this chap had light shoes on. Anyhow he died and I went to his funeral. He was only eighteen and a beautiful bike rider—used to race and everything. The foreman got very depressed about it. There was an investigation and the engineer, who was not an electrician but who used to fix up the electric drills, he was lucky to get out of manslaughter. The following week, *Jim Kennedy*, the foreman (there was a big family of them they used to live round here) committed suicide. He was found in the Yarra.

At Guest's biscuit factory *Harold* saw a man get his head smashed in a mixing machine when his hair caught in an unguarded belt and at Brockhoffs next door he saw a man fall into a tank of boiling syrup. It was rarely the employers who lost sleep over accidents. *Thelma Clark* also saw a boy killed when he was dragged through a machine: 'That was forty-three years ago. We were all told to go home; the man who had the job of cleaning up—he had a breakdown afterwards. They came and asked me to go and tell his mother but I couldn't have done it'.

Workers' compensation was exceptionally difficult to win but some injuries were straightforward. The girls who lost the tips of their fingers at Bryant & May's got £50 (the factory would close when the temperature rose above 100°F. because the phosphorus became too volatile). A friend of *Muriel Thompson* lost her thumb: 'She got £100—a lot for a thumb and she got a fur coat out of it—but she never used to miss it—she just used to imagine it was there'. Not until 1936 was the Workers' Compensation Act amended to cover workers affected by chemicals—*John Brown* remembers the tanners at Kennon's coming down with 'chrome poisoning' and receiving acid burns that went through to the bone. The 1936 amendments granted £750 compensation for the loss of sight, hands or feet or for 'the incurable loss of mental powers which led to an inability to work'.[4] *John Brown* was a leather-dresser at Kennon's for fifty-four years. The work was safe and creative but he often had to work into the night to fill orders. When he retired they gave him a 'decent cheque'; but 'they were in a bad way and it would have been larger—or so they tell me'. Over his long working life he witnessed a dramatic improvement in pay and conditions for which he thanks the trade unions. When he started it was tough:

> You earned your money in those days. They'd have a foreman—he didn't do any work—he used to sit behind you in the one department with all the machinery going. You were not allowed to talk and you'd look round and you'd see the boss falling asleep. Smoking wasn't allowed at work until they got a tea break—five minutes and they'd come and boil the billy.

During the forty-eight-hour week they started at 7.30 and worked till 5.15 with forty-five minutes for lunch. When the forty-hour week came in after World War II, 'if you worked Saturday morning it was extra pay—five days for forty hours—it was good'. Men's working conditions did not significantly improve until World War II when the safety regulations, first aid facilities and tea breaks won by the women in war industry flowed on to the male workers. *Doug Davis*: 'The war improved a lot of things in the factories; they got better conditions and you got a cup of tea in the afternoon; we got hot water to wash our hands instead of having to wash them in cold water in the old kerosene tin—some firms even got canteens'.

Some of the hardest conditions young workers encountered were in the retail trade. In 1919 employees of Swan Street barbers won the right to knock off at 8 o'clock on Saturdays.[5] *Friedrich Smith* worked 'blackfellow's hours' as a young butcher: 7.30 to 5.30 weekdays, 4 a.m. to 1.30 Saturdays, and frequent night work to prepare orders. *Friedrich* had worked part-time in a butcher's shop from the age of ten, so when he left school at fourteen he decided to forgo a formal apprenticeship because of the low wages and, through a family friend, found a job at fifteen shillings a week. He soon picked up the trade and moved from shop to shop to widen his skills. His second job was at Angliss's where his wage leapt from fifteen shillings to 26s 6d, even though he was still only fourteen:

> An old chap came through and was watching me roll corned beef and he picked up my knife and said: 'You've got a blunt knife there'. I said, 'Yes, if you'd teach me how to sharpen it I'm willing to learn'. He said, 'I've been watching you roll corned beef and if you have any trouble with this fellow Mc——here don't leave the firm, come and see my brother in Bourke Street'. I found out afterwards he was Sir William Angliss. Sir William took

> me outside with some sandsoap to the wheel, turned it for me and I turned it for him. That's how I learnt to sharpen a knife.

Such encounters could be the highlight of an entire working life.

Richmond girls had a narrower range of careers in trades or white-collar jobs. *Ruby Kane* was one of the few whose parents could afford to have her learn shorthand and typing and her first job was in the office of the timber merchant who had employed her father. Soon she was doing ledger work, dropped her shorthand and finally worked in a city motor firm as a book-keeper/typist until marriage. *Rose Saddler* was even more fortunate:

> I had to stay home until I was twenty-one—the 'good old days'—our grandparents came back from Warburton to live with us and it was a bit much for my mother. But when I was twenty-one I said, 'that's it—my brother Jim had just been married and I would have been the only one home so I went to the Children's and did nursing. I was a bit older than the others and I found it very hard because a lot of them had gone on at school and I hadn't had the opportunity. I found it hard to study but I scraped through.

Rose never married and served her community as a district nurse, then in her final years at the VD Clinic in Fitzroy.

Most girls were apprenticed to the clothing, millinery and footwear trades. The lucky were apprenticed to large shops and city firms; those without contacts and influence were trapped in the small businesses that proliferated in the inner suburbs. *Margaret Taylor* went into a white-work factory at fourteen and quickly learnt to stand up for herself:

> It was all calico nighties, women's pants, all turned camisoles and petticoats. I started at Barry's in Lincoln Street. You only got 7s 6d to start and after six months you were supposed to get a rise of 2s 6d. Of course, they never offered it to you—you had to ask: 'Oh, couldn't afford it and you're not worth it'. And you had your head down and never let up—you just went like mad. So I got my back up at this and I went home and said to Mum, 'I'm not going back there'. I tried another white-work factory in Lennox Street. They didn't want anyone but they told me to try across the lane. I went up the stairs and they said, 'We only give 7s 6d to start', and I thought—heavens above, how long have I got to stay on 7s 6d? However, there weren't many other white-work factories nearby and I thought that if I had to go to town I'd have to pay fares; so I decided I'd better give it a try. At the end of the first week she said, 'We'll give you ten shillings', and at the end of the six weeks I got 12s 6d, so that was the difference with the bosses. You had to work just the same—they're so grinding some of them—it's dreadful.

She stayed there four years and at seventeen and a half was on adult rates as a sample hand, but the work was exhausting, sitting only on a stool and in agony from crouching over a machine all day. In all her working life before marriage. *Margaret* never belonged to a union, not because of objections to them, but simply because the unions were too often unable to penetrate the sweat shops. One of the special hardships was the denial of holiday pay. In many factories workers were automatically stood down before Christmas and Easter. *Margaret* was paid only for the six designated public holidays of the year, which included Christmas Day, Boxing Day and New Year's Day; and if the factory closed down for a fortnight, the workers had to live off their savings. *John Brown* remembers well being stood down every Christmas and being told to 'come back when we send for you' so 'you were very poor over Christmas'. *Isabel Williams* would save all year just to have enough to get through the Christmas shut-down; a family struck with sudden medical bills could spend Christmas in destitution. *Margaret Taylor* is still bitter that 'my mother died on the Easter Monday and because I wasn't at work on the Tuesday I wasn't paid for Good Friday or Easter Monday—it was just terrible the things that happened, just mean and miserable'.

But those girls who got into the workrooms of the large shops were better protected and better trained. *Monica Rinoldi* was very happy at Myer's making baby dresses, then later at Head's in Richmond where she became a fully trained dressmaker: 'it was a very nice place'; and when she did overtime she was properly paid for it. And *Emma Murphy*, making up to £5 a week turning and pressing shirt collars at Henry Buck's, was one for whom the twenties were gay:

> I bought my first pair of silk stockings and I thought I was made. And I paid off—for £5—a bit of skunk fur. And when my daughter came back from America with a black and white treated skunk fur, I said, 'Oh darling, when I had a skunk no one would come near me—they STINK'.

Morals

Many elderly people see adolescence as the life-stage that has undergone the most profound change in the twentieth century. They recall their own adolescence as a time of greater respect for parental authority, of keener commitment to the responsibilities of life, of tighter control of sexuality. Adolescent culture was more integrated with adult culture and the gap between the dependence of childhood and the self-reliance of adulthood shorter. Contemplated from the vantage point of old age, they applaud their own adolescence as emotionally mature and sexually unsophisticated and deplore the present generation for being the reverse. Perhaps they forget the many who experienced an alienation quite as profound as that displayed today, for adolescence, then and now, confronted young people with critical choices about their relationship to the dominant values of their society, about whether they would rebel or conform. Adolescents faced decisions about respectability that could affect them for the rest of their lives.

The choice over respectability involved both family and society and the family came first in shaping an adolescent's probable moral future. But there were children of unrespectable families who fought their way out and there were children of respectable families who became delinquent. In 1911 the Richmond Court convicted Elsie Myrtle Slack, aged nineteen and 'of good physique and appearance', of being idle and disorderly after her father had complained to the police. Her crime was both moral and racial; for, when Constable Koetsveld made enquiries,

> he found the defendant in the company of four other females at the house of Mrs Wells at 35 Little Smith Street, Richmond. Two of the women were married to Chinese. He asked the defendant if it were true that she intended to be married to a Chinese named Ah Hing. The girl said she was thinking of doing so. She admitted that Ah Hing had given her money and that she had visited the house of Mrs Ah Lee. Her father was a respectable working man and was willing to take the defendant home again.[6]

She returned home with a three-month bond. The following year Frank ('Bull') McCarthy, also aged nineteen, was sentenced to twelve months gaol for being idle and disorderly. His parents had often complained to the police and on this occasion the police found him sleeping on some bags in a shed behind his parents' house. His mother said he had pawned everything he could, including blankets and quilts, and the court found that there was no doubt that he was a heartbreak to his parents who were respectable people. McCarthy was an inveterate two-up player. Witnesses had known him for nine years and during that time the boy had done very little work'. Mr Tatnall J.P. claimed that in all his experience he had never known such a bad reputation as in this young man, who admitted to five previous convictions. McCarthy, in his opinion, should be flogged.[7]

Moral life was worked out on a very public stage. The rich community life of Richmond inevitably limited privacy—just one slip from respectability and everyone knew about it. *Lilian Campbell* had a friend who received particularly unfortunate publicity:

> I had a friend *Gina* who was married as a bride and she had the biggest bouquet—the *biggest* bouquet—naturally it was to hide her condition. And her photo was still in the window of Mason's the photographer in Bridge Road when her baby was running around. Her Mother was the caretaker of — — State School and I went up to see *Gina* there one day and the toilet was outside and I went in and closed the door and there was the full photograph of *Gina* and the entire wedding group on the back door of the dunny. You could sit on the seat and look at the bride. That's what her mother thought of it.

Unmarried motherhood, as ever, was fraught with misery. Many married in haste only to repent; some rough families simply adopted an illegitimate grandchild as another 'one of the kids'; others saw no alternative but abortion.

Richmond harboured its share of abortionists. A few doctors performed terminations and in 1926 Richmond's Dr D. F. MacGillicuddy was arrested over the death of a woman. He was known to look after the prostitutes in Little Lonsdale Street and *Norman Stevens* remembers ferrying 'Corned Beef' Maude and Sailor May in his taxi to Richmond for their regular check-up. MacGillicuddy was caught, as was the saintly Dr Albert Bretherton of Prahran, while treating a victim of a back-yard operator.[8] Both escaped conviction; but the reputable doctors were few who would perform safe and cheap abortions for the poor. Bretherton practised in Prahran from the end of the war until 1937 and made his money from the rich so that he could abort the poor free. He never lost a patient through septicaemia and died from an internal haemorrhage when he refused to stop operating on a difficult case which lasted three hours. Over five thousand people thronged the streets of Prahran for his funeral in 1937.[9]

The working-class woman's usual recourse was the back-yard trade. In Richmond these were commonly midwives who found abortion more lucrative; and they ranged from the most primitive and unsanitary to the wealthy and stylish Nurse Hannah Mitchell of Burnley Street. Between 1928 and 1932 a police crackdown succeeded in sending before the courts a complement of Richmond abortionists from the lowliest through to a local chemist and Nurse Mitchell herself. In February 1928 she appeared before the Richmond Court over the disappearance of a married woman who had become pregnant to a naval officer with whom she was infatuated. Nurse Hannah Mitchell had class:

> Mrs Mitchell wore a frock of biscuit-coloured crepe de chine with a smart grey fur and a small hat trimmed in Oriental colours. Her daughter Queenie and another female relative were in cool white tussore with black hats.[10]

Lilian Campbell remembers Mrs Mitchell's court appearances well: 'When she appeared at the Richmond Court on Monday morning we'd all be standing outside Head's, looking across—we weren't game to walk across, of course'. Gossip and rumour about abortion were part of life and the breeding ground of myth and stigma. *Mary Davis*:

> There was always a lot of talk of abortions. The police could never prove anything but there was always babies' dead bodies around. They said all the bodies were thrown into Albert Park Lake and I remember when our eldest Julie was in the Girl Guides later on they had to row a boat on the lake and it tipped over. And later she said, 'I was too scared to put my feet on the bottom in case there were any dead babies there'. She'd heard all the talk even years later.

A more serious recipient of the stigma was the Royal Women's Hospital where the septic victims of the back-yard abortionists were sent to die. This stigma, reinforce by the care the hospital gave to unmarried mothers, deterred some respectable working-class women from having their babies there, even though it provided the best maternity care for the very poor in Melbourne.

Living under the constant scrutiny of a close-knit community could be stifling. Adolescents, caught between the high spirits of youth and the certainty of a life as poor and as tedious as that of their parents, did rebel and their resentment exploded into Richmond's famous larrikin pushes. Although some girls hung around the fringes of the gangs, group rebellion was essentially masculine. Much of push life was the harmless swagger of youth, an adolescent fraternity with titles and uniforms: in 1910 the Rowena Parade Rats sported slouch hats and 'loud neckerchiefs'.[11] The push was a working-class retaliation at a society that denied equality of opportunity and individual dignity; it was a group raspberry blown at dreary adult respectability. They broke dances and in 1920 police had to be engaged to protect the respectable patrons at vaudeville concerts in the Town Hall. They vandalized the parks the Council tried to 'make nice' for the nice people of Richmond; they jeered at churchgoers and leered at unobtainable girls; they harassed and threw stones at boating parties on the river; they commandeered the best swimming spots; they outraged the Wowsers by playing cards in public and two-up on Sundays.

They were also capable of viciousness. In 1924 larrikins attacked children in a new Council playground in North Richmond, leaving one girl with a broken leg and other children with head lacerations. In 1926 two members of the Hill Mob knocked a youth unconscious in Swan Street when he refused to give them a tomato from a bag he was carrying home.[12] And the great battles between rival pushes could be awesome with flaying bike chains, knives and pickets ripped off fences. (With the combined efforts of the pushes and the unemployed needing firewood, the fencing in Richmond was in a sorry state by the end of the 1930s.) Even respectable youths like *Friedrich Smith* knew the 'basic rule in Richmond'—that 'you daren't walk away from a fight':

> One night my brother and I came home from a game of cards—I was about seventeen, he'd be about nineteen—and this mob stopped us for cigarettes. There was about eight of them. I took one look at them and said, Look, Appy, you couldn't clean us up at school and we don't smoke, so you'd better just forget about it'. Phil said to me, 'Back up against the wall', and Appy made a swing at me and I shifted to one side and he hit the brick wall behind me. I kneed him and cut him down but fortunately for us the firemen came and most of them ran off. We picked them out, one at a time

> and we gave four of them a hiding and I got a black eye myself. Next time they passed us they left us alone and didn't ask for cigarettes.

The police answer to push violence was simply police violence. With full community support, the 'good' policemen bashed and bullied larrikins into fear and hatred of the law. *John Brown* remembers with admiration Constable Strahan, who 'lone-handed' with his baton 'cleaned up' the Crutchy Push of 'Irish Town' near the Church Street bridge: 'we never seen them anymore after that'. Such policing rarely concluded in Court appearances and when it did it was not uncommon for cases to reveal that innocent youths were being persecuted by a crude and demoralized police. In 1924 the Richmond Council was moved to condemn police for charging youths with obstruction when they were simply unemployed and passing time on the streets.[13] Some of these alienated youths became alienated adults, trapped for life in a vicious circle of unemployment, drink, violence, gambling and bravado. One famous Richmond family, the Eddys, saw one of the four sons, Dolph, escape into respectability and enter State parliament. Billy Eddy, however, spent a lifetime at war with the police. In May 1938 he was sentenced to eight months' gaol after a fight outside St James' Hall where Father Godwin had instructed the police to 'keep certain persons' out of a dance. Eddy was seen approaching the hall; the police told him to keep away. Eddy said he was only going to pick up his girl. Eddy was then joined by a group of twenty men that included his father. The police told them to move on, then, according to Senior Constable Feldtman,

> Eddy said, 'Into them chaps. By the time we've dealt with these chaps they won't be able to move anybody on'. To Constable Carter he said: 'I've been waiting for you for a long time and now you are getting what is coming to you'. He clenched his fist, moved towards the police and Constable Carter and witness arrested him. Some of the crowd followed and Eddy, who was struggling, called out to them, 'Kick them to death'.

Eddy's mates clustered round the police. Eddy punched and kicked the policeman and 'used bad language all the time'. The mob followed them to the police station, then in Gardner Street started pulling pickets off a fence and attacked the police. They got out of control, broke into a house, smashed windows and insulted the women inside. Beer bottles were brought out and smashed. Seven others were convicted with Billy that time. Two months later his father was again in Court and was convicted of assault with a beer bottle.[14] Billy Eddy came to maturity as a social enemy in the Depression, when, predictably, adolescent violence and vandalism increased. Dr Jim Cairns remembers him hanging on the fringe of the Labor Party in the 1950s and being used by corrupt elements in the party to beat up and intimidate Groupers. Cairns witnessed the pathetic end of such men and the ambivalence of Richmond people towards their social rebels:

> Dolph was a cut above the others. He was always better dressed. He always maintained a job and lived in Clifton Hill. Bill, on the other hand, was out of work as much as he was in it and didn't care. He always dressed untidily. Billy, I think, is dead now. He had the reputation of being the finest street fighter the eastern suburbs have produced—at about nine and a half stone—and it probably was true. They had a good reputation in Richmond—they were fair dinkum blokes.

Yet for all those who rebelled, many more endeavoured to conform to the disciplines of the family, the church and the community. Many respectable young people would be more involved in church life as adolescents than they would be for the rest of their lives. All of *Hamish Roberts*'s social life revolved around the youth activities at his church, St Bartholomew's Church of England in Burnley Street. There were dances, picnics, sporting competitions and gymnastics, social clubs and music and drama societies. Even the Methodists who deplored dancing ran tableaux vivants and fancy dress parties. *Will Parker* thrived on the library provided by his Methodist Sunday School and still recalls his excitement at some of the speakers who came to the church. He absorbed the inner history of the Methodist movement in England: 'the lay preachers of the Methodist Church were the first people to set up trade unions', even though his father, as an English Methodist translated to Australia, would not vote Labor because 'it was dominated by Catholics'. He experienced a call to the ministry but felt handicapped by his lack of education.

> The local minister, Taylor, tried his hardest to get me to become a student and join the ministry, but I'd only had an ordinary State School education. I got up to the Merit Certificate which was the highest standard in those times. I did have an inclination at one time—if it had been possible—to have become a medical missionary because 1 used to read a lot and David Livingstone was my hero—other people like big sportsmen and so on. I thought that would be a good life to be able to help people and put them on the right track, because it was useless to be a missionary without doing something to help them in their need. I would have if I could, but the war came along and things changed.

The war changed the Methodist Church too; for *Will* first noticed in the 1920s he decline in attendence that would turn into a stampede after World War II. The largest and most enduring youth organizations were in the Catholic church. At St Ignatius' the Catholic Young Men's Society ran debates and lectures as well as sporting and social activities; girls moved from their sodalities into the social clubs. Youth organizations provided a bridge from school to adult church life, keeping adolescents within the disciplines of the faith. A significant educational role of the churches was in music and theatre. St Ignatius' musical and theatrical societies have for nearly a century provided a marvellous opportunity for amateur musicians and actors in Richmond. The Protestant churches' societies began to fade in the 1920s but St Ignatius Loyola Operatic Society still performs Gilbert and Sullivan. In 1941, under the leadership of Leo Collins and supported by the Conservatorium orchestra, the Society performed Stanford's opera *Shamus O'Brien*. And the St Ignatius' choir similarly exposed working-class people to serious music, regularly performing sung masses from the classical repertoire. The Protestant churches' too, provided an opportunity to hear and perform serious music, although it usually meant that a congregation had chanced on an organist of distinction. In 1922 the Lennox Street Presbyterian Church had the services of Herbert Davis and found themselves treated to a performance of the Brahms *Requiem*, accompanied by organ and tympani.[15] All this social and cultural activity meant that working-class people were gaining experience in organization and administration, in financial management, in public speaking and lay preaching, and above all in plain self-confidence. Perhaps this has always been the most important role of the church in the emancipation of the common people, albeit a role that many churchmen might not have intended.

The churches had another not very spiritual value to the poor—they provided free entertainment. It started in childhood as children did the rounds of the Sunday Schools, attending just long enough to qualify for the Sunday School picnic. *Mary Davis* went to all the Protestant churches in South Richmond just for the socials. *Muriel Thompson*, as a young woman, was secure enough in her Presbyterian faith to attend Vespers with her Catholic girlfriend just for the outing: 'There wasn't much else to do—you had to do something'. *Friedrich* and *Florence Smith* occasionally filled a Sunday evening contemplating the bizarre at the Pentecostal, the Tabernacle and Spiritualist churches:

> We went to the Spiritualist Church up in Rotherwood Street. This night they were dealing in flowers and I knew the medium too—she worked in Craven' s Cake Shop in Bridge Road, much to my surprise. There was a pot of geraniums growing in the front so I picked one and went into the church. The first thing she picked on was my geranium: 'Oh, I get a strong signal from this—this flower was grown very close to here'; and of course we got the giggles and had to go out. And we didn't hear the end of it.

This generation remains the most active churchgoers in Australia outside the new ethnic communities, even though many felt their faith diminish over time. These respectable working-class people, however, have lost none of the moral discipline inculcated by church and family: 'It's still in us', says *Lilian Campbell.* And nowhere is this moral discipline more obvious than in their attitudes to extra-marital sex and to drink. It is almost impossible to measure the sexual experience of this generation without causing offence and intruding on privacy. Paul Thompson's massive oral history of Edwardian England, however, made comparable findings which suggest that the late-Victorian and Edwardian generation of respectable working-class people were the most sexually deprived in their youth of any generation before and since.[16] In Australia in the 1920s premarital chastity was regarded as normal, despite the knowledge of contraception gained by working-class men during war service. Contraceptives were on sale in pharmacies and by mail order as never before, but they were expensive; many men were too shy to purchase them in a shop (*Friedrich Smith* used to be asked in later years by married friends to buy contraceptives for them), and the unmarried encountered moral recrimination if they sought the advice of doctors. Moreover, young lovers had nowhere to go. Poverty and convention forced most young people to live with their parents until marriage and hardly anyone had access to a motor car. Enough couples, however, were sufficiently successful for the 1920s to record a proportion of first births conceived outside marriage comparable to those of later more liberated decades. (The rate has hovered around 40 per cent throughout the twentieth century despite the apparent changes in sexual mores and contraceptive practice.) [17] Such pregnancies were more likely, before World War II, to have resulted from impulsive moral 'accidents' and snatched opportunities after factory and office parties than from extended love affairs. In fact, most respectable young engaged couples endured years of frustration as they saved towards marriage, an emotional sacrifice that makes them intolerant of the sexual behaviour of the young today. Similarly with alcohol, many young people, both male and female, were remarkably abstemious. Drink was rarely an integral part of picnics and sporting activities. For one thing, few adolescents earned enough to buy alcohol regularly and alcohol abuse was seen as 'an older man's problem'. The management of alcohol was one of the great dividers between the respectable and the rough and many young people were deeply frightened by the ravages of alcohol only too visible all around them. There were, of course, always unexpected tragedies. *Hamish Roberts* knew a youth who swore one day as they were walking past a local pub that he would never touch a drop but who later became an alcoholic. And not a few respectable people were driven to drink by the Depression only to be saved by the harsh fact that once their savings ran out, the sustenance was barely enough for food, let alone drink.[18] Most respectables, however, partook of the general rise in alcohol consumption after World War II and remain only light social drinkers.[19]

However, as religion inspired, soothed and guided, it also had the power to divide and hurt, for adolescence brought the first painful encounters with sectarianism. Family, church and neighbourhood now became vigilant lest a mixed romance led to 'marrying out'. When *Bill O'Reilly*'s brother married a Protestant he left the family. 'It was a sin to marry out of the Church—the parents called it a sin and they didn't mix at all'. Many young people kept childhood friends who were of the wrong faith but a quiet sorting-out took place over potential spouses. Not that mixed marriages were inherently disastrous: many survived well if the couple were deeply attached and able to compromise. Above all it was the search for work that young people, especially Catholics, confronted the sectarian facts of life. Many Protestant employers refused outright to take on Catholics. Moran and Cato, the Methodist grocery chain, even stooped to warning that 'Catholics need not apply on their job advertisements in the window; the G. J. Coles chain were still discriminating against Catholics in the early 1960s.[20] *Ruby Kane* was given a job at a timber mill because of her outstanding clerical experience until, as an afterthought, the boss asked for his records where she went to school: 'St Ignatius'—and she was 'shown the door'. 'If you were a Catholic you were branded—we did have a battle to get on'. One of her friends blew up when he was asked his religion during a job interview: 'You don't want a clerk—you want a bloody lay preacher'. *Kevin Maloney* recalls the time when no Catholic could get a job in a bank: 'but the direction would come down from the top so you can't blame the rank and file'. When *Lilian Campbell*'s husband opened a barber's shop in Toorak village, the local Presbyterian minister, unaware of their Catholicism, was quick to visit and confide: Isn't it good to have a Protestant barber here at last'. And *Brendan Ryan* found as a medical student at the University of Melbourne that his religion made him a social isolate. Even sport was blighted. *Kevin Maloney* was refused membership of the St Stephen's Harriers, Richmond's only avenue to competitive athletics, and was forced to join the Glenhuntly Club where one of his father's customers enrolled him. And down in Burnley *Jim Saddler* played in the Methodist Church's football team: 'We had three Pages, three Delbridges, three Bentleys, three *Saddlers* and a Murphy and just about every time we won someone would file a protest at our having a Catholic playing—that was funny'. Some Catholics gave as good as they got; and *Isabel Williams*, who ended her working life in the post office, has a vast repertoire of injustices perpetrated against Protestants and instances of Catholic bigotry. But one memory stands out: that of her aunt being visited in old age by both the Reverend Wenzel of St Stephen's and the parish priest. Often the two men of the cloth met at her aunt's and chatted with obvious pleasure. One day the priest confided to *Isabel*: 'One thing I must say of Mr Wenzel—he's a Christian'.

Finally with youth and entry into the workforce came the first perceptions of class-consciousness. *Hamish Roberts* experienced his first face-to-face relationships with members of the privileged classes in the City solicitor's office:

> I think we have less class distinction now. It didn't worry me very much but sometimes I was a bit conscious that someone might appear to be a bit better than I was. I had an inferiority feeling sometimes and as I look upon it now it was really stupid. I felt it most in the Law Courts and in the barristers' chambers—I used to feel very very inferior because I was just an office boy. Later on, I learned that it wasn't like that at all because I was respected by them. But I used to think they were very important and much older than me, even though some were younger. I was still associating mostly with working-class people—all similar types. I never considered myself any better than the others. Practically all the crowd I knew worked in factories—very few were in offices. We have always been Labor people—my father was in the railways and always for the union and Labor. We seemed to be all one of a kind. Sometimes I would have thought that someone working in a bank was superior to me.

Many young working-class people commenced their working lives resigned to a future of poverty and insignificance: 'We were never meant to have money—that's what we used to say', *Jean Fowler* recalls; 'whatever we were in we could never win it'. And *Jean* has no illusions that Australia is a classless society: 'Oh, don't give me that'. Yet a handful did determine in adolescence to escape somehow from the working class. *Thomas Beauchamp* found inspiration at school from Aesop's fable of the Lion and the Mouse where 'the insignificant little beast' proves he can help the 'King of Beasts' who once sneered at him:

> And this comes back to most things in life. We and governments get too big for ourselves sometimes. When it all boils down we are all living on one another. The highest in the land is reliant on the man who clears the garbage away because if he doesn't we'll get a disease and an epidemic of something. So the highest in the land is still reliant on the smallest in the land and we all play our parts.

Thomas Beauchamp has a deep admiration for Margaret Thatcher and corresponds with her. *Will Parker*, blessed with innate self-confidence and the nerve to take risks—they used to say I was the biggest gambler in the family'—also early formed ambition and ultimately realized it:

> I saw so many people when I was young—old people in hovels who hadn't a bean and nothing nice at all—that I thought if I possibly can I'll make sure we have comfort and everything we want when we're old and that the family would be well looked after. That was my main object in life.

Others saw no chance of escape from the working class but refused to regard themselves as inferior human beings. *Margaret Taylor* and her family were not uncommon in that they ignored the social gulf between the bosses and the workers: 'We didn't take much notice—we always considered ourselves as good as the next fellow'. Some like *Monica Rinoldi* actually denied that they belonged to the working class at all. Taunted at school because her mother dressed her well, she later ascribed it to envy: 'I suppose we were really middle class'. Her father was a tradesman in the Gas Company and a keen Laborite but *Monica*'s mother had 'married down' and *Monica* formed a class identity at variance with her family's actual financial and social status. Yet, as these young people formed their values on the threshold of adulthood, they were not to know that history had a cruel blow awaiting them.

Fun

Whatever the difficulties of starting work and growing up, life in the 1920s was to be the most carefree for this generation for decades to come. As they ventured into adult pleasures and relationships, they partook of the host of new urban entertainments and activities that now characterizes modern life. With the exception of electronics, all the major technological inventions had entered everyday life—radio, the cinema, recorded music and motorized transport. And with World War I marking the real end of the nineteenth century, this generation saw themselves as truly modern, emancipated from the social constraints that had afflicted their parents' youth. Women could reveal their legs, use make-up and play on the beach in costumes that clung alarmingly when wet. Some dared to smoke in public, although they were still suspected of being 'fast' or worse. The working girl with her time-payment sewing machine could quickly emulate the fashions of the rich and the film stars. And the young men and women went out as never before—to the pictures, dances, picnics, ice-skating, parties and spectator sport.

It was a time of great crowds at public events. Fifty thousand people turned out on a Tuesday in freezing July in 1924 to watch the Governor, Lord Stradbroke, open the new Church Street bridge and the tramway to St Kilda that brought the beach to the doorstep of the Richmond poor. Empire Night that year drew one hundred thousand to the St Kilda Esplanade to watch the fireworks; and in 1925 sixty thousand thronged the Esplanade to watch the judging of the Sea Nymph Contest. Above all, the extension and electrification of the tramways as well as the economical motorized vans and charabancs that took picknickers to the Dandenongs and the beach increased ordinary people's geographical mobility.[21] Even the very poor partook of the gaiety of the 1920s. The cinema led the evolution of mass entertainment as an industry. Popular entertainment began to appeal to audiences of all social classes and the working class was drawn into modes of leisure and cultural experience patronized by the more affluent. Cultural hegemony was being created by Hollywood and the poor were offered a cheap version of the popular culture that pervaded all Australian cities and towns. The working class was leaving the world where people had to create their own entertainment in the home, in the street and open spaces and where the common people patronized theatres and dancing places disdained by their social betters. Hollywood and jazz integrated the fantasies of the social classes so that a young woman like *Jean Fowler*, brought up in near destitution, dreamed of looking like Clara Bow for her wedding.

The decade opened gloriously when, before the dashing Prince of Wales, the Richmond football team defeated the detested Collingwood to win its first League premiership. It was especially memorable for *John Brown*:

> The Prince of Wales came from the city to Punt Road in the morning that Richmond played Collingwood in the premiership game. It was a frosty morning and the crowd was packed up to the roof, up on the trees and everywhere. I used to get up on the steps of the old pavilion to see the game so that if it rained I was sheltered. There were a lot of people on the roof and there were ten minutes to go. Richmond were a point in front and one of our players, Hughie James, took a sky-scraping mark in the goal square. I didn't see any more—all the people on the roof jumped up in the air and down they came on top of me—the iron and the people came down. I was lucky, though, because the beams that were holding the roof were out in front of me. But I didn't see the finish. They were one point in front and Hughie James kicked a goal from the goal square. And he was the worst kick in the team—he used to kick like a girl. But they won by seven points.

Women and girls wept for joy. 'Premiers at Last', roared the *Guardian* in headlines bolder than those used to announce the Armistice, and at night thousands 'heard the "Eat 'em Alive" call, and poured from the by-ways and highways of Richmond' to process deliriously down Bridge Road.[22] Thus began Tiger greatness and Richmond's most enduring social cement. And when the final siren blew for Richmond's record-making defeat of Collingwood in the 1980 Grand Final, the bells of St Ignatius' tolled out Richmond's joy, cancelling for a brief moment the damage done to community life by the electronic media and the cynical exploitation of the people's game by big business.

Although football had had a big following since the 1880s, it did not develop into the extraordinary spectator sport we know today until the 1920s. Sixty thousand attended the 1919 Grand Final and in 1920 a record was set for a home-and-away match when thirty-one thousand saw Richmond beat Melbourne in June.[23] Tiger fever became a tribal loyalty; a victory brought a moment of triumph over feelings of social inferiority; selection for the team opened the chance of heroism and success. In schools, both State and Church, there emerged a new breed of schoolmaster with a football for a head and impatient of the classroom duties that interrupted training sessions. The Christian Brothers in particular supplied the working-class clubs with tough, skilled and fearless recruits and the Church subsidized the talents of schoolboy stars like Jack Dyer. *Brendan Ryan* played football every day of his life until he went to university. And the players became more than paid professional agents of communal pride—they were 'our boys', family. But the unique social fact about Australian Rules, especially in Melbourne, was that it quickly became respectable for women to be as fanatical followers as the men. Thus it embraced the entire community and was not relegated to being a disapproved masculine weakness like the pub. Pubescent girls displayed sexual hysteria over their idols that matured into maternal pride in later life. *Ruby Kane* passed her Sundays as a teenager sitting in Barkly Gardens with a girlfriend 'making up parodies' about the match the day before. At the age of eighty and on the pension, she would still travel to Sydney to watch her beloved Tigers and on her lounge-room wall hangs a rich tapestry of a Tiger that her grandson in the Navy brought home from Singapore: 'He said he'd brought me a mat, but I couldn't in my heart, loving the Tigers as I do, put it on the floor and walk on it, so I made it a showpiece up there—it's a beautiful thing'. Of course, some girls, like *Phyllis Smith*, went to the football just to meet boys, but most young people went as serious spectators in large groups of the same sex. *Jean Fowler* and her girlfriends took a cut lunch and went straight from work on Saturday afternoons. Still you will see groups of elderly women with their knitting and their thermos out at the 'footy' with their girlfriends as they did fifty years ago. Drink was one reason for the segregation of the sexes: respectable women did not drink in public and football grounds were served by male-only bars. But also, everybody was there for the football—social distractions were for later in the weekend. According to *John Brown*, protective races were installed to save the detested umpires from being speared by the hatpins of outraged female fans. One woman Tiger fan could not bear to be separated from her boys even by the grave:

> A unique ceremony was performed by Canon L. L. Wenzel when he scattered the ashes of the late Mrs E. Schofield over the Richmond Football Ground on Monday. The deceased was an enthusiast supporter of the Tigers, and arriving at the ground with her lunch and knitting, always occupied the same seat in front of the entrance to the footballers' training rooms.[24]

Above all, Australian football is colossal fun to watch. Played on a large ground, the action is open, rough and astonishingly fast. Unlike soccer or rugby, one never needs to have played the game to understand the finer points and appreciate the spectacular skills of big kicking and high marking, dodging and baulking, hand passing and contesting, tackling and playing dirty. Scoring is rapid and in a tight game the lead may change literally dozens of times. The multitude of rules are applied at the umpire's discretion in the heat of the moment, giving spectators the added pleasure of hating the umpires and suspecting darkly that the game is rigged. For many people, especially during the Depression, football was simply the best thing happening in their lives. In terms of the ground facilities, the greatest attendances in the history of the League were in the worst years of the Depression. One hundred and twenty thousand attended the opening round in 1930, thirty thousand alone at the Richmond-Collingwood game. Admission was cheaper than the theatre and boxing: from the mid-1920s to 1933 the hard-up could get into the Outer for ninepence, and children were secreted in by sympathetic adults, free.[25] And the club itself became a focus of community involvement. In the late 1920s a season ticket cost eight shillings and each Saturday members could leave behind them their mean dwellings and enjoy the camaraderie and prestige of the members' stand. Politicians could ill afford to ignore the club, and club balls and annual meetings provided the major community social events of the Richmond year. Becoming a club member was a way a nobody could rightfully feel a somebody. And in watching over 'our boys', anxiously scanning their training sessions, patting their backs as they ran up the race, comforting them in pain, drinking in the perfume of male sweat, eucalyptus and oranges, one could be bathed, for just a moment, in sympathetic magic.

Boxing, horse-racing, cycling, speedway and cricket all flourished as spectator sports in the 1920s, and by 1925, aided by the falling cost of photography, the *Richmond Guardian* had quite transformed its sporting coverage. People were playing more sport, too. All the churches and large businesses fielded cricket and football teams.

George Little worked for an estate agent and was a keen social cricketer:

> I played a lot of cricket in the 1920s and I played with the Swan Street Traders' Club. Bryant & May's and Ruwolt's and the tanneries—they all had their own cricket teams and their own competition and it was more of a social event. You'd go to the Melbourne Sports Depot and there'd be notices like 'Fern Tree Gully would like a cricket match on Sunday the umpteenth of the umpteenth', and you'd write to them. Maples were pretty decent and they lent us one of their furniture vans free of charge, and your wife or girlfriend would come and we'd all go up there and play the locals and have dinner and have a jolly good time. They were more social in those days—we're living in a different time now. People think differently.

The Richmond Industrial Cricket Association was formed in 1922 and in eleven years thirty clubs were to pass through it. At the top of the cricket competitions was the Richmond Cricket Club, one of the oldest district clubs in Melbourne and owner of the Tigers' ground. For older sportsmen, the Richmond Union Bowling Club also had a long history and in

1923 installed electric light on its greens to enable members to play as well as drink after work.[26]

Youth was also the time for romance and the intentions of the sexes, as ever, were somewhat different. Girls wanted husbands boys wanted something a little less binding. This was not altogether a cynical double standard. Marriage offered girls the status of being a married woman, children and release from the tedium and restrictions of the factory. But working-class lads saw marriage as fraught with dangers, heavy responsibilities and traps. Divorce was a disgrace at all levels of society but it was also very expensive and a working-class man paying maintenance could scarcely afford to remarry and start another family. None the less, the Richmond Court's major business before the growth of traffic offences was in maintenance cases. A young working-class husband was expected to support his wife fully from the moment of marriage; and, whatever emotional pleasures it might bring, he did lose control of his earnings and his independence. He was caught between sexual frustration and a substantial decline in his standard of living and freedom. Most young men in time, however, accepted the inevitable with good grace and hoped for the best.

Not that all young men frittered their money away at the pub or the race track. Many had hobbies or perhaps a motor bike that a married man could no longer afford to keep. Many became addicts to the crystal set, persevering even when the shaky floorboards of Richmond homes perpetually threw the cat's whisker out as the family moved through the house. It might take half an hour to find the spot again and God knows what happened in the test match while you were off the air. The coming of motor cars and bikes sent thousands of youths into the delights of tinkering. *Arthur Coombes* and his cousin *Bertie Middleton* bought an old car for £25, stripped it down and rebuilt it:

> What we intended to do we didn't really know. There were a million bits and I said to *Bertie*, 'We'll never get it back'. And when we ran the motor and the engine started 1 nearly wet myself with excitement. I was about fifteen then.

Youths even built their own bicycles and, equipped with wheels, began to explore Melbourne as they never could before. But the ultimate was a motor bike. *Doug Davis* bought a massive AJS bike with side-car, 'like the police used to have then', for £45. According to *Mary*, that bike was the beginning of their relationship: 'He had the motor bike and he'd lost his girlfriend and I used to work with his girlfriend's mate—that's how it started—he wanted someone on the back of his bike'. But to get married *Doug* had to sell it; and the £80 he got for it was all the money they had to start married life.

If wheels were a boy's passport to adventure, the girl's passport to romance was the sewing machine. *Phyllis Smith* took her first pay packet straight to the Singer shop and made a down payment of ten shillings on her sewing machine. The revolution in women's fashions after the Edwardian era suddenly made all bought clothing cheaper and home dressmaking easier. The coming of paper patterns—actually produced in Richmond at Madame Weigall's paper pattern factory in Lennox Street—enabled even the working girl to become a fashion plate. In 1917 alone Madame Weigall sold over a million patterns in Australia.[27] Romance aside, it was deeply important for working-class people to have at least one set of good clothes. *John Brown* observes that in his youth people dressed better than they do today: 'Even if you were poor you had to have one suit—that was for Sunday and when you went out and you wasn't complete if you didn't have a hat—both men and women—I like the hats on the women, there used to be some nice hats'. *Lilian Campbell*'s husband would rather have been seen without his trousers than without his hat. In the 1920s *Will Parker* remembers buying a 'beautiful blue twill suit' for £3 17s 6d (less than a week's wage). (During the Depression suits went down to £2 and £3 and Morrison's offered that great bargain, 'extra trousers free'.) Almost as a gesture of insane defiance at their poverty, young people would allow themselves one absurd luxury. With *Nellie Roberts* it was a hat: 'I can remember my mother having kittens because I spent four guineas for a hat. I was eighteen and I wore that hat everywhere—even to our Sunday School picnic'. When *Thelma Clark* was a single working girl this was her wardrobe:

> For best clothes I had a skirt and a blouse but the coat was long and I eventually had it shortened and I made a costume out of it. I always had a suit—always—like herringbone tweed, beautiful wool. And I had a green beret. The suit had a green fleck in it and I had a green crepe de chine blouse with one of those frilly things down the front. I was very daring with the beret—'You're not going out in that!'

For work clothes, skirts were the most popular, with blouses, a twin set or cardigan and a coat. But like young girls everywhere, they were impractical slaves to fashion and with *Thelma* it was walking to work in high heels:

> You used to change at work into overalls and I would put on slippers because 1 had chilblains that bad that my shoes hurt. I used to crawl to work and then I'd have to put something big on. Then in the afternoon the sun would come through the window and they'd start to itch like mad and so I used to take my slippers off and stand on the concrete to cool them down. So it was a vicious circle from the cold to the heat to the cold.

The saving in costs of shorter skirts was eaten up by the cost of stockings, for they were expensive: 'I liked to get the old—time silk stockings; they used to run but I'd mend them—I'd have the hooks in the knitting machine which I used to get from work and I'd mend them at night—I'd pick up every thread of the ladders'. Poor girls had to be ingenious. *Emma Murphy* lived opposite a decaying terrace house where six daughters of an alcoholic couple were fostered by an elderly uncle and aunt:

> The place was really rough but they had beautiful wallpaper on the wall and it had red flowers. It fascinated me that they'd rub their fingers on the red then rub it on their lips (I can't remember seeing lipstick in the shops then) and of course all the red roses were smeared.

Girls in the clothing trades or with mothers who were skilled dressmakers could look splendid. *Ruby Kane*'s mother would make up a costume that appealed to her girls on their previous visit to the theatre and *Ruby*'s sister was 'recognized as the fashion plate of Richmond'. *Lilian Campbell*, a tomboy in childhood, became 'a dasher' in her teens:

> I was years before my time; there was Worrell's black velveteen and I can remember having a tight waist and a full skirt and tight sleeves; and I can remember big wide cuffs lined with satin tartan and split and when they fell back you could see this rich satin—OH OH OH.

She was a flapper from top to toe. She bleached her hair blonde with peroxide and ammonia and went to the Melbourne Cup as a blonde in black and white, 'with a black hat with a white roll edge and a long black feather going crossways. . . I thought I was fantastic—AWFUL'. *Lilian* and *Ruby* now shriek with laughter at the fashions of their youth:

> Do you remember the hair style, *Ruby*, where they used to put the soap on their hair and bring it down and curl it into a cow lick over the forehead and the side they'd tizzie up? It looked like two packets of Jex—and a black velvet band around. The black velvet band—we used to say—was to keep your brains together—we were jealous because we didn't have a black velvet band. I remember Maisie Burns—I worked with her—and one day I could see a great big grey flea and it wouldn't go over the black velvet band. I was fascinated. It didn't want to go back among the soap.

Now dressed in their best, Richmond girls were ready for romance. Couples met through work, mutual friends, dances, the church, family friends and neighbours. In the St Stephen's Church of England marriage register until World War II over 70 per cent of couples came from Richmond. Around 6 to 7 per cent each decade lived in the same street. The proportions at the other churches, especially St Ignatius', would be higher because St Stephen's active congregation was in decline and many transients chose the church because of its closeness to the city.[28] Young couples also met in the street, although respectable girls had to be careful. Friday night shopping saw a ritualized promenade of flirtation. *Friedrich Smith*:

> It was a common thing for a group of fellows to spread out their arms right around and rope two or three girls and give them a cuddle. There'd be a squeal and they'd buzz off. Sometimes they'd like it and you'd have a girlfriend for the night. But you're speaking to the wrong couple because we stuck together for donkey's years.

Florence's family were strict Methodists but she met *Friedrich* in a game of postman's knock at the Loyal Orange Lodge: 'you went outside and kissed the boy in the dark'. 'Whacko', *Friedrich* remembers. Henley night on the Yarra bank was another time for flirtation. *Friedrich*'s sister, *Phyllis*: '1929 we got engaged. *George* popped the question on Henley night and I remember that I had a blue voile dress with blue and white lace on the bottom and a handkerchief collar—we made it up when I was working with Miss Thompson'. Their romance had started fifteen years before with that fight in the gutter.

Some respectable families had such a dread of their daughters 'getting into trouble' that they placed severe restrictions on them. *Mary Davis*'s father forbade her to go dancing, and 'if you were out late with boys he'd come round the streets looking for you; it was his funny ideas, although they said he used to get out and about in his young days'. *Muriel Thompson* was even more hampered by her aged father and blind mother. Not only could she not go dancing, but she also had to take her little sister around with her everywhere: 'They used to say "Hello baby, how's nurse?"' She stayed home and sung round the piano or went window shopping or down to the beach, but she did find some fun:

> I was a bit of a doer. We used to go up to Bridge Road after the boys—see something. And up near Yarra Park School there's a little reserve we used to call 'Little St Kilda'. But we had clean fun and we used to sit and sing—boys and girls—that to me is clean fun.

Most Methodists and Baptists banned dancing, and *Will Parker* now feels that he missed something valuable. Music and dancing played an immensely important part in working-class life. This Richmond generation still belonged to the tradition of home entertainment and the gaining of accomplishments, and a pianist in the family was a priceless resource for singing round the piano. Many of these old people are still involved in community singing—*Muriel Thompson* and *Monica Rinoldi* both conduct the singing in their Elderly Citizen's clubs. Any family with the cash to pay for music lessons did so and Richmond before and after World War I proliferated in low-priced piano, violin and singing teachers. The more ambitious dreamt of escape from their drab obscurity into the glamour of the stage (as do the children of European migrants today at John Young's Talent School in Lennox Street). And some succeeded: Ivy Schilling, Ida Buller, Lizzie Newbold, Georgina O'Meara. Richmond's dancing schools offered both ballroom and theatrical dancing. Lucy Dolan, Lorna Vesper, Miss Ivy May, Miss Rose Allen and a host of others exhorted and bullied thousands of Richmond children and adolescents into a measure of rhythmic grace between 1900 and World War II. The climax of each year's work was a grand concert and Miss Ivy May, 'the well-known vaudeville actress', always drew a packed Town Hall and exhaustive if not exhausting press coverage of her pupil's individual displays.[29] Other teachers were more modest: 'Who's coming to Lucy Dolan's and bring your own chewy', is the call *May Little* remembers.

Most young people, however, wanted only to hold their own on the dance floor but some did take ballroom dancing very seriously; for, like sport, it was one of the few ways a working-class person could pursue and attain excellence. *Friedrich Smith* deliberately danced with older women at Masonic dances so that he would learn the old dances, and in later life he became a square dance caller. Most people learnt to dance very well indeed and young men were quite as enthusiastic as girls: 'We practically lived for dancing when we were young', recalls *Hamish Roberts*. The choice ranged from the cheap and rough that seemed invariably to end in a fight, to the more respectable Town Hall dances, to church dances, and finally to the great dance halls of the era. At the Palais in St Kilda, dancing pumps and white gloves or handkerchiefs to prevent nicotine and grease staining the girls' dresses were *de rigueur*. Leggett's in Prahran and on the Church Street tram, was more plebeian and valued for the dancing classes that preceded the main event. Richmond even had a handful of private assemblies which hired good orchestras and provided a season of dances for the best people of the suburb.[30]

However good the dancing, romance often faltered under a crippling shyness between the sexes. *Hamish Roberts*:

> When I went dancing, the men got up one end of the hall and the girls up the other and it was only when the music started playing that the men would all make a dash to get a girl who could dance well or who was good looking. It used to be just a rush like a team of draught horses. A lot of our church socials were like that. And when the dance was over you might be polite enough to lead the lady back to her seat, but you wouldn't sit with her, you'd walk back to the men again. It was 'sissy' to talk to women—the tendency was that men were men and the ladies talked about their own things. Of course, if there was a niner [a nine-gallon keg of beer] at a party or function then all the men would be around the niner.

Males and females inhabited separate social worlds and the only common ground was sex. Even with football, women were expected to discuss it in 'a woman's way'. Many respectable young men found girls mysterious beings to be revered rather than ravished. *Hamish* now confesses:

I used to think of some girls as being very tender and you had to be careful as to how you handled them. Of course a lot in those days were not very physically strong, very frail—perhaps it was malnutrition. I can remember some of the girls I took out—I had to handle them very tenderly and respectfully.

When the ice was finally broken the cinema became the scene for courtship. Of course, most had acquired the cinema habit long before. To *Hamish* and his friends, the Burnley Picture Theatre 'was the answer to all our prayers—we thought it was the most wonderful structure':

We used to sit up the front, but occasionally, if we had a girl, we'd go up into the Dress Circle and people would say, 'They must have plenty of money to be able to go upstairs'. Up to the Dress Circle with their box of Old Gold chocolates—half a crown they were then. That was what you did if you wan d to impress a girl.

A popular novel of the day is memorable for one line alone: '"How do you like the film?" "It's luvverly", she replied in a voice thick and clogged with chocolate'.[31] Once engaged, *Thelma Clark* and her fiancé went three time a week. The cinema offered a little warm darkened privacy, the chance for a harmless cuddle. Yet anxious parents like *Thelma*'s mother recruited their younger children as chaperones and spies to guard the virtue of their courting daughters:

That was Mum's safeguard that if my sister went out with a boy then I'd tell Mum—and I did. I can remember walking home and saying, 'If you don't come I'll tell Mum on you', and she finally gave me a big bag of honeycomb to keep me quiet. My sister's favourite in those days was Rudolph Valentino and she used to have a huge picture on the wall of him where she used to work. And every time her boyfriend used to go there he'd put a mo on it and she'd have to rub it off and of course it got real worn.

If romance blossomed into betrothal the life of the couple became strictly disciplined as they saved towards marriage. Every girl who hoped to marry had started early on her glory box, sewing and embroidering household linen, buying sheets and towels on cash order. When *Phyllis Smith* started courting, apart from her sewing machine repayments, 'all my money went into Love and Pollard's'. *Monica Rinoldi* took four years to prepare her glory box: 'You'd never see my sister or I without needlework and our pillowshams would all be starched and embroidered—oh hundreds of doilies, tablecloths—all that sort of thing'. Engagement for the respectable was a prolonged preparation for the financial responsibilities of married life. *Monica* recalls:

Engagements lasted four to five years and in that four to five years your mind was filled with nothing else but your glory box and saving and buying

> furniture and saving up a deposit for a house. It was the done thing—you were getting married and you should have enough money to get married on and you should have a house to go to. You couldn't camp in with Mum and Dad—they'd just throw up their hands in horror.

Not all survived such enforced celibacy and the unlucky and the impatient were precipitated into an earlier union. Not all, also, were on as good wages as was *Monica*'s ex-Light Horse man, doing well now as a foreman upholsterer on £6 18s a week. So *Monica* was especially fortunate to start her married life in a home of her own filled with new furniture. But within eighteen months they had lost their house and furniture and *Monica* withdrew the last of their savings to pay the Bethesda Hospital for the birth of their daughter. *Monica* and her baby and her glory box went back to camp in with her Mum and Dad while her Light Horse man joined the other unemployed 'on the track'.

1927–1939

5

Depression and Decay

Crisis: 1927–1930

As with a cancer, in hindsight the symptoms of the mounting Great Depression can be perceived years before the crisis officially broke. And like a cancer victim, people denied and belittled those symptoms until almost too late. The human toll of the Depression is almost impossible to quantify. First, the dating of the Depression by economists and politicians often differs from individuals' 'own' Depression: for *Margaret Taylor* and her husband their Depression began in 1926 and lasted until 1940; and for Richmond as a working-class community the Great Depression came early, finished late and damaged the physical and social fabric of the suburb for decades to come. Even the raw statistics of unemployment and sustenance relief understate the numbers of people afflicted at some stage during the crisis. In mid-July 1931, the worst weeks of that frightful winter, 2983 applications were made for sustenance in Richmond with 1969 families and 383 individuals meeting the requirements for relief. And on Census day 1933 Richmond was found to have 28.9 per cent of its male workforce and 13.5 per cent of its female workforce unemployed, exceeded in the Melbourne metropolitan area only by Melbourne, Collingwood and Fitzroy. But if we look at the collection of people interviewed for this book we have a glimpse of a very different human toll. This group is not entirely representative of the people of Richmond in the 1930s; their articulateness and interest in history set them apart and the majority achieved comfort and security in later life. Many are people of high intelligence and nearly all have seen their children move out of the working class. All but one—a spinster—have owned their home at some time since World War II and none has suffered irreparable emotional damage from the Depression. Yet, even of this exceptional group, 58.6 per cent were wage-earners who were significantly unemployed at some stage of the slump and 17.2 per cent were self-employed who suffered financial hardship. Less than a quarter of this unusual sample of Richmond people survived the Great Depression unscathed.[1]

The Depression was the overwhelming fact of working-class life between 1927 and 1939. Even the unscathed were affected by the plight of relatives and friends. It was both a private and a communal affliction and like a cancer it poisoned and debilitated the entire body corporate. And as with all crises it brought out the best and the worst in individuals and institutions. It was for many the gravest test of character and principle that they would face in their entire lives.

The early symptoms were there in the cyclical unemployment that pervaded the 1920s. By May 1927 ten thousand were known to be out of work in Victoria and the Hogan government was moved to offer the municipalities pound for pound up to three thousand to fund relief works. After a long debate the Richmond Council decided to create work for twenty-five men while there were over two hundred men registered at the Town Hall as unemployed, half of them being married with families to support. By the end of June the number had jumped to over two hundred and fifty. Soon accusations began circulating of unfair treatment in the allocation of work. Scullin, newly elected as deputy leader of the Federal A.L.P., addressed a meeting convened by the Mayor to raise funds for the unemployed. He blamed cheap imports and 'the insane policy of bringing shiploads of foreigners here when we had such an army of unemployed of our own'. But the meeting drew only fifty people. The slump came in with stealth, hitting first the little luxuries; and, as consumer spending contracted, great suburban shopping centres like Chapel Street, Prahran, were visibly in decline by the end of 1927.[2]

Through the summer of 1927–28 unemployment remained static, then in the autumn it began to surge again. By mid-May the Richmond Ladies' Benevolent Society was broke and closed its books. Little could be expected, either, from the A.L.P. Unemployment Committee founded in 1914 by George Vesper and now in chaos from the factional fighting within the Richmond party branches. With David Murphy as Mayor, the Council hit on the idea of reviving the mayoral ball; and the launching of sixteen Richmond debutantes raised £100 for the unemployed. Again the State government allocated funds for relief works and Richmond was awarded £500. The Council then turned to local businesses and 'interested citizens', and Mr J. H. Archer, president of the Richmond Football Club, was confident that £1000 could easily be raised, but within a fortnight only £300 came forward—cash was scarce. By July the Ladies' Benevolent Society announced that it had never seen such distress in twenty-eight years; by August the Salvation Army's relief kitchen at the Lennox Street Barracks was serving cocoa and bread and jam to two hundred young children every afternoon. Local bakers began donating bread to the Salvation Army and in six weeks the Lennox Street Barracks supplied 17 691 helpings of bread and soup to destitute families. In South Richmond Councillor Jack Goodwin and Mr T. Jackson formed the South Richmond Co-operators using Mr Jackson's large shop in Green Street on Saturday mornings to hand out donated flour and potatoes to the unemployed. Jack Goodwin and the officers of the Salvation Army were to be some of the quiet saints of Richmond in the Great Depression.[3]

As the crisis spread so also did bad debts. Some local identities had their embarrassments paraded through the courts; many more defaulted on their municipal rates. Already burdened with an overdraft of nearly £19 000 three months into the financial year 1928–29, the Council was forced to cut back sharply. In December it voted its allocations from the Mayor's Unemployment Relief Fund to see Richmond through 1929—the year that would be officially accredited as the beginning of the Great Depression-and distributed £2330 14s between the Ladies' Benevolent Society, the Unemployment Relief Committee, the Society of St Vincent de Paul and the Protestant relief organizations. The Salvation Army was given £130.[4] By March 1929 the Council had already exhausted its loan funds and was near the limit of its bank overdraft. There seemed no alternative but private charity. Under the Mayor's leadership a citizens' committee was formed and a fair, celebrating the American wild west with Indians on motor cycles all in 'correct American garb of separate tribes', was held at John Wren's pony racecourse. The wild Indians raised £1450 and Wren's Pony Race Club donated the net proceeds of a meeting—£450 7s 7d. In eight months the mayoral fund raised £3000.[5]

But if you didn't go looking for the unemployed you could pretend that life was going on as usual:

> To celebrate the coming of age of their daughter Winnie, Mr and Mrs G. E. Hughes gave a most enjoyable evening to some forty guests at their residence 'Riverside', Durham Street, Richmond, on March 23. Dancing and games were indulged in until nearly midnight. The supper, which was catered for by Mrs A. Turner of Kew, was of a high order and during this important session fitting speeches were made in reference to the personality and popularity of Miss Hughes, the health of the parents being proposed by Mr W. Perrin. The presents were numerous and of a quality that show how highly her friendship is valued by her many friends.[6]

None the less, through the summer of 1928–29 convictions for vagrancy, normally a condition of winter, rose significantly in the Richmond Court. Soon buskers were to be a feature of city street life. Major Richmond factories and businesses were deeply worried; but most were careful not to publicize their problems and through 1929 there was almost a conspiracy of silence in the local press about the deepening crisis. Pelaco was one of the few large factories whose plight was made public; small businesses especially went down in silence. *Will Parker*'s family soft drink firm started its Depression in 1928—'it knocked our business terrible'—so the fleet of trucks was cut back from eighty to thirty and they kept all the men on by working them three days one week and two days the next—they'd get money which was better than the 7s 6d they'd get otherwise'. But the level of poverty of those on part-time work, let alone on relief, was illustrated by the Minority Report of the 1929 Royal Commission into Child Endowment which argued that the basic wage could barely support a man and wife and one child let alone the three children the Harvester Judgment had set as the minimum standard of living. In June 1929 two Burnley women, Mrs Cowland and Mrs Carter, started a soup kitchen for the poor children of Burnley; and at the end of the financial year the Ladies' Benevolent Society totted up its good works for the twelve months: 4266 people or 676 families relieved for a total outlay of £2423 0s 2d. But if there was no money for the poor there was plenty of gratuitous advice. Dr John Dale, the Melbourne City Health Officer, recommended that for sevenpence a day the unemployed could remain in good health if they ate a loaf of bread containing 1 lb of wheatmeal and 5½ oz of skim milk power, 1¾ oz of butter and one orange. 'The bread', claimed Dr Dale, 'in effect a slightly enriched wholemeal loaf, was palatable, and he would be perfectly willing to live on the diet prescribed for a week'.[7]

As the Depression deepened, symptoms of moral decay appeared. The City Reserve, a park and children's playground reclaimed from a rubbish dump in memory of G. H. Bennett, was now a magnet for listless bands of unemployed men and youths:

> The reserve has of late become a home for suburban tramps, fire fiends, card and two-up parties, spring-heeled jacks and undesirables of all classes. Trees have been destroyed, holes dug in the ground, grass torn up, pickets pulled down from the fences, electric lamps broken, while several attempts have been made to burn down portions of the Council's property. Cricket and football matches have been interrupted owing to unauthorised persons intruding on the arena during the progress of matches. At every football match played during the past season the umpire has been compelled to stop the game and clear the field. Many of the undesirables have also had access to the dressing rooms and have been allowed to mix with schoolboy players much to the disapproval of parents who have come to see them play.[8]

An army of outcasts had suddenly appeared, not carrying leprosy or syphilis but poverty. And if they didn't have the cash to play football they'd wreck the games of those, who had; and they'd smash the trees and lamps and buildings used by people with jobs. One of the most frightful social facts of the Great Depression was now manifest: the unemployed were, consigned to a caste—they were the untouchables. Their desperate want made them dangerous. If an ordinary person helped one there were hundreds of others who might impose their need on one's scarce resources: 'tramps have signals—the word gets round that you're a soft touch'. Relief must be distanced, impersonalized, organized by authorities. The burden of proving that they were deserving poor was thrown back on the unemployed themselves. If they kept the rules of respectability they were safe to help; they would use their sustenance properly and try to keep clean. Above all, their pride would deter them from making excessive demands. And if they stayed respectable they would be first to get jobs when things improved again. But if they were not respectable they deserved to starve. In the public debate leading up to the eight-yearly prohibition poll in March 1930 respectability raised an ugly head in the politics of the Depression. The anti-prohibitionists, led in Richmond by Con Loughnan, the organizer of the Richmond branch of J. J. Liston's campaign, argued that prohibition would throw thousands more into the army of the unemployed and would foster organized crime. The prohibitionists, however, blamed drink for unemployment. The Reverend Wilfrid L. Collins of the Lennox Street Presbyterian Church declared:

> . . . we have to recognize that a great number of men are already unemployable because of the destruction that drink has wrought in their lives and by voting out that which has been their undoing we are giving them a chance to recover their lost status in the community and to become once more decent and industrious citizens. We must remember too that drink interferes with the efficiency of the worker, and that No-Licence would make for more prosperous conditions and help solve several of their problems.

Drink was a class issue; for while 57 per cent of Victorians voted 'No' to prohibition, Richmond's vote against was 71 per cent.[9]

As the winter of 1930 approached, the true meaning of the symptoms could no longer be denied. Small and large business had exhausted their credit. The *Guardian*'s barber shop columnist, 'Figaro', who four months earlier had dismissed the slump as just 'bad talk', confessed at the end of June: 'The waves of depression came up so suddenly that one hardly realized that it would nip so many'. With over nine hundred unemployed registered at the Town Hall, the Mayor estimated that up to four thousand were now out of work in Richmond. Stories of near starvation and heartless evictions were reaching the Council; children were coming to school with only a cup of tea or a plate of soup to sustain them through the whole day. The headteachers' branch of the Victorian Teachers' Union classified all Melbourne State schools according to their need for relief and their capacity to help others. Deepdene State School adopted North Richmond and at Central the teachers themselves started buying the school breakfasts.[10] The pressure was on the politicians—Federal, State and municipal.

People were now looking for political solutions. New members flocked to join the Labor Party and by the end of October 1930 North Richmond had four hundred members and in 1931 was reputed to be the largest Party branch in the country.[11] Scullin was now prime minister and in April 1930 'Figaro' aptly expressed the community's pride and hope in the new administration:

> I knew him to be a clever man, but Scullin and Co. are handling big problems in a way that is rapidly evoking admiration. The prohibition of many imports for the time being is a drastic move, which is going to cause inconvenience and loss to many, but on the whole seems to be about the only practical method of dealing with the fact that we can't draw cheques on our European accounts because we've no funds there and they won't allow us an extension of our overdraft.[12]

But the immediate responsibility for the unemployed lay with the State government and the municipalities. And the State government's intervention in the community depended on the political skill and administrative competence of the Council. Local government was still seen as the primary authority in the administration of social welfare—a burden the Great Depression was quickly demonstrating to be unendurable.

In 1928 the Richmond Council had performed quite well, set an example of careful moderation by the 1928–29 Mayor, H. M. (Bert) Cremean, and Councillors Longfield, Mitchell and Kennedy who had impressed with well-prepared debates. But Con Loughnan had slipped back into Council in a by-election in South Ward in May 1928; and the rising unemployment was strengthening the hand of Geoff O'Connell as spokesman of the industry lobby seeking further encroachments on Richmond's residential areas. North Ward ratepayers were especially apprehensive and Longfield, for one, had no doubt that while industry brought new jobs, 'a certain type of selfish industrial capitalist, residing outside Richmond, was contemptible enough to take a mean advantage of the absence of a zoning by-law, and was commencing to destroy the remaining residential areas'. Twelve months later, in March 1930, Longfield lost the battle and Council voted eight to six to relax land zoning for industrial use, apparently unmoved by a near disaster in January when two massive explosions in a blacking factory in Church Street killed two workmen and threatened the wooden cottages that abutted it on three sides. Cremean's influence on Council had diminished since he had been elected M.L.A. for Dandenong in late 1929; and in October 1930 he was forced to resign from Council altogether, taking with him 'his habit of self-restraint' and leaving unchecked his impulsive brother-in-law, Geoff O'Connell, and his mortal enemy, Con Loughnan.[13]

Cremean was succeeded as Mayor by R. H. Lightfoot, leader of yet another dynastic faction in control of North Richmond, and it was

Lightfoot who—led the Richmond Council as the Depression hit Victoria with full force in the winter of 1930. By the beginning of June the Hogan government's administration of unemployment relief was in chaos. The Ladies' Benevolent Societies were charged with the main burden of assessing individual need and handing out sustenance, but the sheer numbers of unemployed overwhelmed them and the danger of fraudulent claims by people registering simultaneously in a number of suburbs alarmed both the societies and the Minister for Labor, Gordon Webber. The Trades Hall Council, however, wanted the distribution of sustenance transferred to the municipal councils; the government saw the municipalities as an equal partner with the State in the provision of relief jobs. Itself critically short of funds, the government placed a monthly quota on the Societies in each suburb for sustenance and offered the municipal councils funds on a pound-for-pound basis for relief works. The Ladies' Benevolent Societies were appalled at the meanness of their quotas and resolved to cease paying all sustenance as soon as their monthly quota was exhausted. Within twenty-four hours of the cessation of their sustenance payments, the government relented and increased their funds and on 24 June, after being closed for four days, the Societies re-opened their doors and were besieged by desperate applicants.[14]

In Richmond the situation was even worse. The Ladies' Benevolent Society and the Council had both exhausted their funds by early May and Mayor Lightfoot called on the unemployed to help themselves. But when the government offered relief works money on the pound-for-pound basis, Richmond distinguished itself as the only municipality too poor to be eligible. On 8 July Ted Cotter led a deputation to Premier Hogan pleading for special consideration for Richmond so that the sustenance grant could be continued. Hogan demanded that the Council declare its. preparedness to follow the Trades Hall Council's policy of providing work as well as sustenance. This time the Richmond Council changed its mind and agreed to spend £5000 to provide work for 120 men, but still wanted the government to waive the pound-for-pound basis for additional sustenance funds. Preston Council similarly protested that the government subsidy for relief jobs could do little to feed all the unemployed in its community. Hogan was implacable: the government and the councils were not to give employment and sustenance as well, 'although many were trying to get both'. As the political wrangling and confusion persisted, the un employed in Richmond took up Mayor Lightfoot's call and began to help themselves. At the end of June special committees for each ward were formed under the auspices of the combined churches and charity organizations of the suburb. Soup kitchens spread; even St Stephen's opened one in July. By the end of June the Town Clerk, Mr Blazey, was forced to write again to the government that the Mayor's relief fund would be exhausted in less than a week. But now the Council was under another threat—from the organized unemployed who had begun to help themselves.[15]

There had never been a shortage of self-help groups and committees among the unemployed: at one stage there were up to twelve in Richmond. But the demoralization of unemployment made effective organization difficult. Committee members seemed to change weekly; high hopes and firm resolve soon faltered under community indifference. Unemployed workers had no clout, unlike a trade union. The only power they could hope to command was moral power, and to do this they would have to force their plight in a dramatic and desperate way upon the public mind. The one organization that had the mental toughness and the political skill to make such an impact on the 'haves' was the Unemployed Workers' Movement. The U.W.M. was a front for the Communist Party of Australia, but it seems that a majority of its members were not in the Party. C.P.A. policy dictated that Party members conceal their affiliation and the leadership had the common sense to keep a low ideological profile amidst a working class that distrusted Marxism as too intellectual, somehow foreign and un-Australian. The U.W.M. was very good at mobilizing anger and raising morale. It provided a complete alternative life for the unemployed: there was comradeship, entertainment and, above all, action. The U.W.M. had the guts to do something for you. Many ordinary members who went to the dances and the boxing contests, and who joined the demonstrations and the eviction battles, got to the point where they did not care if 'the Commos' were behind it—they at least were behind you, the unemployed, in a time when precious few were truly behind you. The Great Depression changed community attitudes towards unemployment and poverty. Beneath the platitudes of middle-class philanthropy there persisted a moral disapproval of the poor: there was plenty of work for the willing, and they drank and gambled and allowed their children to play in the gutter. And they smelt; 'The poor will always be with us'. But the Great Depression afflicted many who believed themselves immune; there were doctors and lawyers and hard-working businessmen in trouble. It was really the novel plight of the respectable and middle-class unemployed that evoked communal sympathy, and during the worst years of the crisis the militant unemployed were able to exploit this smidgin of moral power to win a few basic concessions.[16]

After Steve Bagley, the experienced and skilful leader of the unemployed, had established himself in the Richmond Unemployed Workers' Movement, a new militancy emerged in the suburb which set the pace for all local organizations. In August 1930 a demonstration almost got out of control when the U.W.M. succeeded in preventing the execution of a distress warrant on the furniture of a house in Lyndhurst Street. And while twenty thousand people had been placed in jobs in Victoria under the government's work and sustenance scheme, the U.W.M. began its campaign for the payment of a money dole on British lines instead of sustenance work and free rations from the Town Hall. Bagley led a noisy demonstration to the Richmond Council with a petition of five hundred signatories calling for a fairer distribution of food according to family needs and for the allocation of work by roster rather than by ballot. Above all, the angry crowd demanded that all women be removed from the investigation committees. The committee ladies refused to deal with male heads of households; and to men robbed of dignity by unemployment it seemed that women were in control. But the problem was also over respectability and the notion of the deserving and undeserving poor. *Ruby Kane*, as a friend of the Mayoress of 1930–31, Mrs Mitchell, was one such committee woman:[17]

> We used to go round and investigate homes, and the people—honestly it'd break your heart. They'd sold their furniture, they'd sold 'everything. And we investigated one place and it was the saddest and most genuine I've ever seen. A chappie and his wife lived on top of a place up in Church Street and they had two little boys. There was nothing on the floor and you could have eaten off those boards—they were scrubbed. And the two little white blouses hanging in the corner with a sheet over them—spotless clean—everything was spotless. And I came back to the Town Clerk: 'It would make you cry Mr Blazey, they're so genuine'. And fortunately I met the man in the tram some time afterwards, and he'd got a job at the *Herald* office and I said, 'I'm thankful, for if anyone deserved to get on you deserved it'. But others lost heart and got so depressed. And we had the crooks too. There was a family at the back lane here—the boozers. She came up and filled the form to be put in and we had the parcel all ready for her and he came up, signed for it and collected it. She came up and the parcel was gone—he'd taken it to the second-hand shop and spent it on booze. These were the sad things you heard. It was a dreadful time. We were amazed at the people filling in the forms. We had a solicitor appealing for assistance—for those men, the money that must have been spent to study to get to that stage—it was pathetic.

Not that *Ruby* did not know what unemployment meant: her own husband had lost his job as a traveller and had become deeply depressed: 'we were practically in the same position—we had nothing but we were just doing the charity work—it kept you going it did'. But to deserve sustenance you had to be respectable. Many who were refused sustenance because they drank were sufficiently sober to write to the Council to 'protest. The control of relief by the community itself inevitably led to injustices and corruption. Neighbours sent anonymous letters to the Relief Committee denouncing recipients of sustenance for false claims to marital status and for immoral behaviour. Accusations of favouritism in the balloting of work for councillors' friends and relatives abounded: 'I know my people have been ratepayers all their lives in Richmond and I can't get a go. It seems funny and things look shifty. In my mind and everybody else's'. And 'A Mother of Four' wrote:

> Mr Blazey,
>
> Dear Sir,
>
> Seeing R. Church is again on the list for two days work (Thursday and Friday of this week). There are legally married men with wife and several young children depending on them it seems most unfair that a man with not even a wife should impose, only to leave little innocent children without nourishment they are entitled to. It is only on account of hard times that I complain.

Desperate need divided the unemployed as much as it united.[18]

Bagley's petition failed and a week later he found himself before the Richmond Court charged with vagrancy. His counsel, Mr Lazarus, accused the police of acting under special instructions to remove Bagley because of his leadership of the unemployed. Bagley had twice refused work in the country because his wife was in hospital and they had four children; also he was suspicious, because while others had been awaiting country work for nine months he had had two calls in three weeks. The police prosecutor seemed to comprehend the law of vagrancy as having something to do with being a Communist, for he asked Bagley if he had been 'giving out Communistic literature': 'I am not a Communist; I have distributed pamphlets'. The police case failed, but Bagley was issued with an order of ejectment from his Henty Street home for non-payment of rent after a stay of three weeks. A month later Bagley shared the platform with Mayor Mitchell and Councillor Con Loughnan at a meeting for the unemployed in the Town Hall. Now families were being evicted for only two weeks' arrears of rent and the militants were organizing to resist evictions and repossessions. Bagley then condemned the proposed changes to legislation regarding 'consorting with undesirables' for it would mean that 'half the unemployed men would find themselves in gaol'. To loud applause he maintained that 'the law prohibited begging but many men were forced to beg to prevent their children from starvation.[19] This united front with the Richmond Council was short-lived.

On Friday 7 November 1930 the 'militant unemployed' sent a new deputation to the Council calling for a reversion to the old system of issuing orders on grocers instead of supplying food direct from the Town Hall depot. Mayor Mitchell refused, arguing that the retail cost was greater than the cost of bulk food to the Council, and the militant unemployed declared the Town Hall 'black'. Pickets were placed on the room where sustenance was issued and all relief was stopped:

> Things came to a crisis on Thursday morning when a well-known resident who has recently been thrown out of work through the absorption of the

> undertaking in which he was engaged, and who is also an expert boxer, was refused admittance to the room by the pickets. The next few minutes were sensational. He had laid out three of his opponents and black eyes came into evidence. It was stated that in revenge a 'push' from Carlton had been ordered to invade Richmond the following day.[20]

The Assistant Chief Secretary, Mr Kiernan, after conferring with the Mayor and Town Clerk, arranged for sustenance to be delivered direct to the homes of applicants to circumvent the pickets at the Town Hall. Mayor Mitchell was shattered: 'I'm finished', he told his committee and wiped his hands of the distribution of government sustenance. The same day the unemployed held a mass meeting on the City Reserve and reaffirmed their ban. Everyone now looked to the government to resolve the deadlock. The next day rations were declared 'white' for the weekend. On the Saturday more than a thousand people queued for sustenance. After another week of the black ban the government capitulated to the unemployed's demands and orders were to be issued on local shopkeepers at prices previously agreed to. With this victory the leadership of the militant unemployed temporarily collapsed; Bagley resigned as organizer and committees were elected only to be summarily dissolved. All they resolved was to distribute Christmas presents to the children. In December 1930 Richmond was in receipt of £2000 a month for its sustenance scheme and the Council revealed its current debit to October 30: £9733 1s 11d after a total expenditure of £99 235 7s 5 d.[21]

Sepsis: 1931–1934

The Depression was taking a terrible toll of political life and morale. As the Scullin and Hogan governments faltered, local government in Richmond, sank to new depths. Fearful of the growing effectiveness of the militant unemployed as the U.W.M. renewed its campaign for a money dole in February 1931, many Richmond councillors became ever more obsessed with the Communist menace while their constituents remained afflicted by the capitalist menace. Council meetings were dominated by the problems of unemployment relief but discussions 'usually led' to 'personal recriminations and nothing in particular'. Some Richmond councillors were labouring under bad consciences and the U.W.M. was whispering in the community about the distribution of government handouts by the Mayoral Relief Committee. The Council counter-attacked in March by forming an anti-Communist organization for the unemployed, the Richmond Unemployed Association. It installed its puppet in a factory in Little Buckingham Street, provided stationery with a handsome letterhead and helped with socials and advertising to raise funds. The officials of the new association were anxious 'to make it clear to the business people of Richmond, that our movement has not at any time been connected with other movements of a similar nature in Richmond'. That same week police had been called to forcibly eject demonstrators against the Mayoral Relief Committee from the Town Hall.[22]

But the allegations would not go-away. In June the North Richmond branch of the A.L.P. called for the abolition of the Mayoral Committee on the grounds that since the Government's Central Relief Board had been established the Richmond committee was superfluous, wasteful and creating 'a lack of harmony.[23] Then on 9 June E. Barry of the U.W.M. wrote to the 'Mayor and Council':

> Dear Sirs,
>
> The recent decision of the Richmond council that all moneys raised for the local unemployed must be handed into the Mayor's fund. I guess that it would go the same as the Million Penny Fund to a few of the pets. Cr Lightfoot opposed it strongly I am not surprised at that because if he has to hand the money in from the Picture night then there would be mighty few boots for the women and children and none for his pets. Then again we see that Cr Lightfoot wants auditors to go into the Books. Did Cr Lightfoot have his books looked over by auditors and let the ratepayers see how he juggled his money. It would be a good thing for the unemployed if that was done. Now we get to another statement. Cr O'Connell talks about the communists. They must be his nightmare as he abuses them whenever he gets the chance. In the past when the U.W.M. asked the council for any concessions the first question Cr O'Connell slings out—are you a communist. I am no communist myself but I would rather be a communist than a twister. Cr O'Connell says that everything must be fair and above board in regards unemployment. I can bring proof regarding how fair and above board that the work is given out at the Reserve. 1 Man has had 6 days in 6 months 2 Men 6 days in 10 months and myself 2 days since August last. I will prove this statement if wanted to do so myself. I think it is run as crook as it can be, and as it has been run althrough the piece. As the Town Clerk stated that he did not care if a man was registered for 2 years it was all fair and above board. I think he is in the swim as well.
>
> I am yours etc,
>
> E. Barry.[24]

'Minds like toads in cesspools', opined Councillor Mitchell; Communist pique over the Richmond Unemployed Association. declared Councillors Lightfoot and O'Connell, and the Council banned the U.W.M. from any further deputations or demonstrations at the Town Hall. Mindful of Councillor O'Connell's advocacy of relaxed industrial zoning, the Council's critics spread other allegations abroad: 'It was said he was a kept man and drew his salary every Monday night. These were dastardly and lying statements as he was never in the payment of anyone as a representative of the Council'. A week later O'Connell as a I.P. presided over the Richmond Court when Patrick Griffen of the U.W.M. was charged with assaulting Vera Alice Nixon, a member of the Relief Committee when she was near the central distribution depot in Church Street. Counsel argued that Griffen had been framed and the incident was a manifestation of the faction fighting among the unemployed. O'Connell was unmoved and found Griffen guilty.[25]

Then perfidy arose in the official ranks of the Richmond Unemployed Association. On 28 June Mrs F. Tomkins asked the Council to receive a deputation from a minority of the committee to make public certain allegations about the distribution of clothing and food sent by the State Relief Committee. On 13 July four members of each of these two new factions met before the Public Works Committee and made charges and counter charges, implicating, among others, Councillor and Mrs Lightfoot in the theft of meat, vegetables and clothing destined for the unemployed. Councillors O'Connell and Lightfoot accused the U.W.M. of white-anting the R.U.A. Then a week later, on the handsome letterhead paper provided by the Council, Mr Keat as vice-president of the R.U.A. wrote to Council alleging that four days after the deputation Councillor Lightfoot and two other men had waylaid Mr Smith, secretary of the R.U.A., and assaulted him. The ex-Mayoress, Mrs Lightfoot, it was claimed, had assisted with 'abusive and offensive language'. Of the flood of allegations and innuendoes, nothing was ever proved and nothing was ever d0ne.[26] In retrospect, *Ted Sullivan* takes a tolerant view of the scandals of unemployment relief in Richmond that persisted throughout the Depression: 'It was rather comical because every week the committee used to change because they would get first selection of the goods that came in—they'd get in and grab for their family and they'd have at least one good feed for a week once a year and then they'd get kicked out and others would get elected'. It was during that same fractious week in mid-July 1931 that 2983 applications were made for, sustenance in Richmond.[27]

In the following month the U.W.M. reached a heroic peak in Richmond, as one activist remembers:

> We had a very good organization to fight evictions and one particular Wednesday there was an eviction in Burnley and we got an awful bashing from the police. People were batoned down. So we called a meeting and decided to do something about it. The evictions were instigated by the estate agents on behalf of the owner. They never let you know who owned the houses and we didn't know how to find out for ourselves, so we decided to take on the Richmond estate agents. On the Friday we met at a certain place and divided up into groups of two people to each estate agent. It was late shopping night and at a quarter to nine there were two of us outside each of nine estate agents

> in Richmond. One chap in each group had a watch and they were all synchronized. At a quarter to nine, "Bang!" We wrecked every estate agent's window in Richmond with lumps of bluemetal. There' was hell to pay the next day. The papers were full of it. Even Mr Sidney Myer came out with a statement that it wasn't right that people could be evicted because they were out of work, and the Government should do something. Well, the Government announced the rent subsidy of eight shillings a week. If you had an eviction order you could apply for this money. This took the sting out of the eviction fights.[28]

One of the U.W.M.'s most publicized eviction protests was on behalf of *Jean Fowler*'s family in Edinburgh Street. *Jean* liked the U.W.M.'s dances in Balmain Street and her future husband used to box in their competitions: 'If he'd win a fight he'd get a packet of tobacco and papers'. But her feelings were mixed about being a subject of the U.W.M.'s political campaign. She was 'still unmarried and the only member of her family in work, supporting nine people on her wages:

> I walked home from work—as usual and when I got home there was nobody in the house. I thought, 'Oh my God, where have they gone?' I didn't know they were going to be put out. My sister came running round from the next street and said: 'We're all around there—a lady's taken us in. But where are we going to go tonight?' Well, I had a friend in South Yarra and I thought I'd go and stay there because we always used to be together. The next thing all the unemployed had got the furniture and they'd taken it down on their shoulders to the Town Hall and stuck them there. And I thought, 'I'll never live it down to see all this furniture and the Holy picture stuck up on front of it'. I didn't know until later that the Unemployed were all Communists. So they put us in Somerset Street—they pushed in the window and we were squatters. We stayed there—evidently they got sick of pushing people out. I was there until I was just about married at twenty-one. There were seven of us there and our parents—I tell you, it was a squash up.

By the closing months of 1931 it was clear that the A.L.P. itself was becoming a victim of the Depression. Party members struggled to justify the cuts in Federal and State expenditure: the North Richmond branch resolved in November 1931 that they were 'dictated by actual necessity and not by choice'. With the defection of Joe Lyons the Scullin government fell and was forced to a general election. In Richmond street meetings sometimes erupted into violence: when Thomas Cress and his brother attempted to break up a 'semi-Communist' street meeting in Lyndhurst Street, an eyewitness reported that 'the whole of the Communists rushed in' and the brothers were so badly injured that an ambulance had to be summoned.[29] Scullin's U.A.P. opponent was John C. Davis of the Smith Street Traders' Association. The crowd in the Richmond Town Hall overflowed into Bridge Road to hear Davis portray the A.L.P. as the betrayer of the working class in its hour of gravest need:

> My reasons for contesting the electorate are simple. I was born and reared in Yarra and I have seen in the Yarra electorate the suffering, the destitution and poverty which has followed in the path of unemployment of thousands of our breadwinners.
>
> I have hitherto voted for the Labor Party and have been a strong advocate of its principles, and I am certain that my objects are still such as will benefit Labor. I have watched this Labor ministry fail on so many occasions to maintain the interests of working people . . . I consider the trust placed in the Labor Party has been sadly abused.[30]

Yet while the nation rejected his administration, Scullin was returned safely, 21 750 votes to Davis's 12 562. Ernie Thornton, the Communist, found only 1033 supporters.[31]

1932 opened with 2406 families and individuals receiving sustenance in Richmond. In May the Hogan government would also fall and in the Richmond A.L.P. branches some members flirted with Douglas Credit as an alternative solution to the economic chaos all around them. Allegations of corruption in the Council and the local A.L.P. persisted and the Labor Richmond Council, willingly supported the new U.A.P. government's use of the Crimes Act to suppress the Communist Party and the militant unemployed. The police banned Communist meetings in Bridge Road and Councillor Bell, the leader of the A.L.P. on Council, informed the Communists that they could only enjoy freedom of speech if they 'played the game' and refrained from attacking the Council.

In August a new scandal erupted when Dr David Rosenberg defeated Councillor H. Davine in the A.L.P. pre-selection ballot for the West Ward candidature. Davine complained of ballot rigging to the Central Executive of the A.L.P. who quashed the result and promptly endorsed Dr Rosenberg as the official candidate, forcing Davine to 'retire' from the Council. Thus did Dr Rosenberg commence his brief career on Richmond Council.[32] He was still idealistic and proud of his working-class roots and he loyally supported the election of Con Loughnan as the next Mayor of Richmond. Loughnan's first speech was a strange one for a Labor Mayor in the depths of the Great Depression:

> The Mayor . . . said he was deeply conscious of the honour accorded to him, and also conscious of the office he was holding. Referring to himself, he said his parents were still alive and his father was born in the same house in Richmond in which he (Councillor Loughnan) was born, while his mother came down as a young girl from the country to this district, so that both were fully acquainted with the growth of Richmond. The City of Richmond he said, was a city of tradition. It has been noted for its art and its industry. It had

> been the home of Melba, of George Coppin, the Hentys and the Millers, and of notable people in the commercial and the political world. People may laugh at Richmond, (he remarked), but we are a pedigreed stock.[33]

He spoke as a man, who in a strange feudal way, believed that his family owned Richmond; he spoke, too, as a man twisted by class stigma. Councillor Bell capped the evening when he expressed the hope that 'the depression would pass away' as though it were a bad smell that a wind change could remove.

One bad smell the Council was empowered to remove emanated from Cork Industries in South Richmond. One hundred and fifty-eight nearby residents petitioned the Council, complaining of carbon dioxide gas' which gave them 'choking sensations' and on still nights settled on their houses.[34] Councillor O'Connell, as the champion of industry, belittled their complaints and described 'the growth of tanning in River Street, and incidental complaints from persons against conditions in which he had lived all his life'. Mayor Loughnan claimed that he would like the Board of Works to take action against the company:

> He knew there was a smell, but the Council itself had abattoirs and other places of its own where there were smells. They had people in Richmond who were always ready to pinprick industry. Anyone would think they were in Toorak.[35]

Even though small decreases in the numbers on sustenance were being recorded towards the end of 1932, the Depression was still in full force in Richmond. The Town Hall set, however, did not let it dampen their fun. When Councillor David Murphy's daughter threw a pre-wedding party for one of her workmates, the Mayor and Mayoress presented the happy couple with a cheque. It was a splendid evening:

> The success of the party might well be credited to Mr Dave Langdon's orchestral, Miss Edna Gosch, Miss Gwen Hull, also the following artists who arrived from the Tivoli: Misses Angela Parselles, Molly Byron, Esme Jong, Peggy Byron, Elsie Geraldine and Bob Graham and Mr John Debbie, leading man in 'His Royal Highness' produced by Efftee films.

The more common private party in Richmond in 1932 was like the birthday party for a Mr Donnelly of Vere Street which had to be held in Mrs Mary Cawsey's home 'because she had the electric light and wireless laid on'. (A common but rarely detected Depression crime was the illegal connection of electricity, gas and plumbing by amateurs. Occasionally the law caught up with them, but much of their handiwork survives to the horror of modern tradesmen called to work in the inner suburbs.)[36]

Ex-Councillor Davine persevered in his allegations about the Town Hall set: industry was being allowed to interfere with the comfort of residents, councillors were squandering ratepayers' funds on hire cars. The car-hire scandal broke in June 1933 when the government auditor took exception to the Council's spending on taxis. Mayor Loughnan advised his colleagues not to panic over the auditor's enquiries: 'The Council had business to conduct in the city and the expenditure was not excessive'. Presumably neither were the tokens of Richmond's regard awarded the Mayor and Mayoress marking the completion of their term of office at the height of the Great Depression. Two hundred guests at a complimentary social at the Town Hall saw the Mayor presented with diamond studs and his good lady with a diamond cluster ring. The city's generosity, however, belied a growing fear of Con Loughnan. Loughnan was sure that he had the numbers for election for a second term, but at the last minute Councillor Paddy Donnelly 'twisted', and Loughnan lost to Chris Fitzgerald. He was enraged, Donnelly insisted that he had a right to make up his own mind and claimed that before the municipal elections, one councillor had told him that in no circumstances would they have Con Loughnan as Mayor again because 'Councillor Loughnan was termed "a problem" '. Amidst loud laughter Con Loughnan conceived a deadly hatred for 'the twister'. One day he would wreak a macabre revenge.[37]

The strange goings-on at the Town Hall were being more widely reported. The Richmond Ratepayers' Association endorsed candidates for the 1933 Council elections and spread rumours that Council employees were being levied for the A.L.P.'s Fighting Fund. With Chris Fitzgerald in the chair there was no improvement in the conduct of Council meetings. By October the 'storm of accusations, interjections and interruptions from spectators' required that the police attend every Council session. The immediate row, instigated by Con Loughnan, was over the supply of chaff to the Council stables by Chris Fitzgerald's family firm. Fitzgerald retaliated by supplying the Melbourne *Herald* with information about the drinking habits of some councillors, in particular of Loughnan.[38] The *Richmond Guardian*, ever anxious about Richmond's public image, rushed to keep the bad publicity under control:

> Richmond is unfortunately obtaining an unenviable and undeserved reputation through too much talk and exaggerated publicity. A speech of that sort which would be brushed off in other cities becomes a whirlwind of black rain when Richmond is mentioned. This week the sensation has been drinking in the town hall. The Council, has admittedly, been too free in granting the use of the town hall. It has practically been an open house for all who chose to come along and ask for its use—except on Sundays. In addition to the cost of the unneeded generosity to all and sundry, advantage has been taken by some to make it an unofficial clubhouse. The Mayor (Councillor Fitzgerald), however, recently took steps to curtail this liberty and ordered a certain room to be cleared, and this incident has been press 'megaphoned' throughout the State, together with a loud report of a meeting of the town hall committee at which

> it was decided to call upon the Mayor, the police and the hall keeper to explain their conduct in clearing the room.[39]

The Council's performance on behalf of the unemployed showed no improvement. The number of those on sustenance was slowly decreasing—by November 1933 it was down to 1152—but in April it had been made public that some people were receiving more than their share of foodstuffs, clothing and boot repairs. Con Loughnan blamed the 'really deserving cases' for not turning up on Saturdays for the distribution—it was 'a shame' that 'the parcels went to others'. None the less it was a mystery why the same fifty to sixty people attended each Saturday while more than a thousand were eligible for relief. Only after persistent campaigning from the unemployed and public criticism by the Minister, Mr Wilfrid Kent Hughes, did the Council begin in November to consider the possibilities of availing itself of State government funds for public works. The destitute fared little better with the Ladies' Benevolent Society, who in assisting 370 families, 11 widows, 22 deserted wives, 14 single women and four single men in 1923–33, remained watchful for the undeserving poor. The secretary, Mrs C. W. Davis, displayed a nice turn of phrase when she warned: 'the poor must be wisely visited, . . . and liberally cared for, so that mendicity shall not be tempted into mendacity, nor want exasperated into crime'. And as the Depression eased the press found that cases of sustenance fraud made better copy than hunger.[40]

The State government had begun to build the great monuments to the men on 'susso'; and the Boulevard, especially, touched Richmond. While some mocked its social utility, the respectable of Burnley hoped that it would reduce the number of undesirables who lurked along the river banks at night. The Richmond Council eventually made up its mind about its civic works to help the unemployed and decided to remodel the Town Hall and the municipal baths. Richmond's filthy and decayed streets, vandalized playgrounds, noisome industrial enclaves, leaking and rotting slums—all were less important than the renovation of Richmond's tangible civic dignity. The municipal baths were a different matter, however. Two to three hundred children bathed there every week—most had no bathroom at home—even though the water was infested with algae and was changed only once a week. The people of Richmond were greatly relieved when in September 1933 the Council declared its intention to renovate the entire facility and change the water daily.[41]

However grave the economic crisis remained, the Richmond Council continued to be diverted by faction fighting and allegations of corruption throughout 1934. In February Dr David Rosenberg (now calling himself Roseby to distance himself from the rise of Nazism in Germany) suddenly announced his resignation from the Council and the Labor Party. Publicly he claimed that he opposed any alliance with Lang Labor in New South

Wales and that he disapproved of the nationalization of banking and credit. His private reasons were entirely local. Eighteen months of real political work on the Council had shattered his faith in the Labor Party. He had been one of the most idealistic founding fathers of the Richmond Labor movement and now his heart was broken.[42] His resignation gave Councillor Lynch, the non-Labor unofficial representative of the Ratepayers' Association, an opening to condemn the Council publicly. At a Ratepayers' Association meeting in Collingwood he declared that Richmond was 'reeking with graft'. The Council demanded he explain himself, and he

> . . . strongly criticized the methods of the Labor Party and the way it forced its representatives to vote against their own minds and views. Many people only used the Labor Party for their own selfish interests, and may of those who were supposed to be representing the working-class people were wealthy men who cared little about the poor worker. There were again many people in the Labor movement in Richmond whom he admired and amongst them he would name the mayor (Councillor Fitzgerald) Councillor Kennedy and Councillor Longfield. No man sitting round the table that night would believe that Dr Roseby had resigned for reasons that were reported in the press.[43]

Councillor Lynch was also to have a short political career; at the next Council elections his backers melted away and he resigned rather than recontest his seat.[44]

Then in the first week of March Judge Macindoe began hearing the case under the Local Government Act of Councillor David Murphy's defeat of Frank McLeod in West Ward, 644 votes to 570. When the Court called for the ballot papers it was astounded to hear that they had been burnt. The Town Clerk, Mr Blazey, swore an affidavit to the effect that on 26 February the Returning Officer, (who was Councillor Jimmy Loughnan, Con's younger and steadier brother) told him to destroy the ballot papers. Blazey protested that they were about to become *sub judice* and asked if the required six months elapsed? Loughnan replied: 'The six months are up and it is your duty to destroy them. Blazey told Loughnan that he needed three councillors as witnesses. Loughnan then brought along his brother Con and Councillor Bell. Blazey still protested that it was contempt of court; Loughnan overruled him and took full responsibility. The ballot papers were put in the municipal incinerator at 10.20 a.m.; twenty minutes later the subpoena to bring the ballot papers was served. Despite the lack of ballot papers Judge Macindoe persevered and in April found that 'there was substantially more than seventy-four excess ballot papers that had been introduced by fraud into the ballot box'. Councillor Murphy's election was quashed. When the West Ward election was re-run in late May, Councillor Jimmy Loughnan was again Returning Officer and this time Murphy defeated McLeod, 651 to 610 votes. Murphy felt relieved and vindicated and declared that 'he would never be afraid to go before the ratepayers again'. Judge Macindoe had exonerated him from direct blame but he had had to bear the legal costs of the trial. Four weeks later a re-count reversed the winning margin from 41 to 14.[45]

March was a busy month for students of the Richmond Council. On 24 March the *Richmond Guardian* published a letter from a Labor supporter, 'Diogenes Junior', attacking the Council for sacking all staff over the age of sixty-five and appointing councillors and their relatives to Council jobs. 'Diogenes Junior' noted that 'Apparently the sentimental desire for municipal representation so ardently desired by some representatives is forgotten when an opportunity of remunerative employment presents itself. He continued:

> One councillor has already secured caucus and council approval to his appointment, and it was most amusing (that is, if the sordid aspect was temporarily forgotten) to listen to the laudations and mutual admiration when the appointment was made at Tuesday's Council meeting and to contrast these with the trenchant and bitter criticism and innuendoes that formerly re-echoed in the council chamber.[46]

The councillor in question was Con Loughnan, who found himself appointed to the salaried post of the Richmond City Council's Permit and Statistical Clerk. Councillor Lynch protested vehemently; the gallery exploded into uproar; the Mayor called in the police. By December the Council would be flooded with complaints from tradesmen and citizens that Mr Loughnan never seemed to be in the office when permits were to be issued. The Council decided to call for another report—the evidence was insufficient.[47]

With around a thousand of their citizens still on sustenance, at least the Richmond Council provided free entertainment, The *Guardian*:

> Two policemen in uniform guarded the Council chamber at the Richmond Town Hall on Monday evening, with strict instructions from the Mayor to eject any interrupter who might be in the audience (miscalled the gallery). Thenceforth the 'gallery' murmured its applause, laughed when councillors excelled themselves in declamatory denunciations, and smoked. Across the table councillors kept up a continuous hubbub, and quite half a dozen heated debates with suggestions of 'corruption' protracted the meeting, so that the Mayor's hammer felt quite worn out at the close and the Mayor's rulings for order were disagreed with as a matter of course. It was pointed out by the Mayor and other speakers that the scribes of the Press were listening, that the real business of the council would not be reported; but that the accusations would be, and in the morning actually 'scare' headlines in the papers chronicled the doings of the Council. Yes, as a fact a group of businessmen could have settled every debatable question in half an hour.[48]

The August Council elections too were packed full of incident as the Citizens' League campaigned to oust Jimmy Loughnan and David Murphy and directed ratepayers to inspect the rolls. Loughnan got home, 800 votes to 712; but in October Mr Justice Lowe again quashed Murphy's victory after he found that

> fictitious votes were cast by unqualified persons, that persons qualified to vote were wrongfully refused ballot papers on the ground that they had already voted, that ballot papers lawfully marked by ratepayers were altered, and that the number of fictitious votes and the number of ballot papers altered were sufficient to alter the result of the ballot. Councillor Murphy again won the re-run in late October.49

Meanwhile the Great Depression was showing signs of remission. It would last another five years for some working-class people but the national economy seemed to be on the mend. It was time to count the cost and nurse the nation through a successful convalescence.

Convalescence: 1935–1939

By 1935 it was clear that the Depression had wrought profound change in the character and structure of Australian industry. Mass unemployment had shattered the bargaining power of organized labour but employers had looked beyond cheap labour as a means of reducing costs; the Depression had in fact accelerated the replacement of labour by mechanization. Over the decade 1924–34 the percentage of wages as the cost of production fell from 58.1 per cent to 55.3 per cent in Victoria and from 53.8 per cent to 49.9 per cent in Australia as a whole. The percentage of interest payments rose at the same time from 41.9 per cent to 46.2 per cent in Victoria and from 44.7 per cent to 50.1 per cent in Australia. Even the Victorian Railways had sought to survive the slump by economizing on human effort and investing in new technology. The Select Committee into the Shorter Working Week recommended in 1935 that the forty-hour week be introduced, not because it would increase employment but because 'the noise, monotony, nerve strain and general tension required in production' imposed 'undue fatigue on the worker' and deprived him of reasonable leisure. But the forty-hour week would not create more jobs. On the contrary, the Committee argued, it would induce employers to speed up production by new technology and accelerate the already declining role of human effort in industry.[50]

Married women in the workforce were another casualty of the Depression as trade unions and the general public lost sympathy for the wives of employed men who also enjoyed the privilege of a job. On the other hand, some adolescents were motivated to stay on longer at school and the Victorian high schools were overwhelmed by the numbers seeking higher education as a means to job security. It was this new pressure on the already scarce resources of the State secondary school system that so alarmed the headmaster who told the 1931 Board of Inquiry into the Education system that they were already 'over-crowding the black-coated professions' with 'disgruntled men of leisure' who were 'socially objectionable' and 'politically dangerous'. Another almost ironical consequence of the Depression was a dramatic fall in the proportion of factory accidents per employee between 1931 and 1933 as small and unsafe establishments closed, and less put off.[51] Above all, the skilled and efficient workers were the first to be Depression drove workers to display a pitiful conscientiousness. *Jim Saddler*:

> Langfords built the Manchester Unity Building in the city opposite the Town Hall in twelve or sixteen weeks. Two floors a week they were doing. But that was Depression days and men would gobble their dinner down and stand at their bench ready to start. You were frightened if you couldn't find a job on the job you'd get the sack. The Manchester Unity was all concrete poured and you didn't have ready-mix in those days. They'd mix it up in the basement, drag it up the skip and tip it out to run down chutes.

For those with capital to invest in property and building, the Depression was a godsend if they were patient. Clements Langford had a steady stream of contracts throughout the crisis and of course had the pick of the workmen. To the firm's credit it always paid award rates: 'They used to say it was like the Bank of England—your money would be there no matter what', *Jim Saddler* recalls. Property values collapsed—the Richmond valuation fell by £55 832 in 1931 alone—and the canny seized the chance to buy houses and vacant land. By July 1935 housing construction was again under way, but costs had fallen dramatically, and consumer expectations had changed—the middle-class flat entered the Melbourne housing market. Housing for the working class was a different matter, however. Builders and investors remained unwilling to erect cheap dwellings 'because of the uncertainty of collecting rents'; throughout 1934 eviction cases for non-payment of rent entirely dominated the business of the Richmond Court. At the same time there was an acute shortage of rental accommodation in the inner suburbs for the unemployed and the very poor, and at the 1935 valuation only twenty-three houses were vacant in Richmond. Yet despite this pressure on working-class housing, Richmond and its neighbours were in steady decline as human communities. From a population of 43 174 at the 1921 Census, Richmond fell to 39 616 in 1933 and to 38 944 in 1938; Collingwood, Fitzroy and South Melbourne all recorded similar falls. The encroachments of industry were reducing the housing stock and the sheer awfulness of daily life in these depressed industrial communities was driving away many who had the economic power to escape. Moreover, the housing stock. had deteriorated alarmingly during the Depression. Absentee landlords were notorious for neglecting their properties but many Richmond landlords were themselves working-class people with no spare cash for running repairs. But the dwellings were not only neglected; in many, destitute tenants were driven to strip woodwork for fuel—*Mary Davis* remembers watching with fascination as an unemployed family next door progressively denuded the wooden toilet in the back garden, preferring a cooked dinner to modesty.[52]

In 1934 the Melbourne *Herald* and its protégé, the researcher F. Oswald Barnett, had begun campaigning for a slum abolition as a means of revitalizing the building industry. thereby sowing the seed for the Victorian Housing Commission. The Richmond Council had also toyed with the idea of worker housing and in 1935 began investigating possible sites on behalf of the new State government committee. The Church of England engaged an architect for a block of flats on land in Church Street granted it by the' government some years before. Then in September the first real opportunity for public housing appeared when John Wren's Victorian Trotting and Racing Association informed the Council that its lease on the Richmond Racecourse was to expire the following February. The Council informed the government, and thus was Richmond's first public housing estate born. There were to be various slips betwixt the cup and the lip before the Racecourse estate was completed in 1941, but the post-war estates rarely matched the charm of this first venture; the only real flaw in its execution was that some of the houses went to the less than needy like Councillor Jack O'Connell M.L.C. The street names honour Frank Tudor and Councillors O'Connell, Lightfoot, Vesper, Longfield and Jackson. (The Loughnans are commemorated in West Ward in the former Little Miller Street where the clan used to own nearly all the properties.)[53]

During the winter of 1935 around nine hundred families and individuals were on sustenance in Richmond at a weekly cost of just over £1000. The Victorian government decided to expand its relief works and thereby abolish sustenance without work, but the Trades Hall Council led a strike campaigning for relief workers to be paid the basic wage. The Richmond Council, still nervous of the organized unemployed, gave token support to the sustenance strikers of £50 a week—the unemployed declared that £200 would have been more appropriate. Then in July the government acceded to the Trades Hall's demands. Meanwhile the Town Hall set were basking in the luxuries of the Town Hall's renovations. The hall had been closed for dancing in 1929 because of the state of the floor, so a splendid mayoral ball was a fitting way to celebrate the return of civic social life:

> Panelled in polished blackwood, the hall has undergone an entire transformation. Above the panels the walls have been artistically shaded in pastel tones, and huge electroliers and modern wall lighting effects combine to make the hall one of the best in the metropolitan area.

But more was to come. The Council splurged on remodelling the façade of the entire building, burying the delicate Italianate brown and cream brickwork under concrete Stalinist grandeur. The work proceeded at a cracking pace, quite unlike the Council's usual projects, and in March the façade and the remodelling of the Richmond Baths were complete. Richmond's civic fathers had spent £30 000 and not until the Town Hall was finished did they discover that it was out of alignment with Bridge Road. The Council had argued that the Town Hall would pay for itself by being hired out for theatrical use, dances, weddings and private functions. A month later there were still no bookings: dance promoters claimed the charges were excessive; the stage was too small for theatrical use; there were no private rooms to serve wedding and similar functions. The Richmond Baths did a little better, with Olympic dimensions, a roof, heating and chlorination and the facility was managed by the noted swimmer and gym instructor Tom Donnet. Attendances were good in summer but the Council's revenue received little boosting—by August 1939 the baths were losing £75 a week.[54]

The great civic projects did provide work for the unemployed on the drainage in front of the new façade but that was an economy for the Richmond Council. In January 1936 'One of the Unemployed' wrote to the *Richmond Chronicle* alleging that once the Council had rescinded its apparently high-minded motion to provide only sustenance without work after three months of agitation from the local unemployed, it had proceeded to replace men in permanent jobs with sustenance workers at less than half the pay. He went on:

> In the quarries conditions are so bad that an unemployed man working in return for sustenance came home for tea at 6 o'clock and dropped dead. All the permanent men have been taken off the crusher and unemployed put in their place . . . Previous to the introduction of work for sustenance, there were five permanent men getting £5 a week each from the Town Hall. Today there are ten sustenance workers around the mixer receiving 28s paid out of the Government Unemployment Tax—cheap screenings for the council. This is hard, exhausting work, and Dr Dale has repeatedly pointed out that an unemployed man cannot buy sufficient nourishing food for 28s. His wife has to be fed also out of that amount. It is time that new blood was introduced into the council.[55]

The Richmond Council denied all charges of overwork or of causing the workman's death. The Richmond Unemployment Committee hastened to assure the Council that it had no knowledge of the writer of the letter. The matter quickly faded from the public stage.[56]

Other embarrassments received much greater publicity. On 8 April 1935 two statutory declarations were submitted to Council by the partners of J. W. Stamp Pty Ltd of Carlton to the effect that a man calling himself

'Carney' had approached them asking for a commission on behalf of himself and five councillors to ensure the acceptance of their tender for a pig de-hairing machine for the Richmond abattoirs. The commission amounted to £12. Councillor Fitzgerald commented: 'It sounds too cheap', and provoked gales of laughter. None the less, the Council had no alternative but to refer the matter to the Solicitor-General. Almost a year later the police charged Bryan Loughnan, bookmaker, of Loughnan Street, with the offence. All the councillors gave evidence at the trial, disclaiming any prior knowledge of the incident—poor 'Carney', it seems, was trying to cash in privately on council business. The 'Carney' affair was one of the few successful prosecutions of corruption linked to the Richmond Council.[57]

Embarrassment old and new persisted throughout 1936. Again questions were asked about the excessive use of hire cars. Again South Richmond residents complained about the stenches from the cork factory and the tip; again they pleaded in vain for road repairs and new drainage because 'stagnant water lay about all the year'. Again strange things happened in the counting of Councillor Murphy's votes in West Ward when he' defeated the Citizens' League candidate by thirty-five votes: two hundred ballot papers disappeared during the luncheon break and the lights failed when the ballot boxes were opened for counting despite the perfect working order of the switches. Again Con Loughnan scandalized ratepayers when he was awarded a pay increase from £5 6s 8d to £6 6s 8d on condition that he attend the office from 9 a.m. to 4 p.m. and not absent himself without permission of the Town Clerk. Again dark hints of corruption and crude personal abuse—enlivened Council debates. To its credit the Council joined Collingwood and Brunswick in implementing the Trades Hall Council's call for a forty-hour week. To its discredit, burdened with uncollected rates and the incompetence and civic vanity of the councillors, Richmond slid further into debt.[58]

In January 1936 the Council announced that it could not raise the £200 000 needed to build the Richmond Racecourse estate and re-zoned fifteen of the 157 acres as industrial so that British Australasian Tobacco could erect a factory. The £30 000 squandered on the Town Hall and the Baths had pushed Richmond's rates to 2s 6d compared to Prahran's Is 9d. Landlords complained that the high rates were forcing them to raise rents and between May and July 1936 rents rose from 2½ per cent to 5 per cent. Most landlords were making it a practice to raise rents each time there was a change in tenants and by October estate agents reported that there were few houses vacant in Richmond under thirty shillings a week. There were still about five to six hundred Richmond families on sustenance—a number that would persist until the outbreak of World War II. Meanwhile, the new State Slum Abolition Commission headed the attack on sub-standard housing. The Richmond Council began to be more assiduous in the condemning of houses unfit for human habitation but was caught by the cruel irony that the worst slums were now the only housing within financial reach of the unemployed, the elderly and the incapacitated.[59]

Slum abolition presented Richmond with another and more tricky dilemma. If housing conditions were to be improved, the working class would have to accept the intervention of public authorities and middle-class reformers in their private life. Moreover, to admit to a slum problem was to admit to being socially inferior. In November the Richmond Council refused outright to provide the Slum Abolition Commission with a survey of Richmond's slums and vacant land and Councillor Longfield truly' spoke for Richmond when he declared: 'As far as I'm concerned . . . we have no slums in Richmond, though we have dilapidated houses'. The South Richmond Debating Society and the Richmond Young Men's Club both deplored the attacks on Richmond 'by medical men and children's health committees' and denied that there was 'evidence of any outbreak of disease or epidemic amongst children in any part of the district'.[60] The *Richmond Guardian* was infuriated by the sensationalist tactics of the housing reformers:

> In the very early days many people settled in the upper portion of what are now Fitzroy and Collingwood, and there was a certain undesirable element at times. Hence the picturesque Richmond Hill became the home of many prominent business and professional men who had much to do in advancing the progress of the metropolis, and for the greater part of the century homes were healthy and comfortable and families happy in Richmond, and the people of Richmond have been foremost in providing facilities for health—baby health centres, kindergarten, public swimming baths, playgrounds and so forth. Many of the original homes have been replaced by modern buildings and the process goes steadily on, for an average of thirty inspections by the health officer are made weekly, and when a home is found to be uninhabitable it has to be renovated or pulled down.[61]

Above all, the poor were quite rightly deeply suspicious of what sort of housing would be thrust upon them by middle-class do-gooders. And again the *Richmond Guardian* spoke truly for the people of Richmond:

> The working man, even if his pay is small, wants a neat little cottage, with, if possible, a bit of garden, as a home for himself and family. They have no desire to be herded into tenements, and it is just because of a desire of a house for themselves alone that so many crowd into small streets.[62]

Herded into tenements they would be, twenty-five years later; tenements, however clean, dry and warm, that would confirm inferiority and diminish their independence; tenements built and supported by Labor as well as Liberal governments and councils.

Through 1936 and 1937 the economic recovery was becoming ever more tangible in Richmond with the rising number of new factory registrations and industrial building permits. Rosella, Peters Ice Cream, the Bethesda Hospital, the food processors Leggetts Products and Julius Kayser the hosiery manufacturers—all erected new buildings. Many of these new premises left the old ones empty and did not create new jobs; but one significant new factory, was Lamson Paragon's, the office equipment manufacturers, who were building a £30 000 new factory covering two and a half acres in Westbank Terrace. Small business, too, was reviving, especially in knitting factories, rubber goods, metal stamping, car body building. The 1938 Richmond valuation saw a rise of £14 092, largely due to rising industrial values especially in East Ward. All this renewed industrial activity placed greater pressure on Richmond's neglected and ill-planned roads. The concrete roads were breaking up and in 1939 the City Engineer claimed that many would have to be entirely rebuilt. By 1939, too, the new Hoddle Bridge fed an intolerable level of traffic into Victoria Street: 'Accidents are numerous and many of them causing the death of pedestrians are due to the large number of parked cars . . .'. Yet despite all this economic vitality, the unemployed would not go away. In the winter of 1939 625 were on sustenance from the Town Hall and 345 were receiving free firewood. The Ladies' Benevolent Society had ceased assisting the unemployed in 1936 and had since concentrated on those made destitute by 'other causes'. The unemployed were not only isolated; they were also being forgotten.[63] In September 1937 the Richmond Unemployed Committee made a deputation to the Council:

> Mr Whitton, speaking of the handout of food at the Depot on Saturday mornings, said it was stated that the handout was getting later and that the allowance from the Council was being cut down. The handout was a quarter of a pound of sugar and a small loaf of bread for a man and his wife with a tin of jam where there was a child. They were told that the bread was made from flour given to the Council. Although the number of unemployed had decreased generally those in Richmond were worse off. The price of commodities had increased and rents had gone up. It had become impossible for most of them to get a home at 15s per week, towards which the Government contributed 8s, but if they had to pay more than 15s the Government grant was withdrawn. The people who congregated at the depot were in dire need and therefore they asked for an increase in the Council's allowance if possible. They also asked for the use of the small hall to discuss, among other things, national insurance, which as outlined would mean that the workers would be worse off than now.[64]

The Council refused.

A month earlier Councillor Jimmy Loughnan had been elected to the first of his record five terms as Mayor. Like all the sons of Richard Ignatius, he had started in the building trades but by 1937 was the representative of the Hospital Employees' Federation on the T.H.C. He later entered the Taxation Office of the Victorian Public Service where he remained until retirement. His first mayoralty coincided with Richmond's 50th Jubilee as city and local history found itself being rewritten to confer on Richard Ignatius the mantle of '*the* founder' of the Richmond Labor Party. Richmond had developed a Labor ruling class, bonded by dynastic and factional loyalties. They even lived near each other, as the *Richmond Chronicle* was not slow to notice, with five councillors living in the prestigious West Ward, three of them in charming Rotherwood Street alone. And, like most ruling classes, they became ever more preoccupied with their privileges and prestige. In January 1938 the Government Municipal Auditor disallowed a range of Council expenditures which included £220 for hire cars and the cost of an illuminated address from Councillor Bell on his appointment as chairman of the Tramways Board. Councillor Loughnan was a passionate advocate of mayoral robes: he had been 'looked upon as a Cinderella' at the mayoral balls of other cities. In vain did Councillor Jack Cremean argue that it was not fitting for a Labor mayor to dress up.[65]

The Central Executive of the A.L.P. had become increasingly alarmed at the conduct of the Party and the Council in Richmond. By 1935 it had set about reorganizing the branches and taken pre-selections for Council out of their hands. The trusted and respectable Jack Cremean was appointed provisional secretary of the Central and North Richmond branches, the experienced George Vesper took control of the South and Mr Nunn-Patrick of the West. In September 1938 the Central Executive, after its own investigations of Council administration, placed the fourteen Labour councillors under 'instructions' which included the strict adherence to the existing factory, business and residential zones in Richmond for three years until the creation of a zoning authority. Councillors were also required to accept or reject tenders at the meeting at which the letter box was opened and the final selection of applications for out-door staff were to be made by drawing lots in open Council. But the Council was under pressure from the newly created Victorian Housing Commission, which had requested a municipal map showing residential zones, commercial and factory zones, open space and noxious trade zones. The Council had consistently opposed the Commission's proposals that no houses face on to the streets less that 30 feet wide on the grounds that it would unduly penalize many Richmond homeowners and poor tenants. Caught between the Central Executive, the Housing Commission and its own reluctance to lose control of factory zoning, the Council prevaricated and procrastinated. It was soon to be saved by the war which would strengthen industry's claim to expansion in the inner suburbs.[66]

The Council had other troubles. In October 1938 the State Government passed new legislation which gave ratepayers powers to prosecute councillors who failed to ensure that the municipal accounts were balanced by 30 September each year. No longer could Councils operate with huge overdrafts: Richmond's was £9045 on 3 October that year and rose to £18 192 three weeks later. Councillor Kennedy moved at a meeting of the Public Works Committee that, for the better control of the City finances, 'officers in charge of various departments should submit estimates of their requirements for the coming year'. Suddenly all was revealed. No proper estimating had been done for years. Councillors preferred to guess and one recent job had been guestimated at £2000 and its eventual cost was £5000. Even Jimmy Loughnan felt forced to condemn the 'fancy salaries' of some Council staff where 'some men were getting more wages than other men who were doing exactly the same work, and it was time that this was put on a business footing'. The legislation had the desired effect. By 30 September 1939 the Council's overdraft had fallen by a third and in 1941 the Richmond Council's finances were in the black for the first time since 1924.[67]

There remained one embarrassment for the Richmond Council to conclude the decade of depression and decay. It was one of the most bizarre events in Australian municipal history and it involved two former Mayors: Con Loughnan, the Statistical and Permits Clerk, and the twisting Paddy Donnelly, now Richmond's Building Surveyor. In late 1938 Loughnan had been absent from work for 'severe pains in the chest and the head'. After 'surgical treatment' he returned to work in December. Then on the evening of 3 January 1939, according to Councillor Jack Cremean who conducted the Council's subsequent investigation:

> P. F. Donnelly, building surveyor, had received permission from the Town Clerk to use the car from the Town Hall garage, the keys for which he was given by the Town Clerk. He went out on his duty as building surveyor. Cornelius Loughnan, statistical clerk, had that day purchased a hacksaw, hatchet, a padlock and two keys and had altered the lock on the Council's garage at 10.20 p.m. Mr Donnelly returned but was unable to obtain admission to the garage as the door was chained. He met Mr Loughnan and it was alleged that Loughnan struck Donnelly with an axe on the ear, necessitating several stitches being put in.[68]

Councillor Kennedy, as leader of the A.L.P. on Council, enquired: 'What jurisdiction have we? It was stated that there was a likelihood of murder?' The Mayor replied, 'definitely'. Luckily for the Richmond Council and Con Loughnan, ten days later the public and the media were diverted by the tragedy of Black Friday, Victoria's worst bushfire disaster; but the incident received enough 'unfavourable publicity' to alarm Councillor Jimmy Loughnan that the Council was being 'held up to ridicule' for what was merely a private dispute between two of its officers. The best the Council could do was to 'forget about it. Let the dead bury its dead'. And so they did. No report was made to the police and no charges ever laid. Richmond legend has it that Con Loughnan later sent Donnelly a card wishing him 'A Happy New Ear'.[69]

Perhaps this was a symbolically fitting end to a decade of disgrace for the Labor movement in Richmond. In its hour of greatest need the working class had found little comfort in Labor, and the kindly but ineffectual Ted Cotter was himself testimony to the intellectual bankruptcy of so many Labor politicians. There were strong suggestions that he was 'paid off' by the Wren interests to support the less than holy alliance between the A.L.P. and the Country Party that brought the Dunstan Government into being.[70] And in a speech in 1938 marking his thirtieth year as Richmond's M.L.A. he told his hapless constituents:

> . . . the democratic system of government still remained the only system for the working class people. The workers themselves were to blame for any faults, as they had everything in their hands, but displayed lack of interest. The Dunstan Government was striving to place on the Statute Book legislation of benefit to the majority of the people.[71]

Ahead lay the war and in the international struggle against Fascism the radical Left would find a new moral authority and a new access to political and industrial power, such as the isolated and impotent militant unemployed had never enjoyed. The real political consequences of the Great Depression still lay ahead and they would ultimately embitter and divide the Labor Movement and working-class communities like Richmond as never before.

6

Young Marrieds

The Depression and Private Life

> *When we were out of work we were over near the Fitzroy Gardens and I remember marching with all these people—I don't know whether they were Communists, it didn't matter to me what they were, you just got in with them. And there was a great crowd of them marching because we didn't have a job. Well the police came through on horses and batoned you everywhere. We had to jump the Yolimont railway to get over the picket fence away from them. They just batoned you down wherever they, came through. They were shockingly cruel then—just because you didn't have a job and were hungry and had nothing. You didn't even have a change of clothes—I don't know how we ever got on—we must have stunk.*

Jean Fowler, half a century later, still feels the anger and alienation she experienced in the Great Depression. But she is unusual. The load of bitterness she has borne throughout her life enables her to remain in touch with the blackest emotions of her past. Many more, who perhaps have coped better psychologically with their struggles and frustrations, find it difficult now to recall their despair and fear. Like old soldiers, they are justifiably proud of having endured and survived, and like old soldiers they have suppressed those memories which now would evoke shame. Many are now so removed from the emotional reality of the Depression that they do not know how they ever managed to survive. One suspects that others are being deliberately misleading. One informant worked for a Richmond estate agent throughout the Depression and claims that there were no evictions. One woman admitted that her husband took to drink when he lost his job but refused permission for the fact to be associated even with her pseudonym. With another woman one sensed that she had found her husband wanting in the crisis and that the marriage had soured. Nearly all would be appalled at the mere suggestion that any Richmond mother was forced to prostitute herself to feed her family; *Joe Grant*, who lived in Gwynne Street. South Richmond, claims it was 'common'. On being pressed, he admitted to knowing of three cases where 'mothers of large families', women 'you wouldn't look at', went down to Princes Street or the Botanic Gardens for three shillings a go.[1] Who is telling the truth? Most people are at pains to recount how they honoured their debts: *Joe Grant* again claims that cheating on rent and clothing was a way of life for many. And there are those who romanticize. The Left romanticize the heroic working-class struggle against the capitalist system, despite the evidence to the contrary.[2] The hardy romanticize the psychological resilience of the unemployed despite the suicides, the alcohol abuse, the social delinquency, the violence, vandalism and petty crime that not only occurred but which were inevitable. The neighbourly romanticize the community support and kindness in the slums despite the ruthless competition for jobs, the petty theft, the informing on sustenance delinquents and the fiddling of relief funds and handouts. The Depression story is a mass of contradictions and a minefield for the unwary oral historian.

All history is the history of the present, as each generation rewrites history in terms of its current values and preoccupations. And so it is with private oral history. We all construct inside our head an autobiography as we progress through life and, like written history, that autobiography not only seeks to record significant events and experiences, it above all serves to make sense of the past and define our evolving sense of identity. It provides a version of ourselves with which we can live and even recount to others—with modifications. And that is the problem; for, in the formation of a personal history that is tolerable to the ego, the line between careful truth and personal myth is easily fudged. This is not to suggest that many people tell black lies; on the contrary, they attempt always to be accurate and fair and do not hesitate to contradict mistaken ideas of the interviewer. But the essence of human memory is that it is selective and, like written history, the basis of that selectivity is value-laden; hence the sins are of omission rather than commission. When the oral historian faces an informant it is in fact a dialogue between two historians, one of whom has complete and exclusive control of the evidence and has already selected and interpreted the story now made public. And nowhere is this more treacherous for this history of Richmond than in the Depression. Most of us find it difficult to be entirely truthful about things of which we are ashamed; and those Depression years were the most testing of their lives for many of these people. Many of the unemployed are now strangely vague or reticent about the day-to-day details of 'finding a feed', for respectable people were driven to theft or to receiving stolen goods. Moreover, as these two historians face each other, each is hoping to make a favourable impression on the other and the informant is telling the oral historian as much about the present as the past. The oral historian is forced to deal in personal myth as much as in private history. But personal myth is no less valuable as historical evidence, for it is the basis of private ideology: it is a window into the way human beings cope with life. *Muriel Thompson* records in her late seventies as her salient memories of the Depression:

> I think it was just accepted and everybody helped each other. And everything was hard to get and I think you appreciate anything that's hard to get—more so than everything that flows in. And everybody sharing it—that's what it was all about—more loving. There was so much love and kindness about. And all our clothes—we used to have jumble sales. And all the people from Toorak used to come over to our little church and they used to take us for trips. And I said, 'They can say what they like about the stuffy people in Toorak—they're ladies when you get right down to it'. They were. They'd take the babies out of our arms, Then they used to bring over clothes. And if the children wet their bloomers at the kindergarten, deaconess would always change them and they'd come home in a nice little dress.

But on 1 July 1931 *Muriel Thompson* wrote this letter to the *Sun-News Pictorial* Appeal:

> Dear Sir,
>
> I notice you are still appealing for clothing. I am one of the unfortunate no home 2 children and husband out of work 3 yrs. We are both in need of cloths the kindergarten look after my girl but I have been cold and wet all the winter I am almost bare footed as I have a baby at the breast I must be kept dry if possible could you do anything for me. I am extra outsize and take 7 in shoes. I find it hard to get anything at all in fact I can't I have never received any help other than the sustenance 11/3 which we try to live on Mr *Thompson* has nothing to wear I can't do any more to his cloths We would be glad to hear from you hoping you will do your best for us.
>
> Oblige
>
> Mr and Mrs *Thompson*[3]

The letter was passed to the State Relief Committee who then passed it on to the Richmond Council who were in turn preoccupied with the allegations against Councillor and Mrs Lightfoot. The letter was not even filed correctly.

Muriel is a truthful woman. Above all, she is one of those rare true Christians: she has seen a lot of life and a lot of suffering and she looks for the good in people and is compassionate about their failings. When she describes her South Richmond you would not think that it was only a few streets away from *Joe Grant*'s world of 'metho' drinkers, prostitution. stabbings and shootings, of foul-mouthed teenage girls who held men down on the banks of the Yarra and forced them to have intercourse. As *Joe* relishes vice and panders to middle-class fantasies about proletarian licence, *Muriel* discounts it. To *Joe* 'the respectable' were 'one in five hundred'; to *Muriel* the proportion is the other way round. Finally, as Wendy Lowenstein found in her massive oral record of the Depression, *Weevils in the Flour*, Australian working-class people have a deep fear of being seen as a 'whinger', of wallowing in their own hardships: 'Oh, we got through'.[4] People are often far more comfortable describing the sufferings of others. The Depression was always tougher for someone else: women claim it was harder for men; men claim it was harder for women. But in the euphemisms, the projections, the evasions and the myths, we can sense the pain and the fear, and comprehend the impact of this most frightful failure of the capitalist system on the total lives of this generation.

Muriel chooses to remember the Depression as Richmond's finest hour as a community when family, friends and neighbours rallied to sustain the afflicted. *Ted Sullivan* now translates this into modern jargon:

> It was a terrific struggle then and the one who had a little bit morewell they shared it. It was like living in a huge commune. Those who had it shared it because they realized that one of these days they'd be without it—they'd be out of work.

The sense of community was forged by the local places of work—'real old home factories', *Ruby Kane* calls them—and by the pubs, the churches, the sporting clubs, the corner shops. Above all it sprang from close living and shared poverty. Not all Richmond streets had *it—Margaret Taylor* once lived in Bromham Place where the neighbours never sat out on hot nights and only spoke in passing in the street. But the 'real loving' that *Ruby Kane* and *Muriel Thompson* treasure in their memories was strongest where life was hardest: 'There was a camaraderie amongst them', *Ruby* recalls, 'and in South Richmond too—they were very very close down there'. 'We were as happy as birds', *Muriel* romanticizes:

> Even though we were all poor we had the fun of the world. That little street of mine—I often sing 'Just a little street where old folks . . .'. You could knock at any door and you'd get 'Come in and have a cuppa'. I always think to myself that's very good.

It was essentially a feminine community in the street; men were bonded through the pubs and at work. And when unemployment kept them at home and out of the hotels the feminine dominance of the neighbourhood networks added to their sense of failure and incompetence. Many of this generation were newly-weds with young babies when the Depression struck them and the street community saved the sanity of many a young mother on sustenance. But the benefits were also material. When *Muriel* did her washing, buckets of the used soda water would circulate among neighbours so that they could clean their toilets. A bowl of starch would similarly do the rounds. So too with food. *Muriel* and *Jean*, *Joe Grant* and many others cannot remember ever going without food: 'Someone would give you something, even a piece of fruit'. Shopkeepers, too, understood and did what they could, says *Jean*: 'All the shops knew what it was like'. If you were liked and respected, as was *Muriel*, 'you was right':

> I'd mag away at the butcher and he'd be talking away and putting in these scraps (three pennyworth of scraps) and I'd be looking and I'd pick out a nice chop and that'd do your husband, and with the rest make a nice 'Cousin Jack's'—a pasty with plenty of vegies.

But where there is intimacy there must also be conflict. Feuds and fights enlivened daily life in the slums: some were diverting, others were terrifying. The Richmond Court often enjoyed female feuds like the battle in May 1928 which led to Mrs Maud Barker of Green Street being fined £5 for using insulting language and blowing raspberries at her neighbour, Mrs Allen. (Less amusing had been Mrs Johanna Mann who was fined in 1903 for emptying night-soil into a drain on her neighbour's property—the police had been alerted by the stench out in the street.) Fights and brawls broke out easily with drink, but even in sobriety there was so much underlying stress among the poor that disputes could suddenly escalate into terrifying violence. *Friedrich Smith*'s brother once became involved in a fight with the son of a nearby dairyman. The dairyman gave *Friedrich*'s brother a hiding and when *Friedrich*'s father later came to see what it was all about the dairyman attacked him with a pitchfork. Festering neighbourhood tensions were only exacerbated by mass unemployment. *Joe Grant*, while thankful for the mutual help of the community, emphasizes that the level of want was so great that people would 'cut your throat for a job'. Resources were so low that people did have to steal from others as hard up as themselves. If money or goods were donated through a third party for the unemployed, they as often as not did not make their destination. Cheating and petty theft were essential for survival, lurks and scheming an absorbing daily challenge: 'Everyone was on the move, everyone was on the look-out for a racket, everyone was proud if he had a scheme on somewhere and he'd skite and boast about it', *Joe* remembers. And even though informing to the police or to welfare authorities was a dastardly crime in a working-class community, people were driven by want and jealousy to risk the enforced social exile if they were found out.[5]

Down in the close-knit slums of South Richmond the Depression to some extent was easier to bear. Those on or below the economic margin of respectability were accustomed to periodic unemployment; they had already acquired techniques of survival; they were used to feeling like outcasts; they were too practical to refuse, charity. *Joe Grant* says his family 'were born for it; *Jean Fowler* however angry she was, cannot remember feeling fear: 'The ones who didn't, have anything before, well they just went along, with X; it was 'those who had money and come down' who suffered. Above all, they were capable of just living from day to day; it was dangerous to look too far ahead. What was different about the Great Depression was its length. Casual and unskilled labour were the first to lose their jobs and the last to find regular work. For some families the father was unemployed for the entire period of dependence of the children and by the end of the 1930s the Richmond pushes were overflowing with violent and alienated youths who had no memory of their fathers being in work and no expectation of a secure future for themselves. On the other hand, the very poor had the consolation that many others were in the same boat; the stigma of being unemployed was relieved—this time it wasn't just their fault.

There are in fact four distinct 'Depression stories'. First, there were the well-off who remained deliberately ignorant of the plight of the unemployed, who insisted that the unemployed were simply not trying hard enough. *Margaret Taylor* had the misfortune to marry into such a family and when her husband lost his job they had to live with his parents. *Margaret* found them 'pretty hard'; her mother-in-law had 'never known hardship, you couldn't tell her anything and she was convinced that there was money in poultry'. She forced them to take on a poultry farm in Edithvale where, in a country already awash with eggs, they failed dismally. They had a cow and brought up three children by living on their own produce. Second, there were those who stayed in work but who did understand what the unemployed were going through. *Thomas Beauchamp*'s skill and loyalty saved him and he was lucky to work for Repco, the motor repair parts firm that flourished through the Depression as new car sales slumped. None the less, he has a vague feeling of guilt like that of a soldier who survived four ye ars in the trenches without a scratch. *Doug Davis*'s family also got through: his father had a 'job for life' as a driver for the Rosella and all four sons were 'kept on' in their jobs in the metal trades. *Lilian Campbell*'s husband earned £6 a week as a hairdresser and she too felt guilt at her good fortune as she saw her childhood friends, who were now young mothers like herself, living on food she could not have touched. *John Brown* was another who found he had a 'job for life' at Kennon's:

> When the Depression come the lot at Kennon's got put off. I was operating a machine that come from Germany—it was the first one in Australia. a big hydraulic press. The works manager said to me: 'There won't be much work going but if anything wants doing, you'll be the only one to do it'. I knew that somebody was going to sing about it—which they did—but I was lucky. I used to get jobs around the engineering shop and I even used to be joining up steam pipes and so on.

Only the very best in skill and character were plucked out of the workforce for jobs for life. The Depression was a cruel lesson in the economic fruits of respectability.

Yet there were many respectables among the unemployed. Much of the poignancy of the Great Depression springs from the fact that in its severity it afflicted many who because of their skill and character believed them selves to be immune from prolonged unemployment. Hence, there are two stories among the unemployed: that of the very poor, for whom it was more of the same, and that of the respectable, for whom it was unimaginable. And many working-class people who were used to hardship felt, as did *Jean Fowler* and *Ruby Kane*, a special sympathy for them. *Dot* and *Edna Wilson*, who had kept apart from the dirty children at Burnley School and whose father had prospered as a builder and moved the family to Malvern, were now thrust back into the ranks of the poor. The sisters had begun to make a name for themselves as high-class tailors, then 'We were hit very hard, we were all out of work—there was no dole or anything like that—we just had to live on our savings and watch our savings go'. After the Depression they would pick up where they left off; they have never wavered in their loyalty to the Liberal Party. And there was *Monica Rinoldi* and her Light Horse man. *Monica*, who despite her father's job and politics had never felt 'working-class', was now destitute and an outcast. Gone was their new home and all the furniture. All they had was their baby, Monica's glory box and each other. Monica and her new baby stayed for a time with her parents in Richmond while her husband went 'on the track' selling notepaper. But they could not bear to be parted and *Monica* and the baby took to the road too:

> We were not allowed to camp in showgrounds or anywhere under shelter because we were what was called 'Ovoes'—down-and-outers. I suppose there were a few bad ones who had broken into places and you were all under the same stigma. And when you're proud it's . . .
>
> My husband was a very very proud man and I can see him to this day going up to the door with a writing pad in his hand and only I know what that must have done to him.
>
> Until we came to Rupanyup and our daughter was very ill with fever and we didn't have any money for a doctor. We went into one of the chemists in the town and he happened to be a Richmond chemist and he recognized my husband and he was horrified. From then on we got on in the world. But up to then, for over twelve months. I wonder how we survived.

Young as she was and still suffering the after-effects of her childhood bout of typhoid, *Monica* more than rose to the challenge. She learnt to make every household need that could be home-made; she learnt to grow vegetables and keep poultry; she thought nothing of going out walking on cold nights to keep warm and save fuel. She still finds it painful to recall her Depression but the experience did not change her political views. She concentrates on individual people who helped them through; it is the relationship of individual to individual that is important to her, not the relationship of the individual to society.

Above all, the respectable saw their unemployment as an injustice. They had kept the rules, they were willing to work. *Isabel Williams*'s uncle was sixty-two when he lost his job and he was never to work again:

> He used to go out every day though, walking round all day. And he used to mend his own boots and they'd be nearly off his feet And I remember once he cried and said, This is bloody degrading to think a man's willing to work and can't get it'.

Isabel herself found it an agony to go up to the Town Hall for her handouts and would hide her billy under her skirt so that no one could see what she had been reduced to. Even those who had work found that they were forced to share the suffering. *Jim Saddler.*

> They brought in a new wage change. We were getting £6 2s and they brought in an unemployed tax and dropped us down to £4 12s. Thirty shillings in one smack and that was one of the things that everyone resented, but you couldn't do anything about it. And where did all that unemployed benefit go to? It was just brought in overnight—bang. That meant a big thing to all the working men in the building trade.

Many were 'glad' to take wage cuts, however, *Joe Grant* claims, for 'if you didn't take it, someone else would'. For those who had amassed a little equity in a house, their weekly payments took such a slice out of their pay packet that a wage reduction, let alone the sack, placed their home in peril. *Jim Saddler* was lucky, though. His bank manager agreed to lower his weekly payments to 2s 6d, and with a little help from his father, he and his new wife kept their home.

But cruellest of all, was that if you owned your home you were not eligible for a money dole. *Joe Grant*'s parents owned their cottage in Gwynne Street, so *Joe* was only eligible for the travelling dole when he went to Mildura for the fruit picking. Proud home-owners, who had faithfully practised the respectable virtues of providence and thrift, independence and responsibility, found themselves dependent on Town Hall handouts. Families had no alternative but to sell all their possessions, piece by piece, to get them through the week. *James Mitchell*, a Burnley pharmacist, remembers one doctor who was notorious for demanding immediate payment, relenting once when he attended a boy with double pneumonia in a house in Coppin Street. The only furniture in the house was a packing case for a table in the kitchen. The desperately sick lad lay on bags on the floor covered by another bag. When the doctor first visited, the father was wearing a coat and vest; when he returned and was given his 10s 6d fee the father had no coat or vest. Ashamed, the doctor returned the money and ordered the father to redeem his clothes. This family were house-owners who had sold all they had.[6] To the respectable unemployed it seemed that all the help was going to the 'no-hopers' who had frittered away their earnings in good times at the pub and with the S.P. bookie. *Ruby Kane*'s husband was out of work for nearly a decade, and when the Depression ended for them, 'we had nothing', but almost miraculously they saved their house:

> When the Depression came we had nothing. We didn't have any dole or anything like that When we got married we put a deposit on the house and we were paying it off. Well, during the Depression we couldn't keep it up, but fortunately I had a decent woman who had loaned the money through the agent, who realized the position and she was most kind—she let us go along and eventually she got paid up every penny.

Ruby's politics have always been respectable Catholic Labor. She worked for the Cremean brothers' campaigns and followed them into the D.L.P. She worries still about Communist infiltration into trade unions and even the Church, but she is none the less aware that some people did very well out of the afflictions of people like herself:

> It was not of our doing—it was the Depression that came and caught the whole lot of us—rich and poor alike. Some people even had to sell their homes and that's where a lot of these bloodsuckers made their money—0h, they did. There were some callous people around at that time. God forbid that they ever have it again.

The respectable at first were ashamed to accept charity and even sustenance. *Joe Grant* now recalls with a certain satisfaction the progress of a snobbish family in Gwynne Street as they learned to swallow their pride: 'The son, he wouldn't talk to us . . . then he lost his job . . . his pockets started to get loose and clothes got bad . . . and he'd start to say "How are you?"' Some lost their reason. Frank O'Brien, a wharfie aged fifty of Bosisto Street, was the devoted father of a young family. His hold on respectability was always precarious and as the Depression dragged on, his age increasingly reduced his chances of finding regular work. In May 1934 he killed his wife and three little children in their beds before taking his own life.

> There is evidence that O'Brien, who was a casual hand, was excessively worried over his inability to obtain employment which prevented him both from sleeping and eating and preyed upon his mind until he became morbid. The unfortunate part of the tragedy is that it might have been avoided if his circumstances had been made known to the Town Hall. The sustenance allowances, supplemented as they are by local contributions, are not large but sufficient to keep a family in food and necessaries. In this case O'Brien had told his friend Mr. G. Brommell last week that he had only 7s 3d to carry his family over the week and could not sleep because of the worry.[7]

At 3 p.m. on 10 July 1932 Mrs Fanny Conlon, the former secretary of the Richmond Ladies' Benevolent Society, opened the door to a young man (who seemed sincere and professed to discuss charity and church work'. It was cold and she asked him in. As they were talking she turned to the bookcase and the nice young man smashed her twice over the head with a rolling pin wrapped in brown paper. He was after the funds for the unemployed girls that she distributed every Monday. Mrs Conlon, with blood streaming down her face, ran out of the house for help and the attacker was apprehended by a neighbour. In court the nice young man was identified as Clarence Alexander Smith, an optician aged thirty-three.[8]

To make it more difficult, the respectable in work were often sternly moralistic towards anyone suspected of spending their dole on pleasure. *John Brown*'s wife 'used to get cross because the people next door were on the dole and they would still go to the pictures twice a week'. *Friedrich Smith* witnessed the Depression from behind the counter of a butcher shop. He remembers with anger the woman who came in with a hard luck story. The boss gave her food and groceries and five shillings for vegetables. That night *Friedrich* and his wife were sitting in the shilling seats at the cinema when he saw that same woman lead her family into the ls 6d seats. Another woman once refused to take some skinny lamb as a free feed and he exploded, 'Madam you're not hungry. During the First World War when my father was unemployed, I'd have given anything for a lump of meat like that—we lived on damn rabbits and fish and anything we could lay our hands on'. 'Bludging' was a terrible crime in the Australian working class. Yet even the very poor who were practical enough to accept charity felt ashamed. *Jean Fowler* was delighted with the clothes she got from the Toc H: 'a beautiful wrap-on skirt and beautiful cow skin shoes—I thought I was made'. But 'you had to get into things like that and no one tried harder than my mother and father to get a job'. And her memories of getting sustenance are still full of humiliation:

> It was really terrible standing waiting for things at the Town Hall. And your shoes would have nails sticking out of them—it was really horrible. All we had was veal and I wouldn't touch veal now. And I'd even have to come home and cook rings of onions and potatoes—make my own tea for the lot of them, because no one had started because they had nothing to start with. And we'd put it in butter and fry it.

The plight of the truly unrespectable like *Norman Stevens* was even worse. The economic slump affected lucrative crime as well and with his criminal record he stood last in the line for proper work.[9] Yet he still had four children and a wife to feed. One evening there was simply nothing in the house to eat. He went to a nearby sustenance baker and pleaded for a job. The baker relented and gave him firewood to stack:

It was getting dark so I worked as hard as I could to get as much as I could. He gave me two shillings and four pies. I run up the street to home and give the wife the two shillings and went out for a while. When I come back she said, 'These pies are rotten—we can't eat them'. One whiff and OH—knock you down . . .

I wouldn't have gone near the man again after he did that but I thought—he give me something and it may be a start and I thought I'd stick to this and stick like glue. So I go back—he runs stables and has the carts going and I thought I might get a job—there was plenty to be done. I think to be correct the Basic Wage at that time was £3 11s. And a fellow said to me, 'You're working too hard'. The idea was—they was single and was working for £2 11s and signing the book for £3 11s. Anyhow I stick to that and I kept going round. Now one day—and this is how prosperous it was for him—he said to me, 'I'm opening up another baker's opposite the Collingwood Technical School and I want the frost taken off the window so I can put a few loaves of bread in it. Do you know how to get this stuff off?' To be truthful at the time I didn't, so I went to a painter and asked. 'That's no trouble', he said; 'caustic soda will take it off, but be careful'. It was a little old pokey window and I had a rag and tied it on to the end of a broom handle and had a bucket of caustic soda. And I put my arm through and it was just scratching it and scratching it. And it was only a small window and I thought, 'God dammit, what if he comes now and sees it—I'd better get a move on'. Now I knew what I was doing—I'm quite clear on that—and I thought, 'here goes', and I pulled the rag off and put me fingers in it—desperation gives you power—and I was rubbing away. Then I finish and the blood was running out of me fingers—which is what I expected. Well God dammit—this would break your heart—I forgot what he give me that day and I went the next day and the wife had got a white sheet and tied it up and he came in gravy-eyed, old miserable man, and said to me: 'What's the matter with your hand?' 'I had a bit of bad luck, I burnt it with caustic soda.' 'Well you can't work for me like that.' Well I could have—you know—but I had to think of my family and think of things the right way—and I walked out that disgusted.

Now in spite of all this happening—this will tell you how tough things were—I went back to him. And he says, 'You're a pretty useful type of man', or words to that effect. I said, 'Thank you', and he says, 'Do you think you could get me a motor car?'

Norman, unlike most unskilled men, not only had a driving licence but also knew a lot about swanky saloon cars. The baker was building a house near Studley Park and needed a car that could climb steep hills. *Norman* did a deal with a city firm and got the baker a second-hand Nash tourer, and 'there was twenty-five lovely quid in it for me'. The car dealer, too, was impressed with *Norman*'s knowledge and cunning and gave him a job: 'All my life all I've had were my wits and strength—in all the days since I was born—I know that'.

The key to survival in the Depression was persistence. The unemployed had to be able to try and try again, day after day. And they had to be flexible. Skilled tradesmen like *Thelma Clark*'s husband learned to take any job going in their general field of work. *Harold Stephenson* was just out of his apprenticeship when the Depression struck him. The daily routine was to look up the paper but it was rarely necessary to know the full address for the crowd of hopefuls in the street soon gave it away. He quickly learnt to lie about his experience and capabilities. Once he claimed he could do metal polishing but he was so slow in his try-out that he failed; walking home later with one of the workmen he was told, 'I knew you weren't one of us by the way you talked'. Another time he even claimed he was a carpenter and in two hours made such a mess that he was sacked. The wages for those two hours, however, were better than nothing. The Depression taught that any job was better than no job. *Bertie Middleton*:

> During the Depression my father got me a job at Kenneth Wright's and I had to work on a sewing machine. I objected strongly to it as a young boy so I came home and said I'd stopped. He grabbed me by the scruff of the neck and sent me back again. When I came home the second time he said, 'You shove off and find a living yourself somehow'—I got the order of the boot.

And it taught toughness. *Bertie* again:

> Going through the Depression as I did—I would have been over the fence and stolen a pumpkin for something for my wife and kids if they needed it. I was brought up in an honest environment but I would never have hesitated. I never had to do it, thank goodness, but a lot of other people would have thought the same.[10]

But when people were forced to take any job they would tolerate the intolerable. *Muriel Thompson*:

> I had to get work. Another girl and I walked and walked and we finished up in South Melbourne and we went to Hoadley's. We did get one there but we got put off 'after a rush'. I finished up at the Union Can and that was supposed to be really tough, but I didn't know much about it. I finished up forelady there. I said, 'Have you got any vacancies?' 'No.' (They used to make tins and canisters—only a small place.) I evidently could talk then like I can now and I said, 'If you could see my shoes—I've walked here from Richmond. I've got to get work somewhere', and I took my shoe off and I definitely had a hole in my shoe. I was at the end of my tether and I practically prayed. My girlfriend didn't need it but she didn't say anything—she come from wealthy people. 'And I haven't even got my fare.' Well, the old grey-haired man said, 'I'll give you a couple of days a week and I'll put youse on'.

> We used to get morning tea break. We used to all be sitting in the lavvy—they didn't have a dining room and a fellow used to be sent into the girls' lavvy to tell us 'time's up'.

Muriel was forelady and in the union but she was still paid as a junior and was again obliged to hide in the toilet when the factory inspector came.

It helped, too, to be resourceful. *Mary Davis*'s father was a plasterer but he had always had a weakness for buying knick-knacks. When the building trade collapsed he took a stall at the Victoria Market and began buying up job lots. He and *Mary* made simple jewellery and he installed a watchmaker, who had become addicted to methylated spirits from blowing his lamp, in the pigeon loft where he repaired broken clocks and watches.

Alice Murphy's husband was a skilled tradesman who had to swallow his pride:

> My husband used to cut the kids' hair around our area and do things for them. And they used to be swimming in the river because they had nothing else to do—there was nothing else they *could* do. They used to go into the market and meet a market gardener and help him weighing in at the market and then he'd bring a cauliflower home for his mother and sometimes two shillings and think that was lovely.

Alice herself, as a top florist, was unemployed for two years. *Harold Stephenson* had luckily kept his newspaper stand in the city and when he did find a job his brother would stand in for him. A third brother had a morning stand starting at 5 a.m. and *Harold* would look after it when he went to get something to eat. When *Jean Fowler* lost her job at the rubber factory, leaving the family with nothing but sustenance, her brothers went panning for gold in the bush to reduce the numbers in Richmond: 'They'd rob beehives and pan for gold—little bottles of bits of gold—they never got anything but they'd be off up there so we could live'. Another time *Jean*'s brothers got hold of an old car with wheels stuffed with straw and she set off with them for Monbulk and the strawberry picking. *Jean* perched atop a ricketty pile of old furniture and the straw-stuffed wheels were going 'plonk, plonk, plonk'—they could have fallen off and been killed, 'but you don't think of these things'. Now she finds it, hard to believe that they were so poor that they set off without a toothbrush, let alone a change of clothes: 'We didn't realize that we had to have a change—we washed our underclothes out each morning'. In the city women would collect empty bottles and get sixpence a dozen from the Bottle-O as he did his rounds. *Muriel* would take the pram and sell her collection at the Marine Yards where the price was higher, and 'I'd pick up all the little bits of zinc and copper—that's another way we got a feed'.

As the unemployed battled and connived to keep body together so too had they to keep the soul. While not wishing to diminish the suffering of women, especially those with children, men not only lost their jobs they also lost their roles. At least the housewife still had a clear function and responsibilities. Men, especially those who found domestic duties threatening to their masculinity, were socially adrift: the family's suffering was in part their fault and many saw little chance of contributing. To make matters worse, in Richmond there was still casual work for women in food processing and both *Muriel Thompson* and *Jean Fowler* found temporary jobs while the men in their families were continuously out of work for years. *Muriel* even worked at the Rosella while she was still breast-feeding and would run home in her breaks to feed the baby. *Jean* would arrive home from work to find her father and brothers waiting for their tobacco money and for her to cook the evening meal. But such apparent male chauvinism was also a desperate attempt to salvage sexual pride and many women understood and tolerated it as that. As wives recall the Depression they tend to pity their husbands more than themselves: 'I think the working men noticed it more', says *Alice Murphy*, her euphemism speaking volumes. And when *Muriel* managed to scrounge a 'nice chop' for her husband in three pennyworth of scraps she was trying to shore up his shattered pride, as though he was still working on the wharves. Yet even in *Muriel* there was an element of condescension, for poverty and unemployment changed the balance of power between the sexes.

In the family on or below the poverty line it was the competence of the mother that determined the family's fate. However acute her anxiety as she waited to see how much of the pay packet or the dole would reach home after the pub, she was the affective head of the household. Men considered it a disgrace if their wives had to work, but amongst the very poor, women were often forced to take things into their own hands and take a job. When a man failed to provide, it was a sexual as well as a material failure. *Muriel*, *Jean Fowler* and *Margaret Taylor* were all forced at various stages in their marriages to take the initiative and earn, and *Muriel* and *Jean* both made and saved the money to buy the homes they now live in. Mass unemployment therefore thrust many patriarchal families back into the matriarchy of the very poor and reinforced the association between success and male dominance and failure and female dominance. Much unemployment relief bypassed husbands and was conducted directly through wives. This was in part to avoid the danger of alcohol-dependent husbands using sustenance to drink but it also was a recognition that women bore the real burden of family care and protection. Nearly all the begging letters in the Richmond Council's archives are written by women and the Mayoress' Unemployment Relief Committee was administered by women who assessed the needs of wives and their dependants without consulting the husbands. The U.W.M.'s demand in August 1930 that all women be taken off the investigating committees was in part a cry of men robbed of their manhood. Hence, when mothers like *Muriel* gave their husbands the only chop or the solitary egg, they bought marital power, nurturing their men as one of the children. But the Depression also forced change upon the balance of the sexes among the secure and successful. As a married couple climbed out of acute poverty the acquisition of a bank account, then a mortgage, transferred power from the wife to the husband; but the *Kanes*, like many house-owning couples, were forced by the husband's unemployment to transfer the title of the house from the husband's to the wife's name as a protection against bankruptcy. Before the Depression all house titles in Mary Street were in the husband's name; by World War II titles were commonly in joint names.[11]

Still, to *Joe Grant* as a young bachelor it seemed that the women had the worst of it:

> The women had a hard time. You were scheming all day . . . from the time he come home you was worried . . . 'What'll I give him for lunch?'—you'd hear that sentence a dozen times day. You'd send one of the kids with a note to get a loaf of bread and pay tomorrow and the kid would come back: 'Mummy, he says you can't have it because you haven't paid for the last lot'—then she'd be worried—how could she get him his lunch for tomorrow?

There is no doubt that many women suffered acute stress during the Depression even though in retrospect many now deny it. *Phyllis Smith* is not uncommon in her boast that 'women in her day' never suffered nervous breakdowns 'like they do today' even though 'they had to put up with things that were far harder'. But Dr *Brendan Ryan* doing his house calls in Richmond during the Depression saw many once disciplined homes where beds were still unmade by mid-day and the housewife had succumbed to despair. And there was the other extreme. Even when the family was destitute, a mother could still keep spotless what little they had. Cleanliness was the last defence against total humiliation, obsessional neurosis the respectable poor woman's path to madness. The family's diminishing wardrobe was washed, starched and ironed to perfection. Floors, tables, front verandas, even front paths were scrubbed white, 'so that you could eat ice cream off it', *Lilian Campbell* recalls; 'that's all they had to do'. *Muriel* and *Jean* have a rich catalogue of housework neurotics from among their neighbours in South Richmond:

> *Jean*: You'd be frightened to go in sometimes—they'd get the brush and if the kids put anything on the floor they'd be right behind you with it.
> *Muriel*: One of my friends' husband got nearly driven away from the house; he said: 'I've got to take my shoes off before I go into the house'.
> *Jean*: There was a woman up here—she was Catholic and had about seven kids and she wouldn't allow them inside—they were sleeping outside in a

> shed. She was never out of her pregnant clothes but the priest reckoned she was the best-dressed woman in the church.
> *Muriel*: I've been into houses and you've never seen such terrible lino and yet in between, where there was a broken bit of lino, it was as white as the living snow—she got on her knees—I was amazed—I don't know that I could be bothered with that.

Jean noticed too, with satisfaction, that many of the rich for whom she did housework were 'dirty people'—cleanliness as a means to self-respect was at least free. But under great stress it could get out of control. *Isabel Williams* remembers one young mother:

> She had three young children and she got pleurisy: 'Oh, I can't let them go to school dirty'; and she got up and was washing while the doctor came. 'You should be in bed.' 'Oh, I've got to keep the kids clean.' Next thing she was dead. There was nothing for those things in those days.

In contrast, unemployed men and youths faced days that flowed into weeks and into years of nothing to do. The cunning and resourceful occupied themselves with 'scheming'—lurks for odd jobs, free firewood, handouts, spoiled food. Yet the gravest danger to the unemployed remained chronic depression and the normal means of solace were beyond their pocket. Even sex suffered. There are hints that many married couples saw little alternative to abstinence and many a marriage was delayed or abandoned for ever. Of course there were prostitutes but they too cost money. Alcohol consumption fell by 25 per cent in 1930–31 and the Strang Brothers of the Royal Hotel ('Noted Richmond Footballers') resorted to advertising Richmond Pilsener at a shilling a bottle as a health drink 'Rich in Vitamines and Yeast'. Many men too poor to drink kept up the pub habit none the less, congregating outside their favourite local, as Jim Cairns observed them, savouring the smell. Those on sustenance who continued to drink imperilled their families; but it was vital for men to maintain their social networks and the pubs were at the heart of them. Those who stuck to their mates during the Depression, schemed and went job-hunting together, swam in the river, and kicked footballs about in the open spaces, found great comfort in troubles shared. *Harold Stephenson* and his mates—'not a "mob" because we didn't go looking for fights'—pooled their sixpences and played billiards for ls 6d or went dancing in the Memorial Hall. They threw birthday parties, 'if the house was big enough'; and 'if there was any nonsense we threw them out'. They even formed a social club with fifty members so that they could hire a hall and run dances and organize picnics to Warrandyte. *Harold* also did a lot of reading—1 read any book I could get hold of'; but he was especially fond of P. C. Wren, Edgar Rice Burroughs, Victor Hugo and Rider Haggard. There has always been a tradition of artisan intellectuals in the industrial working class (*Ted Sullivan* fitted into his busy life the time to read *Das Kapital* and Gibbon's *Decline and Fall)* and the Depression boosted working-class reading. Attendances in Richmond's two municipal libraries in 1933 were double those of 1927 and attendances and borrowings remained high into prosperity with World War II.[12]

All paid entertainment, with the exception of football, was hit by the slump. Talking pictures came to Melbourne in 1929 but even that novelty could not prevent the Hoyts chain of cinemas—the largest in the country—losing £10 000 in 1930 and having to pay its dividend out of reserves. In live theatre J. C. Williamson's had to do likewise; even Luna Park finished 1930 in the red. The host of unemployed musicians and actors found some work, however, in a brand-new mode of public entertainment that grew out of the Depression—community singing. In Richmond the struggling shopkeepers of Swan Street and Bridge Road formed themselves into Traders' Associations. instituted sale days and organized community singing to raise morale and lower consumer resistance. At the Globe Theatre singers, actors. comedians and musicians toiled often to little avail: 'It was a bright and sunny day full of the joy of Spring, yet the balcony sang "All the World is Sad and Dreary"—just like that; but when the lights went out the whole gathering rose to the occasion and sang "Moonlight and Roses"'. Community singing became one of the institutions of Richmond life and still occurs fortnightly in the Richmond Town Hall.[13]

There was one great joy in Richmond in those black years—football. To *Joe Grant* 'the most important thing in the social life was the footy'; men might give up beer and tobacco but they could never give up the Tigers. The Depression years are considered by many as the most illustrious in the Tigers' history: they won three premierships and these were the best years in the playing careers of Jack ('Skinny') Titus and Jack ('Captain Blood') Dyer. Dyer remembers the Depression teams as 'desperate men' and the seconds full of ageing players pushing themselves to stay in the team long after their bodies ceased to cope. Football was the only income for many players' families and an injury meant no money. Jack Titus is reputed to hold the record for the longest time in a team without injury. Dyer played for nineteen years and was idolized in Richmond; when he married in 1939 the crowd of well-wishers could not be accommodated even in the vastness of St Ignatius'. One of Richmond's Depression premierships was in the Jubilee Year of the club, 1934. 'Titus the Great' kicked six goals five and the crowd, which had been waiting since 7 a.m., were dazzled by their Tigers' performance in 'the vital third quarter' when 'South Melbourne stood leaden-footed as though thunderstruck, while Richmond, playing with electrifying dash and system, flashed the ball from man to man with bewildering ease'.[14]

Such triumphs were a brief consolation for the personal and social damage inflicted by the Depression. While major crime including homicide showed little change, petty crime, vandalism and juvenile delinquency flourished alarmingly. With so little cash about—to *Joe Grant* it seemed that 'the mainstay of the economy was the pensioner'—the temptation to deal in sly grog and illegal gambling was strong. By 1937 and 1938 it had become a way of life and almost every week a Richmond publican was before the Court for trading after hours; many more were amateurs selling a few bottles from home or from under the counter of a shop. Unemployment put a lot of otherwise decent people on the wrong side of the law and weakened the authority of the law in the eyes of their impressionable young. *Harold Stephenson* is anxious to distinguish his gang of mates from 'the mobs', because by 1933 the Richmond pushes had turned nasty. The 'Reserve Push and Basher Gang' terrorized central Richmond; they vandalized all public amenities and smashed shops and hotels. They assaulted children and attacked adults who refused to hand over money or cigarettes. They threatened to damage the homes of, and 'deal with' anyone who reported them to the police. By 1938 Mayor Jimmy Loughnan announced that the Council had decided it was futile to repair any of the damage to the public facilities—Richmond by the end of the Depression was laid waste.[15]

But what happened to more constructive anger? Many victims of the Depression seem remarkable for their passivity. The vast majority, including most loyal Labor voters, accepted the Depression as a natural calamity, an act of God. *Margaret Taylor* does not know who or what to blame: 'It just happened and happened terribly'. Working-class history is inevitably dominated by the record left behind of political and industrial activists. The Left has too often been taken as a spokesman for the entire working class, their passionate and intelligent response to the Depression seen as normal. Intellectually the Left found it easier to cope with the crisis: all this suffering did have a purpose if it signalled the collapse of the capitalist system. Working-class conservatives could draw no such comfort; yet the *Wilson* sisters, *Monica Rinoldi*, *Isabel Williams*, *Bertie Middleton* and *Thomas Beauchamp* went through it without missing an ideological beat. Sociological searches for a distinct Depression Generation have yielded little.[16] Perhaps we are asking the wrong questions if we are looking for evidence of significant ideological change as a consequence of mass unemployment. To some extent Australian intellectuals and social critics have been projecting a model of themselves on to the expected behaviour of the working class. Intellectual life in this country since World War II has been profoundly influenced by a generation of middle-class radicals who were shocked as idealistic adolescents by the Depression and who were matured by the subsequent war.

They were a world apart from victims of the Depression such as *Joe Grant*, who feels the same about the Labor Party as he does about his beloved Tigers: it is his team and he wants to see them win. 'Labor' is what you were as a Richmondite; the others were 'bloody snobs': 'He could be the best bloke in the world but to you he was a bloody snob; and if you mentioned you was a Liberal they'd pick a blue with you in a minute'. If his analysis seems crude about working-class conservatives, it is essentially accurate. The working-class conservative was making a gesture of social superiority, a definition of identity as being above and apart from the scum all around him. *Isabel Williams* has mellowed with age and is now shocked at a letter she once wrote to the Richmond Council asking them to clear the footpath in front of her aunt's boarding house of the drunks and dead-beats who urinated in the gutter.[17] The working-class conservative did not expect his team to do anything directly for him; just belonging to the team made him feel better. It is with pride that the *Wilsons* and *Monica Rinoldi* announce that 'we're Liberal, you know'. But many Labor voters like *Joe Grant* did not expect their team to do anything for them either. *Joe*, like *Jean Fowler*, distrusts most politicians, including Labor ones: 'most politicians and councillors were only in it for what they could get out of it'. *Joe* dislikes Bob Hawke for his arrogance; he admired Scullin because he was 'genuine' and 'placid'—'he didn't force himself upon you like most of them'. But *Joe is* not at all critical of governments and councils in the Depression. He has a primitive sense of equity: when he worked during the war he was paying only Is 6d tax; therefore the government had no money and therefore people like himself could not expect anything in return. You were 'glad to get anything' and the sustenance was enough 'in the circumstances because the Government had no money'. And *Joe* doesn't blame 'the system' for the Depression: 'governments don't make Depressions': it is the fault of greedy men and he warns today of trade unions who push wages too high and are 'out to destroy the monetary system'.

The Depression only succeeded in radicalizing people when the radical critique fell on already fertile ground. *Nellie Roberts* was questioning everything:

> For somebody of my age group I would never go through that again . . . I couldn't bear to think of that happening to somebody else. But it will never happen again because it was at that time that Communism reared its head. You had your groups of Communists at pretty well every street corner on Friday night and I don't think that even the most rigid capitalistic system would allow that ever to happen again. The Communist Party was opening up a new vista. It was promising many things and one of the most prominent I remember was Free Love. I wasn't actually in the Party but I went along to all the meetings and for those people older than myself it was opening up a promise—it was fascinating people. After World War II all our social services went ahead and they've gone on even more with the Whitlam government. When I hear young people talking about how bad things are, I think to

> myself: 'You've got no idea of what it was like'. And if it was ever as bad as that again I think that Communism would sweep the world. At that time we knew the money was there—foreign capital—and it was just withdrawn, held, and people were allowed to suffer like that.

Despite the work of the U.W.M. in Richmond the Communist Party made little impact during the 1930s. It was to enjoy a brief interlude of popularity during the war, but most people distrusted it as 'foreign' and 'immoral'.

Yet most agree that there was something they all learned from the Depression, right and left alike: that you had to look after yourself. However kind the neighbours and shopkeepers, you were alone: 'It did mean that everyone had to battle for themselves', says *Nellie*; 'I learnt to look after myself', says *Joe*. Unemployment only intensified the need in conservatives to put as much distance between their new selves and their working-class past as possible. It was a need that Robert Menzies was to exploit brilliantly in the 1950s. And for the very poor, who had been 'born into it', the Depression was not that much worse than what they had already known. They had no expectations for themselves; they only hoped to survive. Politics was not there to change life; it was just about 'teams'. And *Joe Grant*, asked now whether people fought the Depression:

> Not as much as you think they would—looking back now. As I said, everyone was on the move, everyone was on the look-out for a racket, everyone was proud if he had a scheme on somewhere—and he'd skite and boast about it.

Marriage and Childbirth

The Depression could not have come at a worse time for this Richmond generation, for it hit them just as they were marrying and commencing their childbearing. The testing years of early marriage and the crisis of parenthood had to be endured amidst insecurity and deprivation; and love was an inevitable casualty of life on the dole. Engagements were broken off and marriages delayed; some missed the romantic boat altogether as their youth was swallowed up by the crisis. To *Joe Grant* 'the saddest thing I seen in the Depression was the girls shuffling down the street with their high heels worn right down, with laddered stockings and clothes torn ragged'. At the 1961 Census a Depression generation of people who had never married was still discernible. The birth-rate too fell noticeably, but this was part of a long-term decline that had worried politicians and churchmen since the 1900s. In fact the 1929 Royal Commission into Child Endowment had found to its chagrin that it was prosperity more than poverty that was inciting couples to limit their families. None the less, the

Depression did cause many to delay childbearing: by 1937–38 27 per cent of those who had been married five years had not had a child but by 1959–60 the number would be down to 17 per cent.[18]

Of course many took the plunge. *Thelma Clark*'s fiancé lost his job a couple of weeks before their wedding day; but 'I thought we're not going to put the wedding off and we had the breakfast at home'. Yet, however accustomed to poverty they might have been, it was still important to make the wedding something special. *Jean Fowler*'s only worry was that 'I couldn't get a decent dress or anything'. Out of her wages of thirty shillings at a rubber factory she gave her mother a pound, leaving only ten shillings for herself. Yet somehow she saved enough to have a long dress made: I wanted to look like Clara Bow—white dress and cowl neck. I look at it now and think, 'Oh my God—nothing like Clara Bow. Oh, she was beautiful'. *Phyllis Smith* married her *George* at nineteen despite the opposition of her family. *George* had lost an eye in a childhood accident and with a ruthless practicality born of poverty the family argued that if he lost the other eye she would have to support him: 'This, annoyed me a little bit because I loved him very much and I wanted to get married—I wasn't happy at home because of the drinking and all that'. So in 1931 they had a Depression wedding at St Stephen's:

> I thought I can't afford a big wedding because times weren't good, so I made a brown satin dress and I had autumn flowers and gloves matching and was just married in ordinary clothes. My brothers were all rather cross with me but my sister-in-law's dress was a bit short and I didn't want to be married in somebody else's wedding dress. So I just got married in my own. I thought, 'Oh blow them—if they can't all put together and give their only sister a wedding, well I'll just get married'. They all came to the wedding, of course, and it was very nice. We didn't have a reception or anything like that because it came at a bad timemy parents had just separated and my mother had just got a job working for an old lady who was a diabetic who had a leg cut off and she only lived another nine months. Of course, once I was married my mum came and lived with me and I nursed her for eleven and a half years until she died. And *George*'s father lived with me for thirty-three years.

Harold Stephenson was more cautious. He waited until he had a job and £200 in the bank before getting married, but he and *Evelyn* did it in style with a proper reception and an orchestra. They ordered no beer, 'because we thought it might get wild', but *Harold*'s younger brother 'liked beer so went and got a bottle for each couple and then he decided the orchestra wasn't lively enough so started to get them drunk'. The catering cost *Harold* £20, the orchestra £1 a player and the vicar five guineas. Then the lucky couple set off for their honeymoon in a guest-house at Point Lonsdale.

Working-class marriage brought a drastic reduction in a couple's income. *As Harold* recalls, 'it was a disgrace' to have a working wife: 'it's alright now but when you married in our day you lived happily ever after—you didn't tell them about the struggles you were going through'. As *Ruby Kane* says, 'It was very low to go out to work' before World War II, yet the Depression forced many to compromise their standards. To *Monica Rinoldi*, 'you'd have done anything then—ploughed fields'—and Muriel *Thompson* was glad of any work 'on the fruit' at the Rosella. Unemployment forced some married women to take initiatives that were unthinkable in prosperity: they found work and took over negotiations for relief. Marital tensions were inevitable and often endured for the rest of their lives together. *Margaret Taylor*:

> The whole trouble was that the men got so used to you living on nothing that they expected you to live on nothing for ever. The men didn't go without like the women—or very few of them. They still smoked and still had their drinks and poor Mum could just manage as best she could. And you got very little in the way of new clothing. There was [resentment] but what could you do—there was no work about for women. The men were always the wage-earners and they were considered to be the head. Just as well that's changed a lot—though I'm not sure that they're any better off.

Ruby Kane had married in 1923 with good prospects and they moved into their own home. Within four years her husband had lost his job as a travelling salesman and he was in and out of work until the outbreak of war when he put his age back from forty-five to thirty-seven and was accepted into the Army. Their only son had left school by the time the *Kanes* were secure again and Ruby was to have both her husband and only child serving in the same war. The Army was the salvation of her husband and somehow their marriage survived. *Phyllis Smith*, too, had but a short time of married bliss:

> *George* had been working at Henry Berry's the tea merchants and he smashed his hand and that meant he couldn't work. A month after when he went back to work they found they could do without him. Then we were in real trouble. I was pregnant and my job had gone too. We'd taken a place in Buckingham Street, but you had to pay rent for that so his father suggested that we come back to the old home.
>
> I can remember the very day *George* lost his job—he didn't even have the courage to come home and tell me. He went to his father first and they both came round and that backed him up. He just said, 'I went back to work and they don't want me. They gave me a very wonderful reference but the job's gone and the Depression's on'.

George was unemployed for five years and *Phyllis* bore their two children before they were secure again.

The expected joys of marriage—sex and babies—easily soured with life on the dole. Poverty restricted people's freedom of choice about their sexual relations and the number of children they could afford to have. For the respectable, expecially women, sex outside marriage was impossible. *Emma Murphy* laughs now that 'there wasn't much else to do than get married then—not like living together like they do today'. Sex inside marriage became almost impossible too. Good Catholics obviously had a conscientious objection to contraception but so also did some Protestants. Above all, many were ignorant. *Phyllis*, like many girls, could think only of Phyllis getting married and having babies—'I can remember dressing up the doll in the baby's clothes I'd made and try to imagine what it would look like before it was born'—yet even she realized that they had to wait for better times. But she was the last baby in the family and the only girl to survive into maturity: 'Mum didn't talk about babies—they just sort of materialized out of the blue—and she had all boys so with a girl she was a bit lost'. So:

> This was the time of Dr Marie Stopes and being a very modest and stupid girl I sent away for one of these pessaries and I didn't realize it had to be fitted to be right inside. And here I am preventing for four months. vomiting and nauseous and my old maiden auntie said, '*Phyll*, I think you're pregnant'. 'Oh no, auntie, I couldn't be pregnant—I'm using one of Dr Marie Stopes' pessaries.' But sure enough I was.

Margaret Taylor too had to find out the facts of life for herself—her mother died before she married—and similarly turned to the writings of Marie Stopes. *Phyllis*'s brother *Friedrich*, however, received a practical , sex education from his father; and married male friends took advantage of his lack of embarrassment to ask him to purchase condoms for them. Condoms, by far the most reliable of the mechanical methods available at the time, were expensive at sixpence each and a passionate couple could spend as much on contraception a week as they might on meat. The resourceful soon learnt to wash them out and use them again. As *Friedrich* attests, most people became pregnant while trying to find out which method of contraception suited them. Some threw all caution to the winds. *Nellie Roberts*'s mother was appalled by an unemployed couple nearby who cheerfully had baby after baby during the Depression because 'they had nothing else to do'. Those who kept their sexual relationship alive during the worst unemployment preserved a priceless emotional resource; but too often poverty and sex were bad for each other. The obsessional disapproval of current sexual behaviour, especially of the young, revealed by many of these old people suggests that they have experienced little sexual happiness. Yet few will talk about it openly. *Bill Shannon*, a younger man, observed of his parents' generation: 'Sex caused a lot of family breakdown in marriages any normal man has to have a certain amount, they've got to let off steam somehow—only the trouble was they'd let off some steam and there'd be another kid on the way'. Moreover, couples had little privacy. *Lilian Campbell* maintains that the popularity of the Sunday School in workingclass communities sprang in part from the parents' need to have a little privacy together one m orning a week. There was also a lack of privacy from the neighbours. Neighbours could listen in through party walls and sexual peccadilloes were widely broadcast around the suburb. *Bill Shannon* recalls one woman whose husband, unbeknown to herself, was keeping a mistress, even though an alcoholic woman neighbour on her way back from the pub would chant 'Oh you cold-arsed bitch' outside the poor woman's door. Sexual ignorance and fear of unwanted pregnancy presented immense hurdles to marital happiness. *Jean Fowler* and *Muriel Thompson* reflect on the past and the present:

> *Jean*: There's nothing nice about a woman these days—they don't care, they just undress themselves and I think that's vile—that was in the bedroom, that was between you and your husband.
> *Muriel*: I think we were born in the wrong year, *Jean*—they seem to be enjoying it now. Mind you, I do think we had it a bit hard. I mean you were never allowed to talk about that sort of thing at the table—you had to find out everything from everybody else. I think we were a bit backward. I knew nothing. My mother and father were so prudish.
> *Jean*: Neither did I. I was fourteen before I knew anything like that. In fact my mother said to my sister. 'You must tell her'. 'Tell me what?' 'Oh, you'll find out some day.' Well, that sort of thing you come to know the wrong way. A girl once put me up to use a vile thing to a boy when I didn't know what it meant.
> *Muriel*: I don't like the swearing—there's too much swearing going on. But I think that things you find out—well what you don't know you don't miss. I walked straight into it, never knowing a thing and it was good. If I'd known I mightn't have walked into it—but I got a surprise!

As sexual life suffered so also did many couples fear having the children they wanted. *Harold Stephenson* for the rest of his life was haunted by the Depression:

> During the war we had no children at the time and the boss said, Why don't you have a child?' 'Oh. I'm not secure enough. I've been thrown out on my neck so many times I'm not game enough to have a child. We couldn't support it. I don't want to drag a child up the way I've battled up.' So he says, 'You're all right'. I says, 'I've heard that before'.
> We were married twelve months before we had a child and I always didn't feel secure that I wasn't in a constant job—I always felt there'd be a day when I'd be put off.

Harold in fact was to remain in work until he retired, but he and Evelyn only had a daughter. *Muriel Thompson* adores children but bore only two girls—both during the Depression; in later life when her husband found secure work in the P.M.G. she fostered another girl, so she considers herself to have three daughters.

The sacrifice of desired motherhood was painful for many women. For most working-class women motherhood was the most rewarding and creative period of their lives. Childbirth is a great human leveller. Even if parents later fail to raise a healthy and happy child, a desired birth done well is an accomplishment that transcends class and race. Most work for working-class women was ill-paid, exhausting and unbelievably tedious, so marriage and motherhood offered relative freedom and real achievement. *Muriel* looks back on years of acute poverty: 'We seemed to be happy didn't we; our kids made us happy because we sent them to High School'; and she unwittingly reveals how important it was to enable your children to escape from working-class life. *Jean Fowler* agrees: 'People today say, "I'll be glad when the kids go back to school", but I never used to be, because I used to take them out to the gardens and things'. *Jean* found motherhood utterly absorbing:

> You looked to your children for pleasure. I didn't look outside my kids—I lived for them. I was here all the time when they come home—I didn't believe in going out. I never went out to work because I could never let them come home to the place empty. Even when *Bob* was going to university I always stayed home. He would swot in the sleepout and I'd stay home until he went out.

Margaret Taylor was a skilled white-collar worker but she found greater satisfaction and freedom in motherhood: 'I was quite happy to look after the kids and the only entertainment we had was to take the kids for a walk down the beach—with an apple cut in half—and they thought they had a lovely day'. The one mother interviewed who did find early motherhood isolating and frustrating was *Alice Murphy*, but she had left an interesting and responsible job as the manager of a Collins Street florist shop:

> I remember after *Mary* was born I wondered what had hit me. I suppose being thirty I'd been around a long time ['Having a ball', her sister *Emma* adds]. I was in the city and had a lovely send-off, a big do, getting married and all that business. Then you find yourself home and it is so humdrum and you've lost all contact. I used to sit in the kitchen and try to feed *Mary* and it would take me about an hour to try and feed her—which I didn't because I wasn't as clever as *Emma* with the milk—I had half and half which is ridiculous and used to wear me down. But all I'd be waiting for was my mother until I could hear her coming down the side way.

Alice came to terms with motherhood, became deeply involved in school parent committees and 'thoroughly enjoyed their childhood' but it had taken time.

If the achievement of childbirth transcends class, medical care certainly does not. When this generation commenced childbearing the transition from home births to hospital births was still in progress and the seeking of medical and hospital services presented most working-class women with their first major confrontation, since leaving school, with institutions shaped and administered by middle-class professionals. The working-class woman had to choose between home, an expensive and adequate private hospital or a cheap and often nasty private one, and of course between the large public hospitals. *Muriel* had both babies at home attended by Richmond doctors and her blind mother who was a superb natural mid-wife. She had a bad time with both babies but they all survived. And when the time came to pay the doctor he said, 'Take it Mrs *Thompson* and go buy the child a set of clothes—those over in Toorak will pay for what can't be paid here'. 'That's wonderful', she replied. *Muriel* was lucky in her mother's support; many women are still angry that their mothers let them go into childbirth in utter ignorance. *Lilian Campbell*'s mother had had five children before she was twenty-seven but when *Lilian*'s time came

> My water broke on the Thursday and I was putting Mum's washing out on the line and the water running down—my mother didn't tell me. And I went into labour on Friday night and I was in labour until mid-day Saturday and my mother didn't tell me I was going to give birth. It's stupid. I didn't know anything and that's why I believe in education now.

Thelma Clark's mother did not even tell her older children when she was pregnant; all that *Thelma* knew was that her father came out of their bed-room and announced, 'You've got a new little sister'. *Thelma* did not learn the facts of life until she went to work in a factory, 'and by gee I found out in the horriblest way—my girlfriend and I we just thought that that line down the stomach just opened up'. Ignorance and fear condemned many women to appalling experiences, their only salvation being the readiness of doctors to offer pain relief Hospital births offered chloroform and self-administered ether and doctors even took the considerable risk of using chloroform in home births.

There was no doubt that it was medically safer to have babies in hospital but many women, especially working-class women, feared the discipline and indifference of the public hospitals. The public hospitals might send home a healthy baby and a rested mother, but as social institutions they were organized to break the will of the patients.[19] *Lilian Campbell*, *Phyllis Smith* and *Emma Murphy* all had one home birth and one hospital birth and their stories reveal the medical and social consequences of being a workingclass mother. *Emma* had her son at home and had suffered a severe postpartum haemorrhage. She decided that she would not go through that again and went up to the Women's Hospital:

> I was in there twelve days and I never sighted a visitor because they weren't allowed. When I came out my mother and aunt came up for me and they said they had never seen such a beautiful baby handed to them so I had my reward in the end. My husband could only come up to the office and give me maybe a little luxury like a chocolate and on one day he brought our son up, a two-year-old, and the sister took a liking to him down in the office where my husband left the stuff and she said, 'Would you like to come up and see your mother?' and she brought him up by the hand and, Oh dear, it was heartbreaking. He got to the door and then tore away and ran back so I thought afterward you're better off not seeing the little bloke. But I was well and good when I came home from that—different to the other one.

Lilian's first baby was born at home thirty days premature. Her daughter was placed in a bassinet between two heaters and the midwife came daily for ten days. The midwife's bill came to £2 10s out of *Lilian*'s £5 Baby Bonus and with the balance she bought a pram. With a premature first baby she was required to have the second in the Women's where 'the bones were like boomerangs in the fish and the tapioca pudding was like golf balls'. As she observed, working-class patients 'got a pretty rotten time in those days'. *Phyllis* was nineteen with a husband on the dole when she went into labour and took a tram to the Queen Victoria Hospital. It proved to be a long and difficult birth:

> It was dreadful because it had been a very bad confinement and apparently there was something wrong with her—she was jaundiced and they had to operate on her nose. When I went out into the ward, my sister-in-law, whose baby was born two days later than mine, she was in the same ward and holding up a beautiful little blonde baby and I still hadn't seen mine. I used to cry at night and think, 'She's dead but they won't tell me'. Of course she was in a humidicrib and wasn't dead at all. Finally I heard a tap and there's my husband looking through a window—he couldn't bear it any longer. Finally he was allowed to come in and I remember crying and saying, 'Our baby's dead because I haven't seen her'. He said, 'It's not true. She's all right—she's had a nose operation and I've seen her'. Then they brought my baby to me and she was like a little Chinese—long black curls, and I said, 'This can't be my baby'. However, she was my baby all right and they kept me in there almost a week longer to get her well.

Phyllis decided to have her second at home and Dr *Brendan Ryan* presided over a birth so quick that she had to be slowed down—'you could smell the chloroform out in the street'. She haemorrhaged, but this birth was 'much happier'. However, she then decided that two children 'was enough'.

To her lifelong regret *Ruby Kane* refused to go to the Women's because it was 'degrading': 'If you went to the Women's Hospital in those days there was something queer, something wrong, because of the abortions and all that, and the poverty'. They could not afford the fees at the Mercy Hospital or St Vincent's so she booked into one of the small private establishments run by midwives in Richmond:[20]

> It was a slaughterhouse. She was a great big horse—she should have been a horse doctor. See in these days they don't let them suffer- -they don't! I walked the floor all night in agony. Poor old *Fred*—God love him—he came up and saw me in this intense agony, walking up and down in that room on my own. He said, 'I can't sit here and watch you'. I said, 'Go home', and he went to the pub and got full. He couldn't stand me. I was thirty-six hours in labour. I was almost unconscious when the doctor came and gave me an anaesthetic and took the baby away because he was a whopper. When I came to he said, 'you've got to be quiet—you've got stitches there'. I didn't know anything.

Such private hospitals were also notorious as hives of infection, and some even as covers for illegal abortions.

The Commonwealth Baby Bonus helped increase the incidence of doctors attending. births: in 1913 13.2 per cent of births were supervised by doctors and by 1926 the percentage had risen to 79.3.[21] Postnatal medical care was still neglected for many working-class women, however, as *Lilian* recalls: 'They'd neglect themselves—birth, birth, birth until their prolapses would be down between their knees before they'd get medical helpembarrassment more than anything'. Women spent years with their legs swathed in bandages concealing untreatable ulcers from varicose veins and at the Richmond Dispensary and Dr Singleton's clinic in Collingwood a day a week was set aside just for dressing ulcerated legs. (Many men suffered varicose veins as well from excessive standing at work.) And when women did seek medical care they found themselves treated like imbeciles incapable of making decisions about their own bodies. *Lilian* sought help for menstrual irregularities after the birth of her second baby, was put into a bed in the Women's, suddenly given an anaesthetic despite no warning that she was to have surgery, and awoke to find herself sterilized. Luckily she had already decided not to have any more children.

These young working-class mothers then faced getting their babies through the most hazardous year of early life. Even though 'White' Australia and New Zealand had the lowest infant mortality rates in the world by 1926, the working-class baby was still at greater risk than the middle-class baby and the Depression increased the dangers. In 1929 infant mortality in Richmond rose to 78.01 per thousand, the highest in the State. For the next four years it fluctuated between the high sixties and low fifties and did not return to being under fifty per thousand until 1934. In the worst years the infant death-rate was pushed up by an increase in prematurity—a known correlate of low socio-economic status. The Richmond Health Officer, Dr Haynes, had no doubt that the 1929 figures were 'largely' due to 'maternal factors': 'possibly congenital disease, lack of sufficient nourishment, prenatal care and constitutional weakness in the mother'. The birth-rate fell a little in Richmond: in 1929 it was 16.47 per thousand and in 1933 it was 14.74. Infectious disease, however, did not show a close relationship to economic events—the ecological flux of bacteria and viruses was no longer so closely tied to living conditions—and 1933 recorded the lowest incidence of infectious disease in Richmond for many years.[22]

The authorities and the medical profession were united in their belief that the Baby Health Centres were vital to the preservation of infant life. Yet one of the unkindest cuts in the Premiers' Plan was the reduction from £125 to £100 in the Public Health Department's grants to the centres. The Baby Health Centres provided free milk to the destitute and only a special grant of £400 from the Richmond Council maintained the free milk supply for children under two. In 1934 only eight of the 1507 babies who attended the Richmond Health Centres died.[23]

Women were less united than the middle-class experts, however, in their support of the centres. New mothers without nearby relatives to help them cope often deeply appreciated the sisters' instruction, but there was still resistance to these new notions, especially from grandmothers: 'What do you want to go there for? They don't know as much as we do—they've never had babies', *Ruby Kane* was told. Working-class matriarchs quite rightly saw the centres as an attack on their maternal competence, and in a society where working-class women were allowed little chance of expertise at anything, their mothers' wisdom was jealously guarded. The Health Centres were excellent for teaching hygiene and safe artificial feeding, and were essential for monitoring the growth and development of children. And although always intended as well baby clinics, their sisters were often the first to detect serious illness and to assist parents to find adequate medical help. But those grandmothers who knew how to breast-feed on demand were absolutely right about the sisters' too frequent ignorance of successful breast-feeding; and breast-feeding saved many more babies from dying of gastro-enteritis than did any Health Centre. The Health Centres certainly believed that breast is best, but most mothers who fed according to the sisters' instructions seemed to run out of milk. The Health Centres, from inception the agents of 'national efficiency', had become the mouthpieces of medical systematizers like Dr Truby King.[24] Too often staffed with nursing sisters addicted to bossiness and possessed of an unerring knack of making young mothers feel guilty, they insisted that babies be fed fourhourly on the dot and *never* at night lest that breed 'bad habits'; that babies should be left to cry because it was 'good for their lungs'; that 'excessive' physical affection overstimulated infant nervous systems. Few women have the milk supply to hold up under such infrequent suckling, especially if their own diet is marginal through poverty. Few parents have the hardness of heart to sleep through hours of hungry despair: 'I used to go to work with my little bloke's yells ringing in my ears', one father recalls. *Nellie Roberts* was one young mother who knew instinctively that the sisters were wrong and was lucky to find support in an elderly doctor who said: 'What would you do if you woke in the night hungry?' *Lilian Campbell*, with her premature 'skinny little arrangement', attended the Health Centre with a girlfriend, but she never seemed to get it right: one week the baby put on too much; the next week too little. She gave up and listened to her mother instead. For too many women the weekly visit to the Health Centre ended in tears. Ironically, it was often the most conscientious new mothers, anxious to be thoroughly modern, who read the medical sympathizers' books and slavishly followed the sisters' instructions, only to find early motherhood a nightmare of guilt and exhaustion.

Of course many shrewd old doctors and humane nursing sisters held out against the new authoritarianism, but the 1930s saw the beginning of the end of the easy breast-feeding in this country. Necessity and the innate conservatism of the working-class, however, saved many of the babies of the unemployed. In fact a recent study of average body weights of Australian babies in 1933, 1964 and 1980, shows little difference in weight at six months between 1933 and 1980. By contrast in 1964, at the height of the artificial feeding and 'fat is bonny' fashion, the average weight at six months was a kilo heavier and clearly overweight. With what is known now about the immunological properties of human milk and the miseries of allergy, the drastic decline in breast-feeding constituted a significant degradation of the people's health.

With the *Murphy* sisters almost a century of change was encompassed in a decade. *Emma* had her first baby in 1929; she did not attend a Health Centre, took her mother's advice, breast-fed easily on demand and kept the baby in bed with her for comfort. *Alice* had her first baby in *1939;* she attended the Health Centre and lost her milk. *Emma* was advised that circumcision was not important for her son; *Alice* a decade later was ordered by the doctor to give her consent. *Emma* now claims that she was never as good a mother as *Alice* who read books and kept up with the most modern ideas, but *Emma is* the one with the happier memories of early motherhood.[24]

The quiet class battle over infant feeding had a wider significance. By the end of the 1930s middle-class experts had succeeded in cracking an important area of working-class domestic resistance to professional authority. The coming war would usher in the Welfare State which, while providing an essential safety net for those unable to earn a living, would ultimately expose working-class life to further management by middle-class experts. Working-class people were being incorporated into middle-class domestic culture: when *Nellie Roberts* had her first baby during World War II, she would be inflicted with the same advice as her counterparts in Balwyn and Brighton—breast-feeding was 'old fashioned' and 'difficult' and 'not as good for the baby'. Above all, it was 'rude'. Now in the 1980s the wheel has turned full circle, for it is the working-class mother's excessive deference to white-coated experts that is so artfully manipulated by the purveyors of infant formula and processed foods.

1939–1955

7

War and Peace II

War and Welfare: 1939–1945

World War II was the turning point in Australian social and economic development and no section of Australian society was more affected than the urban working class. Even though fears persisted throughout the war that peace would bring another depression on the scale of the 1930s catastrophe, the technological and strategic needs of the war ushered in an expansion of secondary industry and of primary exports that was capable of underwriting thirty years of unparalleled national prosperity. And that prosperity filtered down to even the poorest in Australian society. But it was not only steady work and higher wages that lifted the standard of living. The war, both here and in Great, Britain, ushered in the Welfare State, a dramatic if miserly intervention of government in private life that registered a significant change in notions of social equity and morality. Moreover, this war was the forcing house of mass non-British immigration that dragged Australians out of their Anglo-Celtic insularity; and the cultural impact was felt first by working-class Australians living in inner suburbs like Richmond. Finally, the war ignited ideological conflicts between Left and Right that split the working-class political and industrial movement and ultimately consigned working-class politics to a near quarter of a century of political impotence. To *Muriel Thompson* and *Jean Fowler*, who have lived all their lives in Richmond, World War II was the great turning point in their remembered history, transcending even the Great Depression. *Jean* felt the social dislocation even more acutely than the economic release from the Depression: 'the war finished it all—you didn't know where you were really—you were baking things and sending them overseas to your sons or something'. However frightful the Depression, for the very poor the war brought the first major change in their life experience. In fact, World War II proved to be an even greater historical watershed than was the transition from the nineteenth to the twentieth centuries: the poor of the 1920s and 1930s had more in common with the poor of the 1890s than with those of the 1960s and 1970s.[1]

Civilian Richmond could not fail to profit from a modern total war. Its boot factories, tanneries, textile, clothing and knitting factories and food preservers all won lucrative war contracts. Even more, this war was fought on Australia's doorstep and Australian industry would have to supply war *materiel*, especially aircraft and munitions, on a scale undreamt of in World War I. And this time many of Richmond's males of military age were protected against war service as their skills were needed in industry at home. War industry needed women and girls and their wages enabled some families to get on their feet for the first time in more than a decade. Thus was the stage set for one of the great areas of social conflict during the war as servicemen fought a brutal war against, a sadistic enemy in tropical jungles while civilians at home prospered and lived it up. However grave the threat to Australia in 1942 and however irksome manpower and rationing regulations, the fact remains that many working-class civilians had never 'had it so good'.

The outbreak of war brought none of the excitement of August 1914. For ex-servicemen like *Will Parker*: 'we didn't want to see it happen again; we'd been through it and seen how stupid it was'. Some radicals and trade unionists were wary of the Menzies government's motives in its rapid support of Britain; Communists were forced to explain away the Nazi-Soviet Non-aggression Pact. The two world wars witnessed opposite civilian reactions to the war: in World War I civilians gradually became disillusioned with unthinking patriotism; in World War II civilian commitment deepened as the war came closer to Australia. Air raid precautions, decontamination squads and demolition parties were organized immediately but it would be two years before people took them seriously. But if the war and its dangers seemed remote, the economic benefits were already visible by the end of 1939. In the last two weeks in November alone the number on sustenance in Richmond decreased by a hundred. Although it is now clear that economic conscripts constituted a minority of the Second A.I.F., the mythology remains important for *Ruby Kane*, whose husband was a Rat of Tobruk:

> I would say that at least 80 per cent of those boys that went to the war went to get a job because the Depression was so terrible. I'll be quite honest. We had *nothing* when *Fred* went away to the war. And he got on and rose to a Warrant Officer I which was good money. And when he came back the Army got him a good job. But we had nothing until he went to the war: one weekend I had two shillings—I had to go up the road and buy everything for two shillings.

Certainly in the first year of the phoney war, enlistment was an honourable way out for many unemployed men. Francis Donohue was fined £2 in the Richmond Court in January 1940 for submitting fraudulent sustenance claims and the Court was pleased to hear that he was now a cook in a military camp. As in 1914 some young men were eager for action and anxious to enlist with their mates. In February 1940 a young Spotswood man was arrested in Punt Road for posing as a sergeant in the Air Force, the most glamorous arm of the services in World War II. He told the Court that 'all his old cobbers had joined the Air Force but he had been refused on account of an injury to his hand by which he had lost two fingers'.[2] *Bill Shannon*'s father was desperate to go in with his mates:

> Dad wanted to go in, and his mates—they all come from around Lambert Street where Mum and Dad lived when they first got married. They were real tough sorts of characters—they'd sooner fight coppers than go to school. Dad was at Pizzeys as a tanner and Pizzeys wouldn't let him go, so the old man flattened two of the Pizzeys and went to join the Air Force, but he finished up in the Army.

Not all tough Richmond lads took to Army life, however. Billy Eddy for one was in as much trouble in the Army as he had been in civvy street. And the Depression generation were physically conspicuous. Dr David Roseby took note of Army complaints about the poor physique of many recruits and of the common practice for quartermasters to order over-size uniforms as men put on weight on Army rations.[3] Yet for all their life disadvantages, the character of the men of the Second A.I.F. was impressive. Major *James Mitchell* was also a Richmond man, but a very different early enlister in the Second A.I.F. Too young for service in World War I, he had served throughout the inter-war period as an officer in the militia. A deeply patriotic Protestant, he remains unforgiving of Archbishop Mannix's alleged denigration of World War I as 'a sordid trade war'. And when Australia declared war to support Britain he had no hesitation in leaving his new wife and secure job in a Burnley pharmacy to transfer to the doomed Eighth Division. He was nearly forty when he entered Changi as a prisoner of war:

> They were a terrific body of men. The thing that amazed me was that these boys, including my brother, had come on the labour market at a time when the world didn't want them. They couldn't even get a job to earn some sort of self-respect. There was nothing. Fathers were paying employers to employ their sons so that they could get some sort of experience and be able to get some feeling of purpose in the world.

As in Britain, the working class were so accustomed to stress and deprivation, especially after the Depression, that they coped far better with the anxieties and dislocation of war than the authorities expected. And as the

City of Richmond farewelled its first batch of soldiers in February 1940, Scullin reminded them that they were not only to bring back honour to their country but also to Richmond. War could restore working-class dignity.[4]

Yet for civilians without relatives in the armed forces the war still seemed unreal. In June 1940 a War Savings Rally at the Richmond Town Hall attracted only a handful of locals. Scullin spoke of the evils of Nazism and on its attack on the labour movement; Councillor Jimmy Loughnan declared: 'The workers should think about the war instead of so much amusement'. None the less, the leadership of the Richmond Labor Party and the Council were still more preoccupied with the evils of Communism than with those of Nazism. Back in November 1936 the Richmond Council had voted nine to two to refuse the Communist-controlled New Theatre permission to stage the banned anti-Nazi play, 'Till the Day I Die' in the Town Hall. (Collingwood Council gave New Theatre their hall instead but took out all the seats.) Menzies' opportunistic banning of the Communist Party now gave the Red-hunters on the Council a chance to flex their muscle. The Council withdrew permission for the No-Conscription Fellowship to hold meetings on the City Reserve and Councillor Jack Cremean accused the organizer, Jim, Walsh, of being a Communist. To the embarrassment of all, Walsh turned out to be a member of the A.L.P. The Council also took advantage of State loan funds to spend over £20 000 on 'necessary works in war-time' such as renovation of the destructor and the Soldiers' Memorial Hall, a hot-mix plant, a new house for the Bath Superintendent and accommodation for Council employees over the Gymnasium. The *Richmond Chronicle* was appalled. Yet as the war in Europe progressed, the Mayor's war fund-raising picked up and in September raised £124 7s 6d from a Sunday football match between the Bookmakers' Society and 'Mr Foley's team', despite the protestations of sabbatarian Protestants. Another manifestation of war was the growing drunkenness and violence from soldiers on leave. With Italy in the war, two young soldiers felt justified in throwing a brick through the windows of a fish shop-owner in Swan Street, a Mr C. Nicoli, before bashing him with a chair. And real Italians like Mr Antonio Sesso, a Swan Street fruiterer who had been in Australia for twenty years, also had windows smashed. *Monica Rinoldi*'s father, a second generation Australian of Italian-speaking Swiss descent, received insulting letters: 'It hurt my father, I remember'.[5]

The war was getting closer. By 1941 weekly casualty lists had reappeared in Richmond's local paper. The military service call-up for all unmarried men between the ages of twenty-five and thirty was announced in January 1941 and, haunted by fears of inadequate reinforcements, in May the Army sought permission to broadcast appeals at football matches. It was still difficult for Australians to believe that their country was in peril: in

May the Richmond Air Raid Precautions needed 360 volunteers and attracted only twenty. Once Russia entered the war the Richmond Council had to recant its hostility to the Communist Party and in November 1941 permitted the Australia-Soviet Friendship League and a rally against the continued proscription of the C.P.A, to use the Town Hall. However, the Richmond Council was still no friend of Russia and after a heated debate voted only £10 to the Red Cross Russian Relief Appeal when most municipalities gave £50.[6]

Economically Richmond was booming and the Council was sympathetic to the needs of war industry. Jaques Bros, the engineering firm, pushed aside protests from householders, the North Richmond A.L.P. and the State Housing Commission to win planning permission to extend its premises. The Australian Knitting Mills, growing fat on war contracts and anticipating good times in peace, commenced large extensions to its mills and announced a new share issue of £68 750 which would in part finance the expansion. By April 1941 the boot trade in Richmond and Abbotsford was on full and overtime for the first time in twenty years and reported an acute shortage of labour. Tanners and leather merchants were also stretched to the limit; and union officials reported that some employers were offering good tradesmen high inducements to transfer to their firm. In South Richmond Con Loughnan led a residents' campaign to protect workers' homes: in September and October alone thirty-three houses were demolished for three factory extensions and a fourth factory had purchased fifteen dwellings and given tenants notice to quit.[7]

But there were plenty of jobs and the growing shortage of labour opened industry to women. In industrial metals, machines and implements the Commonwealth figures for female workers jumped from 14 877 in 1940–41 to 23 494 in 1941–42 to 45 307 in 1942–43. Traditional factory work for women, like food processing, also boomed. *Isabel Williams* returned to the Rosella when it got its first Army contracts and when the Americans arrived Rosella became the first Australian firm to install machinery for canning sweetcorn:

> We had women doctors and doctors' wives—all kinds of people working at the Rosella doing that as their war effort. Really very nice people. And a man came from the Army: 'But you're doing a good job here because you're providing food for the services'.

War workers certainly did not have it easy. The shifts were excessive—twelve and thirteen hours—the temperatures always extreme for the season, the noise deafening and the women found the amenities provided for male workers disgusting and inadequate. Women in industry hastened the coming of canteens, washing facilities, even essentials like first aid. And when the women won 90 per cent of the male rate in the metal trades, the money was almost worth it: 'I felt like a Rockefeller', recalls

Rose Cruickshank, who worked in the Government Aircraft factory. *Isabel Williams* was appalled by her sister who left her five-year-old daughter locked in the house alone while she worked the night shift at Maribyrnong. There was so much work for working-class women that Toorak ladies began advertising for domestic servants in the *Richmond Chronicle* offering 'high wages'. Before Japan entered the conflict it was inevitable that the war seemed like a great release and people began catching up on the fun robbed by the Depression. But once war came to the Pacific it was different. The pressure on war workers became intense and began to take its toll. The Manpower Act threw into industry many half-hearted patriots, and conscientious war workers were shocked by the absenteeism, the pilfering of valuable materials like aluminium to build caravans in the back yard, and the making of 'foreigners' in factory time. The long hours and rarity of holidays was wearing for even the most patriotic.[8] Top skilled workers found much was expected. *Thomas Beauchamp* was still at Repco when the war started:

> We went for about two years into the war when we as foremen never got any overtime and we were working twelve hours a day and we were expected to run our departments. Then the men with the higher wages started to get more than the foremen with the result that there were quite a few words about the foremen and I spoke to Mr Russell and he agreed to pay us time—we didn't get time like the men, just time for overtime.

Harold Stephenson as a boilermaker had an exhausting and unglamorous war:

> We had to black out the windows of the factory because we were working at night. I had a push bike and I also had a motor bike but with rationing you only got a gallon of petrol a month so I saved that so we could go down the beach at Christmas. We were instructed in what to do if incendiary bombs were dropped and I used to pedal home at 10 o'clock at night. When we done the job for the Americans' periscope they gave me a holiday because I'd been working thirteen hours a day. We went up to a guest-house at Healesville for seven days and Claire was only a little baby and all the windows were blacked out.

With the news of the Japanese attack on Pearl Harbor and their horrific march through the islands and down the Malay Peninsula, Australian civilians were now right in the war. Brown-out regulations were enforced and a black-out applied in industrial suburbs like Richmond. Friday night shopping was stopped and slit trenches were dug in public parks and playgrounds. South Richmond's oasis of charm, the Barkly Gardens, were desolated and have never been restored to their original state. The slit trenches, of course, filled with water with the first rains and were soon seen to be useless. The authorities found it hard to arouse civilians to comply .with air-raid precautions, and in January 1942, instead of attending A.R.P. trench-digging parties, Richmondites were 'generally making their way to the beaches on hot evenings'. A 'large number of parents' refused to register their children for evacuation. At the end of January the authorities despaired that 80 per cent of the population of Richmond were not observing the black-out. Racist over-confidence in the prowess of the Anzacs lulled some into complacency: 'I don't know why a Labor Government should get so panicky about air-raids coming here; Aussie airmen will settle the Japs'; and a Richmond barber reported: 'Most of my customers scout the idea of raids over Melbourne or even Australia. They are more concerned over the proposed cutting down of race meetings'. Then four days after the surrender in Singapore, the Japanese bombed Darwin and the nation panicked.[9] *Alice Murphy*:

> When Darwin was bombed I can remember letting *Dick* out the back gate—he used to leave here at 6 o'clock to get to Deer Park—and he said to me: 'Now if anything does happen you know what I told you. The hall has got a false ceiling, just get the table and pull it into the hall and you put both of them under the table with you'. When the subs were in Sydney and Darwin was bombed the feeling was dreadful—it was electric.
>
> All of a sudden, wherever you looked there were Americans. This is the thing that's in our generation's mind as far as America is concerned—they just seemed to come from nowhere, just when things were at their blackest. The Stage Door Canteen opened in town and that was for a certain type—an officer's type of thing.

The Americans materialized in a community soaked in Hollywood; they were glamorous, seemingly rich and lonely: 'over-paid, over-fed, over-sexed and over here'. Richmond had two massive American camps on its borders in the Melbourne Cricket Ground and the Survey Park. The Americans dangled nylons in front of girls forced to paint their legs by clothing rationing; lonely Army wives were tempted to catch up on the fun they had missed during the last fourteen years. But Australian girls had their standards. *Bill Shannon*:

> In World War II the big fright was with the Negroes—no woman would go out with a Negro. Then you had Leonski [a white American serviceman] running about killing people. That turned a lot of women off going out. I can remember Mum and one auntie—they used to go to all the dances at the service clubs and Mum was a pretty good looking woman, a good dancer, and she was a real character while she was a nursing sister and so forth. I suppose I'm proud of her in a way. But a lot of my mates' mothers—the fathers were away and they had to do something. Actually we were very lucky—can't remember any break-ups—they battled on.

The Americans' alleged sexual success with Australian women and the privileges they commanded only exacerbated the tension between the men at the front and civilians having the time of their lives.[10]

But the war had become difficult at home too. With the Manpower regulations and rationing, Australians had never been so regimented since convict days. On the first Saturday in May 1943 the officers of the Manpower Department raided Richmond hotels and dances looking for absen tees and soldiers who were Absent wit' out Leave. They interviewed six hundred people and enraged local hotel keepers for singling out Richmond while bigger crowds of young people were to be found at the cinema and the football. However good their wages, workers found the cost of living rising alarmingly—in January 1943 tomatoes reached ls 6d a pound. Rationing, it seems, did not have quite the beneficial effect on working-class diet as it did in Britain where the working class was better fed during the war than ever before. Petrol rationing was more a hardship for the middle class who owned cars and working-class people of course were well acquainted with living on very plain fare. Many small shopkeepers, however, failed as the big retailers monopolized supplies and the empty shops created by the Depression in Richmond were added to by the war. By mid-1942 there were twenty-three empty shops in Bridge Road alone. Everyone felt the shortages of tea and dairy products; and the great wood fuel famine in the winter of 1942 imposed acute hardship. The comforts of alcohol and tobacco were also scarce and in October 1943 all Richmond hotels were forced to close by lack of supplies. The black market flourished and ration books became a currency in their own right. In June 1943 two thousand old ration books, three hundred of them with unused tickets, were stolen from St Matthias' Hall in Richmond. *Bill Shannon*'s uncle *Smokey Smithers*, Richmond's own millionaire, seemed never short of full books.[11] *Smokey Smithers* started his extraordinary career helping his mother with her milk rounds from the family dairy. With S.P. bookmaking, sly grog and selling goods that fell off the back of trucks, he amassed the cash to buy up Richmond properties while they were dirt cheap. Eventually he owned 310 houses and four factories in Richmond plus used car yards and seaside properties around Melbourne. *Bill* continues:

> Uncle *Jimmy* was a very enterprising fellow—he used to have ration books and everything—and he was the baker and he got the permit to make bread rolls for the American mess in the camp in the Survey Park. So he built a big room on the side of the house and he used to have all my aunties making bread rolls during the day, but in the evening the big table they used for making the rolls was turned into a table for baccarat. And Uncle *Jimmy* had an air-raid shelter dug—where Johnson's the carpet people now are—there's a driveway which was a railway easement and underneath that was a big

> cellar, going down a fair way—about sixteen or twenty steps down. The officers used to leave their side arms for security and I can just remember as a kid when they opened it up and it was all full of U.S. Army issue side hand guns.

Smokey Smithers did well out of sly grog, too, selling a dozen bottles of beer in a cement bag and during the war paid all his debts with ration books.

> He was an easy-going kind of bloke, everything he done he done himself—self-made. But he was mean in a lot of ways. He was tough on his family—my aunties who made the bread rolls got paid in kind. There was always something at his place for sale. I'm not saying he was a fence or anything; but he used to be a 'commission man'. At one stage you couldn't get towelling, but we always had towels at home, especially Dickies multi-coloured towels—we got them first.

High wages and rationing meant that people had money on their hands they could not spend. Gambling, despite the cut-back on horse-racing, boomed, but so too did saving. Richmond people were so flush and generous that in January 1943 they exceeded their quota of £10 war bonds by £95 000; and in 1944 theirs was the first municipality to reach its quota for the Victory Loan. By May 1944 the suburb's total contribution had reached a quarter of a million pounds. Fund-raising had none of the hullabaloo of World War I. In October 1942 one of the few patriotic carnivals of the war was held on the Richmond Cricket Ground to raise funds for prisoners of war. As in World War I, brothers and neighbourhood friends had enlisted together and died or became P.O.W.s together, doubling the family and community loss. Unlike World War I, the Richmond Council showed no interest in paying a civic tribute to Richmond men and women in the Services until the secretary of the R.S.L. branch persuaded it to give a certificate to all surviving men and women.[12]

The conduct and competence of the Richmond Council and the local A.L.P. showed little improvement during the exigencies of war. In July 1941 Councillor R. H. Lightfoot defeated Ted Cotter in the pre-selection ballot for the State seat of Richmond. Accusations of irregularities forced the State Executive to order a re-run and in October Cotter won. 407 votes to 404. but as Pat Kennelly, the State Secretary, was leaving the counting room he was attacked, menaced with a gun and deprived of the ballot box. In May 1944 William McGregor, 'a man of parts unknown', was sentenced to three months gaol for the theft. He admitted to a four-year sentence for 'conspiracy' and several other convictions. Kennelly was later told that McGregor had been paid £25 for the job. On Kennelly's advice the State Executive upheld Cotter's pre-selection for the sake of peace.[13]

More than ever the Council needed to be on its toes if it were to protect the interests of its constituents. Early in 1942 it became apparent that industry was taking advantage of the crisis to erect factories and factory extensions with the permission only of the State Government Factories Department. Building was commenced before the Council had time to issue a permit and in peace Richmond was left with some conspicuous industrial blots on its residential streetscapes. A major offender was the Sutex Knitting Mill in Coppin Street which succeeded in persuading the Government that its war contracts demanded extensions even though its products were not of the highest priority. Residents found themselves policed by an A.R.P. warden who ignored the factories on night shift that flouted the brown-out. In South Richmond residents were kept awake by the hammering from the K.M. factory on night shift, but their protests were in vain until the occupants of luxury flats in South Yarra across the river added their complaints and the firm agreed to alter shift times. The massive increase in industrial and military traffic was tearing Richmond's already precarious roads to pieces and in the pitch-black of night, accidents were numerous. Night workers struggled home on crumbling footpaths and risked assaults by 'undesirables lurking about in the dark'. The shortage of materials made road repairs almost impossible, but the Council was not helped by having a lazy and incompetent staff. A full-time City Engineer was appointed only in 1940, after a bitter row between the Council and his predecessor, and efficiency improved. Even so it was the veteran Councillor George Vesper who was the first to notice, albeit eighteen months after the event, that the now waterlogged and unhealthy slit trenches on the City Reserve had been dug opposite the entrance to the gasometer in Gleadell Street and would have been enveloped in a firestorm had there been an air raid. The extent of sick-leave absences continued to anger councillors and some council staff seemed more concerned with gaining exemptions from military service as 'reserved occupations' than with the war effort. The most blatant offender was Con Loughnan, now in a steady decline into alcoholism. His sick leave was a scandal, and in 1943 he was prosecuted for forging a medical certificate for leave on the grounds of 'asma'. In May 1942 he was given a three-year suspended sentence for wounding a sixty-five-year-old pensioner with the rapier in his walking stick. By June 1943 Mayor Ernie Boland was determined to sack him: 'This officer has been standing over several councillors but he is not going to stand over me'. But Loughnan was secretary of the South Richmond A.L.P. and still a power in Richmond; the motion was lost when Councillor Lightfoot, the seconder, was 'persuaded to withdraw'.[14]

As in World War I, war concentrated the Australian political mind wonderfully. Once the Japanese tide was turned, concern about the fate of Australian people in peace grew. Many were haunted by the spectre of another depression and many were determined that peace must bring a correction of the social injustices embedded in Australian society. The Labor Party had earned a new prestige through the brave and dedicated leadership of Prime Minister Curtin, yet many people were seeking a more drastic reform of the economic system and the heroic struggles of the Red Army and the Russian people lessened doubts about Soviet Communism. Ironically, in view of the hysteria created by the Catholic Right in the Labor movement and by Menzies, Australia's flirtation with Communism was very brief In Richmond, 1943 was the only year of electoral success for the Communist Party when Bertha Laidler (later Walker), the Richmond born and bred daughter of the vain and unreliable Percy Laidler, stood as the Communist candidate against Ted Cotter. To a packed Town Hall she called for a speeding up of war production, precautions against the out break of disease, better education and care for youth, more support for soldiers and the decentralization of industry. It was a wise programme and she was rewarded with 6183 votes to Cotter's 13 358 with 6621 abstentions because there was no U.A.P. candidate. In South Richmond where the Laidlers had lived, she polled 1343 to Cotter's 2884. The C.P.A. were ecstatic; the war was winning votes for Communism that the Depression had failed to. But their success was short-lived. Two months later George Frank of the Carpenters' Union stood for West Ward and polled poorly. Thus ended the Red Menace in Richmond. The A.L.P. was alarmed none the less,, and attempted to root Communist sympathizers out of the Party. In 1944 Councillors Lightfoot and Williams were expelled from the North Richmond branch for their membership of the Australia-Soviet Friendship League. They both recanted and returned to the fold.[15]

Real reforms in Australian social welfare were now coming from the Commonwealth and State governments, putting in place a welfare net financed by the new Federal taxation powers. In 1941, to forestall an impending rise in the Basic Wage, the Menzies government instituted Child Endowment to all white children under sixteen being supported by their parents. For large working-class families this added £1 or more to their weekly income. In 1942 the Curtin Government added the widow's pension for mothers with dependants and for all widows over fifty-five, provided they passed the means test and, except in 'special cases', were again not Aboriginal. From 1944 unemployment and sickness benefits were paid by the Commonwealth and the Government took the first steps towards the establishment of a National Health Scheme with free prescriptions.[16]

The other great running sore in Australian society was housing. The decay of the housing stock through the Depression was prolonged by the war as essential building materials were directed to the war effort. By 1944 it was revealed that the nation was short of 257 521 houses: an 'actual shortage' of 175 940 dwellings and an additional 82 031 to replace structures fit only for demolition. Melbourne was found to have the greatest shortage of homes, Sydney the worst slums. Not that Melbourne did not suffer from sub-standard housing. A survey of 7330 homes in the inner suburbs in 1936–37 by the Housing Investigation and Slum Abolition Board had found:

14.40 per cent were in good habitable condition
42.81 per cent were unfit for habitation without expensive repairs
41.56 per cent were incapable of being made fit for habitation
28.19 per cent were without bathrooms
44.82 per cent were without washing facilities
75.76 per cent were without kitchen sinks.

Moreover, Australian tenants had always been required to pay excessive rents for sub-standard dwellings, and the housing shortage pushed unjust rents even higher. In Richmond old age pensioners were paying seven shillings and ten shillings a week for 'hovels' in back yards without gas or electricity.[17] Three houses investigated by the University of Melbourne Social Survey of 1941–42 in Richmond Terrace revealed:

63 Richmond Terrace: a brick, one-storey semi-detached house built early 1860s had one separate bedroom, two living rooms, no sink, a wood stove and an internal bath. The occupants were a twenty-six-year-old boiler attendant at the Australian Paper Mills, his twenty-four-year-old wife and three-year-old son. They had their own gas stove. The interior needed repapering badly. The sewer was always blocking and the landlord seemed unwilling to carry out repairs. The husband's wage was £4 10s a week, his pay the previous week with overtime was £5 before tax. They paid £1 2s 6d rent.

120 Richmond Terrace: a brick, detached, one-storey house built late 1880s had two separate bedrooms, three beds on the front veranda directly on to the street with only an old blind for protection and privacy, a separate bathroom, a kitchen with a sink and tap, no hot water service, both wood and gas stoves. The tenants were a forty-two-year-old man who worked as a casual labourer at Angliss' meat works earning £5 a week, his wife who did not work, her sister who earned £3 16s 10d a week as a textile worker, her seventeen-year-old daughter who earned £2 a week at the Kayser hosiery factory and a twelve-year-old daughter still at school. This second family paid £2 5s board a week. This house was clean and in good repair although the blind on the front veranda kept out the light. The household head's work was seasonal and usually lasted only six months of the year but the war had created more work for him. The rent was 37s 6d a week.

58 Richmond Terrace: a brick one-storey terrace house built early 1880s, had two separate bedrooms, two living rooms including the kitchen, a bath outside but unusable because of leaks, no sink or tap in the kitchen, a wood stove and the tenants were buying their gas stove on hire purchase.

This family consisted of a thirty-year-old timber stacker earning £4 17s a week on regular work after being on sustenance before the war, his wife of the same age, a son of two and a baby daughter. This was a family made possible by the prosperity brought by war. This family were also aware of their rights. They had been in the house only a week and were dissatisfied. The house was dark and in poor repair, the bath was unusable and the combined external bathroom and wash house unsatisfactory. 'The husband has given the owner until the week-end to install a new bath and if nothing is done intends to report it to the Board of Works. This house is one of a terrace all owned by the same man, and although he charges £1 rent for this one, he only charges 17s 6d for similar houses in the terrace. Husband intends to wait for a few months and then ask for a reduction to 17s 6d, with a threat to the Fair Rents Board.'[18]

This last man was unusual in his preparedness to seek official help. The desperate shortage of houses and working-class diffidence prevented many from exercising their rights. These three houses were average for Richmond: there were many worse and not many better. By 1947 1200 houses had been condemned, around 15 per cent of the housing stock, 850 of them being deemed fit only for demolition. However, these statistics must be regarded with caution. M. A. Jones has since thrown doubt on whether the large-scale demolition of houses by the Victorian Housing Commission was either necessary or justified. Careful renovation and the rebuilding of only the irredeemable on their old sites might have made for greater human happiness for the recipients of welfare housing.[19]

With the formation of the Victorian Housing Commission in 1938, political power over housing was being taken away from the local community. The assumption of local government powers over slums by the Commission was badly handled. Richmond councillors feared that 'big government' might carry out drastic slum clearance that would destroy Richmond as a human community and deprive working-class home-owners of what little equity they had. Provisions for compensation were unsatisfactory and the style of public housing to be offered worried many. Councillor Vesper was appalled by the plans for the proposed Richmond Racecourse estate. They were not fit for workers to live in: 'They would be like barracks and built with the cheapest materials with low ceilings, plywood doors and have no passages'. And the Government would be the landlord and collect the rents every Monday morning. Mr Overend of the Housing Commission sought to reassure the workers: the Commission was offering an exciting return to the 'old style' of early colonial architecture (that is with front doors opening directly on to the street, low ceilings and no passages). However, when three thousand people inspected the first eight houses on the estate in September 1941, the comments were favourable and many housewives later assured the University of Melbourne investigators that, while they neglected their present homes, they would look after a new Commission house properly. But with the rationing of building materials, housing would have to wait for peace. All that could be done was to worry. In South Richmond in 1944 Con Loughnan led a campaign to persuade the Richmond Council to use what powers remained under the Local Government Act to borrow money for slum reclamation. Seventy-two houses had been demolished for factory sites in South Richmond since the outbreak of war. All the people of Richmond knew was that the Housing Commission had promised to commence its post-war work first in Richmond.[20]

As peace approached it was clear that the war had brought significant change to Australian working-class life: improvements in income, in job security, in basic welfare payments for those unable to work, in prospects for future housing and educational opportunity. But the war had also seen a decline in old working-class community feeling. In contrast to World War I, the metropolitan press and radio had overtaken the local press as the media cement of Richmond. On 6 July 1945 the *Richmond Chronicle* suspended publication owing to 'manpower difficulties' and the illness of 'Robbo', H. L. Roberts, who had been the guiding genius behind the *Richmond Guardian* in its best years, then the *Richmond Weekly* and finally the *Chronicle.* 'Robbo' had been always a thoroughly professional journalist who had maintained a standard worthy of the best metropolitan dailies. The *Chronicle*'s successor would be a very different paper indeed, reporting a changed post-war Richmond. Richmond's war heroes returned to none of the community honours conferred in 1918. Certainly Mayor Jimmy Loughnan, now resplendent in the mayoral robes he had resumed in wartime, 'threw a Victory Ball in the Town Hall, but peace was celebrated by most people in a new metropolitan style. *Emma Murphy*, who had won two shillings in the Armistice Day picnic races at Burnley, this time joined the delirious city crowds: 'I remember I went into town and I thought I was going to be seized by the crowd and end up in the river'.[21]

Richmond's second war was over.

'Roads, Rats and Rancidity': 1946–1955

By 1945 Ted Cotter had finally decided to retire from State parliament. Two years later he died, remembered as a kindly and unobtrusive man who in his final years in politics had done little other than frustrate the many ambitious locals who coveted his seat. The 'king-maker' of the Victorian A.L.P., Pat Kennelly, believed that 'if anyone deserved a seat in Richmond, one of the Loughnans did', and if the tragically afflicted Con was unsuitable, then Jimmy was the man: 'he wasn't in the rough stuff—or if he was he had the brains to do it the right way'. But when the pre-selection ballot was counted Jimmy Loughnan had lost in 'a rank and file revolt' to a thirty-year-old bachelor, Standish Michael Keon. Keon was a Richmond man; he had left school early and suffered in the Depression. He was intense, ambitious and supremely confident of his ideals and abilities. He had a powerful intellect and was widely read. A devout Catholic, he was passionately opposed to Communism.[22] And he had integrity. His greatest political opponent of a decade later, Jim Cairns, now says of him:

> Keon was a strong driving force. He had an electric character in his voice. Bert Evatt said: 'When I hear Keon talking I can smell the faggots burning'. And he had that very repressed, powerful, internal source of energy. I don't know to what extent he moved people, but he had a powerful oratorical presence.

However impeccable his origins, Keon was ill at ease in the world of ordinary blokes like *Bill Shannon*:

> Stan Keon—he's the luckiest bloke to be alive. It was unbelievable. There was eight of us come home from Puckka [Puckapunyal Army Camp] and we were all in the Swan Hotel—National Servicemen were not allowed to drink beer in uniform—and there was a rally or some flaming thing, and Keon and all that were talking on the corner of Swan and Church Streets. And he come into the hotel and the next thing we know the M.P.s are there. We got away out the back. On the Saturday we went to the football—Richmond was playing at home—and we went past Keon's place and he turned round and said: 'I hope those blokes give you a belting last night'. Well, have you ever seen a bloke with four broken windows in two seconds flat? I don't know where the rock come from—it was in me hand. I missed his head by that much. (laughs)

Yet there were many whom Keon captivated. He was the right man for the right time: a brilliant and seemingly incorruptible leader for a ground swell of lower-class Catholic respectability yearning for a new moral order in Labor politics and inspired by a Holy mission against Communist materialism. Keon was a new man leading a growing army of new men and women. Many were cutting their political teeth as Industrial Group activists fighting Communist influence in the trade unions; some were members of Santamaria's Movement, many were young, educated and poised for upward social mobility. But this 'rank and file revolt' in the Richmond Labor Party faced two enemies: Communism and the Richmond Labor machine. In Richmond it soon proved to be very much a revolt of the respectable.

If the electoral success of the Communist Party was piffling, its industrial power was a different matter. In 1945 Communist-controlled unions had come close to having a majority at the A.C.T.U. biennial conference, and with peace, had embarked on a campaign of strikes to destabilize the country. In 1946 the Victorian Executive of the A.L.P. acceded to branch demands to sanction industrial groups in the unions to fight elections against the Communists. Many had misgivings, however, about encouraging organized Catholic militants to penetrate the industrial wing of the Labor movement. Kennelly, especially, saw the Victorian A.L.P. as a delicate balance between a political wing that was strongly Catholic and white collar and an industrial wing that was Protestant or secular. Sectarian tensions were never far from the surface and could be fatal if ignited, and some militant Catholics had already shown themselves addicted to intrigue.[23] During the war, Movement-inspired watchdogs had tailed known Left militants and Communists and presumably made up dossiers. The Groupers in fact had much in common with their Communist foes. Both were sustained by a conviction of moral rectitude that justified almost any means; both delighted in secrecy; both offered a life that was intense and exciting; both easily unleashed hysteria born of the cabal.

On 21 July 1946 the new and brilliant M.L.A. for Richmond challenged Bert Flanagan, the Communist secretary of the Ironworkers' Federation, to a debate in the Richmond Town Hall. Five thousand people were crushed in and around the Town Hall; the screaming, singing and 'counting out' drowned the debaters. The metropolitan press found it all faintly amusing; for the participants it would become the stuff of legend. In fact it was an ominous and frightening confrontation between antagonists who sometimes abandoned reason for certainties that defied reality. Above all, they assumed a self-importance not shared by the rest of the nation and they would persist in ideological warfare long after the danger was past. Later the Groupers would allege that a 'Labor rat' had opened the side door early so that the Communists could take up all the seats 'with all the riff-raff they could dredge up from around Melbourne'. 'Armed with knuckle-dusters, batons, etc., the Red strong-arm squads were all set for trouble', but the Reds had made a tactical error by sitting down and they soon found themselves surrounded and contained by 'good, sturdy Australian Laborites' filling the aisles and 'ready to see that the local member got a fair go'. The 'Labor rat' who had opened the door for the Reds was named as Con Loughnan.[24]

Loughnan had been the first victim of Keon's army of crusaders. Early in 1946 they began moving into his stronghold, the South Richmond branch, signing up new members until they had the numbers to elect Miss Monica Slattery as secretary. Loughnan suddenly found himself expelled and all that remained of the old guard was the president, Councillor Albert Huckerby, the eighty-year-old secretary of the Theatrical Employees' Union and reliably anti-Communist. The next year he was succeeded by a young returned soldier from the engineering section of the P.M.G., Bernard Callinan. Then Monica Slattery left to be married and a young protégé of Keon, Francis Raymond Scully, took over. Unlike Keon, Scully was a member of the Movement, one of its inner circle, and was distinguishing himself as a tireless and intelligent secretary of the Railways Industrial Group. While he did not like Keon, Jim Cairns warmed to Frank Scully's humour and common touch; Kennelly admired Keon and distrusted and detested Scully. In 1948 the reformed South Richmond branch outpaced even the Movement when it placed a motion on the Victorian conference's agenda paper calling for the banning of the Communist Party.[25]

On 12 September 1946 the first edition of the *Richmond News* appeared, filling the vacuum left by the *Chronicle*. It was an entirely new type of suburban weekly: provocative, melodramatic, it often abandoned journalism for propaganda. For the next twenty years it served up to the people of Richmond an unrelieved diet of Grouper politics and sport. It was linked to a chain of four private libraries in Richmond, where advertisements could be lodged, and each week the *News* ran reviews of recommended books from their shelves. In 1949 it wrote of *The Nazarovs* by Markoosha Fischer:

> Using his diverse characters skilfully, the author paints a vivid picture of the growth of the [Bolshevik] revolution, its final victory, of the early joy and virility, especially of the youthful rebels, of their faith in their leaders. of their gradual disillusionment as clamps are placed on one freedom after another. Then come the purges. No one is safe, not even the O.G.P.U. husband of the prostitute grand-daughter of the respectable Nazarovs.[26]

In State parliament Keon soon revealed himself to be a fearless and troublesome addition to the embattled Cain government's back bench. He embarrassed with his attacks on Communist union officials and with his campaign for faster action by the Housing Commission to abolish slums. He had a talent for headlines and in Richmond each speech was rewarded by a flurry of articulate, even eloquent, letters to the *News* by grateful constituents.[27] Then in March 1947, under the banner 'ROADS, RATS AND RANCIDITY', the *Richmond News* turned its attention to the Richmond Council. Ratepayers, it said, had patiently borne with Council neglect during the war, but with peace it had done nothing other than raise the rates by threepence in the pound. Highly literate letters to the editor told the people's story. Mary Barkald of 350 Mary Street wrote:

> May I point out that this end of Mary Street has received no attention whatsoever in the ten years we have been here, and that my own friends prefer to leave their cars in Church Street and walk here rather than subject their car's springs to the appalling surfaces of these streets; that this whole area is rat-infested; that to my knowledge all that portion of the quarry face being filled in by the South Yarra bridge authorities, is being used as an unsavoury tip by all and sundry, and that the Council has made no effort to clean out the rats flourishing there; that this whole area is atmospherically polluted by a

> revolting odour from the official tip leased to the Prahran Council if the wind be from the north or east, or from the not so very Hygienic Meat Depot if the wind be from the west or south.[28]

And Mrs Harden of Docker Street on the Hill confessed: 'of late years I have been ashamed that we live here'. Councillors were outraged. Councillor Ryan accused the *News* of faking its photographs; Councillor Loughnan protested that they had just spent £100 on the City Reserve and only a year before had filled in the air raid trenches. The next week Councillor Jack Cremean blamed as the 'root' of the Richmond Council's 'squalid record' the nominee system that enabled councillors' relatives and friends to get Council jobs: certain 'old hands' were notorious for 'taking things easy on the job' and those who were willing to work were 'branded as bosses' men or black legs'.[29]

The *News* kept up the campaign about the condition of Richmond while the South Richmond branch began to press the Council to redefine its zonings to protect Richmond's threatened residential areas. Keon publicly accused the Housing Commission of discriminating against Richmond by concentrating on building new estates in suburbs like Highett and Reservoir. Then on 25 June Keon struck in parliament: 15 per cent of Richmond's houses were unfit for human habitation and Bill Barry the Housing Minister should come and inspect them for himself Throughout July the *News* backed him with a graphic exposure of Richmond's worst slums. The Council's housing inspector protested that only 12 per cent of Richmond's houses were condemned but Stan Keon and the *News* were on to a winner. Keon was in fact the first parliamentarian in Richmond's history who had the nerve, the commitment and the skill to fight for Richmond people's immediate and daily needs, even if it meant embarrassing his own Party. He may have been an intellectual and something of a puritan, but he earned enormous respect for his political courage. He did not take Richmond's loyalty to Labor for granted: he was out to transform the Labor movement and he had to win hearts and minds.[30]

The State Executive, in particular Pat Kennelly and Arthur Calwell, were worried by the crusaders' progress in Richmond. In January 1947 *Truth* spilled the rumour that Jack Dyer would be set up by Kennelly to challenge Keon at the pre-selection. Dyer, however, showed little interest in the proposal, but the speculation made business even 'brisker' at his milk bar. In May Kennelly declared that the Richmond Labor branches were 'too crook' to hold pre-selections for Council and the State Executive re-endorsed Jimmy Loughnan for West Ward. The *News* whipped up outrage among the crusaders and in June. Kennelly, with the sole support of Jimmy Loughnan, faced two hundred A.L.P. members at the Town Hall who received him in 'frigid silence' as he endeavoured to explain his stand. It was a fatal move. Kennelly and the State Executive were seen to protect a machine and its Council that dismayed and disgusted many ordinary, unpolitical, respectable Richmond citizens. Loughnan spoke angrily of that 'scabby rag', the *Richmond News*, that had created so much trouble in Richmond and alleged: 'There's a lot of faces here tonight that I have not seen around working for Labor before'. 'You mean we're not in the clique', called out a woman. Then Bernard Callinan rose to speak and issued a dire warning: 'Since I and quite a few of those here tonight were away from Richmond at the war for the past five and a half years, it is quite probable that Councillor Loughnan has not seen us around, but now we are back and determined to do the job for Labor and clean things up'.[31]

At the State election Keon held on to his majority despite the defeat of the Cain government. He intelligently supported Chifley's plan to nationalize the banking system: the money supply could not be left in private hands with safety; those who controlled the money supply of the nation controlled the life-blood of its economy and the nation was at the mercy of 'a small group of men, directors not only of banks, but also of the largest monopolies'.[32] On reform of the Legislative Council, he expressed a keen sense of class grievance:

> The people of Richmond did not need to go back further than the depression to get a thorough grounding in the type of men who occupied seats in the Council. They would remember how they blocked bills for unemployment relief. It was abundantly clear that these men had spent their lives amassing money for themselves and that they now sat in the chamber to protect their vested interests.[33]

And at the declaration of the poll he called on the A. L. P. to stop 'coquetting with Communists': to re-define its socialization objective to distinguish it from Communist tyranny, and to assert that 'personal, responsible ownership by the workers, either individually or co-operatively within the framework of a State-guided economy is the Labor Party's programme. . .' It was a masterly performance and timely, for Scullin, broken in health and prematurely aged by his prime ministership, had announced his retirement from Federal politics. A job in Canberra was vacant.[34]

1948 was a year of pre-selections in Richmond. The factions lined up as Keon's crusaders versus the Loughnan/Cremean/O'Connell machine, with John Wren lurking in the shadows. The crusaders lost their first round when their Maurice Sheehy was defeated in the pre-selection for the Melbourne Province; they complained of ballot rigging but Kennelly insisted that the winning margin was too handsome to warrant an investigation. Next came the R.C.C. pre-selections. The State Executive could not decide whether or not to concede to the pressure from the old machine to forbid pre-selection ballots; then in late May Kennelly proposed that the membership of the Richmond branches be frozen to prevent the crusaders stacking branches in preparation for Keon's Yarra pre-selection contest.[35] A month later the Cremean/Loughnan ticket swept the poll for each ward pre-selection and the *News* screamed:

> With local thugs reinforced by gangs from Collingwood, intimidation impersonation, forgery, bashings and the boot disgraced the A.L.P. election ballot for the Richmond Council on Saturday, Gangs in cars, with pockets full of union tickets, alternated between local pubs and polling booths. Even the cemeteries yielded up their dead who voted early and often.[36]

If the crusaders gave as good as they got in branch stacking and the smear, they were 'not very good at violence', according to Jim Cairns:

> Whether it was their Catholic morality—and if it was it was the first time it had reacted on an Irishman in that way—but they didn't seem to me to be much responsible for violence. The Eddys could always clean up two or three twice their size, it seemed. In one State Election Scully got hold of some fellow who'd won the light-heavyweight championship of the Australian universities, to go round with him as a bodyguard. And that of course was silly because it was like a red rag to a bull. And I think it was Billy Eddy who cleaned him up somewhere around Highett Street polling booth on the afternoon of the election.

A month later Keon did the unthinkable—he attacked John Wren in the parliament: 'It is no secret that because the Labor government took night trotting away from Mr. John Wren that he had set out to destroy that Government and he financed the campaign of the Country Party'. He seemingly took a bold risk, for his most serious rival for the Yarra pre-selection was Councillor Jack Cremean who was close to Wren. Cremean had been regarded as the heir apparent to Scullin for years. A fortnight later a redistribution was announced that created the seat of Hoddle, for which Cremean was the logical contender, and leaving Keon with a new Yarra that now encompassed middle-class Hawthorn. Keon probably knew what was afoot, and his attack on Wren could only endear him to his new electorate. The speculation, rumour-mongering and numbers game went on for months. Keon continued to make the headlines and at the end of November was banned from the parliament for the rest of the year when he gave a Nazi salute to the Speaker after a debate on the Mental Hygiene Authority Bill was gagged. By March 1949 it seemed that the anti-Keon forces had failed to get the numbers. Police supervised the pre-selection ballot: Cremean and Councillor Jack O'Connell had to be ordered out of the booths on several occasions; Keon won handsomely.[37]

In April 1949 the Richmond Council finally voted to sack Con Loughnan, his brother Jimmy, loyal to the end, being the sole dissenter. The outbursts of violence and the drinking had become intolerable. He was to have one more part to play in the Richmond political drama before he died in July 1954. In death even the *News* was sensible of the tragic waste of

> undoubtedly the most colourful figure in the history of Richmond's municipal affairs. As a young man Mr. Loughnan was hailed as a coming leader in the Labor movement. But the destiny promised by his forceful personality, his brilliance as a speaker and general ability was never to reach its rightful peak.[38]

The crusaders seemed to be carrying all before them. Then in May the leading Richmond Communist, Ken Miller, appeared on a morals charge over a young gir . He was acquitted, and the far Left, ever ready to suspect the worst of the far Right, were convinced that he had been framed. The Richmond Council pre-selections, however, brought the crusaders sweet success. The Central Executive cancelled the ballots but did appoint two crusaders. Gus Coloretti for West Ward and Bill Moran for South. Coloretti was an especially good choice. The son of Italian immigrants, he had known discrimination and poverty. Through night study he had acquired an array of qualifications and as a chiropodist had risen to the presidency of the Hospital Employees' Union. A gentle man, his integrity and devotion to duty had earned him wide respect. And at the Council elections the West Ward ratepayers returned him with an absolute majority over two opponents, the A.L.P.'s best vote in the ward for decades. On Council Coloretti and Moran joined with three sympathizers to form a new faction of 'reform' councillors. The new Mayor was Paddy O'Connell, nephew of the first Geoff and brother of Jack. He had entered Council in 1945 and, as a father of nine, his driving ideal was a Baby Health Centre for Burnley. As the *News* noted ingenuously: 'In attaining the Mayoralty, Councillor P. O'Connell has realized an ambition he said he has entertained since he began work as a council employee at the age of sixteen'.[39]

The reform councillors lost no time and began asking awkward questions about excessive overtime payments to council staff; the Cremean/Loughnan faction retaliated by using closed caucus meetings for debates. Tension mounted as the pre-selection for the State seat of Richmond approached. Frank Scully was the crusaders' candidate; Councillor Ernie Boland his opponent. The contest was hotly fought. The *News* tried to suggest that Boland was a man who had compromised his loyalty to Richmond and to the working class. Boland's supporters saw that more charitable accounts were published in the *Truth* and the *Sun*. The reform councillors kept up the pressure and the dramatic headlines; Scully and Keon conducted highly conspicuous wood-cutting expeditions to supply Richmond pensioners with firewood. And in November Scully swept the poll, doubling Boland's vote.[40]

Keon opened his 1949 Federal election campaign before a modest crowd of six hundred at the Richmond Town Hall. Again he took pains to distinguish the socialization objective of the Labor Party from Marxism, this time injecting more of the pulpit:

> The socialization objective of the Labor Party simply means that theA.L.P. believe that the goods of this earth were pro ided by God for the benefit of the people as a whole. That greed and exploitation of the means of production, distribution and exchange should not be allowed to be used in an anti-social manner. The Labor Party is not Communist. It was based on the fundamental principle that every human being is precious in his own right and that the protection and full development of the human personality was the purpose and measure of social policy.[41]

He needed to take pains for his Liberal opponent did not hesitate to liken the Labor platform to the Communist Manifesto. Advertisements throughout Richmond and Hawthorn warned: 'Only a few days left for you to decide between freedom of choice or regimentation of your whole life'. The Chifley government went down but Keon held firm in the new Yarra electorate, with an anti-Labor vote in Richmond below that of Scullin in 1946. Two candidates lost their deposit—the Communist and a Mr Vines, a Protestant-Democratic candidate. The Labor Party's internal battles had enticed some militant Protestants out of the woodwork and Mr Vines found 361 supporters in Hawthorn and 555 in Richmond.[42]

So Standish Michael Keon was a 'forty-niner', going to Canberra at the beginning of a twenty-three-year reign by the Liberal Country Party coalition, a political wilderness for the A.L.P. for which he would ultimately bear much of the blame. Yet Keon would lose also, Pat Kennelly, the king-maker:

> A tremendous shame—he'd have been prime minister of this country. I told Ben Chifley when I was giving him an outline of the fellows who had won in '49: 'You keep this fellow on the rails and he'll take this seat'.

Back in Richmond the crusaders were in full flight. On the Council Coloretti, Moran and Williams began attacking the re-zoning of residential land as industrial when Richmond's greatest need was for housing. They made allegations that some councillors and their relatives were doing well by selling property for high industrial prices after recent and judicious re-zonings. Coloretti so embarrassed Council over accusations of building permit graft on one site that work was stopped in April. As the August Council elections approached, the Cremean/Loughnan faction was on the run. The crusaders had successfully stacked all Richmond branches and Jimmy Loughnan was tipped off that he no longer had the numbers. Preferring an honourable retirement to a humiliating defeat, he decided to withdraw in favour of Ray Donovan. He had been twenty years a councillor, and Mayor three times, and had achieved much. Now an officer in the Taxation Department, he was a senior J.P. an M.M.B.W. Commissioner since 1936, leader of the A.L.P. in Council. a member of the committee of the Richmond Free Dispensary, and a Life Governor of every major metropolitan hospital. At the August elections the crusaders won every ward; only in the North Ward did an Independent who would later join the A.L.P. Dave Lewis. make a good showing.[43]

The next four years were the jewel in Richmond's municipal crown. Much was expected of the new Council and it made haste to honour its Christian commitment to the family and the needy. In November 1950 it announced a five-point plan to 'help family life in Richmond': a home help service, scholarships for the poor but clever, a community centre, special assistance for families in dire need and a wider commitment to charitable work. More was to follow as the crusaders put in place Richmond's first co-ordinated social welfare infrastructure. The Council even initiated a housing scheme in Mary Street—James Scullin Court. In Coloretti's mayoralty alone in 1952–53. with additional funds raised from the temporarily legal 'Housey' (Bingo), Richmond adopted the South Melbourne Council's free meals service scheme and was the first to put it 'on wheels'; it financially assisted the Elderly Citizens'Clubs and bought land for a boys' club (now the Jim Loughnan Memorial Hall), and it bought properties to enlarge the facilities of the Dame Nellie Melba Kindergarten and the Creche. Coloretti even found the time to donate his services free to perform chiropody for old people at the Dispensary. In 1952 the Council was able to economize and prevent a rate increase. Yet the crusaders were undoubtedly lucky in that they could raise funds from Housey that were unavailable to their predecessors and successors: in Maurie Sheehy's mayoralty of 1951–52 Housey yielded £8123 and the Citizens' Ball £3 10. The crusaders were not insensible of the propaganda value of their reforms. The *News* was incapable of criticism and broadcast every triumph. Scully co-ordinated his parliamentary speeches on housing with the Council's statements of policy and programmes. The undoubtedly useful collection of free firewood and briquettes for the pensioners saw Scully and Co. in high profile getting their hands dirty with the best of them. But is was not all success. While the Council persuaded the State Government to give £6000 for a sports park in the Survey Paddock, it had no more success than the bad old Council in obtaining outside financial aid to maintain the arterial roads that ran through the suburb. Then in March 1953 the Council issued a new zoning plan. The only dissenters were the two remaining 'machine' men on Council, Paddy O'Connell and Roy Jackson, who were dismissed as 'all for industry and nothing for residents'. The new zones largely conformed with existing areas; and factories in residential areas were guaranteed an unrestricted existence provided that they did not change their type of manufacturing. It was a conservative, even timed, plan and would invite criticism in later years that would help discredit the crusaders' administration of the city. They had chosen to freeze rather than reform Richmond.[44]

For all the surface calm of Richmond's political life, violence and disorder were never far away. Many of the old guard now found themselves expelled from the party and the Left acquired some unlikely allies: Ernie Boland for one, now residing in Mathoura Road, Toorak, took up the cause of the Communist Party in its campaign to obtain use of the Richmond Town Hall. At a Central branch meeting in March 1951 the police had to be called to eject 'undesirables' who 'had 'infiltrated' the meeting. And in June 1951 Councillor Ray Donovan was 'subjected to a violent attack' in a hotel by a man 'well known in Richmond'. But above all it was the crusaders' obsessive hounding of the Red Menace that promised disaster for the Labor Movement. Menzies' Communist Party Dissolution Bill drove a wedge into the A.L.P. between the Catholic Right and the rest of the Party. Keon was placed in an impossible position: he either disobeyed his Party or he relinquished his credibility as a fighter against Communism. Initially he wavered on the Bill, ostensibly unhappy about the possible injustices that could arise from its deliberately vague definitions of Communist sympathizers; then in September 1950 he abandoned all such reservations. With the unanimous support of the Yarra Campaign Council, he worked to have the Bill passed. At the 1951 double dissolution election Keon increased his majority over the Liberal candidate: 21 800 to 12 836. Ken Miller the Communist attracted only 1493 supporters in Yarra.[45]

Frank Scully, too, maintained the pressure. Doing well as a back-bencher in parliament and newly appointed to direct the Young Labor Association, he was given the responsibility of delivering the Labor Hour broadcast for Australia Day 1951. He warned Australia that Moscow had sent a message to Communists all over the world ordering them to sabotage the Western powers' industry and 'Communist Trade Union leaders in Australia are planning for a general strike to paralyse Australian industry and smash production'.[46] A month later Keon told his Richmond branch members:

> To any unbiased observer looking at the state of affairs in industry today, it can only appear that we have all contracted some collective madness and are determined to destroy what, compared with other countries is, or rather ought to be, a paradise. Nothing but strikes, stoppages, shortage, hardship, and trouble in a country where our only real worry should be the threat from the East. No matter what the import of miners' or wharfies' grievances, nothing can justify workers cutting their own throats at the dictation of a gang of Communist thugs who have muscled in to control all the key unions.[47]

But the crusaders, too, were losing touch with reality. The *Richmond News* became ever more intemperate. Anyone against them must be a

Communist or a Communist stooge. The paranoia infected the workplace as well as the union, and invaded the lives of ordinary people quite uninterested in Labor politics. *Isabel Williams* was by that time a mail sorter in the P.M.G.:

> If you didn't vote with the Catholics you were a Communist. There was a big hullaboloo when the men came back from the war and they reckoned the Post Office was a hotbed of Catholics and Communists—there was no centre line; you were one or the other. Then they had a Royal Commission about the Post Office being ant-ridden with Communists. We were called up and had J.P.s laid on for a week and had to swear allegiance to the King, which I'd done all my life because I'd been brought up a strong Royalist.

Isabel attended union meetings at the Trades Hall and at one sat on 'the Catholic side' with a friend from Richmond, who was howled down when she rose to speak 'about paper towels or something'. A fortnight later *Isabel* sat on the other side of the hall for the union meeting.

> I sat with my friends on the Left side. They were good Protestants and very loyal and they joked about being on the 'Left side', the 'Communist side'. The next day when I was clocking on I heard a chap talking to the time-keeper about my friend Mrs Fraser: 'She's one, she's a Com'. She didn't hear him because she was deaf, but she would have tom him to pieces. I didn't say anything because she would have made such a scene she would have ended up getting the sack. We weren't permanent so we had to tread very warily. On the Friday, up at the cafeteria they used to have lovely fish, so I used to have that for a change. At the table that same fellow asked to sit with me. He was having fish too. After ten minutes he said: 'I owe you an apology'. 'Why?' 'I thought you were a left footer.' 'What do you mean? I don't play football.' Then he said that he'd seen me sitting with the Communists at the meeting, but now I was eating fish on Friday so I must be all right.

The meandering and inconclusive Lowe Royal Commission threw little light on the Communist Party in Richmond. Only three activists were identified but Richmond did provide some prominent witnesses against the Communist Party: the local solicitor, Laurie L'Estrange, Scully and even Con Loughnan who, ironically, gave evidence on violence and intimidation, secret members, fellow travellers and disputed membership. It was his final appearance on the political stage.[48] But the crusade against Communist materialism was re-opening old sectarian and class wounds. As the crusaders became locked into a mad little world of their own, they drew on decades of class and religious grievance, tapping a vast reservoir of lowerclass Catholic resentment against secular sophisticates and the Protestant establishment. In an obituary for a Mrs Newcombe who had helped organize charwomen into the Miscellaneous Workers' Union, the *News* wrote:

In these days, when the loud-mouthed viragos of the Communist Party prance around in slacks doing nothing but talking of militancy and the working class, it is refreshing to recall the spirit of these grand old Labor women, of whom Mrs Newcombe was an exemplar. All of them were deeply religious women, but their faith inspired their fight for justice, courage and solidarity rather than weakened their courage and solidarity as the Reds would suggest.[49]

And in 1956 the *News* commented on the defeat of the 10 o'clock closing campaign:

With 'No' happily triumphant and the wowsers planning their next onslaught, we wonder what will happen when the 'Old Boys' of the Church Public Schools apply for a late licence for their Annual Ball. We were most impressed by the eloquent pleas of the leaders of these churches to protect young people from 'the Evils of Alcohol', but if you want to see young people of both sexes really 'pie-eyed' from the effects of the demon grog, we can recommend any public school ball. We have been to boozier turns but they were in the shearing sheds.[50]

1955 marked Richmond's centenary as a municipality. It was also the bitterest year in its entire history. Every Labor voter and every Catholic in Richmond would have to make a decision: a decision that divided families and friends, that ruined political careers, that consigned working-class politics to the wilderness in Victoria for twenty-seven years. As Keon and Scully went forth to do battle with the 'Kennelly gang' and the 'Communist stooge Evatt', the *News* and the branches cheered them on their missionary way. When they returned from the fateful Hobart Conference, three thousand branch members gave them 'thunderous applause' at the Richmond Town Hall as 'they gave an account of their fight against the bushranging tactics of the Evatt-Stout-Kennelly clique'.[51] When the Split actually came it seemed easier for the crusaders at first. To Gus Coloretti 'it didn't seem painful at the time because so many of my friends were of the same opinion: it *was* painful later and it ended my calculation about getting parliamentary endorsement'. Coloretti was later to blame anti-Catholic prejudice in the A.L.P. as the true impulse behind the Split. In Richmond the great Labor families were divided. The Cremeans went with the D.L.P.; their relatives by marriage, the O'Connells, went with the A.L.P. as did the Loughnans. The discredited O'Connell/Loughnan machine thus had an honourable path back to power landed in their laps and they would make much of being A.L.P. stalwarts,, heroes in a sea of D.L.P. rats. The pressure put on Labor leaders like Kennelly and Calwell is well known. Kennelly:

They nearly offered me the world. I don't know what I wasn't offered to go with them because I am a Catholic. I'm not a bit sorry at the stand I took, and I can tell you lady, I had some pressure—some pressure. But I said No.

> They were *mad*—I tried to tell them—they were mad and they had much more control than people think. It was a waste and even today, it's left such a bitter feeling in the Party that for a Catholic to get a good seat in this State is virtually impossible.

Yet however much their ostracism by the Church hurt leaders like Kennelly and Calwell, they were better equipped to cope than were most ordinary Party members. The pressure persisted for years after the Split, given terrifying force for simple people by the 'missions' where priests from other parishes would visit Cain Labor Catholics in their homes, calling them 'Communists' who were doomed to eternal damnation. Jim Cairns:

> In the 1958 campaign when they had their missions and all sorts of things, they had apparently been working on Bernie O'Connell and he was going straight to hell and all that. And he was very afraid and very aggressive. At a small street meeting we were having in South Richmond on the corner of Cotter Street, some bloke called him a Communist. And Bernie, even though he was smaller, flattened him—just like that. We had a truck with an amplifier in it and Gwen was sitting in the truck and Bernie came round and he was crying about it. He didn't really regret having knocked him down, but he was crying about the whole incident.

The State election in May 1955 was terrifying in the bitterness and hysteria unleashed by the Split. As Robert Murray has found, everyone who took part in the campaign has stories of being spat upon, of doors slammed in faces, of fights and whispering campaigns. Cain Labor Catholics were snubbed at church, their children hounded at school. At St Ignatius' the Jesuits lent eloquent support to the crusaders. Threatening telephone calls and letters abounded; some leaders received dead rats in the mail. The Split devastated the Richmond A.L.P. Not only had all Richmond's parliamentarians gone over, but so also had almost the entire active membership of the Party. Only in East Richmond, where the O'Connells had maintained control, did anything remain of an organized Party branch, and it was from the O'Connell clan that Pat Kennelly had to choose a candidate who could defeat the charismatic Frank Scully. Kennelly later considered it one of the greatest mistakes of his career that he chose Councillor Paddy O'Connell, brother of Councillor G. J. (Jack) O'Connell, instead of Jack Dyer to fight Scully. Jim Cairns was one of many A.L.P. members from other suburbs who were called in to letter-box in Richmond. Despite his years in the Police Force, he knew nothing of Richmond and the thought of standing for Yarra had never entered his head. During the letter-boxing he had met no one from the Richmond A.L.P. so he decided to attend Paddy O'Connell's Richmond Town Hall meeting:

> I went into the Town Hall and I saw this little stocky fellow talking on the platform and went away thinking he was the candidate. But the candidate hadn't turned up at that main meeting—that was Paddy. Paddy would never speak from a platform. He'd have a nail in his shirt too, instead of a button.

It was brother Jack who gave the speech for Paddy. Cairns was later impressed by Jack O'Connell: 'He was neat and tidy, quick-footed, never drank much; he was one of those people who make use of a hundred per cent of their capacity'. Paddy, however, 'never did much; he'd never do any door knocking or canvassing—he really did lack confidence'. The A.L.P. campaign was disfigured by fights at Scully's Town Hall meeting and accusations of his campaign workers being bashed while letter-boxing at night. Council out-door staff were implicated in the violence and Scully traded on the crusaders' record against the bad old machine on the Richmond Council. And when the votes were counted Scully had held enough Protestants to win, with 8053 to O'Connell's 7979 in the two-party-preferred votes. He was the only D.L.P. candidate ever to win a Lower House seat in a State or Federal election.[52]

Next came the Richmond Council elections. The A.L.P. lost no time, and gained little kudos, in reinstating some of the discredited local identities who had been expelled by the crusaders. The A.L.P. (Anti-Communist) councillors campaigned on their impressive record: since 1949 when the first two crusaders had entered Council, the loan liability had been reduced from £131 020 to £84 616; the bank overdraft of £13 707 had been converted into a credit balance of £24 738; while public works expenditure had grown from £19 251 to £33 199. Yet they lost two seats—North Ward in a close result and East Ward with a massive majority to Jack O'Connell. The *News* alleged electoral fraud and saw nothing ominous in the result: the crusaders faced the Federal election in December full of confidence that Stan Keon would be returned to Canberra to help lead the new and purified Labor Party.[53]

This time Kennelly did not make a mistake. Over the heads of Richmond hopefuls he spirited in Jim Cairns to take on the intellectually formidable Keon. Once presented with a *fait accompli*, the Richmond party accepted Cairns 'strangely well when you consider it was someone who didn't live in the electorate, an ex-policeman, academic—it could hardly be worse'. Kennelly advised Cairns to go straight to the people in the steets. Friends, fellow academics. the Melbourne University Labor Club, A.L.P. activists and trade unionists descended on Richmond to work for Cairns. The Richmond Communists, too, threw their weight and experience behind the A.L.P. campaign and one Norm Gallagher, in particular, made his presence felt. Cairns held seventy-two street meetings in Yarra—later claimed to be a record for a single electorate in any election. Keon was hampered by his responsibilities as a deputy leader in the national campaign, but he was also very confident. Both sides deluged Yarra in so much election literature that Richmond was said to be looking forward to its first 'White Christmas'. It was a nasty campaign. The *News* dubbed Cairns's Richmond Town Hall meeting a 'Hate Keon Rally'; when Keon finally began to campaign in Richmond, 'the only thing he did was this behind the hand stuff, says Cairns: 'He had an expression that if anyone mentioned how I'd left the Police Force I'd turn white'. Old sectarian flames flared again. *Isabel Williams* was disgusted by 'the scurrilous papers they used to put in the door about Dr Cairns: don't vote for him, he's a lecturer in economics at the university and what would he know about the working class—not knowing that he had worked his way up to those jobs by sheer ability', and *Isabel*, for the first time in her life, voted Labor, because of the way he stood up to the D.L.P.' Such votes were vital. The street meetings, too, were vital, Cairns again:

> Sometimes I'd have a thousand or fifteen hundred people, say, on the corner of Coppin and Wall Streets. Once we had Arthur Calwell who got a bad reception, but I didn't ever. It was fortunate that I was an outsider, but I also mesmerized them a bit. They were impressed by the way I could talk—with what education could do—and they thought I was a nice fellow, and they couldn't believe the stories they'd heard like being an ex-copper.

In Richmond's narrow streets Cairns's campaign workers could hear chuckles coming from the darkness as families sat on their verandas on hot nights and listened. There was violence, too, though Cairns was kept ignorant of what was being perpetrated in his name. And when it came to the count it was very close: Cairns won with a margin of 791 after the distribution of preferences. He knew that had his name not come above Keon's on the ballot paper he would have lost. As for Standish Michael Keon, 'who would have been prime minister', he would contest many elections yet, but his political career was finished. He had gambled all and lost; he was barely forty years old.[54]

8

Middle Life

Making Good

Muriel Thompson:	*The war made a difference. When the men come home they seemed to have a lot more money—they got their gratuity money and they got regular money.*
Jean Fowler:	*All the Australians have gone out of Richmond—they've gone out further.*
Muriel Thompson:	*They've all made good.*

In the summer of 1941–42, as the Japanese bombed Pearl Harbor and made their sweep through the Islands and Malaya, Professor Wilfred Prest's workers were out in Richmond, investigating the housing and income of the people for the massive University of Melbourne Social Survey. A small number of further interviews were conducted in June and September 1942, hence Richmond was surveyed before the Manpower Commission commenced the conscription of labour. The findings on housing confirmed the 1936–37 study undertaken by the Slum Abolition Commission; but the evidence collected on income and work was truly astonishing. No fewer than 90 per cent of those households with breadwinners capable of participating in the workforce and looking for greater income security had already benefited from the war. Only two injured returned servicemen and a group of small shopkeepers, struggling against the shortages of goods, had suffered a decline in income as a direct consequence of the war.[1]

In a total sample of 228 households who furnished sufficient information for analysis, 110 or 48 per cent appeared at first sight to have been unaffected by the war. However, thirty-nine of these were old age and war pensioners, invalids, or retired people living off annuities, savings, rent or investments. Then of the remaining seventy-one unaffected households, fourteen were permanent government employees, nine were self-employed, three were white-collar workers and twenty-seven were 'job-for-life' workers who had suffered little or no unemployment in the last decade. (The Manpower Commission would later draw some of these workers into war industry.) Only eighteen of those households with members capable of entering the workforce or the armed services had not been touched by the war: that is 10 per cent of the eligible households.

Of the remaining 118 households who were drawing new or improved income from the war, only fifteen had members in the armed services. These were families at risk, of course, of losing financially through the death or disablement of a breadwinner. The Prest Survey found only one war widow in Richmond, but one family of butchers in Mary Street by 16 January 1942 had two sons as prisoners of war. The father and the remaining son were in the militia and a fourth son had died at nineteen. Non-combatants, however, could find new horizons in the services. A former tramway employee of Buckingham Street was doing dispensing work in the medical division of the R.A.A.F.: 'He finds it very interesting and would like to continue in similar work after the war'. Another ten households had representatives in both the armed services and war industry: by far the largest change had come in civilian jobs and wages.

Thirty-five households were benefiting simply from the general improvement in the economy. A thirty-six-year-old plumber from Bridge Road who had earned £5 a week before the war could bring home over £8 a week by 1942. In Wall Street a working couple had a net income of £13 a week and fourteen shillings board from their son who was an apprentice fitter. The father, also a fitter, had been unemployed in England thirteen years before and then for two years in Australia. His wife ran a mixed business and found she was selling twice as much milk as before the war, plus more butter, cream and breakfast cereals. Yet while her Richmond clientele were spending more on food, she was disgusted at how much more they were spending on the horses: 'Women in the streets laying bets with bookies'. This family was saving up for their own home and an escape from Richmond. In Gardner Street there was another family saved by the war. On sustenance still at the outbreak of war, the forty-nine-year-old father had by now managed to get into the Victorian Railways as a permanent labourer. The week before he had brought home £5 and handed nearly all to his wife. The family paid 12s 6d for an old three-bedroomed house that was almost beyond repair. The landlord would do nothing; the Housing Commission had paid a visit but had not come back. During his seven years on sustenance the father had scrounged the bricks to pave the back garden. The bath in the outside bathroom had a hole, the house had no sink or inside tap, and 'the facilities for storing food are very bad being in a small enclosed part which must be gone through to get into the yard'. They had four children: one ten, one eight, then a telling gap to the three-year-old and a new baby. At forty-three the mother was determined to catch up on the years of childbearing denied her by the Depression. This was a loving family: 'the mother appeared a better type than some visited and evidently cared for the children exceedingly well considering the conditions of the house'. Above all, the investigator was struck by the sight, on arrival, of the mother playing with the children. In a community of harried and worn-out women, few had the time or the energy for the joys of motherhood.

Some workers found that once-casual jobs became regular in wartime; others were elevated into good money by the growth of overtime: a moulder who had been on sustenance for nine years found his income raised from £5 3s to £7 2s. Another moulder went from a pre-war wage of £6 to £9 12s by January 1941. A coppersmith at the Newport Workshops with overtime raised his income from £6 6s to £8 2s. These were wages that could generate real savings, building a financial launching pad for a post-war escape to the garden suburbs and a home of their own. Three household heads were old men able to re-enter the workforce to make up labour shortages. One from Hunter Street was a sixty-nine-year-old wharf-labourer. With two days work a week he made £3 10s 4d which was more than double the old age pension. Five households had wives in the workforce who had been occupied at home before the war. And in one family of a thirty-six-year-old woman and her invalid father, where there had been 'a frightful struggle to keep going' while she earned just over a pound a week from domestic work, a new job making airmen's goggles promised that 'things should be different'.

Direct employment in war industry above all had made the difference for the majority of these households. Ten households—a fifth of the war industry group—were dependent on the boot trade alone. One fifty-eight-year-old man had been earning thirty shillings to £2 before the war doing casual boot repairs at a market; now he was a finisher in a Collingwood factory and bringing home £5 a week. Another bootmaker in his fifties from Somerset Street had been unemployed for twelve years before the war. This family owned their own house so could not draw sustenance: 'They just managed to live as best they could'. Their only son was seven years old. Now the father was earning £5 12s a week as a stuff-cutter and the family's sights were set on fleeing Richmond and its memories 'as soon as they can afford it'. In general war industry there was a former dray driver, unemployed for ten years in the Depression, who as an iron-worker now earned £5 10s with overtime. A boilermaker from Stanley Street, after overtime, took home £9 a week. His two teenage children were in good jobs and paid an additional £2 a week board to the family income. And a furnaceman of forty-four took home £7 a week after a seven-day week, and his new bride of twenty-four earned £2 15s making comouflage nets in Burnley. This man was paying £1 a week maintenance to his two children by an earlier marriage. Before the war he had been on £4 5s as a railway ganger and scarcely able to afford divorce. Finally, a once-poor family in Rooney Street, paying twenty-five shillings for a house that was 'very old and about to fall down', but 'clean and adequately furnished', had 'hit the big time' through its sons. The father, an iron-worker, was on the basic wage but one son, just out of his apprenticeship as a moulder, was clearing £7 a week and the other, on £4 10s before the war, now earned £10 before overtime in the same engineering job. Such young working-class men could only gain from the war; for however desperate their desire to enter the armed services, government Manpower regulations kept them safely and honourably at home.

By contrast there were those still in dire poverty. A strict poverty line is hard to determine in this sample. Some old age pensioners were struggling; others appeared to be coping. As always, survival on a low income depended on tough self-discipline, and the senile, the simple and the incapacitated were doomed to deprivation. Drink, too, could make all the difference between survival and suffering. A family of six in Railway Crescent had three breadwinners: the father a railways labourer ostensibly on the basic wage and two teenage sons earning just over £1 a week each; but the father had brought home only £2 4s that week and the house was in a 'dirty and untidy condition'. By far the worst house the survey found in Richmond was at 104 Cremorne Street. A seventy-seven-year-old man paid 12s 6d for a structure that 'doesn't deserve to be called a house'. The electricity had not been connected for years; only a single gas jet shed a feeble light in the kitchen. In every room there were great holes in the plaster, rats had gnawed away the skirting boards, floor boards were missing or buckled. The old man had covered up the rat holes with tin as best he could. The only touch of home was a picture in his bedroom of Moses being handed to Pharoah's daughter: 'Has had it thirty years without knowing what it was—was quite pleased to have a reminder of the days when he heard "Bible stories"'. The old man hadn't been to church for thirty years but lived 'a good life—don't have anything to do with women'. He could neither read nor write.

Now with full employment, the causes of poverty that would endure for the next four decades were brought out in sharp relief: old age, infirmity, the loss of a male breadwinner and low wages with too many dependants. The role of the casual labour economy was quickly fading in working-class life. Only three male household heads remained trapped in a low income derived from irregular employment. The plight of the fatherless family, however, was as acute as ever. The Commonwealth widow's pension was a moral improvement on the old system of declaring children 'neglected', but it was still inadequate to support a family. At 17 Pearson Street lived the widowed mother of eight children. Four were living away from home; two were still at school. With her pension and child endowment, her income was £2 7s a week. A twenty-one-year-old daughter paid £1 board and so did the seventeen-year-old-son. They paid 17s 6d rent for a house 'in a very bad state of repair'. The mother was further handicapped by being very deaf: she was dreading the day her twenty-one-year-old daughter married. And at 108 Balmain Street lived a thirty-eight-year-old widowed mother of three. The eldest boy earned £1 8s 2d a week as a railway bookseller, the next son was an invalid, the youngest was eight. With superannuation, her widow's pension, the invalid son's pension (six shillings) and child endowment, her unearned income was £2 12s a week. They paid 17s 6d a week for a 'very old' house in 'poor repair'. At 8 Hodges Street lived a widow who was 'an example of people who have seen better days'. Her son was seven when her husband died; now she lived on his £2 military allotment. Her only other support was in free eggs and cream she received for helping her brother in his dairy for two days a week. She suffered from bad varicose veins. She apologized for her house; her son 'did not like bringing friends home'. It was damp, the foundations had collapsed, the lavatory was 'very poor'—the seat was always too wet to sit on. The yard was a 'mire' in winter. The landlord was prevailed upon to install a new copper—at a cost of £1 2s—and promptly increased the rent by ls 6d. Now paying 16s 6d rent a week she could scarcely afford to demand any further improvements. When women were forced to work to support a family, they were no better off than those on the pension. With the coming exception of women war workers in the metal trades, all female wages condemned working mothers to dire poverty. A widow in Rose Street made only £2 a week from dressmaking; a widow in Mary Street was bringing home £2 14s in good weeks as a press hand in a canister factory, after twenty-three shillings a week before the war from domestic service. Only one female head of a family had entered war industry by the time of the survey.

Finally there were the big families. Big families could go from acute poverty to comfort once enough older children were in the workforce; but while they were still young, fecundity brought disaster. The prize-winner of the Richmond survey was a family at 71 Abinger Street. The thirty-year-old mother had already borne ten living children: the eldest was twelve, the youngest eighteen months. The thirty-eight-year-old father had been on sustenance for four years in the Depression and now cleared about £5 a week driving a Yellow Cab. The family income was boosted by £1 15s in Child Endowment, but that was paid annually. They paid £1 1 s a week for a single-fronted house of three bedrooms and one living room. There were no sleep-outs to ease the congestion. When asked their residential preference, they expressed a wish for a 'bigger place'. The house had no sink or inside tap; the bath was outside, and there was no hot water.

The couple and the baby slept in one room, four children in another, two in the third. The three other children slept in 'different houses in the neighbourhood'. (One other vast family in the survey similarly accommodated excess children in a second house nearby.) Part of the house had been damaged by fire caused by the previous tenant and had not been repaired. Water poured in the roof, the water pressure was terrible, the yard a morass in winter. The children had 'measles and whooping cough'. The mother wanted the rent reduced but had not yet 'screwed neighbours up to the pitch of signing a petition to present to the Fair Rents Court'.

This then was the profile of comfort and poverty in war-time Richmond. Around 8 per cent of the sample of 228 households appeared to be in dire poverty, but a realistic measure of poverty must include those who, while appearing to be managing, had little margin for error. If we include all pensioners and retired people on small incomes, and all household heads on wages near the basic wage, we have a group of people with a perilous hold on survival. If they appeared to be coping at the time of the survey, it was only because of good luck and good management. Hence for those in or near poverty, the true figure for Richmond in 1941–42 was 43 per cent. But the war had already made an astonishing difference to this working-class community. Those who had the skills and the health to take advantage of the war economy were building a financial base for escape into home ownership in a garden suburb. The war was in fact driving a wedge into the working class between the affluent worker and the unskilled and the unemployable. The old division between the regular and respectable, and the casual and rough, had mutated. The casual economy was declining and trade unions were winning better wet-weather pay and attendance money for out-door workers and stevedores. However, a widening income gap divided the skilled and the unskilled, the employed and the unemployed, the male and the female breadwinner. Women remained in the ranks of the poor and the absence of a male breadwinner continued to be the most significant cause of family poverty. The much vaunted Welfare State failed from its inception to sustain in dignity and decency the old, the sick, the unemployed, and the widowed or deserted. Only the skills developed during a lifetime in poverty enabled so many to survive on their pensions. And as the newly affluent moved into 'middle Australia', the decaying industrial suburbs became the refuge of the old and the failed. The working class was being divided both economically and geographically.

The flight from the inner suburbs was, of course, nothing new. It had accelerated in the 1920s but the Depression had driven many young couples like *Monica Rinoldi* and her Light Horseman back to the inner suburbs after they lost their homes. During the Depression those who stayed in work or found good employment quickly after the worst was over were often able to take advantage of the collapse in property values.

In outer suburbs like Box Hill and Moorabbin, vacant blocks had reverted to the local council after the owners had defaulted on the rates and were sold off at just the value of the rates. *Hamish Roberts* was one of many who moved to Box Hill: 'the payments on a home were not very high and as long as you had a regular income, you could do it'. *Lilian Campbell* and her husband were another couple who got through the Depression unscathed and 'made good' with reasonable ease. *Lilian*, none the less, found leaving Richmond painful. First they moved to Sandringham where she was desolate with loneliness. By 1938 her husband had the capital to take on a hairdressing business in Toorak village and they moved into a house in Grange Road. One day *Lilian* walked down to the river and it suddenly dawned on her that Burnley was on the opposite bank and that she was within walking distance of her mother's house. She cheered up at once: Richmond had provided such a complete world for her as a child and young woman, that she had only the haziest knowledge of the outside world. *Lilian* took Toorak in her stride:

> When we went to Toorak in 1938, we would have been considered 'in trade'. It wouldn't matter about the upper strata—they could make their money out of boot polish and biscuits, but we were 'in the village', we were shopkeepers. Thirty years there and thirty of the best years of my life, and I used to say to my husband: 'When we're in, we're in it; but when we're out, I'll be out of it', and I would have willingly, gladly, lovingly gone back to Richmond.
>
> The very top strata, the oldest ones, were the nicest ones—they are the most secure. But the newly rich were the ones that made you feel that you were there to wait on them. Maybe it's my early childhood where I'm Richmond born and bred and I'm Richmond still in my blood. I could gladly go back to Richmond tomorrow and feel at home.

Lilian never did go back but she lives close enough to be able to look at the Pelaco factory on the Richmond skyline every night before she goes to bed.

It was everyone's ambition to own their own house, but there were houses for sale for a song in Richmond if you wanted one. These people were in fact fleeing working-class life itself. Putting Richmond behind you was putting bad memories behind you. And it was only natural, especially after the Depression, that people wanted to put as much distance between their past and new selves as possible. *Margaret Taylor* now feels so remote from the Depression that she wonders how they ever survived it: 'You put it past you and forget it and think aren't I lucky—I'm much better off than my mother and grandmother'. *Margaret* and her husband put a deposit on a house, 'but it was still a struggle; you hardly spent anything on clothes and nothing on luxuries—you'd buy some second-hand furniture—our oak extension table cost 37s 6d'. *Mary* and *Doug Davis* found the 'hardest part' was getting the deposit together for their house in Fairfield, even though *Doug* was never out of work. They ended up paying it off at twenty-five shillings a week which taxed all their skills of saving for years: 'You thought you'd never see the end of it and the kids were little and everything'. *Monica Rinoldi* and her Light Horseman also bought a house in Fairfield in their first step back towards dignity, but many couples went further out into new communities that were free of history and class associations. All but one of the *Smiths* made good and left Richmond. Once *George* was in work again, he and *Phyllis* sold his father's house and with the proceeds bought a new house in Mentone. For *Phyllis* Richmond was 'starting to change'; it was getting 'congested'; there were rumours about the Housing Commission's intentions; and the children had come down with diphtheria and whooping cough while *George* was on sustenance. Mentone, by contrast, seemed like a paradise. There were gum trees and wild gladioli and mushrooms outside the front gate. You could leave the front door open without fear of thieves and 'stay down the beach until 10 o'clock at night': 'We thought the children won't get sick here'. But, once in Mentone, *Phyllis*'s tolerance of hardship changed. In the Depression she had resigned herself to *George*'s absences on sustenance work; now she deeply resented his being manpowered and sent interstate on construction jobs. They had escaped Richmond and all its association; they had 'done their bit' of suffering and it was unfair that they should have to make further sacrifices of their family life.

The seeming miracle of World War II was that the economic growth carried over into peace. After the inevitable dislocations of the demobilization and the retrenchment of munitions workers, there were soon plenty of jobs. In 1947 the District Employment Office found jobs for 1273 people in Richmond; by June 1948 the Commonwealth Employment Service had 42 789 vacancies on its books in Victoria, 2064 of them in Richmond alone. And the vacancies for males almost doubled those for females—there was no shortage of jobs for returned soldiers as after World War I. Not surprisingly, in June, Alexander's store in Richmond broke all previous sales records and one Friday the store's doors had to be closed three times to control the crowd. With money in their purses now, working-class matriarchs took up the sport of bargain-hunting on sale days in the big city stores, where ample backsides and the judicious use of the high heel got you first go at the tables groaning with bargains. At the Central State School, where eighteen years previously the teachers were buying breakfasts for the children of the unemployed out of their own pockets, the children could now donate a hundred dozen eggs for the Hospital's Egg Day appeal.[2]

Of course there was hardship. There was still rationing and Menzies would win the 1949 Federal election almost on the promise of ending petrol rationing alone. Working-class incomes were rising but so also were prices and after a vigorous campaign by Keon, who addressed workers in their lunch breaks, Richmond recorded the biggest 'Yes' vote in the country in the 1948 referendum on price control. The Richmond Council appalled ratepayers in 1948 when it raised its rates to the maximum allowable under the Local Government Act so that Richmond was taxed at nearly double the rate of Toorak. The great coal and maritime strikes of 1949 afflicted Richmond people both as workers and consumers. *Bill Shannon* remembers the wharf strike as 'the hardest thing I had—Dad was out for nearly sixteen weeks and I knew we were going bad. It was in the winter but we never went without a feed'. That bitter winter of 1949 polarized Australia, creating in many a lasting distrust of the Labor movement. Old class sympathies tended to fade when you were in a nice home in a new suburb.[3]

The greatest hardship remained in housing. Melbourne desperately needed new homes and, with the shortage of building materials, both government and private enterprise preferred to concentrate on building new houses in outer suburbs while the housing stock of the inner suburbs continued to deteriorate. Housing Commission homes enabled the *Clark* sisters to leave Burnley: *Thelma* and her husband and two children into a detached concrete house in Chadstone; *Irene* twenty years later, and against her will, into a high-rise flat in Prahran. The housing crisis temporarily slowed the exodus to new pastures and the continuing poverty of the old, the sick, the unskilled and the fatherless forced many to stay. Some chose to stay, of course, reluctant to cut ties of business, political power and family in Richmond. And Richmond still had good streets and good houses. *Alice Murphy* and her husband owned a large brick house in one of Burnley's riverside streets and *Alice* was to walk by the river nearly every day for the rest of her life. Jimmy Loughnan lived in a handsome brick home on the Hill which he renovated sumptuously; Gus Coloretti built a modern cream brick veneer home on the Hill; Stan Keon, despite the end of his political career and his having business interests outside Richmond, bought in prestigious Erin Street and turned his house into one of the most elegant Victorian restorations in the suburb. Such fortunates were able to pursue a privatized middle-class existence in Richmond; most Richmond people would have to move out before they could enjoy such comfort and space. Those who stayed in Richmond's poor streets usually had no alternative. The *Kanes* owned their house but they had come out of the Depression with a mountain of debt. *Jean Fowler*'s husband now had more money but he kept it for himself. Once her sons had grown up, however, she went out to work and made enough to commence buying their house from the landlord. When her husband died his life insurance paid off the balance. *Isabel Williams* left factory work for good in 1943 when she entered the Post Office as a mail sorter. She overcame sectarian prejudice and, by the sheer force of her high examination results, won permanency and promotion. She now cared for her younger brother and decided to buy a house, but with her low wages as a woman and high deductions for superannuation, could afford only to buy in Richmond. *Harold Stephenson* also bought in Richmond: he wanted to be near his ageing mother and the chance of a spacious house in the good part of South Richmond appeared in 1951. It was to be only temporary but somehow it became a permanent commitment. *Muriel Thompson* also had to go out to work to build up the savings to buy their own home. Her husband had left the waterfront for permanency as a ganger in the P.M.G., but after his superannuation was deducted and he took his allowance for cigarettes and beer, there was still precious little cash each week. *Muriel* was content now: 'as long as it was regular I was happy and things began to brighten up a bit after being on the sustenance'. Then the *Thompsons* were afflicted by a piece of bad luck that is a nuisance for the comfortable and a catastrophe for the poor: the Taxation Department informed them that the P.M.G. had made a clerical error and had not been deducting enough tax from her husband's wages. They had to pay off the debt at two to three shillings a week and *Muriel* was back on the scrounge:

> I went to the grocer to tell him that we would only be getting tea and sugar from now on—not biscuits or any extras, and the grocer said: 'Mrs *Thompson*, you come any time you like. Get what you want and when you do get your money, pay it back'. They were all the same like that—wonderful people. There were a lot of scrags around and they wouldn't care anything, but we was never like that and we was always looking for the best. Though I suppose I was a bit cunning what with begging for a job and finishing up forelady almost.

But if it was beyond some to 'make good', perhaps their children could. Despite being Depression babies, those children were the first Australian working-class generation since the children of the convicts and new settlers in the 1830s and 1850s to achieve some significant upward social mobility—not much, not enough, but some. Economic growth and greater Government spending on education arrived just in time to enable the very bright to stay on longer at school. Parents like the *Stephensons*, the *Thompsons*, the *Fowlers*, *Friedrich Smith* and his sister *Phyllis*, the *Murphy* sisters, would see their children enter the middle class. Teaching proved the best recruiter of working-class brains; the expensive professions remained closed to all but the most gifted and ambitious.

A mother like *Muriel Thompson* had nothing but herself to give to her children; her only resources were her mental and physical capacities and she used them to the full. Perhaps unwittingly, she broke with working-class values and privatized her family life: 'We used to tell them to bring their friends in—not let them play around in mobs in the street because Richmond was full of mobs'. What had been good enough for her as a child was not good enough for her daughters:

> Both my children got good jobs—one worked in a bank and the other in Lane's Motors, in offices—that's where I failed. There was no offices about in our time because the school education was up to sixth grade, then they began the seventh and eighth and I went on to the seventh and eighth but you couldn't get to university or anything. And I thought if I have children—but of course I married a man who wasn't very flourishing—he was all right but work wasn't too good at that time. I didn't have anything but they learnt dancing and elocution and I put them at the piano—they both played the piano. Of course, they were good kids and I could do that. Even though their Dad drank. I think they must have followed me and I took them to church all the time—well not *all* the time because I'm not—well, I play Bingo and cards.

And *Muriel* was well rewarded. One daughter entered the élite MacRobertson Girls' High School; the other is now very 'lah-di-dah' and to her delight at a recent 'back to Richmond' day people could not believe that they were related. *Muriel* has realized the ambition that came to her as a young mother while she was raising money to buy shoes for the children in the kindergarten: 'I didn't want them to be like me'.

Painfully aware of her own lack of education, all she could do academically for her girls was to involve herself in raising money for their school. Charity work of all sorts became almost an obsession with *Muriel*: as a recipient of charity herself she mitigated the humiliation by reversing roles for the rest of her life. Her work for Brighton Street State School continued for decades after her daughters had left the school and she was president of the Parents' Committee from 1938 to 1958.

> I didn't have many good times but I had the fun of the world. I was on the committee up at Brighton Street State School and we used to run a ball every year. And when the war was on, we bought shoes and things for the children with the money. We used to make their dresses out of paper, with frills, and we used to have the minuet and all those dances. We made Easter bonnets out of paper and in Apple Blossom Time we made hoops stuck with paper flowers. Every factory in Richmond knows me because I'd collect rubbish and left-overs for all this school work and charity fêtes. At Christmas we gave every child a toy and I was Father Christmas and they'd say: 'It's not Father Christmas because she's wearing a wedding ring'. But the men on the committee couldn't get off work. And the rubber boots got stuck because I've got big feet and big legs. We had a mock wedding one day and we dressed up as a minister with collar at the back, and in a night-gown we had a funny old bride.

She treasured the prestige of office; she was fascinated by the school, and could not keep away from it, driven perhaps by unacknowledged yearnings:

> Then there was the Opportunity Grade. I used to go in—'Good morning, Miss'—that was me. The teacher was a friend of mine, see, and she'd say: 'Look at Woodsy over there'. Woodsy was a bit—you know—and he used to come and tell her about Mum and 'Uncle' in the front room and there wasn't enough room for the kids. They used to open their little mouths a little too much. He couldn't do his sums or anything, but he had a paper round and there's Woodsy, under the desk, reckoning up his paper round and he wasn't a penny out. She knew, but he didn't know she knew, and she said: I'll let him continue on, *Muriel*, because he's learning and I can't teach him'. But that was teaching him marvellous.

Muriel was a godsend to Brighton Street School. By 1958 her committee, with their twice-weekly card parties and stalls, had bought the school a projector, radios and loudspeakers, sporting equipment and library books. And they had continued to organize the school ball, provide sports trophies and act as the governing body of the school.

Jean Fowler, too, threw herself into the Parents' Committee; her sons were her whole life. And *Jean*, who was more conscious than *Muriel* that the only thing she had learnt at school was shame, was similarly determined that her boys should not repeat her own sufferings. She broke with her church and sent the boys to the State School, but events began to take an unexpected turn:

> The first one—he was a terror—I used to have to open the gate and all the kids were after him. He was a demon, but Mr Hunter said: 'He's a bright boy—he's going over to Toorak Central'. And he got better as he went along. He went further and further.

And so *Jean*, who had sat in school as 'the dumbest thing on earth' because she could afford no books, saw her first son gain entry to Melbourne High School and then to the Law Faculty at the University of Melbourne:

> It wasn't too much of a struggle, but his father always said: 'I went without pants to get him there'—he used one pair of pants and kept washing them out. When you see them go on like that—I couldn't go on—there was nothing like that—to go to university—they were snobs. But since *Bob* got there on a scholarship, things have changed a terrible lot. I had to leave school about thirteen and go to work—we went to the box factory. I put my age up a year—I crossed it out of the birth certificate so I could go there and earn some money. But there was nothing else for us then and I thought that my kids were going to go on if they wanted to.
>
> We never let *Bob* down. He got his books but we had to pay his fares and we gave him some money for morning teas because we couldn't see him out of it with the other kids buying theirs. And he was always kept in a beautiful suit—we made sure of it.

> Holidays he'd get jobs—working at the rabbit place, carting little towels to the factories, as a shopwalker—he'd get into anything, he wasn't a snob.
>
> When he was at uni the floor had a big hole and he'd bring his friends home. 'Oh, you can't.' 'Why worry', he said and they just made a habit of jumping over the flaming hole. And he used to make pancakes for them and sit here of a night.

And at the graduation in the new Wilson Hall:

> Oh I felt lovely. I took a photo in a little box camera under the mural in the hall. I was that proud. I was thrilled to bits to see him come up and get it.

Then came another surprise. He was due to start his articles when he announced that he wanted to study theology:

> I thought, 'What the hell's theology?' 'I'm going to be a Presbyterian minister.' 'Oh, how did that come into my family?' Good heavens, if you'd known his father you'd wonder how the heck it happened.

For *Jean*'s second son things went very differently. He was beginning to show even greater academic promise than his older brother:

> He was a real clever kid, dux of the school over here, then Toorak Central and Melbourne High. He was doing Leaving when he had an accident on a kid's truck. He hit his head on a bridge and was unconscious in hospital for nine days. He came out having fits. He had to leave school at Leaving—he demanded it at the time. Now he really regrets it. But they couldn't push him because of the tablets and the head, Woodfull [the former Australian cricket captain] told us that when the day's finished he's tired and because of the fits thinks that everyone is against him and he wouldn't go on with it. With *Rick* it could have been worse. He could have been a drinker, but he doesn't drink or smoke and he hasn't had fits for years. He's got eight kids and he's a good father, a good provider and a good worker.

Bill Shannon grew up with *Jean*'s boys: he is in awe of *Bob*, but '*Rick*—he's one of us'.

So much depended on luck, both good and bad. Working-class parents had little of the control over their children's education and social destiny taken for granted by the middle class. Had *Bob*'s teacher simply dismissed him as just another pest then he may not have got anywhere. Although there was a path to higher education, it was still unnecessarily complicated and daunting to the poor. Richmond's central schools were down-graded by 1937 and local children wishing to sit for the Intermediate Certificate had to attend central schools outside Richmond. Then in 1939 the seventh and eighth grades in all Richmond schools were abolished, and concerned Richmond parents suddenly realized what had happened. The *Richmond Chronicle* took up the cause:

> Richmond parents see no harm in [central schools being the sole means of entry to High School] but they are protesting strongly against the Department in refusing to establish at least one of these central schools in Richmond when the real object of them being established was to cater for the poorer class children of the industrial suburbs. There is only one of these schools to do the four big industrial suburbs of Carlton, Fitzroy, Collingwood and Richmond. On the other hand, the residential districts such as Hawthorn, Toorak, Malvern, St Kilda and Brighton are over-run with them. Statistics show that the majority of children attending them in those suburbs are mostly one-child families living in flats or comfortable homes.[4]

Much of the blame rested with Ted Cotter. In the twilight of his parliamentary career, he had failed to provide the leadership needed when the various Richmond school parent committees could not agree on which school should have the honour of becoming Richmond's central school and, while Richmond dithered, the Education Department went ahead with other plans. Twenty-seven years later, after decades of citizen agitation under doughtier political leadership, Richmond High School finally opened its doors.[5]

But if successive State governments had been unwilling to help Richmond children enter the middle class, the gaining of technical education to produce a skilled working class had been easier. Even so, it was still more than half a century after the inception of 'free, compulsory and secular' education that Richmond Boys' Technical School opened in 1926, after a sustained campaign led by a younger and keener Ted Cotter and the Richmond Council. The Council provided the land and £1000 from its meagre funds and even had to clear and prepare the site for the Education Department's builders. The Government still stinted on the school's facilities and within a decade its 498 day students and 442 night students were severely taxing the existing accommodation. Girls fared even worse. In 1928 the Richmond Girls' Secondary School was opened, sharing temporary accommodation with the dwindling Central State School in its decrepit and unsafe premises. The *Richmond Guardian* stormed at the height of the Depression after reporting the Speech Night of its three hundred girls in 1933: 'Should bridges and boulevardes be built with public money when there is such a crying need for healthy and adequate accommodation in our girls' schools'. Some additions were made in 1934, but by 1948 the old buildings were so dangerous that large falls of plaster forced the principal to send the girls home. It took another eight years before the Richmond Girls' Secondary School opened in the premises it should have had twenty-eight years before. Victorian Government schools were conspicuous victims of the Depression and the war. By the 1950s many schools had not had a lick of paint for twenty years. The post-war baby boom children, so fortunate in many ways, will remember State School days where it seemed normal that lavatories and shelter sheds stank, that classrooms were barely if at all heated in winter, that classes were small if they had forty-five students. The neglect and decay were worst in the old industrial suburbs, and while the Government rushed to build new schools to cater for the growing outer suburbs, the schools of Richmond and its fellows were to remain a scandal into the 1960s.[6]

Richmond parents and their children could not be blamed for concluding that they were at the bottom of the social heap. One man who attempted to do something about it was Cecil C. Mullen. Mullen was a clerk, living alone in Abbotsford, who took upon himself educational reform and the plight of working-class children. Considered an eccentric by many, he formed the 'Lantern Bearers' Boys and Girls Club' in 1922 so that he could inspire and coach poor children for scholarship examinations. By 1943 C. C. Mullen's 'old boys' were Richmond's only rival to St Ignatius' list of illustrious ex-students: 'Twelve old boys of his club are school teachers, ten are fully qualified accountants, while there are two civil engineers, a doctor, two chemists, a clergyman, two architects and a number of musicians'. His boys had won scholarships at Melbourne Grammar and to Wesley, Xavier and Scotch Colleges. But at the club's twenty-first birthday in 1943 Mullen warned:

> If the Church, Governments, Municipalities and Education Departments continued to neglect the youth of Australia in the way they have been doing in the last thirty years, then other organizations would soon get control of the younger generation and use them for their own purposes as the Nazi and Fascist Movements in Germany and Italy recently showed.[7]

Peace meant that Mullen's fears were not realized. Economic growth prevented the mass youth unemployment that had drawn the alienated and the embittered to Fascism. The people left behind while the rest of Australia 'made good' in the 1950s and 1960s fell victim to the age-old perils of poverty and class stigma. *Bill Shannon*:

> We were the war-time babies and the blokes that grew up with me—there's not many of us left actually. My era of the late forties and fifties—in them days it was all the bad boys and the sly grogs and some of the funny things that used to go on in the pubs after six o'clock was unreal. I was fourteen when I was picked up for nit-keeping for a bookmaker and I had to front the Richmond Court. And one of the old characters, 'Dirty' Jackson, was on the bench. I gave the name of 'Bill Sheehy'. I was sitting in the Court and old 'Dirty' is sitting there and they were calling this 'Bill Sheehy' and I don't wake up and then old 'Dirty' turned round and said: 'Is that you *Bill*?' 'Oh, yes.' 'Oh—five pounds.'

If the role of the casual economy in working-class life was coming to an end, the divisions in behaviour between the respectable and the rough were proving more resistant to change. The old respectable skills of saving and self-discipline remained essential for escape to the suburbs and social advancement through education and the respectables made a smooth transition from working-class life to suburban middle Australia. Where once the scrubbed veranda and doorstep proclaimed that respectability reigned within, now the immaculately tended garden performed the same function. By the time these émigrés reached old age they would be indistinguishable from their neighbours except in their memories. Back in Richmond, however, remained the less capable. As more and more respectables effected their liberation from the slums, Richmond became more rough and went bad.

Going Bad

The new prosperity could not reach all. Not only did it fail to help the unemployable, but also it offered little for the unskilled. In September 1951 the Richmond Employment Office had 1164 vacancies on its books for males, but only 27 were for process workers and 26 for labourers. The match factories, a major employer of unskilled female labour, were in serious trouble by the end of 1952 as Federal and State taxes placed a crushing burden on their products. Keon received a petition from eight hundred Bryant & May's employees who were on a three-day week and in Federal parliament he eloquently defended the efficiency of the Australian match industry which had smoothly adjusted from a forty-four-hour week to a forty-hour week with no loss of production. But there were also people who seemed to be psychologically incapable of seizing the new opportunities for making good—people trapped in a culture of poverty.[8]

As the old and the incapable were left behind, so too were the old industrial suburbs themselves. Richmond now seemed locked into irreversible social and physical decay. By 1955 its shopping centres remained scarred with vacant and dilapidated shops; some shops had been converted into tiny factories, their owners indifferent to the state of the façade. Bridge Road was never to recover as a prime shopping area: all it could claim now was notoriety as the most pot-holed and ragged arterial road in all Melbourne as the Richmond Council deliberately allowed it to deteriorate in the hope of blackmailing the Country Roads Board into assuming responsibility for such arterial roads. Richmond's roads remained a disgrace; but the Council could be partly excused by the fact that the maintenance of services to industrial areas far exceeded the cost of purely residential streets. In the parenthood of this Richmond generation, the streets that had been their delight as children were now death traps. War and economic growth had afflicted Richmond with an intolerable burden of traffic. The narrow streets that had been intended only for pedestrians and horse-drawn carts now carried trucks, semi-trailers and a rapidly growing mass of passenger cars. Few houses had the land for off-street parking and as residents themselves became car-owners, the kerb-sides became packed with cars seven days a week. Children could run out quite unseen and be under the wheels of a passing car in seconds. In April 1948 eighteen people were killed on Richmond's roads; in April 1949 no fewer than thirty died—nine of them in Punt Road, another nine in Bridge Road, three in Swan Street and nine elsewhere in Richmond. In April 1954 alone two students from Yarra Park State School were killed in separate accidents while crossing Punt Road, and the tragedies impelled a local businessman—a Mr Jones of Singer Sewing Machines in Bridge Road—to take it upon himself to shepherd the children over Punt Road each morning and afternoon. The children's street world that had bonded the street community had died a brutal death, and with it much of the heart of old Richmond.[9]

In all services and amenities the inner suburbs seemed to be bottom of the list. Few working people could afford a telephone but, in 1947, some Richmond people could be up to a quarter of a mile from a public telephone. Many saw the state of the great Richmond railway station as a tangible reminder of the class stigma inflicted on them by the wider world. In 1946 it had not been painted in fifteen years. The lavatories were filthy and rat-infested. The subway was perpetually damp, subject to flash flooding and barely illuminated by 40-watt globes: 'the cracked walls, crumbling plaster, unsightly and narrow entrances, dark subways, steep steps, smelly urinals and narrow platforms are not in keeping with Richmond's being one of Melbourne's most important railway stations', declared the *Chronicle* in 1944. But the rebuilding of the Richmond station would not commence until 1955, nine years after it had been condemned by the Richmond Council.[10]

In the public mind the inner suburbs seemed doomed: they were no place now for normal people to lead normal family lives. The slum abolitionists, led by Oswald Barnett and the *Herald*, had inevitably depicted the inner suburbs as reservoirs of disease and dissolution. In 1946 the *Herald* tugged at the heart-strings of Melbourne with 'Slum Kids'. It could only evoke shame in Slum Parents and righteous indignation in Garden Suburb Parents. Barnett was a devout Methodist and social reformer whose socialist convictions were growing in the 1930s. He believed that the physical environment determined the moral environment, slum homes bred slum morals. In his Master of Commerce thesis at the University of Melbourne in 1931 he had argued that slum babies should be taken from their parents and placed in the Methodist Babies' Home for adoption into suitable Christian families. Of course, this was already being done, without the least qualm, to Aboriginal children all over the country. The instrument of reform, the Victorian Housing Commission, remained preoccupied with the concrete rather than the human problems of welfare housing, with the sanitizing of the poor through technological efficiency. The Commission's architects and engineers applied techniques for the erection of prefabricated concrete houses and high-rise flats developed in the Soviet Union and on the Continent. And public opinion fully supported the assumptions of the slum abolitionists. Australians were obsessed with the new; the old should be razed as quickly as possible. The Prest Social Survey investigators tended to think that the only good news about a very old house was that it was soon to be demolished. One in Johnson Street, North Richmond, was a sand-brick cottage built in the very early 1840s and must have been one of the oldest extant houses in Melbourne. It was run down but liveable and surrounded by an old-world cottage garden. Everyone was delighted that it was due to be demolished any time. Public opinion, too, was prepared to tolerate a little redistribution of income through tax-funded public housing and welfare benefits, but it would never countenance a redistribution of income that would put enough cash into the pockets of the very poor so that they could solve their own housing and social problems. It would take the coming of the 'New Australians' and later the 'Trendies' to reveal that Richmond's cottages and streets could be renovated and restored into a fine human settlement.[11]

As more and more escaped 'to the suburbs', Richmond seemed to be dying. Some of the big 'family' factories left, too, taking with them their workers. As each well-known Richmond family made good, the community seemed to die another little death. In 1940 Richmond's population stood at 39 750; by 1952 it had fallen to 36 441. The birth-rate fell below the metropolitan average; the death-rate climbed above.[12] Those who were left behind inevitably felt betrayed. *Bill Shannon*:

> I did. I'll admit that myself. A lot of my friends moved out—in them days my father never had a car. We had to depend on rich uncles to take us out. You had to make a lot of new friends—you wouldn't just lose a family—you'd lose all your mates and girlfriends.

The stayers desperately hoped the emigrants would live to regret it. *Ruby Kane* relishes every story of later regrets: 'They leave and go out buying houses, and they can't get back quick enough—they miss the friendship and the warmth of Richmond'. Many who leave have a part of their heart that is forever Richmond; but very few go back. And the more families that left, the less reason there was to remain. *Rose Saddler* hung on until she was sixty-five and by then 'her Richmond' had quite disappeared: 'I was happy enough there, but to go back now there's nobody I'd really know'. *Jean Fowler* is still in Richmond, but 'you go down the street now and you never see anyone; the woman up here said "I don't know—either they must be dead or they've all gone out somewhere, because I never see anyone I know"'. *Jean*, too, clings to the belief that the deserters will live to regret it and come back: 'people started to go out of here when they got on their feet and it's just deteriorated bit by bit—but I believe that they're all going to come back'.

Yet if those who stayed in Richmond made a virtue of it, it does not disguise the fact that many families were emotionally locked into the culture of poverty. As *Muriel Thompson* reminisces, her Richmond divides into the boozers and the respectables. She and *Jean* were respectable women married to men captivated by the rough. Both are unforgiving towards their men who squandered so much hard-earned money on drink and gambling. *Muriel*'s recollections of the Depression blend into and confuse her memories of better times and it is not just old age that plays tricks on her memory: also it is the fact that her world in South Richmond was left behind as the rest of society made good. She remembers Green Street where her sisters lived:

> There were no back yards—pocket handkerchief—but they were brick and they were terraces. And the fun those women had. They were always buying something on the cheap and stuff that was pinched—fell off the back of trucks. They had the fun of the world—everyone was joining in. And I don't really remember seeing many people without a feed. They had no money but some way of getting it. People stayed there in South Richmond for years and they never had any money to move—they were just struggling. But the whole point was, when the husbands did get money the wives never got half of it—they wasted it in the hotels.

Unskilled family men could not really afford to drink at all, but even non-addicted drinkers believed that their right to enjoy a few beers was inviolable. For many their time in the pub at the end of each day was all that made life bearable; life without beer was unimaginable. And few would admit that they ran the risk of alcoholism: you weren't an alcoholic until you got 'on the wine' or 'the metho'. Beer was safe and it was good for you. Tired and depressed men who found 'the missus' little fun these days with all the kids and the nagging; men who watched childhood mates make good and get out of Richmond; men who feared that they would fail in the outside socially mobile world—for such as these that hour of shouting, riotous swilling before six o'clock was a biological necessity. It was as fundamental to survival as food and sleep; it was more cathartic than sex.

If in a patriarchal society women suffer, so too do men who fail. *Isabel Williams* and *Jean Fowler* were both in later life to pity their brothers as broken human beings, crippled from childhood by lack of self-confidence, only to be maimed in early adulthood by the Depression. *Isabel*'s brothers did get something out of their war service; *Jean*'s only brother who went to the war had 'something happen to him—they never found out—and he stayed at home and his wife went out to work; but we could never make him out—they reckon he fell off something when he was in the Islands'. To *Jean* during the Depression her brothers had seemed nothing but 'bludgers' and when she got married she told them: 'Well, you've got to do something now'. When jobs eventually came their way, however, they showed her that they really could work and 'they worked for the rest of their lives'.

> That's what was wrong with me—I had no confidence—when people are standing on you all the time, at the school and that sort of business. And probably, but we didn't realize it at the time, that was what was wrong with out brothers.

Richmond offered safety to the failed: the familiarity of old haunts, mates of a lifetime, family pubs, 'contacts', 'schemes', fun. The poor were disadvantaged in pleasure as in everything else and they were forced to seek much of their light relief from life in the sub-legal. Six o'clock closing, brought in for the benefit of the weaker-willed classes, forced otherwise law-abiding men to patronize the sly-grog trade: their cramped cottages were no place for drinking with a crowd of mates, and wives who resented wages going in amber fluid while the children needed new shoes were hardly welcoming. Likewise with betting: a run of good luck brought into a poor home a little windfall and a momentary triumph, but the only means to an off-course flutter was through an S.P. bookmaker. And through 'contacts' in your local you might pick up for a song something that your wife needed because it had 'fallen off the back of a truck'. (It could be said that the Richmond Council's greatest contribution to the social welfare of its poorest citizens was that in keeping the roads in such poor repair, things fell off the backs of trucks easily. This was almost true in South Richmond where S.E.C. truck drivers delivering briquettes to the Green Street power station would take corners too fast so that briquettes could fly off on to the street. *Bill Shannon* can remember up to twenty or thirty people waiting on the corner of Mary Street for the briquettes: 'Women with prams—when you think of it, it sort of makes you ashamed'.) In a society where the main body of the law is there to protect the possessions of the wealthy, the poor are often forced to break the law to obtain the essentials of life. And in their neighbourhood they have grown up with people who have become real criminals, and informing on them is emotionally difficult. Similarly local lads who join the Police Force are somehow class traitors:

> You're not as friendly as you used to be. You're careful what you say to them. Not that you're doing anything wrong, but it's a good thing to live by—watch, listen and keep your mouth shut. In a lot of ways you could say that they're betraying the area when you think that the biggest turnover at Pentridge were blokes you went to school with and here you are looking after them. It's like family looking after family.

Bill had a mate who became a warder at Pentridge and when asked how he had found his first day there: 'Oh, I knew everyone there'. Thus were many basically decent people placed into an uneasy relationship with the law.

The supplying of entertainment in drink, sport and gambling was really the only way to make big money out of a working-class community. Publicans who kept off the grog themselves did very well; talent at football opened up new economic vistas on retirement from playing and numerous footballers were able to find the capital and the backers to go into a hotel or a business (Tom Hafey and Jack Dyer both became milk bar proprietors); clever bookmakers could make a fortune both on and off the course. The big names comprised a local aristocracy of 'sporting gents'. The funeral procession of the bookmaker, Jack Miller, in 1951 took nearly a quarter of an hour to leave St Ignatius', for 'when success came his way, he remained a loyal and generous friend to his early associates'.[13] But beneath this legitimate entertainment industry festered a vast and complex sub-legal economy. At the top of the S.P. bookmaking tree were the sophisticated operators with their fronts, agents and 'contacts' in the P.M.G. who installed telephone networks. In 1958 a Royal Commission into Off-Course Betting was told by the reforming chief of the Gaming Squad that the industry had flourished only with the complicity of corrupt police. Inspector Healy went on to provide profiles of the big operators:

> Most of them, apart from violating the gaming laws, have no criminal records. Some of them have children at expensive schools and almost all of them admitted they feared the disgrace of being imprisoned and would give up bookmaking entirely if they thought there was a prospect of a gaol sentence for them. It is to avoid such a prospect that, after a first or second conviction, the bookmaker generally employs an unconvicted agent to carry on the business whilst he himself goes to golf or the races on race days.[14]

The money made was extraordinary. One street bookmaker in Richmond had an annual turnover of £40 000, a Camberwell operator had a turnover of £80 000 and one in Bentleigh of £75 000. The bane of the street bookmaker was the standover man, but S.P. bookmakers could hardly complain to the police that standover men were demanding protection money. One gang operating at the time of the Royal Commission comprised seven men all with criminal records, who would 'visit a particular district on a race day, and by force of numbers or threats, extract money from the bookmakers operating in the district'. Those who resisted ran the risk of 'vicious assaults' and even murder. S.P. bookmaking was part of the fabric of Richmond life and most of it harmless. In June 1956 the police were conducting a blitz in Richmond and the *News* noted: 'If the raids continue, there are at least two respectable Richmond businesses which will have to find new ways of balancing the budget, as they have found the letting of rooms and phones to S.P. bookies a very profitable sideline'.[15] For many families, too, S.P. bookmaking meant the difference between comfort and poverty. *Bill Shannon*:

> Mum used to run a book for the ladies and call around, and Dad used to work in with *Billy Bolton* at the pub. Dad used to take all these little phone bets—we were the only one in the street that had the phone—virtually we were *the* bookie. Mum used to take bets at Mrs *McKay*'s on Saturday morning when they come in for their groceries: 'That's for *Mollie*' (that was Mum), and I used to go and pay out on Saturday night. Mum did make enough out of it to send my sisters to school, sort of thing. They done pretty good out of it. And there were other things—hidden costs: I lost a sister, she had meningitis (lost two sisters actually) and in them days you had to pay for your medical costs. I admire my Dad and his mates. When I was born in 1938 he was earning thirty bob, and he bought his own home and saved and saved and saved. We never went without—but he did.

And this extra income enabled the *Shannons* to extend a helping hand to neighbours down on their luck. The 'respectable' S.P. bookies comprised an unofficial welfare agency for the street:

> That was people like Mum, Mrs *McKay*, Mrs *McIntyre*, Mrs *Edwards* (*Jim Edwards*' wife—she was a bookmaker too), the *Williams* (*Peggy Williams* married my brother-in-law's brother, she was a top contortionist, she lived in James Street) and Mrs *Williams* used to have a junk shop, an antique place, but you could never move in the shop because it was a front for a bookmaker anyway. We had more bookies than we had workers.

The star of *Bill*'s extended family was of course *Smokey Smithers*, who had fingers in many sub-legal pies apart from S.P. bookmaking. As a boy, *Bill* had a good job with Uncle *Jimmy* for a time: 'There used to be all this Richmond beer when the old brewery was going, and my job was to soak them in the bath and stick the Abbotsford Brewery label on them to sell as sly grog.' *Smokey* invested his ill-gotten gains legitimately, but often his methods remained unorthodox:

> In them days he'd buy a house for £200, then buy four, then the whole terrace. One place, Milton Place, which is no longer in existence, he bought all the houses and when they were condemned he had to pull them all down. But it was costing him a fortune—sixteen bob a day to get them pulled down. He had a couple of blokes doing it and they'd get a bit of lead or something and sell it at the pub. So one Saturday morning he got me and said: 'OK—we're going to start a fire'. He'd already tied it up with the Fire Brigade. Next thing he was on one end and I was on the other. It was all burnt out by the time the Fire Brigade got there—it was an hour late, they come via St Kilda. It was the quickest demolition job you ever seen.

Bill Shannon is, of course, a child of this Richmond generation; but he grew up in this sub-legal rough Richmond world and has never left it. He now contemplates the male pub culture with the clear but nostalgic eyes of a sobered alcoholic. His gift for story-telling comes of years of propping up bars, absorbing and retelling the lore of Richmond:

> Richmond's like Port Melbourne. My great-uncle used to be one of the fishermen on Sandridge beach—I spent most of my time there during the war. You walk around Port Melbourne and once you get in Bay Street, if you knew anyone there, you was *it*, and any stranger, no matter who you were, you was stuck.
>
> Mum used to scream at Dad and me when we went Saturday morning shopping. By the time we'd walked from Rose Street up to where the Great Britain Hotel is, you'd start meeting blokes going to the pub and so forth. We'd leave home at 8.30—the shops wouldn't be open—get down to the shops like Dickins (there was no Safeway or that kind of caper)—it would take you nearly an hour to get to Ball's corner. You might have worked with a bloke on the Friday—you'd start talking; you might have gone to school with him—you'd start yakking.

As a child and a teenager, *Bill* felt honoured to go to the pub with his Dad and the men on Saturday morning. Like many regulars, they had an 'act' which made them part of Richmond lore, their 'famous dog' who drank:

> He had his own seat in the pub, his own mug. He'd get into the Swan, and they'd all be sitting round, the bookmakers'd be there, and Nigger'd walk in and if anyone was sitting in his seat he'd walk out. And if they didn't move, he'd go back and bite them. And if anyone won, especially in the football season if Richmond had won, he'd come home blind as a bat and we used to have to carry him. He had his own round of People he'd visit—lived in Toorak originally then attached himself to us. The local policeman used to take Nigger with him on his night rounds. He visited butchers and shops who'd give him bones and biscuits—a regular round, and Sunday morning he'd go down to the Abattoirs, where they'd all be drinking beer, to get his bit of liver.

The pubs each had their characters and reputations:

> The 'Anchor and Hope'—Jack Titus' pub—old Ma Titus—she was a character. And next door there was a terrace of three houses: the first one was a sly-grog, another in the second and a brothel in the next one so you done all your shopping in the one area. The police would come into the rough pubs but they wouldn't come on really strong. One publican I remember he committed suicide down at Rosedale Racecourse, but his wife—he'd be in the bar working—and his wife would be out picking up blokes and taking them upstairs. Then there was the famous Dick

> O'Riordan's, the 'Central Club'. In the Olympic Games there was only two TV sets—one at the 'Rising Sun' and one at Dick O'Riordan's. He had only a little lounge, you'd get about thirty people there. It was during my National Service and I was an usher at the Olympic Games and we'd come back and there'd be all these blokes watching the TV and they'd turn the TV set off half-way through and they wouldn't know what was going on anyway.

The seven-day-a-week drinker needed somewhere to go on a Sunday. If you were in with the Abattoirs crowd you could go there, but one of the most famous places in Richmond was Ma Titus's Sunday Morning Club at the South Richmond Baby Health Centre:

> They used to all meet there and sit on the low fence and start a game of cards. That would be about 10 o'clock, then old Ma would open up the sly-grog and you'd go in and have a few drinks. Then up the lane and you had old Brown's hay and grain and wood and fuel, then there was another yard, Kingstons, and they used to hire out horses and at the top on Brighton Street was *Edwards'* (old *Jim Edwards*, a real character in himself—his son was one of Australia's top ice skaters), and in between that was a vacant block with no fence on it. There used to be a place at the back, *Bert Phillips'*, used to have a beautiful garden and I used to play two-up there. We used to be the nit-keepers. As kids growing up in the area we used to know every police car, but the Gaming Squad used to wear riding breeches and we would pick them out straight away. One day it was hot and we were supposed to keep nit but we all took off down the river for a swim. When we come back the fence into old *Bert Phillips'* was down and his garden was all trampled. When coppers had raided there was about two hundred blokes playing two-up and they'd all gone straight through *Bert*'s fence into a paddock next door and killed his crops and everything.

This minutely remembered world was the essence of the masculine community in Richmond. It thrived on gossip, legends, secrets, boasts, schemes and lurks. And it was the cradle of the conspiracies and petty corruption that cast a shadow over working-class politics. If you were considered to 'belong' to Richmond you were a somebody: you had an identity and a role that helped mitigate your insignificance in the eyes of the outside world. And although the number involved in serious crime remained small, the proximity to big crime gave an edge of excitement to life. *Bill Shannon* remembers Ronald Ryan, the last man hanged in Victoria: 'He could look after himself—there used to be some really tough boys like the *Skinners* and the flaming *Briggs* and he used to keep his own with that crowd and drink at the Saxon'. And of the *Briggs* mob who had terrorized *Florence Smith*'s family forty years before:

> Old *Billy Briggs* and uncle *Willie* (one of the three bookmakers at the Saxon), they were a family unto their own—they'd sooner fight than walk.

> *Willoughbys* the same way. Old *George* (my godfather), him and his three boys was always barred from Dick O'Riordan's Central Club while old Marie was alive—she was the only one who could control them. She was a little woman—a real fire-eater, and they'd be fighting and she'd be amongst them and old Dick would be behind the bar grinning: 'hmmm, hmmm—have a beer, boys'. There used to be a horse trough outside and every Friday night one of the *Millers* or one of the *Waltons* would finish up in the horse trough.

Much of the evil reputation foisted on Richmond by the outside world sprang from press publicity given to its occasionally wild street life. Fights outside pubs were especially prized as free entertainment: in June 1944 four hundred people watched a family fight between two men and two women outside a Swan Street hotel. And when Richmond went rough it did so on a grand scale: in December 1958 the police raided a party in Lincoln Street where over three hundred men and thirty-six women were gathered round 171 gallons of beer on a Sunday afternoon to raise bail and defence money for a popular local lad on a 'serious charge'.[16]

Bill divides his schoolmates into those who made good and those who went bad; and some went very bad:

> One just got out of gaol after doing seventeen years for armed robbery. He wrote himself a play and now he's one of the top boys in radio. He was a character. He used to rob banks and put the money under the bed. Never spent a cracker—had £100 000 when they arrested him.

But more were dead by the age of forty:

> A lot of my schoolmates have died early. I was given up for dead when I was thirty-nine. Next Monday I'll be forty-three and the doctors say I'm a walking miracle.
>
> Let's face it—in our era we were allowed in hotels at eighteen. I know now four or five blokes that I went to school with are hanging around Gordon House—the grog caused a lot of it.
>
> Another thing too. We had no incentive. There was nothing to fire for. There was no ambition. What could you be? Not that we lacked education—we never went on with it. It's our own silly bloody fault. It was follow the leader sort of thing. One bloke got a job, left school early and he'd got money. You were going to school and you can't afford to take out girls and so forth, and he's having fun and he might have a new bike or something like that.

With full employment, young blokes had money in their pockets. At first it seemed quick and easy. For *Bill* and his mates their greatest ambition was to own a house, and many succeeded; but their psychological needs for self-esteem and social dignity went unfulfilled. As the working class divided into those who made good and those who went bad, extended families came to include close relatives with good jobs and nice homes in the suburbs, and the failures stuck in the slums. And even though the failures' material poverty was less than that suffered by their parents in the bad old days, the pain of social failure had become more acute. Young men who had never known success at school, at work or on the sports field, found that they could at least have one accomplishment—the capacity to drink vast quantities of beer. *Bill* at thirty-nine was drinking over twenty glasses of beer a day and weighed over twenty stone. He drank away his two houses, his jobs and his health. He suffered a massive heart attack, survived and was dried out in hospital. Then he discovered that he had leukaemia. He contemplates his fellow victims:

> One is a real pitiful case with the grog. He had everything to gain—top Richmond footballer. He went interstate coaching—now he's lucky to get a job. He's in the horrors every day. That's the way things go.

Bill lives with his father who is also paying a frightful price with emphysema so bad that he must kneel all day to breathe.

Bill Shannon's subjective observation of so many lives foreshortened by drink and failure is borne out by the mortality statistics. Drs John Powles and Robert Birrell of Monash University have analysed the mortality rates for Melbourne from 1969 to 1973. They found Australian-born males from Richmond, Collingwood and Fitzroy to have a mortality rate two to three times higher than in the middle-class suburbs. Richmond is part of a working-class ghetto, with death-rates comparable to the black ghettos of New York and Chicago. Certainly air pollution—in Richmond and Footscray the worst in Melbourne—is a threat to health, but the great common causes of death remain the stress-related diseases of ischaemic heart disease, hypertension and diseases of the lung caused or aggravated by smoking. It is not the high-pressure executive who runs the gravest risk of premature death; it is the poor and the insignificant. Australian-born females similarly die too young in Richmond, but too many also face long widowhoods.[17]

Australians deluded themselves in the 1950s and 1960s that theirs was a classless society, open to talent and hard work. The humiliation and envy of those left behind testifies to the class stigma that endured and crippled generation after generation. *Bill*:

> We're a funny sort of race, the Australian—he's an individualist but he likes to be a con man.
>
> I've always been envious of people who've kicked on in their own thingo—good luck to them but I've always been envious. Then you see the way I've done it myself. I've had a lot of friendship, I've had a lot of hard times—but the hard times, I'll admit. I've brought on myself.

The critical difference between *Bill* and his parents' generation is that he blames himself, not society and not 'destiny', for his personal failure. *Jean Fowler*, when young, hated the people behind the social system that condemned her family to poverty and powerlessness and she saw it as destiny that 'we were never meant to have money'. *Bill*, growing up a generation later amidst the post-war boom, assumes that it was a deficiency of character that kept him at the bottom of the heap. As the respectable made good and left for the garden suburbs, Richmond contracted into a ghetto of the rough. Behind the warmth, the high spirits and the intimacy of the pub culture lurked the dangers of alcoholism and serious crime. Moreover, there were threats from progress itself to the street life and community that had always sustained the poor in their hardest times. But as old Richmond fell victim to the motor car, the television and the supermarket, into the cottages vacated by the successful moved a new people who signalled a rebirth.

1956–1965

9

Death and Rebirth

This final decade was to be momentous for Richmond. Much of the political, economic, social and technological groundwork laid out since the war would finally bear fruit in Melbourne's old industrial communities. Most working-class people would become private motorists; most would acquire a television set until access to television would become a necessity for even the poorest; all would benefit from antibiotics, many from psychotropic drugs and some from advanced surgery on vital organs and diseased joints. Those who stayed in Richmond would see their old community irrevocably dissipated by new modes of shopping and leisure, transport and communication. And there were two changes peculiar to the old inner suburbs: slum clearance for welfare housing and the cultural invasion of foreign immigrants. Then in the 1970s old Australian Richmondites would be amazed to find their once stigmatized habitations being coveted by young middle-class sophisticates enchanted by the old and the cosmopolitan. The social wheel would turn full circle as the Hill became once again stylish and select, but so too would the political wheel turn full circle as the old Labor machine recaptured the political life of Richmond.

Cars and trucks had already killed the children's street life and with it the maternal social network of the neighbourhood. Now came the supermarket to finish off the little corner shop where housewives met daily for a gossip. For *Bill Shannon* it was the New World Supermarket that did the greatest damage to South Richmond: 'It broke it—like the shopkeepers knew everyone and everyone knew each other; Natoli's the fruiterers—you'd walk into the shop and know them all. It's become very impersonal'. Some of Richmond's great stores faded away. Love and Pollard's was deeply mourned in 1956. Miss Dixon, who had worked there as an accountant for forty-three years reminisced: 'Sales in those days were apparently vigorous affairs in which no quarter was requested or given. [I] can remember hats being torn to pieces by eager bargain hunters in the popular millinery department upstairs, where as many as twenty girls used to be employed in the work rooms'. Now all that are left of Richmond's great old stores are Ball's and Dimmey's in Swan Street. (In 1983 the unthinkable happened when Alexander's Menswear store on the corner of Bridge Road and Church Street announced that it too was leaving Richmond.) The Traders' Associations tried valiantly to stop the rot, but the commercial development attracted to Richmond was increasingly industrial and administrative. By 1965 the Chamber of Commerce was driven to supply give-away prizes like stereograms to attract Christmas shoppers to Richmond.[1]

Television permeated all Australian life and broke down community everywhere. *Hamish Roberts* blames television for much of our modern social isolation:

> If I walk round any of the streets of Box Hill on the way to the station after tea-time, there's not a soul anywhere. The sun would still be out and you'd think that everyone would be out in their gardens, but house after house, everybody is watching TV. I can recall the time when everybody would be out on a beautiful summer evening with their hoses and the kiddies would be playing out in the street. This has been the big change. All the halls there were in Richmond—there'd be dances, functions on, parties. None of these halls would be available now—they're all gone.

He is appalled that even members of his own generation who grew up in a socially richer world, have fallen victim to suburban isolation:

> The people next door here—the chap's retired and his wife never goes anywhere at all. She suffers from asthma but he never takes her anywhere. He goes every day to the pub—that's his only entertainment. Their lives are so limited—they turn on the TV and read the paper and that's all. They're Roman Catholics and go to Mass but that's their only contact. But she's only one of many. *Nellie* will tell of all the ones who go to Yoga—they're all suffering from tension and nerves and some of them have shocking lives, matrimonial troubles. They're going to their doctors and taking valium and the doctors don't know what to do with them. I don't recall that sort of thing years ago. My mother lived to a ripe old age because she was always interested in things, had her church and her friends and relations. And she had a happy life—she enjoyed herself. She had hard times and hard work but it didn't kill her.

As the street community disintegrated, so too did the informal welfare network of relatives and neighbours. Paid professionals from outside had to provide the support and guidance in life crises that once had been the spontaneous expression of communal concern. Predictably, the Richmond Council was slow to employ a social worker: in 1971 Councillor Fred Smith was to report that the Council was having difficulty in finding the 'right person' and admitted that 'Richmond being a working-class area, we naturally have some poverty and social problems'. The Richmond Dispensary compensated for the Council's indifference by appointing its first social worker in 1961, giving her a wide brief to attend places of work as well as the homes of the Dispensary's patients. Richmond's parliamentarians found they had to perform welfare duties that rightfully belonged to the Council. Jim Cairns's wife Gwen organized a free dry-cleaning service for pensioners which was conducted from Cairns's electoral office. Once Gwen had to get a ladder to scale the fence of a house in Bridge Road where she suspected an old man was bed-ridden: 'He'd been on a wire-bed for a week'. He gave us a painting—it's out there—which was one of his most treasured possessions'.[2]

While the Catholic churches continued to thrive, drawing a new congregation from the New Australians, Richmond's Protestant churches were dying. Anticipating the Uniting Church by fifteen years, the ninety-three-year-old Lennox Street Presbyterian Church closed its doors in 1965 and joined its tiny congregation to the Church Street Central Methodist Congregation. *Phyllis Smith* was heartbroken when she attended the 125th Anniversary of St Stephen's:

> When we used to go there the congregation was three to four hundred and the balcony would be full. When we went to the Anniversary there were only forty people there and no choir. Really since the high rise buildings all those homes have gone and they're nearly all Orthodox Greeks or Italians, so St Ignatius' is going very well.

At least football seemed untouched by this decay of the old Richmond community, even though the Tigers were in a slump in the late 1950s and early 1960s. In June 1962 the Tigers ended a losing streak of fifteen games, but at the beginning of that season Graeme Richmond had become secretary of the club and Richmond would soon return to being one of the most successful clubs in the history of the Victorian Football League. Church and football were deeply intertwined. Father Flynn of St Ignatius' said prayers for the Tigers each week and unofficially canonized Francis Bourke, Richmond's gentlemanly and courageous full-back.[3]

The loss of street community altered patterns of adult social intercourse. Social contact became more formalized. Chatting in chance encounters in the street, at the corner store, at church, became more unlikely. Conversation became increasingly pursued inside houses, by invitation, and perforce, less frequently. Even Richmond was becoming middle-class in its social style. The only significant social intercourse to grow outside the home was in the pubs once 10 o'clock closing was introduced and the prejudice against women in hotels abated. Certainly, people began to eat a meal with their drinks and they drank more slowly, but overall they continued to drink more and more. It now was the pub that was the natural meeting place of the young, not the street corners, the dances and open spaces that attracted the adolescents of the 1920s, and alcoholism that had always seemed an older man's problem years ago, began to afflict the young, both male and female.[4]

But there remained one large piece of old Richmond community that proved remarkably resilient—the A.L.P. and its dynasties and machine. In 1955 Cairns's hair's-breadth win in Yarra had been the A.L.P.'s sole victory in Richmond. The Council was in D.L.P. hands, as was the State seat of Richmond, and Cairns had no cause to feel safe in Yarra. His preselection had been so sudden and the Federal campaign so feverish, that he only now began to get to know his electorate. For the next five years he and Gwen knocked on every door in Richmond, Abbotsford and Collingwood and it was on the doorsteps that he felt the full bitterness unleashed by the Split:

> By now the Groupers were really working. The Santamaria mob was really doing its stuff, and the Church with its Missions—they had everything. We found a significant number of people who just wouldn't speak to us—closed the door as soon as we came, and I don't think that we changed many of those. Keon got 27 per cent of the vote in 1955 and about 17 per cent in 1958. There would have been Catholics in that 10 per cent drop, but there would have been mainly non-Catholics who voted for him in 1955 because he'd been Labor and so opposed to the old machine. The old machine was bad and we always carried the stigma with us—always. And we always lost a lot of votes around Bennett Street, North Richmond, because they couldn't accept the old machine.

Cairns himself decided to accept and tolerate the old machine. He excused its corruption as a lesser evil than the commercial advantage taken by many councillors in better-off municipalities. He decided that the Richmond machine itself 'worked because of "jobs"—jobs on Council and other things the Council could do—not a bad sort of corruption, I suppose'. And Cairns found himself learning a lot about the Australian working class that he had not expected. He warmed to the social intimacy: 'it was a quality of life that had been absent in places where I'd been before'; he was chastened by its deep conservatism:

> I came into Richmond with very great local activity, street meetings and so on. They treated that as a game—it was exciting. They can be involved in play, as long as it is, remarkably enough, masculine physically or cerebral. But any other kind of involvement they're conservatively against—more so than the middle class. That activity went on for another five years after we won

> the election, until we'd cleared the D.L.P. out of the Council. It then became more conventional and after about 1961 Richmond Labor Party activity was similar to Labor activity everywhere.
>
> Some of them used to think that that five-year period was what it used to be like years ago. They dug out a bell—Jack O'Connell used to have it. They made a box to stand on—those things were supposed to have happened in Richmond in the 1890s. I kept up street meetings for quite a while, but they were not effective after a while—not many people came. They used to know all the issues and say: 'It doesn't matter Jim, we know how to vote—go somewhere else where you can win votes'.

And once Cairns began to dedicate himself to the anti-Vietnam campaign, the local Labor stalwarts lost interest: 'At first, like almost everyone else in the Labor Party, they thought it was dangerous politically and they thought we were going too far. People like Dave Langdon, Ted Sanders, Charlie Evans, Alan Bain and the Loughnans and the O'Connells—they never got involved'.

Richmond found 'the Doc' strange: 'the Doc and I have always been good mates', says *Bill Shannon*, 'but he was a funny bloke—he never let anyone get on top of him, standoffish'. People admired his ability and were even flattered to have such an educated man as their member of parliament. *Bill* again: 'His education was self-taught; he learnt while he was a policeman and a lot of coppers I knew who were in the same time as him used to tell how they'd be out on raids and Jim would be in the back of the car studying'. Cairns sensed their ambivalence: 'A lot of these people now, when I pass them in the street, will lean out of their trucks and wave: they regret me because in a way I triggered off [the idea] that there's something better'. But on the night of 30 August 1969 five young men and two women gatecrashed a fund-raising party at Cairns's home in Hawthorn and brutally bashed Cairns, his wife, stepson and daughter-in-law, and four others. Cairns was never interested in his assailants being prosecuted: this sort of violence, he argued later, stems partly from people's need to be noticed. Some people received attention through their creative efforts; non-creative people sometimes felt they had to make an impact through aggression and violence. The only answer was better education. There is no doubt that the assault originated from deep within Richmond; the motives and the actors are known but lips are sealed.[5]

The battle for Richmond between the A.L.P. and the D.L.P. after the Split commenced with the 1956 Council elections. The tension in the community was acute and the leading protagonists of both sides invited hatred and surreptitious violence. Both sides indulged in bogus voting and Jim Cairns found himself arrested by an over-zealous policeman when as a scrutineer he challenged an intending voter who looked suspicious. Cairns is certain that Keon and Scully knew nothing about his arrest as it could only harm their cause; in fact the young policeman was a convert in Catholicism who in the heat of the moment lost his head. When the vote were counted four D.L.P. councillors had been defeated and their majority on the Council was down to one. Council meetings now became ugly The *Richmond News* made a meal of every incident: 'Basher gangs were once again present in force at the Council meeting'; and dramatic photographs of Councillor Peg Slattery of the D.L.P. being escorted under police protection from a Council meeting appeared in the metropolitan dailies. Both sides excelled in nastiness and petty insults. Some local politicians now began doubting the wisdom of a lifetime in the political wilderness. One of the first notable defections from the D.L.P. was Councillor Roy Jackson, who by becoming an Independent in June 1957, held the balance of power on the Council. In the 1957 elections the D.L.P. lost in every ward except Centre Ward and Jimmy Loughnan returned to the Council for the second half of his record career in local government. Coloretti was now the leader of the D.L.P. on Council and his final year in office was a nightmare. The A.L.P. councillors froze out their opposition by conducting all debates in caucus, using Council meetings only for formal voting:

> Council work was really done inside caucus and sometimes general business items wouldn't be on the agenda paper in precis, so then I'd demand my pound of flesh. They did it so I did it—it was fair enough but they made a welter of it at the time.

In 1960 Coloretti left the D.L.P. and in 1969 was again elected to Council, this time as an Independent. Even so it was not until he was returned in 1973, with a majority of two hundred, that he felt he was accepted by the Labor councillors.[6]

The Split poisoned every area of Richmond public life. In April 1958 even the Brighton Street State School Committee had A.L.P. Councillor Alan Bain and the Communist Ken Miller trying to unseat Herbie Tye in the largest meeting of parents on record. Then in June came the State election. Scully campaigned well and 'made the speech of his career' at his Town Hall rally. His campaign workers said that they were 'quietly confident' but Scully secured only 35.5 per cent of the vote. Wally Towers of the A.L.P. won Richmond convincingly with 54 per cent; the Liberals attracted a tiny 10.5 per cent. The shock was so great that the *Richmond News* did not appear at all for 4 June. In December Maurie Sheehy lost the Legislative Council election to Jack O'Connell. The *News* alleged that Protestant Liberals were voting Labor out of sectarian spite at the D.L.P., but that did not alter the fact that the D.L.P. had been routed in Richmond. The great crusade had been relegated to the political fringe. Wally Towers served a quiet term as M.L.A. for Richmond then in 1962 he died suddenly. Over sixty hopefuls—including Lou Richards—were believed to have their eye on the seat, but the pre-selection was won by Cairns's candidate, a Hawthorn lawyer, Clyde Holding. The *News* took stock of Richmond's parliamentarians: 'A Professor from Toorak-Brighton; a TV and radio performer from Essendon (Doug Elliott); a solicitor from Hawthorn; and *one* worker from Richmond (Jack) O'Connell.[7]

The Richmond Council was soon back in form. Rumour and innuendo again dogged the Council and its staff. The out-door staff saw their role as political agitators rather than as servants of the ratepayers: disrupting DLP meetings, painting graffiti, harassing the enemies of the machine were all so much more fun than cleaning streets. Some employees were quite out of control, drinking on the job and punching foremen and councillors who attempted to discipline them. A handful of men were primitives, who, while often an embarrassment, were undoubtedly useful for political dirty work. And some councillors were now under investigation. In October 1957 Councillor W. W. Williams was aquitted of accepting a £100 bribe from a used car dealer; in September 1960 a jury failed to agree on whether Councillors Eric Conway and Roy Jackson, both JPs, were guilty of extortion when they claimed a £20 'fine' from a butcher at the Richmond Abattoirs who was killing a kosher beast after hours because of an incorrect slaughter the previous day. In the sad campaign to rid Melbourne of all its elegant Victorian shop verandas, two Richmond councillors were said to have a keen interest in their speedy demolition and were seen at work in new demolition businesses of their own. And when the Totalizator Agency Board was being proposed, there was said to be strong opposition from certain Richmond councillors who were established SP bookmakers. In 1960 the Council received harsh treatment at the hands of *Truth* and the Central Executive of the ALP again took council pre-selections out of the hands of the Richmond Party branches.[8] In 1963 the Executive issued a report on ALP machines in local government:

> . . . seeking endorsement for local government seems to bring out the very worst in people. All the baser elements of greed, jealousy, spite and pettiness rush to the surface . . . In some areas the A.L.P. councillors have organized themselves into a nice little clique to prevent any potential threat to their existence ever emerging . . . If 'Tammany Hall' exists in Australia, it is to be found in municipal politics.[9]

The most enduring legacy of the Split for the working class, however, was that it put the Liberal/Country Party coalition into power in Victoria for twenty-seven years. Consequently it was a conservative government that administered the provision of welfare housing in the inner suburbs. Under Cain Labor the Housing Commission had concentrated its efforts at building new communities on virgin land; now the Bolte government turned to slum clearance. The 1956 Royal Commission into the Housing

Commission had praised the technical quality of the houses built by the Commission but found it wanting in understanding of the social implications of its policies: 'It has shown no sign of recognizing its broader responsibilities to its tenants and the people of Victoria generally'. It went on:

> We feel we must warn against the danger of putting family after family into individual houses in large estates, collecting their rent and otherwise forgetting about them.
>
> It is reasonable to expect that Victoria will eventually eliminate its slums and have sufficient houses for all. It must be a tragedy if, when that time comes, we cannot point to thoroughly well-planned cities and towns where all the elements of the community are provided for in a proper balance, and people can get conveniently from home to work and do their shopping and find their relaxation close to home.[10]

Public relations had never been one of the Housing Commission's strong points and when Horace Petty, the new Minister for Housing, announced that a new estate was to be built in North Richmond on a block bordered by Church Street, Lennox Street, Anderson Street and Elizabeth Street, house-owners panicked. Would every house in the area be demolished; what about rehousing; what would the compensation be; what would happen to old age pensioners who owned their homes but were too old to start afresh? Frank Scully and the *Richmond News* rushed to reassure them. A meeting was called at the Richmond Town Hall and nearly every person affected heard Scully and Maurie Sheehy M.L.C. explain the Bolte government's programme. They explained that 'it is definite that not all houses in the area will be pulled down, only those declared by the V.H.C. after inspection'. And on compensation: 'The Commission has made it clear that it is not interested in driving hard bargains. Two independent valuers will be engaged to value all houses affected and a system of ex-gratia payments over and above such valuations may be exercised by the V.H.C. in some areas'.[11] People were not convinced. The *News* started a 'Don't Panic' campaign:

> Calling all Residents! Don't fall for the rumours being circulated at the present time that 'hundreds of good houses' throughout Richmond are listed for demolition in the next few years.
>
> These rumours have no foundation in fact, and are aimed solely at creating an atmosphere of panic in order to obscure the truth about the Anderson Street area reclamation scheme.[12]

Frank Scully and the D.L.P. were trapped. Before the Split the crusader-controlled Richmond Council had done a deal with the Housing Commission under the Cain government recommending fourteen areas in Richmond for slum reclamation. Jim Cairns gives his version of the story:

> These fourteen areas were in all parts of Richmond. I think it was about fifteen hundred that were involved. They were all workers' houses. At that stage what they intended to do was to pay them the value of the house at the date of proclamation which meant that any increase in inflation would not go to the owners. In principle, some cases that had been fair enough, because for instance in North Richmond where the big multi-storey things are now, there must have been two or three absentee landlords who owned three of four hundred houses between them, and it was fair enough to seal those off. But all around there were individual owners, workers, and it was all they had. So there was a tremendous amount of resistance to that—it was wrong from a housing point of view and the Commission has been forced to recognize that. So I decided we'd fight it—it went all over Richmond and it was very effective political campaign. I think it was justified too as a matter of principle—though I had some doubts about it from time to time. We had street meetings and told people what was happening and we argued that the kind of things the Housing Commission was going to put up would be the slums of the future. And that no one should be expected to live in those boxes, one on top of each other—and they shouldn't. And that they weren't going to get fair valuations. And even when it happened, as it did in North Richmond, we fought them on the valuations. I think we increased all of them by 50 per cent. So we had a lot of involvement—it was in the interests of the people and they could see it.

There were lighter moments:

> At one meeting in North Richmond, Scully came along as the State member trying to hold his vote and so on, but always having to support the reclamation of the Housing Commission. At one stage, Bob Charles's wife said something to Scully and he gave an equivocal answer, so she got him by the tie and said: 'Mr Scully—you're a slimy skunk', and he said: 'Mrs Charles, you're exaggerating'.

Yet even Cairns's individual victories on behalf of North Richmond home-owners did not deter the Housing Commission from effectively cheating people out of compensation that could replace the homes they had lost. And although the first flats on the Anderson Street estate were walk-up and innocuous, in 1964 the Housing Commission confirmed Richmond's worst fears when it commenced the high-rise towers. As the president of the Richmond Ratepayers' League said in 1966: 'It's obvious that the Housing Commission see people as statistics to be stuck in monstrous 22-storey blocks of flats that resemble huge beehives more than human habitations'. And once the hapless tenants had settled into high living, it became clear that the tower blocks were worthy successors to the slums they eradicated: they increased morbidity especially among children and young mothers; they strained and cramped family life; they exacerbated social isolation and class stigma. The only discomforts they abolished were rising damp and lack of sunlight. They became a towering testimony to the fact that the problems of the poor came not from bad housing but from low income and class stigma. It was not slum houses that bred slum minds; it was slum wages.[13]

But in the death of old Richmond there was rebirth. The coming of the post-war migrants from Europe, then South East Asia and South America, has constituted the most significant demographic transformation since the gold rushes. As Victoria was made on gold in the nineteenth century, so would it now be re-made by the New Australians. One of the first to foresee Australia's future as a multi-cultural society was Richmond's Dr David Roseby, himself the son of poor Russian Jews. Honoured with the presidency of the Victorian Branch of the British Medical Association in 1944, he concluded his presidential address with prophetic words:

> There remains for me to speak of the refugees. This country, if it is to remain white, has problems of immigration that will tax all the energies of those who govern us. We have been told that Britain herself will need all its artisans to repair the damage there. It is possible that we shall have to comb Europe for surplus population—if we can get it. We must make up our minds, however, on our attitudes towards foreigners. At the earliest we must enfold them into the Australian nation and make them feel they are among friends. Their children must be welcomed among our own children. We must welcome them and their families, not merely grudgingly admit them. Among the immigrants there will be medical men; we must amend our registration laws so they may practise freely. The Australian community as a whole, and to its credit, has given refuge to thousands of the persecuted. I am the son of such parents who came to Australia sixty-five years ago. The health of our country and the conditions of medical practice are better than when I entered the profession. I am proud that I contributed to these results and that you have honoured me by electing me to the highest office in the branch.[14]

White Australia was founded in bloody conquest and peopled by immigrants, but it soon found it difficult to cope with foreigners. Even English-speaking immigrants encountered a raw intolerance from an insular people struggling for identity. That a Jewish liberal like Dr Roseby could defend 'White Australia' without a second thought testifies to the race consciousness that pervaded every section of Australian society. Inevitably the response of Old Australians to New Australians whose first language was not English, was initially racialist. And the migrants' first resting place would be among the least-prepared part of the community—the old working class of the industrial suburbs.

Most working-class people did not have their prejudices tested by face-to-face relationships with people of different cultures, religions and appearance until the 1950s. This Richmond generation, if it had not had overseas war service, had seen only a few Chinese or 'Celestials', a smattering of Europeans, and hardly ever an Aborigine. Aborigines were so rare in Melbourne, they were not even persecuted—they were figures of fun. Generations grew up seeing Pelaco shirts that were made on Richmond Hill, advertised by a blackfellow without trousers and clad only in an oversize shirt, declaiming 'Mine tinkit dey fit'. Yet when a notorious metho drinker, Eva Pearson, was found 'consorting with a black man in Kent Street' in September 1930, she was immediately arrested for vagrancy.[15] *Monica Rinoldi* knew one Aboriginal family at school who were accepted by the whites, but the few Aboriginal families who stayed in the city were easily alienated and demoralized. *Bill Shannon*, growing up in the 1940s, claims that the only truly destitute family in his street in South Richmond was part-Aboriginal—'which was rare in our area':

> They brought it on themselves, really. The mother was on the wine and I don't think that any of the boys knew who their father was. They used to thieve and we had a saying that if you ever saw them around the place you'd have to search them before they'd leave.

To the astonishment of their white neighbours, two of the boys achieved distinction in later life.

Europeans could only hope for social acceptance if they repudiated their cultural origins as quickly as possible. When H. J. Barcelo first stood as a Political Labor Council candidate for the Richmond Council in 1912, a vicious rumour was circulated that he was a foreigner. He protested: 'It was quite true that he conversed in several languages, but as a matter of fact he was a native of Victoria and was proud to be an Australian'—as though he had been convicted of theft as a child but had gone straight ever since. But it was always rising unemployment that ignited working-class hostility towards migrants. The Edwardian wave of British immigrants aroused dark, even official, accusations that they were raising the incidence of insanity, tuberculosis and crime in Melbourne. In 1913 the Burnley Progress Association claimed that immigrants were threatening the health of the community because of the 'herding together of a number of families in one house'. Hughes's 'populate or perish' immigration programme in the 1920s raised the Australian workforce by 40 per cent, but whereas Hughes had intended them for rural life, most were incorrigibly urban and stayed in the capital cities. Richmond House was converted into an immigrant hostel and the 'immies' were much noticed in Richmond. When two young Englishmen were convicted in 1927 of stealing £1 15s from an elderly woman in Richmond, the *Richmond Weekly*'s headline screamed: 'Send them Back'. In 1923 the Richmond A.L.P. mounted a vigorous protest with trade union support against the Tramways Board for giving preference to migrants in jobs. In 1925 Councillor Con Loughnan made it Council business that a Maltese had been taken on by the Albion Sand Company while real Australians were looking for work. In April 1928 the arrival of a French ship with 15 Italians, 69 Yugoslavs, 3 Bulgarians, 32 Poles, 66 Greeks, 45 Albanians and 9 Palestine Jews was greeted derisively by the *Weekly* with 'White Australia?'; and in July Richmond citizens protested in a deputation to the Council against 'unfair competition from aliens in the fruit trade who worked longer hours and for less money'.[16]

Anti-Semitism certainly existed and Richmond's Dr Roseby had battled within the A.L.P. against Frank Anstey's vociferous anti-Semitism, but the historical victims, apart from Aborigines, of systematic racism from urban Australians had always been the Chinese. Fear of cheap Asian labour had politically justified hostilities that drew deeply on physical repugnance at racial and cultural differences. In 1913 *Labor Call* called for the prohibition of 'unnatural alliances' between white women and Chinese: Melbourne's Little Bourke Street was a 'sink of iniquity where hybrid children are seen playing in the gutters and filthy lanes'. This generation of working-class people grew up eating their meals off tables stamped with 'European Labour Only'. Not until the Allies liberated the Nazi concentration camps did it cease to be respectable to be racist in Australia.[17] *Lilian Campbell* recalls her adolescent impressions of Little Bourke Street:

> When Her Majesty's Theatre would open the doors early so that you could dash up the countless steps to the gods, you'd be standing there waiting and you'd see the Chinamen pattering along. And you'd see a white woman who was probably a prostitute in Little Lonsdale Street and Little Bourke Street, and you just stared and stared and stared. It was another world and you'd be frightened out of your life.

In Richmond the few remaining Chinese were laundrymen or market gardeners on the river bank. They were taunted by children and reviled by adults. A Mr Chong Lee and his wife Olive of Burnley were openly persecuted in 1912 when they engaged a 'young white girl to nurse their half-caste child'.[18] When *Lilian* was just nineteen and newly married, she had to take her husband's collar to a local Chinese laundry:

> It was eerie. You'd step inside the door and it was all enclosed—there was just a little peephole and all the collars were up on the shelves with little bits of paper. And you'd hear him padding down the passageway with his slip-ons. I presented my ticket. He opened his mouth—all his gold—and as he put the collar over the tiny counter he pinched my tit. Well I fell out of the shop. I never went back. I was terrified he'd kill me the next time.

Lilian can be frank about the racial prejudices of her youth because she has lost them. She has travelled overseas and developed a 'softness for the Asians'. She is proud to number among her grandsons-in-law a Burmese, a Lithuanian and an Irishman. She is delighted by the new multi-cultural

Australia—'I love that ethnic mix'. But many of her fellows were not to find it so easy to adjust.

Australia was hardly welcoming to the first New Australians who came after the war. No planned accommodation, no language courses, no specialized welfare services were provided to ease the first terrifying months. Moreover, many of the early arrivals were refugees, burdened with an emotional baggage of appalling memories. Serge Liberman has written of his mother:

> What she brought then to Australia, descending the gang-plank warily at Princes Pier, was a near-empty package—little of matter, less of spirit, nothing of faith . . . From the beginning then, Mother and the new alien lukewarm country offered nothing willing to each other; or where they offered, and gave, the exchange was coldly equal—the country providing Mother with work in a drab airless factory in Flinders Lane, Mother in turn giving up her labour, eight, ten, twelve hours a day of her energy, without love, enthusiasm or cheerfulness. It was need, desperate urgency that drove her, for love, enthusiasm and cheerfulness were a part of the rubble left behind and part too of that long Russian exile of which her translocation to Australia was a mere continuation . . . That the sun shone over Australia, I knew, but that was my legacy, not hers.[19]

Even though the 'sun shone' for the children of Jewish refugees as they took advantage of education opportunities never available in central Europe, many Australians remained insensitive to the survivors of the Holocaust and feared Jewish cleverness. To *Jean Fowler* there were good Jews who kept to themselves and bad Jews who 'get into a city and take over everything—no wonder Germany threw them out'. When Europeans conversed in their native tongues, many Australians felt intellectually inferior: if Europeans had to come here they should be 'forced to speak English'. People felt deeply threatened by cultural differences. Hence for old Australians the semantic shift from 'Reffoes', 'Balts', 'Dagoes' and 'Wogs' to 'New Australians' was a marked improvement. Old Australians demanded a high price for acceptance: the jettisoning of personal history and identity.

The *Richmond News* first used the term 'New Australians' in October 1950 when it reported a successful Fair Rents' Board action brought by Stan Keon against a Richmond boarding house that was charging non-English-speaking migrants £5 2s a week for two rooms. The Board reduced the rent to £1 2s 6d. The housing shortage made the new settlers fair game for bad landlords. In 1951 the Richmond Council took action against a seven-roomed boarding house in Mary Street that housed forty-two Cypriots, many of them in the five garages on the property. With short memories of the Depression, the Council demanded that Scully seek the declaration by the State government of 'emergency measures to meet the threat to Australian living standards due to overcrowding of homes'. And if the New Australians were fair game they were also good for a laugh: the *News* delighted in the story of a new arrival with little English who refused to leave the ship after he overheard an Australian on the wharf announce that he was 'fed up with New Australians': 'the migrant believed that the man was a cannibal who had come down to choose a victim'.[20] And in 1956 the *News* found the following incident worthy of print:

> This happened in a Bridge Road delicatessen on Monday. New Australian asked for a breadroll, had it sliced down the middle, and then asked for a rasher of fresh bacon to be placed between the slices. No amount of persuasion could make him change his mind. Then came the finishing touch—'Plenty of pepper on it please', he asked. (Funny thing, I like it with horse radish sauce, myself.)[21]

The old Australians were not to know that many migrants found them equally peculiar.

Keon and Scully had always taken an interest in the new arrivals, but after the Split the D.L.P. became their conspicuous champions. Certainly the Catholicism of many New Australians motivated the Church to promote their welfare, but there were also political profits as the D.L.P. recruited central European refugees from Communist totalitarianism. Sadly, in Richmond the New Australians became a political football kicked about by the two embittered Labor parties and in March 1956 an ugly row erupted in the Council over the removal of some trees by the Wilhemina Soccer Club from their new pitch.[22] The *News* worked hard to re-educate its old Australian flock. In 1958 it counselled:

> Most Australians would naturally prefer British migrants and every encouragement should be given, as it is, to bring them in big numbers, but for various reasons this source is drying up. At the same time, it would be a retrograde step if we were to allow recial and religious prejudices to turn off the flow of non-British migrants, and also heap on these people the responsibility for the housing shortage together with the fluctuations in employment.[23]

Gradually by the late 1950s New Australians began to leave their mark on Richmond public life. In 1958 St Ignatius' began posting church notices in Italian; in 1959 Italian children were among the winners of the Richmond Council's scholarships; in 1961, only five years after the nastiness over the Wilhemina Soccer Club, a local girl of Dutch parentage was chosen as 'Miss Richmond' at a 'gala cabaret ball' at the Town Hall. That year, too. Rockman's store in Richmond began employing interpreters to encourage custom from the migrant community. The Commonwealth Bank took another three years, however, before it appointed a multilingual officer. Then in 1966 the first 'ethnics' stood for political office in the Richmond Council elections and the Federal election.[24]

But if the public record in the local press suggests a reasonably smooth transition to incorporation, what was going on in the privacy of people's heads is a different matter. Many of the first migrants were anxious to blend inoffensively into the Australian social fabric; their war experiences were too fresh to allow them to thrust their cultural differences upon Australian life. But during the 1960s the character of the migrants began to change. As the Italians increased they began to leave their mark on food and leisure yet, they too, were wary of open political commitments. Then came the Greeks, intensely proud of their culture and identity and incorrigibly political. The Greeks confronted old Australia with the legitimacy of ethnic differences, and by the 1960s the Ethnics had the numbers to force their cultural rights upon their reluctant hosts. When the 1961 Census was taken, Richmond was 40 per cent 'New Australian', a third of them already naturalized. The young migrant couples were starting their families and with around a thousand births a year, Richmond was experiencing an annual natural increase of approximately 3 per cent. The Health Centres were having to use Greek women by 1959 as voluntary interpreters. Overall, however, Richmond's population was still falling and since the 1952 Census had declined by 6 per cent to 33 789. The number of voters was down by 30 per cent and Yarra's eventual obliteration in a redistribution loomed. In 1959 no fewer than nine hundred of Richmond's houses were sold, a tenth of the housing stock. Richmond had divided into two: an Old Australian community, disproportionately elderly and female, and a New Australian community, young, vital and fertile.[25]

Old Richmond had to adjust to a new social landscape. In a society where gentlemen and most others preferred blondes, Richmond seemed to be over-run with swarthy strangers 'jabbering in their own lingo'. Some reacted with humour. *Lilian Campbell*'s Irish immigrant mother observed one day: 'It's funny, but I haven't seen a good mop of ginger hair for months'. But *Phyllis Smith*, the daughter of a persecuted German immigrant, worries from the one-time safety of Mentone about the future of old Richmond and old Australia:

> I feel a little bit anxious about St Stephen's church because there's very few white people there now. Even here in Mentone we've got Pakistanis and Turkish. Every time, a white person moves out they're there. And they don't mix very much. We had some Spanish people here for a little while but it was very hard to get to know them. They say we don't mix with foreigners but I find them very hard to mix with. Still there's no problem—they give you a friendly nod when they go by. But its happening all over again: families are moving out and Greeks and Turks and coloureds are moving in.

Jim Cairns's worst experience of racial intolerance came while canvassing in Hawthorn. A fat Australian woman living behind the railway station declared that she didn't know whether she was going to vote Labor because 'they'd brought all these blacks to Australia'. 'Blacks?' 'Yeh—like the people next door.' They were Italians. *Ruby Kane* is too old now to cope with social change. She lives in her little house in Richmond in a state of siege:

> There's Greeks everywhere, all around here. You've heard that the biggest percentage of Greeks outside Greece is in Richmond. They're all around. But fortunately I've still got Australians on either side. It's really very sad to see Richmond changing.

She hates their loud music and their noisy children, but the Greek men frighten her too much to complain. She disapproves of the middle-class 'Trendies', too: their morals are suspect and their children undisciplined and dirty.

The New Australians, however, not only looked different and sounded different; they were also successful. *Jean Fowler*:

> When the immigrants came out they got into the jobs. Good luck to the people who get into their damn jobs—they're not going to starve to death because the Australians are stuck in the pub. I say serve the Australians right.

Bill Shannon has not only had to cope with the childhood friends that have made good and got out, but also with the New Australians he once ridiculed who have since done well:

> At Brighton Street school the first New Australian that come there was a Balt. He was a funny type of fellow. We used to poke fun at him—couldn't speak our language and that type of thing—he made us all laugh. He finished up being general manager of Moulded Products, Nylex Corporation, so he sort of kicked on.
>
> And in the Thomastown area are all the Italians who were in Richmond in the 1950s. If you don't know who to say 'chiao' to you're in trouble. They've got beautiful homes that make Toorak look sick.
>
> Now we've got the Greeks and they're moving out too.

Bill insists that he's 'an easy-going bloke' with 'no hates', except for the Yugoslavs who are 'a more emotional lot', but he has a catalogue of gripes against migrants who pretend 'they canna speaka da English' when there are bills to be paid. He likes the way the Italian families pay back the church and its schools with donations once they have established themselves: 'They pay back and they do it when you're not expecting it—they've been doing it that way for centuries'. But 'If you do the wrong thing by them, they'll come out and cut your throat—that's the way they've been brought up'. *Jean* too is angry towards ethnic groups who bring their historical conflicts to a new country: 'I don't like the way the Vietnamese are bringing their politics with them—send them home if they're going to start blues over here. They're supposed to be very timid sort of people, then they start all that blue over here—no wonder they threw them out'.

Yet when Old Australians came face to face with New Australians friendships were inevitable and mutual prejudices melted under intimacy. *Jean* feels every bit as swamped in a Greek sea as does *Ruby*, but 'there's one Greek woman around here—she's lovely, she says "I'm Australian, that's all there is about it" '. Migrants could be accepted if they enthusiastically became 'more Australian than the Australians'. Gus Coloretti was an old New Australian who had done that and he found himself impatient with the post-war immigrants who would not forget 'home' and 'do it our way'. *Muriel Thompson* is touched by the rivalry between her neighbours, Greek on one side, Italian on the other, and divided by ancient antipathies, as they try to outdo each other in their solicitude for the old lady on her own now after her husband died. But occasional friendships do not compensate for the grief at the death of old Richmond. *Jean*:

> There's no longer anybody here that we know. Just three families left of real people that's always been here. They're all Greeks. I get that way that I just hate Richmond now because there's no one to talk to. In the old days they were all neighbourly, all lovely people. They'd all come out into the street and stand out the front and talk together. We used to go over to the school and play cards and that—there was always somebody around. They'd do anything to help you. But they're greedy now—they don't want to give you anything. People are now all trying to tread on you to get what they want. It's changed and what's going to happen to the kids today?

Yet in the death of old Richmond there was a rebirth, but the story of the varied peoples who re-made Richmond belongs to another and new book.

10

Old Age and Reflection

The social condition of Mary Street Central by 1965 neatly summarized some of the fundamental changes that had occurred in working-class private life since the turn of the century. In 1900 32 per cent of the occupants owned their house; in 1965 85 per cent did. In 1900 a Dutchman was the sole household head not of Anglo-Celtic ethnic origin; in 1965 38 per cent of Mary Street Central was owned by New Australians. In 1900 Mary Street was a family street with 24 per cent of the household heads being women, most of them widows; by 1965 47 per cent of the Old Australian household heads were women, all of them classified as undertaking home duties only. By 1965 the slum landlord had all but disappeared and thirteen of the seventy owner occupiers were long-term tenants who had purchased their homes from the landlord. In his place had emerged the property developer who descended on elderly people to offer sums of money for their crumbling cottages that, measured by the values of the 1930s, seemed like a fortune. Only when these old people moved into the outside world did they realize that they had been duped. In 1965 six houses were empty and in the hands of developers at the time of the municipal valuation. This left thirteen houses with traditional tenancies, that is but 10 per cent of the whole street. And by 1965 Mary Street contained a complex of flats for old people, built by the Richmond Council and now administered by the Housing Commission. 'James Scullen Court' today lives up to one Richmond tradition, however: that of enshrining misspellings in local nomenclature as in 'Botherambo Street' that marks the Reverend Joseph Docker's homestead, 'Bontharambo', near Wangaratta.[1]

The growth in home ownership was the most significant change in the material condition of the inner city working class. It grew quietly during the Edwardian economic recovery and the 1920s until the Great Depression, which saw a rapid turnover of tenants and the forced sale of some workers' homes. Then came the war and the economic growth of the next two decades completed the transformation of Mary Street from a street of tenants to a street of property-owners. However, this rise in home ownership did not necessarily mean that those approaching the end of their working lives faced an old age of financial comfort. On the contrary, many had emerged from the Depression with a burden of debt that took years to shift. Some people, who had been buying a house when they were hit by unemployment, now had increased instalments to cover those missed during the crisis. Many who had known prolonged unemployment simply had hardly any possessions: few clothes, little furniture, no household appliances. Above all, many were unable to generate enough income before they reached retiring age to build the savings to see, them through old age.

The Henderson Poverty Inquiry released in 1970 found many old people in poverty because they had never been able to earn enough to save. One case study was of a couple who had reared an only child who had left school at fourteen to go to work: the husband had worked all his life, his wife for thirty-one years; they had never bought a house and lived in a Housing Commission flat, which cost them, after allowing for their rental rebate, three dollars a week plus a dollar for heating. Despite all this their joint assets amounted to one hundred dollars. Another case study was of a childless couple who had bought a house. They had both worked all their lives and neither had suffered any unemployment or ill health. They had bought their home in 1957 for the equivalent of $3900, with a deposit of $600 and were still paying it off in instalments of eight dollars a week. This couple's total assets, apart from their equity in the house, amounted to 80 cents. A third case study dealt with a single woman classed as 'in need' because her only income was the Old Age Pension plus Supplementary Assistance. She paid $7 a week rent for an unfurnished bed-sitting room and kitchenette. She had worked all her life from the age of fifteen until she retired at eighty-seven. Finally, the study instanced the case of a man who was supplementing his pension with part-time earnings of $14 a week. He paid $15.50 rent. He had been in two superannuation schemes during his working life but had lost the accumulated benefits in each on changing jobs. *Jean Fowler is* infuriated by those critics who insist that working-class people should have saved for their old age: 'How could we—we had NOTHING'. When *Jean* and *Muriel Thompson* both declare that they have never been so well off since they 'went on the pension', it is not a tribute to the generosity of the Federal government, but an indictment of the poverty inflicted on them throughout their entire lives.[2]

Home-owners without savings were unable to carry out even the most basic repairs; tenants without savings could not cope with rising rents and living costs. *Jean Fowler* worries that she does not have the $1000 to repair her house; but, even worse, she has nothing put aside for a rainy day: '$200 in the bank would be enough', she says. Yet even those who were able to save have seen their nest-egg eaten away by inflation. *Thomas Beauchamp*:

> I feel that the modern generation is living on the old because we saved up and I considered that when I retired I had enough to live comfortably for the rest of my life and now you reduce me down to the pension. The simple reason is that you've inflated the costs of everything so much. The prosperity that comes round like this is only robbing the older people. I'm getting more on the pension than I ever earnt before but I was getting good wages and all my earnings have been reduced down to 25 per cent of what they were worth.
>
> We don't get bitter because we understand you're living through time and change. You've got to take things as they are.

Government employees who had contributed to a superannuation fund came into their own on retirement. *Isabel Williams* had felt the loss of her superannuation deductions from her weekly wage but in retirement had enough to take two small trips overseas. Even the *Thompsons* had some cash for the first time in their lives; yet, as working-class people quite inexperienced in finance, they were unable to make the best of it. There was also a surprise in store for Muriel, after married life of tension over her husband's drinking:

> I had a good husband, even if he did those things—he was good. And when he got his 'super' I said to the children: 'Your father's going to have a bust-up now—he's sixty-five and he's retired and he's got this money to come'. And when he said, 'The money will come next week, love', I said, 'Well, you better put it down at the bank'—I didn't know then that we should have invested it. So he took me down to the bank and I was wondering 'Now we should have half each'. 'No', he says, 'I paid it'. 'Yes, but I've had to go on the breadline all my life so I've got to get a bit.' So he took me down to the bank and he used to have a few beers with the bank manager, and he said: 'Here's my money—I want to put it all in the bank. Put it all in the wife's name but give me a few hundreds that's over' (it was a few thousand). Well I nearly collapsed. I thought, (you're not bad after all'.
>
> That man never asked me for a penny and I've still got some of it because I'm a bit tight—I don't waste much—you've got to keep it for rates and taxes.

Throughout their marriage, *Muriel* had borne full responsibility for expenditure and family decisions: 'He never once paid a bill', but 'he let me go my own way'. He also never asked her for extra drinking and gambling money after he had deducted his allowance from his wages, but she is still angry that he continued to drink heavily and to smoke while they were on sustenance in the Depression. They seem to have lived separate lives: he in the pub, *Muriel* in the church, but affection endured to the end: 'He was kind to me and he used to like to hear me sing'. The only decision he forced upon her was to have no more children: even though he was a Catholic, on the dole with two babies was as much as he could take. The gift of his superannuation was an acknowledgement that she had provided him with a home and a family despite his diffidence and failure. So in old age Muriel was able for the first time in her life to have a hot water service, a washing machine and some carpet. She also was able to pay off the house. She lies in bed in her brick house in a street with trees and counts her taps: 'I only ever had one tap in that little house in William Street and now I've got thirteen and to me that's fantastic'.

But the complaints and dissatisfactions of the old are not really material. As long as they remain physically mobile and mentally alert, they survive on their pensions and savings because they are utterly frugal. The one Depression scar they all admit to is that they are incapable of waste: *Ruby Kane* hates throwing bread out for 'every time I throw a bit out I think of all those little children scavenging in rubbish tins in these countries where they're so desperate—isn't the world so badly divided up in food and that'. *Margaret Taylor* discards nothing: 'The Depression made you very careful with money—it must have learned a lot of people to live on very little'. Depression victims like *Harold Stephenson* were never again to feel secure in their employment so that the certainty of the pension is some consolation for its miserliness. Of course they are short of money but they are used to that. *Jean Fowler*:

> I'm easily satisfied—I couldn't care less about what next-door's got, if they've got washing machines and all that sort of thing. I've got a gas copper and I wouldn't be without it but as long as I've got enough. Money's never mattered to me. If I won Tattslotto it'd be all given away to hospitals and people who've been good to me, kids who've been good to me. All I'd keep would be a couple of thousand and do up my house. But money doesn't matter to me—to my daughter-in-law or my sons.

No: their complaints are social and emotional.

First, they are lonely. Too many women face long widowhoods, not just because of the custom of men marrying younger women, but mostly because male mortality in the working class is so high. The preponderance of women among the elderly means that society is more geared to accommodate widows; when men lose their wives the consequences can be catastrophic. When *Bill O'Reilly*'s wife died the light went out of his life: with her died their home and he was rootless. He attempted unsuccessfully to make a home with one of his daughters. Finally he returned to Richmond after more than half a lifetime away. Of course many marriages were unsatisfactory, but some couples, estranged for years by sexual frustrations and daily conflicts, find a new companionship in old age. Some feel only liberated by the death of their spouse. Children and grandchildren rarely live round the corner as once they did and regular contact means travelling and formal visits. And they have lost the street community that had been the working class's greatest social resource. Those who made good and moved to the suburbs found no substitute for old Richmond's warmth; those left in Richmond cling to its remnants. Even so this Richmond generation, either out in the suburbs or back in Richmond, have not lost the 'doing and joining' habit. They flock to Elderly Citizens' clubs, they remain involved in their churches and lodges, and for as long as their legs will permit, they get out of the house or flat every day. Most are readers, and, although they deplore the modern decline in family conversation, they value television. They are discriminating viewers and yearn for documentaries and dramas that depict and make sense of the lives of the common people; (they were glued to the dramatization of Frank Hardy's *Power Without Gory*). They certainly feel that television has opened a door into an outside world of different lands, peoples and times. Some have found new opportunities in old age. For once, *Jean Fowler* has been lucky and she has begun to realize, albeit belatedly, some of her talents. Eight years ago she decided that she wanted to learn to paint; but, as always, her lack of confidence once she left her working-class community interfered:

> I've always been timid about that sort of thing in case I couldn't do it. I went once to a place in East Melbourne to learn, but I got there and they never even looked at me. It was for people who knew how to paint and I was left like a shag on a rock.

However, an oil-painting class was started by the Y.W.C.A. at her church in Richmond and she has never looked back. Then two young men on the dole, Stephen Henderson and Tony Mahood, appeared at the Richmond Elderly Citizens' Club as self-appointed community artists and persuaded the members to allow them to stage a musical show. Some natural extroverts were eager from the beginning; most, like *Jean*, were terrified of performing in public. It took weeks to build self-confidence as the young men taught them singing, dancing, stagecraft, costuming and make-up. Eventually they were ready and took Melbourne by storm in 'Tombola'. A commercial television station made a documentary that was screened in prime time and they took the show on tour to the country. The excitement proved too much for some, including *Jean* who suffered her second heart attack, but none would have missed it for the world.

Few have such opportunities in old age, however. Perhaps the saddest thing these old people say is 'In my day . . .', as though they have no place in the present. Life belongs to youth, not age. The old seethe with resentment towards the young who ignore their needs and their knowledge. Instead of being community elders to be respected and consulted for their wisdom, they are a nuisance. They universally condemn the young for their selfishness and ingratitude, for their sexual licence and emotional carelessness. They seem to think that the modern school syllabus consists almost entirely of sex education, at the expense of spelling, handwriting, mental arithmetic and obedience. In old age many are immensely sensorily deprived and angry that ignorance and fear robbed them of sexual fulfilment in their prime. They cannot understand why the young, who start out life with all the opportunities and material advantages denied themselves in the bad old days, are so bored and dissatisfied. 'The young start out today with all that we finish up with', *Alice Murphy* complains; 'Somehow we were very happy because we got everything the hard way and learned to share', says *Muriel*. Yet when they deprecate the materialism and greed of the young they fail to acknowledge how much of it is of their own making. Poverty forces people to be materialistic: because they have so little, the absence of money and things dominates their perceptions, and the slow climb out of poverty by those who made good is a domestic chronicle of saving for the gas stove, the refrigerator, the washing machine, the carpet and the car. In their determination to give their children all that they had missed, they sometimes spoilt them, and their incomprehension of why the young can be so miserable amidst plenty testifies to their own spiritual limitations.

The old do have compassion for the young as they see them being afflicted by the depression of the 1980s, even though they do not believe that the young unemployed today have the mental toughness to survive as they did in the 1930s. Many are uncomfortable about people being on the dole for long periods: even Pat Kennelly at the end of his life believed that the unemployed should have to do sustenance work for the good of their character. Forgetful of the victims of alcohol they saw all around them in the slums, they see the alienated young as all falling victim to drugs. As this older Depression generation contemplates the new depression generation, the scars of the 1930s are brought out in sharp relief They distrust life. Your safe and secure private world can be brought crashing down around your ears by uncontrollable external forces. Depressions and wars afflict private life as acts of God; you can do nothing to prevent them. It is remarkable how unpolitical these people are: only those who are members of the Labor party or passionate thinking conservatives have attempted to formulate an intellectual explanation for the catastrophe. One of the uses of oral history is that it reveals just how little politics matter in private life and reminds us that less than 3 per cent of Australians are members of political parties. However much the working-class community eased the burdens of the unemployed, the Depression taught people that in the end they were utterly on their own.

Yet if many ordinary people invoke eschatology rather than political theory to explain history, they do have a consciousness of class. And they understand class in its naked truth. When *Jean Fowler* regrets what she might have done in life, if 'we had had money', she reduces the meaning and consequences of poverty to its essentials. The poor have no money and thereby no power. The only way they can exercise power that can have an effect on the rich is through a trade union and it has been the victories of compulsory and legally protected trade unions in the industrialized nations that have won the real improvements in life for the poor. Class feeling within the working class is a culture of shared experience, of similar problems, of common history. It is above all a sense of belonging. And within that community of feeling and knowledge the individuals who are honoured are not the talented and successful but the honest battlers. Everyone knows what each individual and family is up against and those, who endure the worst while keeping their self-respect, are the real working-class heroes.

But the working class's relationship with the classes above them devalues the achievements of respectability and battling. The working class claim on money and property rests only on the value of their labour and the vast majority have little or no value in the eyes of the possessors of capital. The unskilled, the female, the old, the feeble in body and mind too often found that the outside world had no use for them at all. And in the 1930s the skilled and respectable joined the ranks of the economically useless and socially dangerous. However, when the privileged intervened to alleviate the distress of the underprivileged, it was at a terrible social cost. Middle-class social reformers and middle-class institutions taught the poor to be ashamed of being working class. Educational opportunity for the clever poor was a sop for middle-class guilt, so that the champions of talent and hard work could congratulate themselves that they allowed equality of opportunity, while doing nothing to reduce the discomfort of indignity of those left behind. Upward social mobility through education for the few condemned the remnants of the working class in the 1950s and 1960s to see themselves as a demoralized residuum of failures, excluded from the 'Lucky Country' by weakness of character and deficiency of intellect. If in the lifetime of this generation we have seen the worst of material poverty abolished, we have done nothing to remove class stigma. We may shrink from the nineteenth century terms of deserving and undeserving poor, but such notions remain embedded in our social consciousness. Why else should a remarkable and successful woman like *Muriel Thompson* return obsessively in her conversation to the fact that she has done well in life because she 'made friends in Toorak' through her church. And why does *Bill Shannon* shoulder the full blame for his alcoholism and feel honoured by friendship in a hospital ward from men who have been to university: 'I got above me station'. Why do Australian-born Richmond people die so early? The collective depression and despair that White Australia believes is confined to Aborigines continues to afflict, as it always has, all people who are denied dignity and hope.

The essential problem of the poor is that they have no money; but the privileged in this country have never been prepared to sacrifice their economic advantage in a just redistribution of wealth. By the end of World War II they were willing to tolerate, however, the nationalization of philanthropy in the form of the Welfare State. Like charity workers of old, taxpayers resented supporting the undeserving poor and insisted that welfare payments be too low to encourage bludgers. And also like private philanthropy, the givers seemed to profit more than did the recipients. The greatest beneficiaries of the Welfare State have been the middle-class professionals and bureaucrats who have found new careers in the extraordinary explosion of the service sector since the war. And while not denying the necessity for a welfare net for those unable to work, the Welfare State has effected a drastic invasion of working-class life by middle-class experts. Teachers, doctors, health workers and social workers, however dedicated and caring, have stripped the working-class family and its community of many of the life skills that were the foundations of self-esteem and independence. While the Welfare State barely pays the rent and the bills, it contains dissent and delivers the poor into the hands of middle-class social managers.

This Edwardian-born generation has witnessed more change than any human generation before or since; and it is not just the transformation from the horse and buggy to space travel, from germ theory to genetic engineering, from the letter and the newspaper to the telephone and the television. The working class have seen the class into which they were born steadily incorporated into the culture and influence of the economically dominant. They were born into a working-class community that was complete unto itself: it provided its own leisure and entertainment; it created its own lore; it measured human actions by its own standards; it sustained its members by its own emotional resources. Certainly most of the important gains by the labour movement still lay ahead and relationships between the classes in the workplace were still deformed by deference and exploitation, but in private life the working class had a culture that was of their own making. It might be divided by sectarianism and weakened at the edges by better opportunities for upward social mobility than in, say, Britain, but it still could provide a total and satisfying world for its members. It broke *Lilian Campbell*'s heart to leave Richmond for better things; her equivalent today finds the parting easier.

World War I, despite the ambivalence of the working-class commitment, drew all classes into a national enterprise. Even so, for Richmond people and their newspaper, it was the suburb rather than the nation that went to war. By World War II Richmond was just another part of

Melbourne as Australia fought for its life. The cinema and the radio drew working-class patrons and listeners to the same entertainments as the middle class. Respectable working-class dancers rubbed shoulders with middle-class couples at the great dance halls of the 1920s. Poverty and unemployment of course delayed the impact of commercial popular culture; but *Isabel Williams*, for instance, was able to afford to buy her first radio during World War II. If it was good for the nation to pursue common tastes in leisure, it was even better for business as the poor came to pay for the diversions they had always created 'for free' in their homes and streets, churches and pubs. The rise of bought entertainment signified an improvement in working-class real income, but something valuable was lost and is deeply regretted by the old who remember how family life and public fun used to be. The common people have relinquished one of their oldest social resources and the poor, who today cannot pick up the tab of modern pleasures, live on the margin of 'the action', savouring the smell as did the unemployed outside the Vine Hotel in the 1930s.

In fact it was the Great Depression that dealt the fatal blow to the old working class and its communal culture. The Depression was a cruel lesson to those working-class respectables who believed themselves immune to destitution and disgrace. It may have been Richmond's finest hour as a human community, but afterwards most people only wanted to escape and forget. When the war and the following boom made escape possible, they took their savings to the suburbs: Richmond seemed finished, irreparably blighted and beyond salvation. And with the respectables went much of the steel of the old working class. Once in the suburbs, the habits of respectability enabled them to blend inconspicuously into Middle Australia, but removed from class stigma and the daily companionship of poverty, the living faith that had been working-class respectability often degenerated into a dead and suffocating dogma. From the safety and loneliness of the suburbs, many escapees began to mourn a world we have lost. *John Brown*'s sister-in-law interrupted his interview with:

> I now live in a better suburb, Hawthorn, in fact in a pretty posh area, but the people are not the same as Richmond people. They're the ones who are kind, they're the ones who help everyone else.

And *Will Parker*, who early in life was terrified by the destitution around him and determined that his wife and children should never suffer like that, sat in his two-storeyed cream brick veneer home near Wattle Park and paid this tribute to the slums of *Struggletown*:

> We used to sell soft drinks to a lot of small houses in Richmond and Collingwood, just little joints, but the people in them were happy. I came to like those people very much. They had their own back door and their own

> front door and no one could say 'Nay' to them—they could do what they liked and what went on inside their door, it was their affair. But these wretched things that they are put in today and the kids can't get outside and scratch in the dirt like kids like to do—they're like prisons. I liked those people in Richmond and Collingwood in those 'hovels'—they weren't hovels, they were happy.
>
> Oh, they were funny. I'd go round—'Hullo, Mr *Parker.* Come in and have a cuppa'. You often wondered if the cup had been washed recently or not. Oh, they were good people. And they were damp hovels, some of them—you'd almost hear the water trickling down the wall. Why should they have pulled them down—I reckon it was a terrible crime.

Such nostalgia founders on a paradox: the problems of the poor were caused by their poverty, but so too were their greatest assets. The truly admirable qualities of old working-class life—the intimacy, the caring, the resilience and the vitality—all were the products of shared poverty and class stigma. We cannot, therefore, dream of returning to that world we have lost if it has to be at such a price. However, we can learn to respect the under-privileged for the competence and courage with which they faced their manifold anxieties, deprivations and humiliations.

The old working class was thus divided and morally weakened. And by the time the Labor Party returned to power in 1972 for the first time since 1949, it too had become a captive of the middle class. *Harold Stephenson* and *Jean Fowler* both observe that the Whitlam government made no difference to their lives. This working-class generation learned a long time ago, however, not to expect much from politicians. Politics is about 'teams', not actions, and still today old Richmond continues to vote for the Labor machine rather than for the educated reformers, because it prefers to stay with a devil it knows rather than go with one who makes it feel inferior. But something of the old spirit of *Struggletown* endures in the dogged fatalism, something of the Aussie battler. *Bill Shannon* opened this book with the pain of class stigma, and he shall end it with his reflections on the remembered history of his parents' generation, his community and his class:

> Let's face it—we're a funny people, the Australians. We're always for the underdog and so forth but all the history I've read on the American side of the Depression—Steinbeck—they had it hard but we had it a damn sight harder here. Australia—she's not a friendly country; you've got to battle to get a quid. It's a hard country and a lucky country too—although I shouldn't say that because that's a Liberal idea.
>
> Every thirty years there's something to try you—even going back as far as written history—there's always been something. It seems like Nature's way of saying: Right, now—you've had your bit of fun; it's my turn.

Notes

1 BIRTHPLACE

1 *Bill Shannon* (pseudonym) bachelor, interviewed by author 7 February 1981.
2 E. C. Buley, *Australian Life in Town and Country* (London, 1905), p. 75.
3 Dr Jim Cairns, interviewed by author 6 and 20 December 1980.
4 *Richmond Guardian*, 21 November 1903.
5 *Richmond News*, 7 April 1954.
6 *Richmond Guardian*, 26 February 1916.
7 Ibid., 12 January 1901, 8 February 1902.
8 *Victorian Municipal Directory*, 1901, pp. 175–6; *Richmond Guardian*, 17 October 1908.
9 *Richmond Guardian*, 16 November 1901.
10 Ibid., 6 September 1902, 26 February 1916, 7 May 1904.
11 Ibid., 26 February 1916.
12 *Census of Victoria 1901; Richmond News*, 17 November 1966.
13 *Census of Victoria 1901.*
14 Interview with author—confidential.
15 Interview with author—confidential.
16 *Richmond Guardian*, 13 July 1912, 1 October 1921, 6 September 1913, 4 April 1914, 5 September 1903, 7 April 1923, 9 August 1902.
17 *Bill O'Reilly* (pseudonym) widower, interviewed by author 6 September and 1 October 1978.
18 *Richmond Guardian*, 1 April 1916, 7 April 1928, 2 August 1930.
19 Ibid., 21 October 1905, 28 August 1927; *Richmond Chronicle*, 14 August 1936.
20 *Friedrich and Florence Smith* (pseudonyms) married couple, interviewed by author 24 October 1980.
21 *Richmond Guardian*, 11 July 1903, 13 January 1900, 18 January 1902, 5 November 1910.
22 *Lilian Campbell* (pseudonym) widow, interviewed by author 11 September 1980.
23 Interviews with author—confidential.
24 *Richmond Chronicle*, 31 January 1936.
25 Dr *Brendan* Ryan (pseudonym) married man, interviewed by author 4 and 11 October 1978.
26 *John Brown* (pseudonym) widower, interviewed by author 10 June 1980.
27 Figures extracted from the Richmond City Council Rate Books for the Centre Ward section of Mary Street.
28 *Hamish* and *Nellie Roberts* (pseudonyms) married couple, interviewed by author February 1978.
29 *Dot* and *Edna Wilson* (pseudonyms) spinsters, interviewed by author 21 August 1978.
30 *Emma* and *Alice Murphy* (pseudonyms) widow and married woman, interviewed by author 10 February 1981.
31 *Kevin Maloney* (pseudonym) bachelor, interviewed by author 17 November 1980.
32 *Richmond Guardian*, 1 October 1910.
33 See my 'Respectability and Working-class Politics in Late-Victorian London', *Historical Studies*, vol. 19, no. 74, April 1980.

34 P. W. Kingsford, *Victorian Railwaymen: The Emergence and Growth of Railway Labour 1830–1870* (London, 1970); Brian Harrison, *Drink and the Victorians* (London, 1971), pp. 37–63; John Vincent, *The Formation of the Liberal Party, 1857–68* (London, 1966), pp. xiii–xiv; G. Kitson Clark, *The Making of Victorian England* (London, 1965), pp. 251–74.
35 Henry Tuckley, *Masses and Classes: A Study of Industrial Conditions in England* (New York, 1893), p. 151.
36 N. A. Humphries (ed.), *Vital Statistics: A Memorial Volume of Selections from the Writings of William Farr* (London, 1885), pp. 300–2.
37 Henry Mayhew, *London Labour and the London Poor, 1861–2* (New York, 1968), vol. I, pp. 104–18; M. Durey, 'The Survival of an Irish Culture in Britain, 1800–1845', *Historical Studies*, vol. 20, no. 78, April 1982.
38 *Statistical Register of Victoria 1901*, p. 585.
39 E.g. *Richmond Guardian*, 17 June 1911.
40 *Isabel Williams* (pseudonym) spinster, interviewed by author 7 August 1980.
41 R.C.C. Ratebooks, Mary Street, Centre Ward.
42 Report of the Board of Inquiry on Unemployment, *Vict. V&P*, 1900. vol. 2, p. 8.
43 *Jean Fowler* (pseudonym) widow, interviewed by author 12 May 1980.
44 *Muriel Thompson* (pseudonym) widow, interviewed by author 27 March 1980.
45 *Richmond Guardian*, 27 June, 28 December 1903.
46 Ibid., 1 August 1903.
47 Ibid., 2 August 1902.
48 *Ruby Kane* (pseudonym) widow, interviewed by author 23 September 1980.
49 *Friedrich Smith*.
50 *Richmond Guardian*, 28 September 1912, 3 April 1915.
51 *Victorian Year Book* 1940–41, Convictions for Drunkenness in Victoria 1874–1940, p. 61; A. E. Dingle, 'The Truly Magnificent Thirst: an Historical Survey of Australian Drinking Habits', *Historical Studies*, vol. 19, no. 75, October 1980.
52 *Richmond Guardian*, 11 December 1909, 30 March 1912.
53 Ibid., 13 December 1902.
54 Report of the Royal Commission on the Operation of the Factories and Shops Law in Victoria, *VPP*, 1902/3, 31, Evidence, pp. 674, 491.
55 Ibid.; Evidence, p. 298, Report, p. xxxvi; Evidence, pp. 676, 681–2; Report, p. xi.
56 Ibid., Report, pp. liii-lvi, Evidence, pp. 217–20, 504, 226–30.
57 Ibid., Report, pp. lxiii-lxiv; N. G. Butlin, 'Some Perspectives of Australian Economic Development, 1890–1965', in C. Foster (ed.), *Australian Economic Development in the Twentieth Century* (London, 1970), pp. 266–327; Report of Board of Inquiry on Unemployment, op. cit., pp. 6–7.
58 R.C. on . . . Factories and Shops Law, op. cit., Report, p. xl, Evidence, pp. 655, 675, 382–4, 567–9, 652; *Richmond Guardian*, 9 September 1905; *Labor Call*, 13 February, 4 September 1914.
59 *Richmond Guardian*, 27 February 1909, 8 January 1910, 28 September 1901; *Richmond Advocate*, 27 September 1972; *Labor Call*, 2 January 1913.
60 *Richmond Advocate*, 27 September 1972; *Richmond Guardian*, 24 September 1900, 19 March 1904, 16 May 1914, 17 February 1923.
61 *Richmond Advocate*, 27 September 1972.
62 *Richmond Guardian*, 10 April 1915, 24 September 1910, 1 July 1911.
63 R.C. on . . . Factories and Shops Law, op. cit., Evidence p. 529; *Richmond Guardian*, 10 February 1912; R.C.C. Ratebooks, Mary Street, Centre Ward.
64 *Richmond Guardian*, 2 November 1912.
65 *Census of Victoria* 1911; Royal Commission on National Insurance, *APP*, 1926/8, Second Progress Report, pp. 7–8; *Labor Call*, 27 February 1914.
66 The Hon. P. J. Kennelly, interviewed by author 2 March 1981.
67 *Richmond News*, 14 September 1955; *Richmond Guardian*, 12 March 1904, 12 September 1908; Graeme Davison, *The Rise and Fall of Marvellous Melbourne* (Melbourne, 1978), pp. 62–3; John Rickard, *Class and Politics* (Canberra, 1976), pp. 115–17, 223, 229; *Labor Call*, 9 January 1913; *Richmond Guardian*, 1, 15 August 1925.
68 R. A. Crouch, 'Political Reminiscences', MS 9599–74, La Trobe Library, pp. 233–7; *Labor Call*, 27 March 1913.
69 *Ted Sullivan* (pseudonym) married man, interviewed by author 5 November 1979.

70 *Richmond Guardian*, 7 June 1913, 12 September 1914.
71 *Richmond Guardian*, 23 February 1901. 5, 19 July, 23 August 1902.
72 Ibid 16, 23 August 1902.
73 Ibid., 30 August 1902.
74 Ibid., 13 September 1902, 3 December 1904, 7 March 1908.
75 Ibid., 6 August 1904.
76 *Labor Call*, 9 July 1914.
77 *Richmond Guardian*, 13 February 1915, 13 September 1913, 4 April 1914; *Labor Call*, 25 September 1913.
78 *Richmond Guardian*, 9 March 1912, 18 January 1913.
79 *Labor Call*, 18 December 1913, 25 March, 1 April, 30 December 1915; *Richmond Guardian*, 19 June, 13 November 1915.

2 CHILDHOOD

1 Joint Select Committee on the Housing of the People in the Metropolis, *VPP*, 1913/14, D. 4 (v. 1), Report and Evidence. p. 23.
2 *Richmond Guardian*, 16 April 1910, 21 March 1914.
3 *Phyllis Smith*, married woman and sister *of Friedrich* (pseudonyms), interviewed by author 2 July 1980.
4 *Richmond Chronicle*, 21 September 1934; see Thomas Laqueur, *Religion and Respectability, Sunday Schools and Working-Class Culture 1780–1850* (Yale, 1976), pp. 170–1.
5 R.C.C. Ratebooks, Mary Street. Centre Ward; A. E. Dingle and D. T. Merrett, 'Home Owners and Tenants in Melbourne, 1890–1911', *Australian Economic Review*, vol. XII, no. 1, March 1972; *Richmond Guardian*, 15 October 1921, 8 April 1922.
6 Royal Commission on the Housing Conditions of the People . . ., *VPP*, 1917, no. 291 Minutes of Evidence (v. 2), p. 25.
7 *Richmond Guardian*, 16 May 1914, 9 May 1908.
8 *Muriel Thompson:* 'There was a terrible lot of bugs and lice about . . . people were clean and I don't know what it was, but I remember scalding my mother's bedstead. And lice in the kiddies' hair', R.C. on Housing Conditions. . ., op. cit., p. 25.
9 Ibid., p. 78.
10 *Richmond Guardian*, 15 August 1936, 16 May 1914.
11 Douglas Gordon, *Health, Sickness and Society: Theoretical Concepts in Social and Preventative Medicine* (Brisbane, 1976), pp. 171, 105, 162–3.
12 Second Report of the Commission *of* Public Health to the Minister of Public Health, *VPP*, 1924, 11 (v. 1), pp. 25–6; J. W. Springthorpe, *Therapeutics, Dietetics and Hygiene: An Australian Text-book* (Melbourne, 1914), vol. 1, pp. 527–34.
13 *Richmond Guardian*, 16 March 1901, 22 June 1912, 15 February, 15 March 1913, 16 January, 17 April 1915, 15 April 1916, 5 January 1918.
14 *Census of Victoria 1901*, Education *of* the People, pp. 12–13; *Richmond Guardian*, 16 March 1901, 16 April 1910.
15 Michael Roe, 'The Establishment of the Australian Department of Health: Its Background and Significance', *Historical Studies*, vol. 17, no. 67, October 1976, pp. 176–92; Desley Deacon, 'Taylorism in the Home: the Medical Profession, the Infant Welfare Movement and the Deskilling of Women', paper delivered to the SAANZ Conference, Melbourne, August 1983; Report of the Royal Commission on Secret Drugs, Cures and Foods, 1907, *APP*, 1907/8, vol. IV, p. 71; *Richmond Guardian*, 28 March 1908.
16 *Richmond Guardian*, 22 October 1910, 4 May 1912, 18 March, 6 May 1911, 26 September 1914, 5 May 1917, 5 January, 6 July 1918, 17 July 1920.
17 Gordon, op. cit., p. 105; Ronald Mendelsohn, *The Condition of the People: Social Welfare in Australia 1900–1975* (Sydney, 1979), pp. 72–7.
18 *Richmond Guardian*, 1 April 1905; Royal Commission on National Insurance, *APP*, 1926/8 IV, Third Progress Report, III Destitute Allowances, p. 9; Progress Report *of* the Select Committee on Widows' Pensions and Child Endowment, *VPP*, 1936, D. 1 (v. 1), pp. 4–5.
19 *Doug* and *Mary Davis* (pseudonyms) married couple, interviewed by author 15 January and 8 February 1980.

20 *Monica Rinoldi* (pseudonym) married woman, interviewed by author 23 January 1980.
21 *Thelma Clark*, widow, and her sister *Irene*, spinster (pseudonyms), interviewed by author 4 August 1978.
22 *Will Parker* (pseudonym) widower, interviewed by author 10 November 1980.
23 *Richmond Guardian*, 16 September 1911.
24 Ibid., 6 August 1904.
25 Ibid., 19 January 1901.
26 *Labor Call*, 25 February 1926.
27 *Albert Perkins* (pseudonym) married man, interviewed by author 30 August 1978.
28 *Richmond Guardian*, 10 June 1916.
29 *George Little* (pseudonym) married man, interviewed by author 15 August 1978.
30 *Arthur Coombes* (pseudonym) married man, interviewed by author 21 March 1978.
31 *Harold Stephenson*, and wife *Evelyn* (pseudonyms), interviewed by author October 1978.
32 Testimony *of John Brown*'s sister-in-law who was present during interview; *Richmond Guardian*, 26 July 1913.
33 *Richmond Guardian*, 30 March 1912.
34 W. E. Adams, *Memoirs of a Social Atom* 2 vols (London, 1903, reprinted New York, 1968), pp. 110–11.
35 R. J. W. Selleck, *Frank Tate* (Melbourne, 1982), pp. 261–2.
36 *Richmond Guardian*, 7 June 1902, 4 February 1905, 18 May 1901, 17 May 1902, 12 May 1906, 2 April 1910, 22 April 1911; *Richmond Chronicle*, 16 April 1943.
37 Royal Commission on Technical Education: Second Progress Report, Manual and Practical Instruction in Primary Schools, *VPP*, 1899/1901, no. 51 (v. 4), pp. 69–74, 88–90.
38 *Richmond Australian*, 23 December 1882.
39 *Richmond Guardian*, 20 December 1913, 24 May 1919, 31 October 1903, 7 October 1905, 21 March, 10 January 1925, 13 May 1922, 6 November 1926, 10 December 1927.
40 Selleck, op. cit., p. 154.
41 *Richmond Guardian*, 28 October 1922.
42 Board of Inquiry into Certain Matters concerning the Education Department, *VPP*, 1931, no. 17, vol. 1, p. 17.
43 Brother Ronald Fogarty, *Catholic Education in Australia, 1806–1950* (Melbourne, 1959), vol. II, pp. 334–40; *Richmond News*, 21 November 1946.
44 *Richmond Guardian*, 20 January 1900, 24 February 1904, 4 February 1928.
45 *Thomas Beauchamp* (pseudonym) married man, interviewed by author 16 July 1980.

3 WAR AND PEACE I

1 *Richmond Guardian*, 8 August 1914.
2 Ibid., 13 February 1915, 7 September 1918, 18 March 1916; *Labor Call*, 11 February 1915.
3 *Richmond Guardian*, 11 May 1918.
4 Ibid., 8 July 1916; *Labor Call*, 1 February 1917.
5 *Richmond Guardian*, 16 September 1916.
6 Royal Commission on High Prices, *VPP*, 1919 (v. 2), Final Report p. 6; *Richmond Guardian*, 6 January 1917, 10 July, 18 September 1915.
7 *Richmond Guardian*, 15 January 1915, 6 January 1917; George Johnston, *My Brother Jack* (London,1964).
8 *Richmond Guardian*, 23 January 1915, 6 January 1917.
9 Ibid., 4 April 1916.
10 Ibid 23 January 1915.
11 Ibid., 8 January 1916.
12 Michael McKernan, *The Australian People and the Great War* (Melbourne, 1980), pp. 116–49; *Richmond Guardian*, 21 August 1915.
13 *Richmond Guardian* 22, 29 August, 10 September 1914, 28 September 1918, 27 March 1915; McKernan, op. cit., pp. 14–42.
14 *Richmond Guardian*, 27 March 1915.
15 G. M. Dening, *Xavier—A Centenary Portrait* (Melbourne, 1978), p. 109.
16 *Richmond Guardian*, 8 May, 17 July 1915.

17 Ibid 17 October 1914, 15 May, 5, 19 June 1915.
18 Ibid., 13 March 1915, 3, 10 July, 16 October 1915, 29 January 1916.
19 Ibid., 2 February 1911, 27 May 1916, 6, 13 January 1917, 26 January, 2 February 1918.
20 Bill Gammage, *The Broken Years* (Melbourne, 1975), p. 14.
21 *Richmond Guardian*, 10 July 1915.
22 Ibid., 21 August 1915.
23 Ibid., 11 September 1915.
24 Ibid., 25 September 1915; McKernan, op. cit., pp. 98–105; *Richmond Guardian*, 9 October 1915.
25 *Richmond Guardian*, 30 October, 24 December 1915, 8 January 1916.
26 Ibid 15 January 1916.
27 Ibid., 29 January, 12 February, 11 March 1916.
28 Ibid., 4 March, 15 April, 6 May 1916.
29 Ibid 20, 27 May 1916.
30 Ibid., 29 July 1916.
31 Ibid., 12, 19, 26 August 1916.
32 Ibid., 16 September 1916.
33 Ibid., 17 November 1906.
34 Ibid., 14 June 1913, 21, 28 November 1914, 1 May 1915, 9 September 1916; Celia Hamilton, 'Catholic Interests and the Labor Party, 1910–1916', *Historical Studies*, no. 33, November 1959, pp. 68–70.
35 *Richmond Guardian*, 23, 30 September, 14 October 1916.
36 Ibid., 14 October 1916.
37 Ibid., 4 November 1916.
38 Ibid., 6, 27 January, 3, 24 February 1917.
39 Ibid., 10 March 1917.
40 Ibid., 8 February 1917, 5 February 1916, 18 January 1919; *Richmond Chronicle*, 1 October 1943.
41 *Labor Call*, 8 February 1917; *Richmond Guardian*, 10 February 1917.
42 *Labor Call*, 15 February 1917.
43 *Richmond Guardian*, 28 April 1917.
44 Ibid., 12 May 1917.
45 Ibid., 9, 16 June, 25 August, 28 July, 29 September 1917.
46 Ibid., 24 November, 22 December 1917.
47 Ibid., 8 June 1918.
48 Ibid., 17 August 1918.
49 Ibid., 9, 16 November 1918.
50 *Rose Saddler* (pseudonym) spinster, interviewed with her brother *Jim* by author 29 January 1981.
51 Douglas Gordon, *Health, Sickness and Society* (Brisbane, 1976), p. 194; The Senate Select Committee on Intoxicating Liquor: Effect on Australian Soldiers, APP, 1917/19, Final Report and Minutes of Evidence, pp. 685–890.
52 *Richmond Guardian*, 25 January, 8 February, 1 March, 12 April 1919; Gordon, op. cit., p. 90; William H. McNeill, *Plagues and Peoples*, (New York, 1977), pp. 185, 255.
53 *Richmond Guardian*, 8 November 1919.
54 Ibid., 12, 19, 26 July, 13 September, 10 October 1919.
55 Russel Ward, *A Nation for a Continent: The History of Australia 1901–1975* (Melbourne, 1977), p. 142; *Richmond Guardian*, 8 January, 19 February 1921, 19 June 1920.
56 *Richmond Guardian*, 10 November 1923, 9 February 1924, 1 April 1922.
57 Ibid., 4 August 1923, 10 May 1919, 1 May 1926, 7 October 1922; Royal Commission on National Insurance 1927, *APP*, 1926/8, Second Progress Report, pp. 2–7; N. G. Butlin, 'Some Perspectives of Australian Economic Development, 1890–1965', in Colin Foster (ed.), *Australian Economic Development in the Twentieth Century* (Sydney, 1970), pp. 281–3.
58 R.C. on National Insurance, op. cit., Third Progress Report, p. 6.
59 *Richmond Guardian*, 13 January 1923, 27 January, 6 September, 15 November 1924, 29 November 1919, 28 August 1920, 11 February 1922, 29 September 1923, 27 May 1922, 17, 24 January 1920; *Labor Call*, 30 September 1936.
60 *Richmond Guardian*, 19 March 1927, 14 August 1920, 20 September 1924, 22 April 1922, 16 February, 9 March 1929.
61 Ibid., 11 June 1921; Hugh Anderson, *The Rise and Fall of Squizzy Taylor* (Sydney, 1981), pp. 74–5.
62 *Norman Stevens* (pseudonym) married man, interviewed by author May 1978.

63 Anderson, op. cit., pp. 4–5; *Richmond Guardian*, 25 February 1908.
64 *Richmond Guardian*, 5 April 1919; *New Spectator*, 22 January 1919.
65 *Richmond Guardian*, 22 November 1919, 14 August, 11 September, 28 August, 18 December 1920, 19 March 1921.
66 Ibid., 16 April, 14 May 1921.
67 Ibid., 21, 28 May 1921.
68 Ibid., 4 June, 23 July, 3, 17, 24 September 1921.
69 Ibid., 28 January 1922.
70 Robert Murray, *The Split: Australian Labor in the Fifties* (Melbourne, 1972), p. 92; Frank Hardy, *Power Without Glory* (Melbourne, 1950), pp. 259–66; Anderson, op. cit., pp. 13–21; *Richmond Guardian*, 29 August, 26 December 1925.
71 *Richmond Guardian*, 18 August 1923, 14 June 1924.
72 Ibid., 17 January, 18 April, 9 May 1925, 9 April 1927; *Age*, 9 January 1925.
73 *Labor Call*, 15 April 1926; *Richmond Guardian*, 6 March, 10 April, 7 August, 11 September, 9 October 1926, 18 June 1927; *Labor Call*, 21 October 1926.
74 *Richmond Guardian*, 25 July 1925, 19 May, 17 March, 28 April, 11 August 1928.
75 *Richmond Weekly*, 23 December 1927; *Richmond Guardian*, 26 June 1926; *Richmond Chronicle*, 9 June 1939.

4 YOUTH

1 Comment made by *John Brown*'s sister-in-law who was present during the interview with him.
2 *Richmond Guardian*, 4 January 1919, 24 March, 17 February 1923.
3 Ibid., 18 November 1922, 28 July 1928.
4 *Richmond Chronicle*, 7 February 1936.
5 *Richmond Guardian*, 1 February 1919.
6 Ibid., 29 July 1911.
7 Ibid., 13 January 1912.
8 Ibid., 10 April 1926.
9 Wendy Lowenstein, *Weevils in the Flour* (Melbourne, 1978), pp. 290–4.
10 *Richmond Weekly*, 24 February 1928. She was later acquitted of the charge because of insufficient evidence and the judge recommended to the jury that they regard the victim's husband as an accomplice.
11 *Richmond Guardian*, 15 January 1910, 1 June 1912: 'Ivy Maine was convicted with offensive behaviour, drinking in Yarra Park with larrikins. Mother was alcoholic. Dr Agnew J.P.: "This poor girl never had a chance. She went back to a home that was full of drunkenness and misery, and when she went out there was only the paddocks and the picture shows".'
12 Ibid., 25 September 1920, 29 January, 12 March 1921, 27 September 1924, 23 January 1926.
13 Ibid., 13 September 1924; *Labor Call*, 19 August, 11 November 1926.
14 *Richmond Chronicle*, 27 May, 8 July 1938.
15 *Richmond Guardian*, 18 February 1933, 5 November 1921; *Richmond Chronicle*, 25 July 1941; 16 *Richmond News*, 30 May 1957, 24 May 1961; *Richmond Guardian*, 21 October 1922.
16 Paul Thompson, *The Edwardians* (London, 1975, 1977), pp. 77–80.
17 Douglas Gordon, *Health, Sickness and Society* (Brisbane, 1976), p. 113. This figure includes ex-nuptial births and birth within eight months of marriage.
18 Confidential interview material.
19 A. E. Dingle, 'The Truly Magnificent Thirst, Historical *Studies*, vol. 19, no. 75, October 1980, *passim*.
20 The personal experience of a secondary school history teacher who attended Our Lady of Sion Convent in Box Hill in the early 1960s.
21 *Richmond Guardian*, 12 July, 29 March 1924, 7 March 1925.
22 Ibid., 9 October 1920.
23 Ibid., 18 October 1919, 19 June 1920.
24 *Richmond Chronicle*, 29 January 1943.
25 Leonie Sandercock, 'Playing the Greater Game: Australian Rules Football in the 1930s', *Australia 1938*. Bulletin no. 1, February 1980, pp. 29–30.
26 *Richmond Guardian*, 10 June 1933, 24 February 1923.

27 Ibid., 27 January 1917.
28 St Stephen's Church of England Marriage Register 1900–1962, Australian Manuscripts Collection, La Trobe Library, MS 10880.
29 *Richmond Guardian*, 27 March 1915, 5 August 1916, 4 June 1927, 30 January 1926.
30 Ibid., 17 May 1913, 13 October 1923, 14 September 1929.
31 Recollected by Wal Dickson, a friend of the author's father.

5 DEPRESSION AND DECAY

1 Peter Spearritt, 'Depression Statistics', in *The Wasted Years?*, Judy Mackinolty (ed.) (Sydney, 1981), pp. 204–5; *Richmond Guardian*, 18 July 1931.
2 *Labor Call*, 15 April 1926; *Herald*, 21 August 1926, 17 May 1927; *Richmond Guardian*, 11 June, 2 July, 3 December 1927; *Richmond Weekly*, 27 June 1927.
3 *Richmond Guardian*, 18 February, 19 May 1928, 28 July 1923, 18 March 1926, 16 June, 14, 28 July, 1, 15 September 1928; *Herald*, 27 April 1928; *Age*, 12 June 1928.
4 *Richmond Guardian*, 6, 20 October, 22 December 1928.
5 Ibid., 2, 16 March, 6, 13 April, 11 May 1929.
6 Ibid., 13 April 1929.
7 Ibid., December 1928, January, February 1929 *passim*, 18 January 1930, 16 March, 31 August 1929; Report of the Royal Commission on Child Endowment and Family Allowances 1929, *APP*, 1929, 11, Minority Report, p. 105; *Richmond Weekly*, 21 June 1929; *Age*, 1 June 1929.
8 *Richmond Weekly*, 25 October 1929.
9 *Richmond Guardian*, 18, 22 March, 5 April 1930.
10 Ibid., 28 June, 10, 31 May 1930; *Herald*, 10 June 1930.
11 *Richmond Guardian*, 15 March, 12 April, 18 October 1930.
12 Ibid., 12 April 1930.
13 Ibid., 5, 12 May 1928, 2, 16 March 1930, 23 June 1928, 16 February 1929, 8 March, 11 January, 4 October 1930.
14 *Herald*, 10, 12, 20, 21, 24 June 1930.
15 Ibid., 17 June, 29 July 1930; *Age*, 9 July 1930; *Richmond Guardian*, 28 June 1930; *Richmond Weekly*., 27 July 1930.
16 Stella Barber, Community in Crisis: Richmond and the Great Depression, 1930–1932, B.A. Honours thesis, University of Melbourne, 1983; for an account of the politics of unemployment relief see Les Louis, 'Unemployment and the Trade Unions in the Depression: Victoria, 1930–1932', in *Australian Welfare History: Critical Essays*, Richard Kennedy (ed.) (Melbourne, 1983), pp. 167–98.
17 *Richmond Weekly*, 8 August, 19 September 1930; *Herald*, 3 September 1930; *Age*, 16 September
18 Richmond City Council's Archives, Carringbush Library, Town Clerk's correspondence file 1931, *passim*.
19 *Age*, 24 September 1930; *Richmond Weekly*, 24 October 1930.
20 *Richmond Guardian*, 8 November 1930.
21 Ibid., 22 November, 20 December 1930; *Herald*, 12 November 1930; *Richmond Weekly*, 12 December 1930.
22 *Richmond Guardian*, 7, 21, 28 March 1931; *Age*, 21 March 1931.
23 *Richmond Guardian*, 13 June 1931.
24 Richmond City Council Archives, Town Clerk's correspondence file 1931.
25 *Richmond Guardian*, 20 June, 3 July 1931; *Richmond Weekly*, 10 July 1931.
26 Richmond City Council Archives, Town Clerk's correspondence file 1931.
27 *Richmond Guardian*, 18 July 1931.
28 Wendy Lowenstein, *Weevils in the Flour* (Melbourne, 1978), p. 407.
29 *Richmond Guardian*, 21 November, 5 December 1931.
30 Ibid., 12 December 1931.
31 Ibid., 26 December 1931.
32 Ibid., 14, 18 May 1931, 25 June, 13, 20 August 1932; *Richmond Weekly*, 13 May, 24 June 1932.
33 *Richmond Guardian*, 3 September 1932.
34 Ibid., 24 December 1932.
35 Ibid., 15 October 1932.

36 Ibid., 10, 24 September, 17 June 1932; *Richmond Weekly*, 28 August, 16 September 1932.
37 *Richmond Guardian*, 4 February, 8 April, 10 June, 26 August 1933; *Richmond Chronicle*, 1 September 1933.
38 *Richmond Guardian*, 29 July, 14 October 1933; *Herald*, 11 November 1933; *Richmond Chronicle*, 24 November 1933.
39 *Richmond Guardian*, 18 November 1933.
40 Ibid., 4 November, 15, 22 April 1933, 3 November 1932, 12 August, 27 July 1933.
41 Ibid., 9 December 1933, 23 June, 21 July 1934, 21 January, 23 September 1933.
42 Ibid., 17 February 1934.
43 *Richmond Chronicle*, 16 February 1934.
44 Ibid., 3 August 1934.
45 *Richmond Guardian*, 3 March, 28 April, 2 June, 7 July 1934.
46 Ibid., 24 March 1934.
47 Ibid., 31 March 1934; *Richmond Chronicle*, 21 December 1934.
48 *Richmond Guardian*, 12 May 1934.
49 Ibid., 28 July, 25 August, 6, 27 October 1934.
50 Progress Report of the Select Committee on the Working Week . . . (Shorter Working Week), *VPP*, 1935, D. 1, (v. 1), pp. 4–6.
51 *Richmond Guardian*, 9 February 1935; see chapter 2; Report of the Chief Inspector of Factories and Shops for year ending 31 December 1940, *VPP*, 1941, No. 17 (v. 1).
52 *Richmond Guardian*, 24 November 1934, 27 July, 26 January 1935; *Richmond Chronicle*, 20 December 1935; *Age*, 15 August 1935.
53 *Herald*, 15 February 1935; *Richmond Guardian*, 28 September 1935.
54 *Age*, 11 June 1935; *Herald*, 4 May 1935; *Richmond Guardian*, 13 July, 17 August, 28 March 1936; *Richmond Chronicle*, 29 September 1935, 24 April, 6 November 1936, 25 August 1939; Lowenstein, op. cit., p. 446.
55 *Richmond Guardian*, 11 January 1936; *Richmond Chronicle*, 31 January, 14 February 1936.
56 *Richmond Chronicle*, 14 February 1936.
57 Ibid., 12 April 1935; *Richmond Guardian*, 20 April 1935, 14 March 1936.
58 *Richmond Chronicle*, 10 July, 9 October, 22 May 1936; *Richmond Guardian*, 1 May, 29 August, 6 June 1936.
59 *Richmond Chronicle*, 22 May, 6 June, 11 July 1936; *Richmond Guardian*, 1, 15 February 1936.
60 *Richmond Chronicle*, 27 November, 17 July 1936.
61 *Richmond Guardian*, 15 August 1936.
62 Ibid., 26 January 1935.
63 Ibid., 1, 15 February, 22 August 1936; *Richmond Chronicle*, 20 November 1936, 9 April 1937, 18 November 1938, 26 May, 23 June 1939, 1 April 1938.
64 *Richmond Chronicle*, 17 September 1939.
65 Ibid., 28 August, 3, 24 September, 7 January 1937, 7 October 1938.
66 Ibid., 20 December 1940, 16 September 1938, 31 March 1939, 17 February 1938, 2 June 1939; *Richmond Guardian*, 14 December 1935.
67 *Richmond Chronicle*, 22 April, 28 October 1938, 30 June, 6 October 1939, 10 October 1941.
68 Ibid., 13 January 1939. Ibid., 10 February 1939.
70 Kate White, *John Cain and Victorian Labor, 1917–1957* (Sydney, 1982), testimony of A. A. Calwell, p. 78.
71 *Richmond Chronicle*, 18 November 1938.

6 YOUNG MARRIEDS

1 I am grateful to Stella Barber for permission to quote from this interview with *Joe Grant* (pseudonym) bachelor, taped by her at Richmond 1 May 1983.
2 Wendy Lowenstein, *Weevils in the Flour* (Melbourne, 1978); see Sheilah Gray, 'An Evil Long Endured—Newcastle's Depression', in Judy Mackinolty (ed.), *The Wasted Years?* (Sydney, 1981), pp. 58–75, for a defence of the unemployed in Newcastle. The responses in the industrual suburbs of the capital cities were less united than in single industry and mining towns.
3 Richmond City Council Archives, Carringbush Library, unfiled letter in the Town Clerk's Correspondence file 1931. It should have been in the Mayoress' Relief Committee file.

4 From conversation with the author.
5 *Richmond Guardian*, 5 May 1928, 5 September 1903. (Three months later Mrs Mann's unmarried sister, who lived with her in Elizabeth Street, suddenly fell ill with acute vomiting and died. Her mysterious death was reported to the coroner in December 1903.) *Richmond Chronicle*, 21 May 1937; *Bill Shannon*; R.C.C. Archives, 1931. Mayoress' Relief Committee file.
6 *James Mitchell* (pseudonym) widower, interviewed by author 13 July 1981.
7 *Richmond Guardian*, 2 June 1934.
8 Ibid., 16 July 1932.
9 Ibid., 6 January 1934.
10 *Bertie Middleton* (pseudonym) married man, interviewed by author 21 March 1978.
11 R.C.C. Ratebooks, Mary Street, Centre Ward.
12 *Richmond Guardian*, 24 October 1931, 10 December 1927, 11 March 1933; *Richmond Chronicle*, 8 April 1938.
13 *Richmond Guardian*, 21 February 1931, 12 September 1931.
14 Leonie Sandercock, 'Playing the Greater Game: Australian Rules Football in the 1930s', in *Australia 1938*, Bulletin No. 1, February 1980, pp. 25–6; *Richmond Chronicle*, 1 December 1939, 19 October 1934.
15 *Richmond Guardian*, 23 March 1929, 11 February 1933, 2 November 1935, 30 September 1930; *Richmond Chronicle*, 28 January 1937, 18 March, 10 June 1938.
16 Don Aitkin, Michael Kahan and Sue Barnes, 'What happened to the Depression Generation?', in Robert Cooksey (ed.), *The Great Depression in Australia* (Canberra, 1970), pp. 174–83.
17 I am indebted to Stella Barber for finding this letter in the R.C.C. Archives.
18 Douglas Gordon, *Health, Sickness and Society* (Brisbane, 1976), pp. 112–13; Royal Commission on Child Endowment 1929, op. cit., Majority Report, pp. 78–9.
19 Gordon, op. cit., p. 72.
20 *Richmond Guardian*, 23 March 1927.
21 Report of the Royal Commission on Health 1926, *APP*, 1926–28, IV, p. 31.
22 Ibid., pp. 36–7; *Richmond Guardian*, 5 April 1930, 24 March 1934, 23 March 1935.
23 *Richmond Guardian*, 21 July 1934.
24 Desley Deacon, 'Taylorism in the Home: the Medical Profession, the Infant Welfare Movement and the Deskilling of Women', paper delivered to the SAANZ Conference, Melbourne, August 1983.
25 Nancy E. Hitchcock, Elizabeth N. Owles, Michael Gracey, 'Breast Feeding and the Growth of Healthy Infants', *Nursing Mother's Association of Australia Newsletter*, vol. 18, no. 3, April 1982, p. 4.

7 WAR AND PEACE II

1 Russel Ward, *A Nation for a Continent* (Melbourne, 1977), p. 254; Michael McKernan, *All In, Australia During the Second World War* (Melbourne, 1983); Arthur Marwick, *Britain in the Century of Total War* (London, 1968).
2 Ward, op. cit., p. 234; McKernan, op. cit., pp. 20–1; *Richmond Chronicle*, 8 September, 1 December 1939, 26 January, 16 February 1940.
3 *Richmond Chronicle*, 23 October 1942; Dr David Roseby, 'An Address as Retiring President of the Victorian Branch of the British Medical Association', delivered 6 December 1944, *The Medical Journal of Australia*, 6 January 1945.
4 Tom Harrisson, *Living Through the Blitz* (London, 1976); *Richmond Chronicle*, 1 March 1940.
5 *Richmond Chronicle*, 14 June 1940, 27 November 1936, 15 March, 3 May, 19 July, 6, 27 September, 15 November 1940, 28 February 1941.
6 Ibid., 24 January, 9, 30 May, 14, 28 November, 15 December 1941.
7 Ibid., 21 February, 7 March, 4, 11 July, 10 April, 17 October 1941.
8 Ibid., 19 December 1941; Muriel Heagney Papers, Box 1160/1 (c), Australian Manuscripts Collection, La Trobe Library; oral testimony of Hélène McCalman and Rose Cruickshank, metal workers at the Government Aircraft Factory, Newport Workshops; McKernan, op. cit., pp. 207–38.
9 *Richmond Chronicle*, 19 December 1941, 9, 30 January 1942; McKernan, op. cit., pp. 207–38.
10 McKernan, op. cit., pp. 185–206.
11 *Richmond Chronicle*, 7 May 1943, 17 November 1944, 31 July 1942, 8 October, 11 June 1943;

McKernan, op. cit., p. 164; University of Melbourne Social Survey, 1941–2, Melbourne University Archives, Richmond Schedules.

12 *Richmond Chronicle*, 8 January 1943, 12 May 1944, 2 October 1942, 17 September 1943.

13 Ibid., 4 July, 10 October 1941, 5 May 1944, 4 September 1942; interview with Pat Kennelly.

14 *Richmond Chronicle*, 20 February, 24 April, 10 June 1942, 8 January, 5 February 1943, 21 August 1942, 11 June 1943, 7, 21 April 1941, 20, 27 March 1942, 18 June 1943, 15 May 1942, 18 June, 10 September 1943.

15 Ibid., 15 October, 7 May, 18 June, 27 August 1943, 18 February, 24 March 1944.

16 Ward, op. cit., pp. 255, 269–71.

17 McKernan, op. cit., p. 261; Ronald Mendelsohn, *The Condition of the People* (Sydney., 1979), p. 261; Fourth Interim Report from the Joint Committee on Social Security 1942, Housing. *AAP*, 1940–3, 11, p. 22.

18 University of Melbourne Survey, op. cit.

19 *Richmond News*, 3 July 1947; M. A. Jones, *Housing and Poverty in Australia* (Melbourne, 1972), pp. 71–92.

20 *Richmond Chronicle*, 16 February, 22 November 1940, 7 February, 12 September 1941, 15 September, 24 November 1944.

21 Ibid., 6 July, 29 June 1945.

22 *Richmond News*, 25 September 1947, 29 January 1948; Robert Murray, *The Split* (Melbourne, 1970), p. 73.

23 This section owes much to Robert Murray's *The Split* and Kate White's *John Cain and Victorian Labor* (Sydney, 1982).

24 *Age*, 22 July 1946; *Herald*, 23 July 1946; *Richmond News*, 23 June 1949.

25 Murray, op. cit., pp. 76, 80; *Richmond News*, 19 September, 8 April 1948, 10 October 1946, 13 February 1947.

26 *Richmond News*, 12 May 1949. The O.G.P.U. was the Soviet Secret Police.

27 *Age*, 5 August 1946; *Herald*, 29 November 1946; *Sun*, 29 November 1946, 22 June 1947; *Richmond News*, 12 December 1946.

28 *Richmond News*, 6 March 1947.

29 Ibid., 6, 13, 20 March 1947.

30 Ibid., 27 March, 3, 10 April, 3, 10, 17, 24, 31 July 1947; *Labor Call*, 5 June 1947; *Sun*, 26 June 1947.

31 *Richmond News*, 9, 23 January, 22 May, 28 June 1947.

32 Ibid., 18 December 1947.

33 *Age*, 21 October 1947.

34 *Herald*, 21 November 1947; *Richmond News*, 27 November, 11, 18 December 1947.

35 *Richmond News*, 29 January, 5, 19 February, 6 May, 3 June, 15 April 1948.

36 Ibid., 1 July 1948.

37 *Argus*, 29 July 1948; *Sun*, 24 November 1948; *Richmond News*, 5, 19 August 1948, 17, 31 March 1949.

38 *Richmond News*, 7, 14 April 1949, 7 July 1954.

39 Ibid., 12 May, 11 August, 8 September 1949; the late Augusto Coloretti, interviewed by author 17 February 1981.

40 *Richmond News*, 28 September, 6, 13, 20 October, 10, 24 November, 11 August 1949.

41 Ibid., 1 December 1949.

42 Ibid., 15 December 1949.

43 Ibid., 3 November 1949, 19 January, 2, 16 February, 2 March, 6 April, 13 July, 31 August, 7 September 1950.

44 Ibid., 16 November 1950, 12 December, 17 September 1952, 26 July, 18 October 1951, 1 April 1953, 17 March, 22 September 1954.

45 Ibid., 15 March, 26 April, 3, 25 May, 7 June 1951, 28 September 1950; Murray, op. cit., p. 89.

46 *Richmond News*, 18 January, 8 February 1951.

47 Ibid., 8 March 1951.

48 Report of the Royal Commission into . . . the Communist Party of Australia, *VPP*, 1950–51, No. 12, (v. 2).

49 *Richmond News*, 21 July 1954.

50 Ibid., 28 March 1956.

51 Ibid., 30 March 1956.

52 Ibid., 11, 18 May, 15 June 1955; Murray op. cit., pp. 252–3.
53 *Richmond News*, 20 July, 24, 31 August, 7 September 1955.
54 Paul Ormonde, *A Foolish Passionate Man* (Melbourne, 1981), pp. 48–50; *Richmond News*, 30 November, 7 December 1955.

8 MIDDLE LIFE

1 University of Melbourne Social Survey, 1941–42, Melbourne University Archives, Richmond Schedules.
2 *Richmond News*, 29 January, 3, 17 June, 21 October 1948.
3 Ibid., 16 December 1948, 18 December 1949, 9, 16 July, 24 September 1952.
4 *Richmond Chronicle*, 5 March 1937, 26 January 1940.
5 Ibid., 27 March 1940; *Richmond News*, 23 September 1959, 26 April 1961, 26 May 1965; June Hearn, The Richmond High School Campaign (M.A. Preliminary thesis, Political Science, University of Melbourne, 1968).
6 *Richmond Guardian*, 24 June, 28 October 1922, 9 February 1924, 22 July 1933; *Richmond Chronicle*, 11 December 1936; *Richmond News*, 8 April 1948, 22 August 1956.
7 *Richmond Chronicle*, 9 April, 6 August 1943.
8 *Richmond News*, 25 October 1951, 17 December 1952.
9 Ibid., 2 March 1955.
10 Ibid., 17 July 1947, 30 October 1946, 25 September 1957; *Richmond Chronicle*, 4 February 1944.
11 M. A. Jones, *Housing and Poverty in Australia* (Melbourne, 1972), pp. 5–9; F. Oswald Barnett, *The Poverty of the People in Australia* (The Good Companion Christian Social Order Group, Melbourne, 1944).
12 *Richmond News*, 25 February 1953, 14 September 1955, 4 June 1952.
13 Ibid., 18 October 1951.
14 Royal Commission into Off-Course Betting, *VPP*, 1958–59, No. 33 (v. 2), pp. 15, 20.
15 Ibid., pp. 33–4; *Richmond News*, 7 June 1956.
16 *Richmond Chronicle*, 16 June 1944; *Richmond News*, 16 December 1958.
17 John Powles and Robert Birrell, *Mortality in Victoria 1969–1973* (Environmental Research Associates, Department of Sociology, Monash University, Melbourne, 1977), esp. pp. 7, 15.

9 DEATH AND REBIRTH

1 *Richmond News*, 26 April 1954, 1, 29 February, 16 May 1956, 18 November 1965.
2 *Richmond Advocate*, 29 September 1971; *Richmond News*, 6 September 1961.
3 *St Stephen's Richmond, 125th Anniversary* (Richmond, 1976); *Richmond News*, 17 June 1965, 6 June 1962; *Richmond Advocate*, 27 September 1971.
4 Douglas Gordon, *Health, Sickness and Society* (Brisbane, 1976) p. 286; Basil S. Hetzel, *Health and Australian Society* (revised edition, Melbourne, 1976), pp. 122–41.
5 Paul Ormonde, *A Foolish, Passionate Man* (Melbourne, 1981), p. 112.
6 *Richmond News*, 7 June, 8, 15, 29 August, 24 October, 12 September, 28 March 1956, 12 June, 14 August 1957, 3 September 1958.
7 Ibid., 30 April, 11 June, 25 December 1958, 28 March, 11 April 1962.
8 Ibid., 29 November, 4 October 1961, 28 September 1956, 10 July, 1957, 29 April 1959, 28 September, 20 January, 21 December 1960.
9 Ibid., 10 July 1963.
10 Report of the Royal Commission into . . . the Administration of the Housing Commission, *VPP*, 1955–56, No. 45, (v. 2), p. 67.
11 *Richmond News*, 30 May 1956.
12 Ibid., 1 August 1956.
13 Ibid., 20 September 1961, 2 April 1964, 19 May 1966; Gordon, op. cit., p. 334; M. A. Jones, *Housing and Poverty in Australia* (Melbourne, 1972), pp. 171–97.
14 Dr David Roseby, 'An address as Retiring President of the Victorian Branch of the British Medical Association', *Medical Journal of Australia*, 6 January 1945, p. 8.
15 *Richmond Guardian*, 3 February 1900, 27 September 1930.

16 Ibid., 17 August 1912, 15 March 1913, 24 February, 28 April 1923, 25 July 1925, 28 July 1928; Report of the Inspector-General for the Insane, 1912, *VPP*, 1913–14, No. 19, (v. 2), pp. 59–60; *Richmond Weekly*, 17 June 1927, 5 April 1928.
17 *Labor Call*, 3 April 1913, for example *Whither (sic) Away: A Study of Race Psychology and the Factors Leading to Australia's National Decline*, by a Psychologist and a Physician (Angus and Robertson, Sydney, 1934) and Harvey Sutton, *Lectures on Preventative Medicine* (Sydney, 1944), 18 pp. 1–27.
18 *Richmond Guardian*, 25 January 1913, 27 April 1912.
19 Serge Liberman, *On Firmer Shores* (Melbourne, 1981), pp. 201–2.
20 *Richmond News*, 12 October 1950, 13 December 1951, 20 May 1953, 21 September 1955.
21 Ibid., 9 May 1956.
22 Ibid., 7, 14, 28 March 1956.
23 Ibid., 5 February 1958.
24 Ibid., 15 January 1958, 24 April 1959, 30 April, 26 July 1961, 25 June 1964, 10 November 1966.
25 Ibid., 30 November 1960, 19 February 1962, 18 October 1961, 11 November 1959.

10 OLD AGE AND REFLECTION

1 R.C.C. Ratebooks 1900–1965, Centre Ward, Mary Street.
2 Ronald F. Henderson, Alison Harcourt, R. J. A. Harper, *People in Poverty: A Melbourne Survey* (Melbourne, 1970), pp. 82–3.

Index